LIBERTY LADY

LIBERTY LADY

A True Story of Love and Espionage in WWII Sweden

for Amy,
Pat DiGeorge

PAT DIGEORGE

Liberty Lady

Interior Design: Stephanie Anderson, Jera Publishing
Cover Design: Jason Orr, Jera Publishing

ISBN: 978-0-9982570-0-6 (paperback)
ISBN: 978-0-9982570-1-3 (hardback)

Library of Congress Control Number: 2016956749

Published by:
Beaver's Spur Publishing, LLC
Vero Beach, FL USA

www.LibertyLadyBook.com

Contents

Prologue

In 1944, as World War II raged in Europe, neutral Sweden was thick with espionage. Representatives of all the combatant nations moved freely throughout the country. The American Legation in Stockholm sat at the center of one of the most important listening posts of the war. The Allies and the Germans openly conducted business in the same locales, wining and dining at adjoining tables in the restaurants and bars of the capital. Information critical to the war effort was being bought and sold, and anyone could be a spy.

At 1900 hours on Friday, the 18th of August, a handsome young American airman stepped out of an apartment building on Skeppargatan, one of the oldest streets in Stockholm. Barely five months earlier, Lt. Herman F. Allen's B-17 *Liberty Lady* had force-landed in Sweden after it was crippled by flak during a bombing run over Berlin, the most fiercely protected city in Europe. Along with the rest of the crew, Herman was placed in an internment camp in rural Sweden. Then, 30 days later, the military air attaché recruited him to work at the American Legation in Stockholm.

On his first day, Herman met Bill Carlson, a commercial attaché whose office was tucked away in the back hallway of the legation. The two men hit it off at once, and Herman quickly learned that Carlson was not an attaché at all. Instead, Carlson headed the counterespionage division of the United States intelligence agency, the Office of Strategic Services (OSS). One of Carlson's jobs was to identify and catalog persons who might be working for the enemy and then, if possible, feed them false information to pass on.

By this time of the war, more than 900 American airmen had arrived in Sweden. As their bombing missions took them deeper into Nazi-occupied countries, more and more crews were forced to divert to the neutral country when their battle-damaged planes could not make the flight back to England. Once in Sweden, the airmen were interned in camps and ordered not to leave the country. Once a month, they traveled to Stockholm with a weekend pass. Carlson asked Herman to determine whether enemy agents might be consorting with these Americans.

After each visit, the internees met with Herman for a debriefing, and he questioned them about their weekend activities. If they had been with a woman, he wanted to know, "Who was she, and what questions did she ask?" If the same name and questions came up again and again, the lady landed on a watch list of probable spies.

Before long, Herman was so busy that he begged for secretarial support. Carlson assured him that help was on the way. Hedvig Johnson, known to be extremely efficient, had worked with the OSS since its inception and could speak and write Swedish.

On this Friday in August, Herman wore a new suit, civilian dress as required by the official rules of internment. It was a seasonably mild Stockholm evening, and the sun would not set for another 30 minutes. Herman did not have far to walk, his destination being less than four city blocks away. When he reached Linnégatan, he quickly stopped to lean against the tall corner building and then peered back around to confirm that he wasn't being followed. If he had left from the legation on Strandvägen, someone from the German offices across the courtyard would likely have tailed him.

As he resumed his stride up Skeppargatan, Herman thought about the beautiful secretary who had just arrived from London. Even though he immediately noticed the close relationship between Miss Johnson and her boss, Herman had invited her to a legation wedding scheduled to take place in two days.

When he got to Kommendörsgatan, Herman took a right turn and began to focus on the task at hand. Carlson had asked him to go to the apartment of a middle-aged Swedish businessman. Well educated, this man was often addressed as "Doctor." When Herman got the assignment, he immediately picked up a telephone to set up a time for the visit. He remembered meeting the doctor and his wife at a popular Stockholm restaurant. Herman knew how to turn on the charm, and even in this short telephone conversation, he was able to arrange an invitation for dinner.

Carlson showed Herman the intelligence reports. There were several. The doctor had a suspected association with a person in the United States charged with delivering sensitive defense information to the government of the German Reich. In another report, a British passport control officer had passed on to the Americans information that this same Swede had allegedly been involved in a scheme for making money by arranging fake marriages for German Jewish women in order to obtain for them Swedish nationality.

Two days earlier, an associate had given Herman the name of another internee, now back in England, who visited this gentleman in April and supposedly left his raincoat. The forgotten raincoat became a convenient pretense for this visit. Herman could retrieve the coat and, at the same time, find out more about the doctor's interests and possibly obtain evidence against him.

As Herman approached his destination, he glanced back again to ensure no one was behind him. All clear, he thought, but then he spotted the two men, casually smoking and leaning against the building across the street. They were from the Swedish police, alerted by Bill Carlson to stake out the apartment during this arranged meeting. Herman pretended not to notice them.

The doctor's address, number 42, was a typical tall apartment building, six stories high. As Herman walked into the small deserted entryway, he read the nameplates and then hurried up the stairs to the third floor hallway. A deep breath tamed the butterflies fluttering in his stomach. This was his first time in the field, a chance to prove himself to Carlson and to the OSS.

Before Herman reached the doctor's door, he heard footsteps behind him. A man wearing a felt hat appeared at the top of the stairs. Herman didn't know what he should do, so he decided to do nothing. He leaned against the wall and pretended to check his watch. The man nodded to him, unlocked another door down the hall, and disappeared.

Believing the encounter to be only a coincidence, Herman stepped up to the doctor's door and rang the bell. A woman, apparently a maid, promptly opened the door and invited him inside. Herman was surprised to see the portly gentleman who stood up to greet him. This man was not the person he had met on the previous occasion. Had it been a case of a mistaken identity?

Herman recovered quickly, and the two men shook hands, introduced themselves, and immediately began to make conversation.

The maid brought out schnapps and a tray of Smörgåsbord and then the pair sat down to a delicious dinner of lamb chops, raspberries, cold beer, and cognac. Working hard not to drink too much, Herman found it more and more difficult as each round of drinks came out. He knew he needed to stay focused and remember every detail and each topic of conversation.

Dinner over, the doctor brought out his cigars. Herman remarked about the dozen framed photographs of attractive women on the sideboard. His host explained that he knew several Swedish girls he would like Herman to meet, and at 2100 hours, a brunette and two blondes showed up at the door.

It flashed through Herman's mind that the new secretary would have to type up this report in the morning. Nevertheless, he decided to make an evening of it.

Chapter 1

Heart Hospital

It was the Monday before Thanksgiving, 2007. When I heard the phone ring, I glanced at the clock. Almost noon. My sister Kathy spoke quickly, "Patti, Mother is on her way to the hospital in an ambulance. She dialed 911 from home. I'll call you after I get to Providence."

Providence Heart Hospital in Columbia, South Carolina, is where our mother had been treated nearly a year before. She'd had two heart attacks, and a courageous young cardiologist put stents in the arteries around her heart. Since then she'd made two or three more trips to the emergency room. Each time it had been a false alarm, nothing serious. I said a quick prayer that this time would be the same.

When Kathy called back a couple of hours later, she explained that Mother was resting quietly in the emergency room but was still in pain. "Patti," she told me, "you know Mother never complains. It must be bad." Her doctor had scheduled a cardiac catheterization for later in the afternoon.

"How is Daddy?" I asked.

"Antsy. Bored," Kathy answered. "The nurses have already asked him not to wander around outside the room. I'm not sure he understands that he's not the patient."

Our mother, Hedy Allen, was 86 years old, still beautiful with dark brown hair and not a speck of gray. She visited her hairdresser each and every Friday. After an hour, she returned home with her perfect hairdo and walked into our dad's office. Herman would be sitting at his computer reading emails. The minute Hedy walked in, he'd whistle and say, "Come here. Turn around, and let me have a look at you. Beautiful!" Hedy smiled and twirled, and he'd give her an affectionate pat on the behind. This happened every single week, and neither tired of their little ritual.

Herman, 91, had been diagnosed with Alzheimer's six years before. He remembered little of years gone by, but he did as well as could be expected in the moment.

There are five children. I am the eldest. My husband, John, and I have a home in Roswell, Georgia, one of the northern suburbs of Atlanta. Barbara, two years younger, lives in Florida with her husband Larry. David is in New Hampshire, married to Karen. Bill is in Asheville with wife Barbara, and Kathy is the baby, 18 years younger than I. A long-time single mom, Kathy lives in Columbia, a mile from our parents. Hedy and Herman's Christmas cards bragged about their five children along with dozens of grandchildren, step-grandchildren, and great-grandchildren, a bigger number nearly every year.

All of Hedy and Herman's children and many grandchildren planned to gather in South Carolina for Thanksgiving. I finished packing, and then around dinnertime, Kathy called to tell me the catheterization showed Mother had not had a heart attack. Her doctor found a blockage and cleared it. He said everything looked good, but he wanted her to stay in the coronary care unit for another day, just to be sure.

The next morning, I left early for Columbia and telephoned for an update the minute I was safely on I-20 heading east. The news did not sound good. At 5:00 a.m., unable to sleep, Kathy had called the hospital. When the nurse described her patient's terrible night, Kathy jumped into her car and drove the three miles to Providence.

As Kathy walked down the hall toward Mother's room, she saw the nurse, white as a ghost, outside her door.

"We almost lost her," the nurse, obviously shaken, explained. "Her blood pressure was down to nothing. I had to call a code. She's stable now, but we can't give her any more pain medication because of her low blood pressure."

Kathy rushed into Hedy's room, and Mother opened her eyes. "Oh, Kathy," she said, "where have you been?"

When I finally arrived in Columbia, I headed straight for the coronary care unit. As I walked into Mother's room, I found Kathy and Daddy sitting next to her bed. Mother's eyes were closed, but she opened them when she heard me and said, "Hi, Patti." We hugged gently and spoke for a moment. She said she still had a terrible pain in her back. The doctors were giving her what medication they could.

Herman sat quietly next to her. "Daddy, how are you?" I asked.

"I'm fine, Patti. She's in good hands."

Kathy told me Bill was on his way from Asheville and should be there in less than an hour. Our brother is a physician, and when he arrived, we sighed a breath of relief as we all looked to Bill as the authority. He hadn't been there long when Hedy's cardiologist walked in.

"Hedy, your EKG looks fine," the cardiologist explained. "You should be able to go home tomorrow."

"Doctor, I'm still having a lot of pain right here, in my back." Hedy showed him where it hurt.

Her doctor shook his head in puzzlement, "Hmmm, you shouldn't be having pain."

Bill asked, "Have you x-rayed for a dissection?"

The doctor answered, "No, we haven't." His expression seemed to say it would be a long shot, but he went to the nurses' station and ordered a CAT scan.

Kathy took Daddy home, and Bill and I went downstairs to the cafeteria.

"Bill, this is a sign," I said. "We've got to get serious about finding a place for them to live. Mother doesn't need to be taking care of Daddy and that house. And she shouldn't be driving." We had all had this conversation many times, but our parents would never consider so drastic a change. It was too overwhelming to leave their home of 40 years. Every room was filled to the brim with books and memories.

By the time Bill and I returned to Mother's room, she was resting after the CAT scan. Shortly, her cardiologist came in, nodded to us, and spoke directly to Mother.

"Mrs. Allen, we have found bleeding around your aorta. That is what is causing the pain."

Mother nodded with a smile, oh, so politely.

The cardiologist went on to explain the anatomy of what he described as an aortic dissection, a tear in the wall of the aorta. "Because you are on Plavix," he said, "your blood may not clot as well as we need it to. I'm afraid to take you off Plavix because then your stents could close. Open heart surgery is one option, and I am going to call in a surgeon to speak with you.

"In the meantime, if you are having any discomfort, I'll leave orders for the nurses to give you pain medication through your IV. You'll be able to sleep. I'm sorry the news couldn't be any better, Mrs. Allen."

Mother nodded again. I glanced at Bill to see his face, white and expressionless. He walked closer to the bed. "Mother, do you understand what the doctor said? We've got to keep you quiet and pray it clots."

Hedy closed her eyes.

Chapter 2

Hedy's Story

Hibbing

In 1998, Hedy wrote a short history of her family. Her words are in italics.

I was named after Hedvig, the Queen of Sweden. We loved hearing this story from our mother as we grew up. And there was the other Hedy, Hedy Lamarr, the glamorous movie star of the 1930s and '40s, known as the "world's most beautiful woman." We thought there was an uncanny resemblance between the two women with the same first name. Our mother, Hedvig Elizabeth Johnson Allen, was the most beautiful woman we knew.

My parents were born in Finland, but they were Swedes. Both came from Närpes on the western coast of Finland where only Swedes reside.

Their families were farmers, and times were hard. Life centered around the Baptist Church. In my father's family, both parents had tuberculosis. His father died when his mother was pregnant with their ninth child. When the baby was two years old, his mother died. He and his brothers worked in a sawmill and were somehow able to raise the smaller children.

In 1907, my father came to the United States, the land of opportunity. He arrived as Johan Alfred Bärnas, but ten years later he changed his last name to Johnson because he thought Bärnas sounded too German. His first stopover was Denver, Colorado, where an uncle lived. Then he decided to try Florida and purchased land near Fort Walton Beach. There he farmed and planted orange trees.

Plans had been made upon Alfred's departure in 1907 that his sweetheart Helena Gustava would join him. But, via the grapevine, word reached her that Alfred was smoking cigarettes and drinking beer. This delayed any thought of departure on her part.

Finally in 1917, after ten years of letters back and forth, Helena and her niece sailed for the United States. The trip was a nightmare. Storm conditions almost swept Helena's niece off the top deck of their ship, and upon arriving at Ellis Island, they were incarcerated for several days like cattle.

At last, Helena reached her Swedish-Baptist friends in Worcester, Massachusetts. My mother immediately got a job housekeeping for a wealthy Jewish family. This was a new experience, with so many different foods to learn to fix and a white kitchen floor to keep spotless.

In the meantime, word got to my father that Helena had arrived. At about the same time, the government came in and burned his orange grove. The trees were diseased. Alfred almost had a nervous breakdown, and this is how Helena found him, so dejected, all those years for naught.

She accepted his proposal of marriage, and they headed for Chisholm, Minnesota, where my Uncle Eric and my father's sister Anna resided. They were married in the Swedish-Baptist Church on September 7, 1918. My father got a job as a laborer in nearby Hibbing on the iron range with the Oliver Mining Company, part of U.S. Steel.

The Johnsons' new hometown, named after pioneer Frank Hibbing who discovered iron ore there, was flourishing. The three-mile-long open pit mine had become the largest in the world. Alfred and Helena purchased a one-story company house on the north side of town and settled among the many immigrants who moved to Hibbing from all over Europe.

However, the Oliver Mining Company had discovered rich deposits of iron ore underneath Hibbing's residential neighborhoods. The company negotiated with the local council to move the village two miles south. Some homeowners objected, but the steel company's interests won out after they agreed to make many public improvements, including parks and community buildings.

So the houses in the neighborhoods were moved. Helena threatened that the company would have to move her home with her sitting in it, and, according to family folklore, they did.

As an additional gift to the citizens of Hibbing, Oliver Mining Company built a new high school, complete with marble floors and a grand auditorium. Construction on the school began in 1920 at a cost of $3.9 million, in today's dollars, nearly $50 million.[1] In the 1950s, a local student later known as Bob Dylan performed on the auditorium stage.

I was born in 1921. My mother was thirty-eight years of age. My brother, Hedley, was born in 1924, and my sister, Ruby, in 1927. By then, my mother was forty-four.

Hibbing was a melting pot for European immigrants from Czechoslovakia, Italy, Poland, Sweden, Norway, Finland, Ireland, Greece. All kinds of foreign tongues were spoken, and we had friends of every nationality.

My mother learned to speak some English right away and even went to night school, although we spoke only Swedish in our home. She would never admit to being a Finn. "There was a world of difference between Finns and Swedes," our mother insisted.

When Hedy entered school, she learned to speak English. The first grade teacher asked each student to recite a nursery rhyme. Hedy recited "Veenken, Bleenken, and Nod" with the same accent and inflections as her mother, and everyone laughed. She never again wanted to get up and speak in front of a group.

Then came the Depression. The years were tough on our parents. To feed and clothe us was a constant struggle. Most of the time, our father only worked part time, perhaps three days each week. Our clothing was purchased at rummage sales. My mother would take the dresses apart and remake them to fit us. In my junior year of high school, I had only one dress to wear to school. I pressed it every single night.

We always had a garden and also a large potato patch rented from the mining company. My father kept chickens in a hen house, so we had chicken, eggs, and homemade rye bread (never, ever fluffy white bread.) Friends who lived on a farm delivered milk every day. My parents always said if we had not owned our own home during those years, we never could have come through.

Unemployment across the country reached 30 percent. Franklin Delano Roosevelt, governor of New York and a popular Democrat, decided to throw his hat in the ring for the 1932 presidential election. Hedy's sister, Ruby, remembered, "To our mother, FDR was Christ come again. Hoover was a dirty word in our house, and Republicans were hated. They were the only ones who had any money."

Hedy and Ruby came home from school one day to see their mother sitting at the kitchen table crying. Helena had stood all day in the charity bread line. She was devastated, but the children were thrilled to see good food in the house, especially the apples.

During those Depression years, there were never birthday parties and few presents. One Christmas, Hedy got a hairbrush. Another year, the fire department left a big parcel on their front porch. It was a box for poor families, full of toys and presents, a reason for the children to celebrate.

Behind our house, my father built a small wooden steam bath. There were two rooms, a dressing room and a second room with a series of benches. Our neighbors came every Saturday, and my mother kept the schedule. Everyone brought their own wood for the fire. Water was thrown on the hot rocks, and the steam would rise up around the benches where we all sat. Some would whip themselves with willow switches, as the Finnish people liked to do. It became a neighborhood gathering spot.

Our mother was completely in charge of the three children. All permissions came through her, except for the Model A. I started pleading to drive it early in the morning, and, usually by noon, Papa relented. I was the only girl among my friends who could use the family car. I would pick up four or five girls, Sub-Debs no doubt, and we would take off to Sturgeon Lake, Chisholm, or Keewatin.

The Sub-Debs were Hedy's school friends who partied together. According to her good friend Agness Ricci, it was not an official high school organization. "Just a group of fun-loving friends, nothing like debutantes," Agness emphasized. One summer, the Sub-Debs rented a cabin on nearby Sturgeon Lake, a popular beach for the people who worked on the iron range. In the vicinity was one of the Civilian Conservation Corps camps, a work program for unemployed young men, part of Roosevelt's New Deal. When the boys visited one day and surrounded their cabin, the girls laughed and laughed and thought it great fun.

During the Depression, when there was little or no work available, the CCC gave jobs to young men aged 18 to 25. They worked for $1 a day and sent $25 from their monthly paychecks back home to their families. The boys labored to build roads, string telephone lines, plant trees and complete other forestry projects. They lived in barracks similar to army camps, and the government provided three hot meals a day.[2]

The CCC became a godsend to families who had little or no other income. By the end of the program, it had given work to more than 3 million young men. The money they sent home helped support many more people. In addition, the communities where the almost 2500 camps were located profited from the funds spent on the construction and on running the camps.[3]

I had a lot of part-time jobs in high school—keeping books at a filling station, babysitting, cleaning the city recreation rooms (this took a special ticket from a city commissioner and the tickets were rationed out,) and marking test papers.

We all grew up in the Presbyterian Church as there was no Baptist Church in Hibbing. There was more prejudice between the Catholics and the Protestants than between different nationalities. Italians were looked down on. The Irish were Catholics too, but they weren't looked down on like the Italians. Our mother's favorite expression was, "Don't marry a hot blooded Italian."

Many of my boyfriends were Catholic, and this my mother found frightening. She always warned me of the problems that would lie ahead. She classified every person. Not prejudice really, but she was suspicious of different groups, especially Catholics. There was a lot of talk about the Pope. Many believed the Catholics had tunnels under the churches, and they kept guns and would take over the country someday. They also thought the local priest got all the nuns pregnant, and that was why they wore habits.

When Bruno Hauptmann was caught for kidnapping the Lindbergh baby, my mother wouldn't believe he was guilty. She thought it was anti-German sentiment. If he had been an Italian, she would have thought him guilty right away.

People were involved in politics because they knew it affected them a great deal. Mother thought John L. Lewis (president of the United Mine Workers of America) was the greatest man who ever lived, next to FDR. When the union finally got some strength in the late thirties, she gave all the credit to him.

Our Uncle Charlie joined the Communist party. When he came back from the First World War, he owned a theater that burned down and had a lot of bad luck. His name was put on a blacklist, and he couldn't get a job with the mining company.

Coming from the iron range, you really felt different if your parents were first generation in comparison to those whose parents weren't. My parents felt inferior, especially my mother. She never went to a PTA meeting.

After graduating from Hibbing High School, I entered Hibbing Junior College and graduated from their business school. My friends and I took the civil service course so we would qualify for a job with the U.S. Government.

Then came the war in Europe. The first call from Washington, D.C. was an offer of a temporary appointment with the War Department. I was not ready to leave. Next came a call from the Internal Revenue.

Hedvig (Hedy) Johnson in high school.

Hedy always had boyfriends. During the time these job offers were arriving, she was enamored of a young man named Dick. When he gave her an engagement ring, Hedy cried and cried after she got home. Dick's mother came to their house and demanded, "What in the world have you done to my son?"

It was all so dramatic. I was engaged for one night, then decided I wasn't ready to get married. I wanted to go to Washington, D.C.

Washington, D.C.

Conflicts in Europe had been festering since the end of World War I. In 1933, the fanatical Adolf Hitler became chancellor of Germany. The National Socialist German Worker's Party, the Nazis, came into power, and Hitler promised to lead the Germans into glorious prosperity. Under his guidance, he said, their country would rule the world.

By the time Hedy was called to Washington, it had been nearly two years since Hitler's armies had taken over Poland, causing England and France to declare war on Germany. Since then, President Roosevelt and Congress had committed various levels of aid to the struggling countries of Europe.

Most Americans were strongly opposed to going to war. They had barely recovered from World War I. However, if the country was to prepare a proper defense against potential enemies, the government had to get busy.

In late June of 1941, Hedy took a train to Washington's Union Station. On his payday, her father had given her $2 for a new dress, and that is what she wore. She was ready to begin her job at the Internal Revenue.

The city was jam-packed. Thousands each day were coming in from all over the country. From what everyone could see, there was no more

Depression in Washington. It was a boom town. Hotels were so crowded that some visitors had to spend the night in the lobby and then shower and shave in an area especially prepared for this purpose while they waited for a room.

Hedy's first day on the job at the IRS was July 1. As a junior stenographer, she earned a salary of $1440 per annum. From her office, she could easily walk to the White House, the National Mall, and the legendary monuments.

It was a thrill to be in D.C., a city unlike any Hedy had ever seen except in movies and newsreels. Barely 20 years old, with her dark shoulder-length hair, slender figure, and beautiful smile, she could have passed for a film star.

The capital city was first in the country per capita in department store sales. As soon as Hedy arrived, she put three suits on layaway and paid each store a dollar a week until the suits were hers. This was a wonderful extravagance for the young girl who, for one entire school year, had but one dress.

For most people, finding an apartment proved nearly impossible. Fortunately, a friend from Hibbing had already come to town, so Hedy had a place to live. Three roommates, then four, shared one room in a small house on 5th Street, less than five miles from the IRS building.

At one point, the girls were sharing the apartment with three young men who worked in the evenings, one being a roommate's brother. During the day, the boys slept in the bed, and at night the girls slept there. Once the landlord found out, the daytime guests had to leave.

In March of 1941, *Life* magazine reported, "President Roosevelt is well on his way to taking the capital of the world away from London and bringing it to Washington." Hedy had left her small town on the iron ore range of Minnesota to work in the center of all the excitement.

The roommates had little money, so Hedy did the same thing her mother had done during the Depression. She saved her coins in a jar for emergencies. After payday, the girls would host a big dinner for all their friends and then eat like mice until the next paycheck. Money would get tight at the end of some pay periods. One week, all that the girls had left was pancake mix. They couldn't afford to buy much coffee and used the same grounds for two or three pots. Hedy learned to drink coffee black because she could never afford cream and sugar.

At least three nights a week, their boyfriends invited them out to eat. Leftover rolls would be stashed in their handbags. They asked their dates for a dollar to pay the ladies' room attendant and then stood out of sight for a few minutes and kept the dollar.

In the summertime, the nation's capital might have been the nation's hottest city in more ways than one. There was little air-conditioning and certainly none in Hedy's apartment. Air-conditioned movie theaters brought some relief, and Hedy was thrilled when she had a date who could afford to pay.

The roommates soon moved to larger quarters in the Slaughter Guest House near Dupont Circle, a wealthy residential area where mansions and bigger homes had been converted to apartments. The new address was closer to their jobs, a huge boon in the city that imported so many federal workers each month. Traffic was terrible, often paralyzed. The girls traveled to work any way they could, by bus, by taxi, or best of all, by someone with a car driving by to pick them up.

The Slaughter Guest House was a typical rooming house with an ornately trimmed front porch, much like the ones still in the neighborhood today. Hedy made fast friends with a young man, five years older than she, named Lee Bean. With his dark eyes and dark complexion, he could have been Italian.

Lee's apartment was on the first floor because a few years earlier he had contracted polio. With Lee on his crutches, he and Hedy often walked together to catch the bus or a taxi. Soon they were having dinner or going out to the movies. Their friendship grew.

Fresh out of college, Lee worked in the legal division of the Department of Agriculture. He flew all over the country to settle disputed contracts.

Lee's father's full name was Lorenzo Lee Bean, known simply as "L.L."[4] He and his wife's third child, Lorenzo Lee, Jr., had always been known as Lee. In 1933, he entered Hampden-Sydney College in Virginia and joined the football team and a fraternity. He had a reputation for being a prankster and whatever he did, he had a lot of fun doing it.

The summer after his freshman year, like thousands of young people all over the country, Lee was stricken with polio. After two years of excruciating exercise, his arm muscles grew strong again, and he learned to walk with crutches and metal braces. During this period, he kept up his schoolwork and miraculously graduated with his class in 1937. There was no handicapped access at the school. When it was impossible for Lee to get to seemingly inaccessible classrooms, a friend from the football team named Moose picked him up and took him where he needed to go.

Next Lee entered law school at the University of Virginia. He needed financial assistance and got a job as assistant to the dean of the Law School, F.D.G. Ribble.[5]

Near the end of Lee's second year in law school, President Roosevelt was scheduled to give the commencement address. His son, Franklin, Jr., was a law student at the school, and it was time for him to graduate. Unfortunately, Junior was a terrible student.

One day, as Lee sat at his desk outside the dean's office, he heard Ribble exclaiming loudly to one of the professors, "You are going to graduate Franklin Roosevelt because his father is going to give the address at graduation!"

The next thing Lee knew, Dean Ribble called out to him, "Bean, get in here. What do you know about contract law?"[6]

So Lee became the tutor. This was no easy task, but on June 10, 1940, Franklin Junior was ready to graduate with his class. When Dean Ribble made certain the president knew of Lee Bean's important role in his son's graduation, Roosevelt wanted to thank Lee personally.

The movements of President Roosevelt were always carefully planned, taking into consideration his own disability from polio. Most Americans had no idea he could not use his legs. His staff sent instructions for Lee to wait at a predetermined spot.

When the limousine pulled up, the chauffeur walked around and invited Lee into the back seat next to the president, where the grateful father expressed his appreciation. The two men talked for a few minutes and quickly discovered they had something in common. No, it wasn't polio. Neither of them needed to talk about the disease that now framed their lives. What they shared was the love of stamps. Each had been a collector since childhood.[7]

The president left Lee and was driven to Memorial Gymnasium where he gave his impromptu "Stab in the Back" speech. That morning, Italy had declared war on Britain and France. President Roosevelt spoke with unmistakable anger, "On this tenth day of June 1940, the hand that held the dagger has struck it into the back of its neighbor." His speech, noting the delusion of isolationism, was broadcast over the three major networks and even overseas by shortwave radio.[8]

Three months later, when the mail arrived, Lee received a huge bag stuffed with stamps from all over the world. With it was a letter from

Postmaster General James Farley stating that the president had personally wanted to thank Lee with this gift.[9]

Lee Bean and Hedy's friendship soon came to an end. Lee was transferred to St. Louis, Missouri, and Hedy was destined to have other adventures.

On a Sunday early in December, the roommates heard the newsboys hollering, "Extra, Extra, Read all about it!" The Japanese had bombed Pearl Harbor. Because of this "date which will live in infamy," their country was at war with Japan. On December 11, Italy and Germany declared war on the United States. Almost immediately, the U.S. retaliated and declared war on them both. There was no more uncertainty. President Roosevelt had to mobilize every resource possible to get airplanes built and soldiers trained. The country would be forever changed.

An immediate fear was that the city of Washington would be invaded. Before Japan bombed Pearl Harbor, people had been casually walking through the White House gate without even a question. Now, blackout curtains were ordered and installed, and machine guns were set up on top of the president's official residence. Quadruple the number of Secret Service agents were assigned to him.[10]

Staff members and even Roosevelt were issued gas masks. The Secret Service needed to find a bulletproof limousine for him. Fortunately, the Treasury already had in its possession a huge armored limousine that had belonged to the gangster Al Capone.[11] It worked just fine.

Meanwhile, things were heating up at the IRS. Hedy was having to circle her boss's desk to avoid his flirtatious advances. Then he asked her to go on a junket with him. One week later, she filled out an application to work as a stenographer at a newly organized government agency, the Office of the Coordinator of Information.

Why did Hedy really decide to change jobs? *Except when we ran across movie stars who were delinquent in paying their taxes, the Internal Revenue was a bore.*

The Coordinator of Information

Long before the United States entered the war, the ever-increasing threat existed that the country would be drawn into the conflict in Europe. President Roosevelt realized the critical need for stronger intelligence-gathering capabilities. He wanted to facilitate cooperation and sharing of information among the existing intelligence organizations. These included the FBI, the State Department, the Office of Naval Intelligence, and the War Department's Military Intelligence Division.[12]

On July 11, 1941, Roosevelt appointed Wall Street lawyer and former Assistant Attorney William J. Donovan to be Coordinator of Information (COI)[13] for a centralized intelligence agency. Donovan, a member of the Republican Party, would report directly to the Democratic president.

William Donovan's nickname was "Wild Bill" because of his heroic leadership of the Fighting 69th infantry unit during World War I. He had become the most decorated soldier in this country's history. Now in his late 50s, Donovan was a go-getter who had learned through the years how to confidently and quietly present his ideas.

The year before, at the president's request, Donovan had gone to London to study what was happening in Britain. He was even received by the king. Donovan met with government and military officials and discussed topics important to the country's defense, including German fifth column espionage activities.

Donovan learned the British had been successful in capturing German agents and turning them into counterspies. The experienced

British Secret Intelligence Service was more than helpful to Donovan. They gave him access to highly classified information, sent him home with valuable reports, and hoped America would develop a spy organization modeled after theirs. Donovan reported to Washington that, with American support of military equipment, Britain should be able to survive against Hitler.[14]

While on his travels abroad, Donovan was able to collect postage stamps for President Roosevelt's beloved personal collection, including a Himmler stamp from the Third Reich.[15]

The surprise attack on Pearl Harbor made it painfully clear why the United States needed to bring its intelligence operations up to date. FDR told Donovan at 2:00 a.m. on December 8, "It's a good thing that you got me started on this."[16]

Donovan began by hurriedly putting together his staff. Even British Naval Intelligence Aide Ian Fleming, who later wrote the James Bond thrillers, sent him suggestions in this regard.[17] There was no time for long drawn out interview processes. Donovan went first to the people he knew and trusted, the circle of contacts he had built during his years as a lawyer. He hired professors, writers, clients and friends, many of them Ivy Leaguers from the country's most prestigious universities.

New recruits weren't all Ivy Leaguers. Donovan looked for people who could benefit his organization. Film stars and athletes were among his recruits. If they had the skills he needed, he hired them, and he didn't even shy away from hiring men with prison records. The mixture of racial, political and national backgrounds led to ridicule by Hitler and his propaganda chief Goebbels, but these were the men and women Donovan wanted because they could get the job done.

Donovan told his personnel that they "could not succeed without taking chances," and he took plenty of chances himself. In fact, his aide said Donovan was "unwilling to ask anyone to take a risk that he himself would not take."[18]

According to a secretary who recruited women for the organization, Donovan was looking for a "cross between a Smith College graduate, a Powers model, and a Katie Gibbs secretary."[19] His staff also looked for women who could speak a foreign language. Applicant Hedvig Johnson hadn't graduated from an exclusive college nor had she attended the renowned Katherine Gibbs School for secretaries. Nevertheless, her two years at Hibbing Junior College had prepared her to perform essential secretarial duties in any workplace. She could speak Swedish, and the fact that she was beautiful probably didn't hurt.

After a favorable character investigation, Hedy resigned from the IRS and on April 1, 1942, began her position with Donovan's new group, the COI. Her official title was Assistant Clerk-Stenographer at a salary of $1620 per annum. Hedy had secured a raise as well as an exciting new job.

The prior September, the COI had set up their offices in the Public Health buildings, a 13-acre complex west of the Lincoln Memorial. The official address was 2430 E. Street, NW, but no signage identified who worked there. Buildings were linked by underground tunnels.

On one side of the compound was an old brewery, and on the other side was the Naval Hospital. This was a good out of the way spot for Donovan's new agency.[20] Donovan's office was on the main floor of the white-columned administration building. If you climbed the steps and turned right, you might find him in the corner room at the end, working at his large mahogany desk. Individual offices were identified only by numbers, not names, and Donovan's read 109.[21]

When Hedy came to work each morning, she was dropped off in front of the administration building. Before the armed uniformed guard allowed her to enter, he would carefully study her laminated photo ID.

As a first order of business, Hedy signed an oath of secrecy never to reveal what went on within the top-secret organization. She was ordered not to speak of her activities with anyone. Hedy took this oath seriously her entire life. Many times she said, "I could *never* talk about what happened during the war."

Huge maps hung on the walls of the COI offices. As a constant reminder of the requirement of secrecy, posters in the corridors cautioned "Loose Lips Sink Ships" or "The Enemy is Listening." If anyone asked where she worked, Hedy had to answer vaguely, saying "Oh, I'm a file clerk with the government."

In the beginning, Hedy worked near "109" in Personnel Management but soon moved to the Executive Branch's Budget and Finance division. At the end of her first year, she received an excellent efficiency rating. She was a fast typist and could take and transcribe difficult dictation involving technical words and phrases. Shorthand was a skill she would use the rest of her life.

On June 13, 1942, in an effort to garner military support, the Office of the Coordinator of Information was brought under the authority of the Joint Chiefs of Staff, which included representatives from the various branches of the military. The organization's name was changed to the Office of Strategic Services, in short, the OSS.[22]

Donovan and his staff organized the OSS into several working branches, including:

- Research and Analysis (R&A), which did the background research for planning covert operations.
- Secret Intelligence (SI), which obtained secret information primarily through agents out in the field.

- Special Operations (SO), which implemented the subversive activities meant to disrupt the enemy.
- Operational Group (OG), which was composed of commando teams, primarily paratroopers highly trained in sabotage.
- Counterintelligence Branch (X-2), which executed counterespionage activities to keep track of enemy intelligence operations.
- Morale Operations (MO), which created propaganda campaigns to mislead the enemy.

These groups were served by a top-secret communications center located in the basement of the administration building at the E Street complex. There, coded messages were sent and received from all over the world. As the organization grew, branch offices were set up in at least ten additional buildings throughout Washington.[23]

As time went on, the OSS expanded its operations into cities all over the world. Offices were established in New York, San Francisco, Seattle, and Honolulu. In North Africa, undercover agents gathered intelligence to prepare for Operation Torch, the invasion of French North Africa. Then from London, operatives were sent into occupied France and later into Germany. Because Sweden was a neutral country, Stockholm would become an important listening post for the surrounding Nazi-controlled countries. These were just a few of the outposts where OSS agents in the field worked to gather intelligence and send it back to headquarters in Washington.

Once the information arrived, the secretaries on staff would sort, decode, file, write and type page after page of reports and then send the material to the proper branches. Afterward, these women had to forget what they had read and never mention it again. They might not have been the agents out in the field, parachuting behind enemy lines, but the secretaries knew what those agents were doing, and they cared what happened to them.

In October of 1942, another young woman left a position in the Office of War Information to join the OSS as a junior research assistant, working in the same area as Hedy. At 30 years old and a Smith graduate, Julia McWilliams was also an efficient typist. Her job was to review the reports and documents flowing through Donovan's office.

Julia left headquarters to work at the OSS Emergency Sea Rescue Equipment Section, where she helped develop shark repellent to protect fliers who had ditched into the sea.[24] The repellent was also coated on bombs that targeted German U-boats to prevent curious sharks from setting off the explosives.

In 1943, when Julia volunteered to go overseas, she was sent to Ceylon, present day Sri Lanka, and to Kunming, China. With her top security clearance, she served as Chief of the OSS Registry and managed secret messages and documents.[25] In later years, she would be known all over the world as "The French Chef," Julia Child.

As Hedy's roommate Thelma Kane explained, she herself worked in the accounting part of the organization, but Hedy worked on the "quiet side." According to Thelma, "She was right there with Donovan. She could never talk about her life at work because everything was so secret."

Thelma's job was to issue the paperwork for travel vouchers requested by persons doing work for the OSS. "I remember once Hedy brought Donovan's papers home so I could help her finish them," Thelma said. "These were his travel vouchers, and we had them spread out over the bed. We had to make sure the forms were filled out correctly so he could be reimbursed."

By March of 1943, Hedy had been promoted from Budget and Finance to the Counter Intelligence (CI) division as senior clerk, working for William H. Sherwood. The files Hedy handled were marked "Top Secret" and involved reports on what enemy agents were doing all over the world. In the absence of Mr. Sherwood, she was authorized to sign for all personnel matters for the CI division.

Although the women greatly outnumbered the men, Hedy had her share of dates to escort her to the popular restaurants and clubs. Hedy's friend Lee Bean had already left Washington. Another of her "dear friends," as she wrote on the back of his photograph, was Paul Paterni with the OSS. He left Washington to go first to North Africa and then to Italy. President Roosevelt telephoned his mother upon Paul's arrival in North Africa to reassure her that her son had reached there safely. After the war, Paterni became deputy chief of the Secret Service under President Kennedy and was very much involved in the investigation following Kennedy's assassination.

OSS officer William Casey, who in 1981 became director of the CIA, described Donovan's office as "the most exciting place in Washington."[26] Thelma Kane concurred, saying "There was always something going on. So many well-known people came through who wanted to do their duty for the war. Do you remember the movie *Sergeant York*? I did the paperwork for the actor who played the Sergeant. He didn't talk much, and he wore a funny hat, I think hoping nobody would recognize him."

In 1939, Gary Cooper went to Germany with his father-in-law, an economic adviser to Roosevelt, to research German finances. They met with Albert Göring, the anti-Nazi brother of Hitler's commander of the German Air Force, Hermann Göring.[27] It is interesting to imagine that a few years later Gary Cooper might have undertaken some type of undercover assignment himself.

Another prominent person Thelma came in contact with was J. Robert Oppenheimer. He needed to travel somewhere quickly, but the airplanes were overbooked. Oppenheimer called Thelma and asked if she could kick someone off a plane so he could fly instead. Thelma, who had been told this was not the thing to do, refused. The furious physicist asked for her supervisor who, unsurprisingly, allowed it. Thelma bragged later that she was chewed out by the "father of the atomic bomb."

One weekend Hedy asked Thelma to go to New York City. Mr. Sherwood wanted Hedy to go with him, and she preferred to have Thelma along. Thelma didn't know the reason for the trip. After all, Hedy worked on the quiet side.

Thelma remembers, "When we got to our hotel, Hedy cautioned me about talking on the telephone. It might be bugged, she said to my surprise. Hedy explained I would hear beeping in the background. Earlier in the day, a large bag of cash had disappeared from headquarters. No one was above suspicion." Thelma met Hedy and Mr. Sherwood at the famous Astor Hotel for drinks and dinner. She never did hear any beeps.

London

At the end of 1943, Roosevelt, Churchill, and Stalin met at the Soviet Embassy in Tehran. The Big Three confirmed there would be a cross-Channel invasion of France during May of the following year. Gen. Dwight D. Eisenhower was appointed supreme commander of the operation, code name Overlord. Britain became a massive camp for the troops as forces began to gather, and for the Allies who were there, Great Britain was the center of the universe.

After working for the OSS for more than a year, Hedy received official notice in July of 1943 that her headquarters had been changed. She was going to London! Her salary by now was $2600 per annum. A medical exam found her fit for Foreign Service.

Only a small percentage of the women who worked for the OSS were sent overseas. That Hedy had such good secretarial skills and could also speak a foreign language were undoubtedly factors considered in her selection.

It would be six months before Hedy would leave for her new post. A secret monthly progress report from OSS London described the difficulties in obtaining adequate staff from the United States. The report noted, "The Army will not allow these women to be transported to London." The challenge was to find secure transport, as the Germans were a threat to planes and ships alike.

Finally, Hedy's orders came through. Along with others from her office, she took a train to New York City where the group spent the next ten days making final arrangements for their trip across the Atlantic.

Hedy spent most of her time in New York with Debbie Stowe, also traveling overseas to OSS London. For the two young ladies, it was an exciting hiatus. Sidewalks were packed. Alongside the holiday shoppers were servicemen from all branches, celebrating as hard as they could while they waited to be shipped out.

During the evenings, the girls went to the movies or jitterbugged in one of the popular nightclubs. Just opened on Broadway was *The Voice of the Turtle*, a comedy focusing on the challenges of a single woman living in wartime New York City. By the time they were ready to sail, Debbie announced she had spent nearly every dollar she had. In fact, she arrived in England with 32 cents in her purse.

At Times Square, the news zipper wrapped around the *New York Times* building and kept the gathered crowds informed of the progress of the war. On New Year's Eve, the rules were relaxed for the merrymakers, and the neon lights remained bright until ten o'clock at night.

The next morning, January 1, 1944, Hedy and her companions were at Pier 86 to board the four-stack *Aquitania*, a massive British luxury ocean liner gutted and converted to a troop ship. This was not the first time the *Aquitania* had served at war. During World War I, she was at various times an armed merchant cruiser, a troop ship, and a hospital ship.[28]

As the 900-foot long vessel left the dock, servicemen and women hung over the railings and waved good-bye to the cheering crowds on the pier below. It was a scene right out of the movies. As the ocean liner pulled out, the waters were swarming with freighters, tugboats, ferries, boats of all kinds. It was a remarkable sight, but soon the city and the other boats were left far behind, specks on the horizon.

The price of Hedy's warship ticket was $165, including tax. The ship was crowded with soldiers who slept stacked like sardines in their bunks. The women were housed separately, and Hedy's orders stated that she would travel with the same privileges as an officer. That meant crowded quarters with barely enough room to walk around and two meals a day.

The trip across the Atlantic took 11 days, with much zigzagging in order to evade German submarines. Despite the potential hazards, this voyage was the most exciting adventure yet for the 22-year-old from a small Minnesota mining town.

After disembarking at Glasgow, Scotland, Hedy followed specific written instructions on how to proceed. She was to report to "JRM" for duty:

a. If you are permitted to use a telephone at the port of debarkation, telephone the US Embassy at 72 Grosvenor Square and then ask for JRM. If he is not there, ask for Colonel B and leave a message for JRM as to what station you will arrive and the arrival time of your train.

b. If for any reason you cannot reach JRM or Colonel B by telephone, proceed to London.
c. Upon arrival in London, telephone Mayfair 8444 (if daytime) or Grosvenor 2495 (at night) and ask for JRM.
d. If for any reason you cannot reach JRM by telephone then proceed to 43a Hays Mews by taxi. If no one is there, then proceed to Claridge's or Grosvenor House and arrange for a room for the night. Then call Mayfair 8444 next morning and ask for JRM.

After a bite to eat in the dining room at Glasgow's Central Hotel, Hedy was able to use a telephone to alert JRM of her estimated arrival time. Then she and Debbie boarded the all-night train to London. As tired as they were, it was impossible to sleep sitting up in the dark, unheated car.

They were met at the London station by a young man, an American, who helped them with their bags and found a taxi for the three of them. Hedy was shocked by her first views of the city. Even though she had seen photographs and newsreels, nothing prepared her for the extent of the bombed ruins, in some areas block after block after block. The streets were clean, however, the debris hauled away.

London was cold and gray. There was no snow, and the temperature was about the same as it was in Washington. Hedy still hadn't been anywhere as cold as her hometown of Hibbing.

All over the city were barrage balloons suspended by long steel cables. They looked like enormous blimps floating in the sky and were there to ward off low-flying German bombers. Sandbags were piled up against buildings and lampposts as protection against a bomb explosion. The windows of many of the stores still open for business were boarded up.

Before she left New York, Hedy had been issued a small gas mask and four anti-gas eye shields. Because gas had been such a terrible weapon during World War I, these protections were issued as a precaution. Hedy wasn't sure what to expect, but she knew she could be fined if she went outside without them.

Her destination, Grosvenor Square in exclusive Mayfair, was a garden green surrounded by grand offices and residences. The formerly manicured gardens had been transformed, and this plot of ground was now the American nerve center. Military vehicles were parked anywhere their drivers could find space.

Number 1 Grosvenor Square housed the American Embassy. Number 20 was General Eisenhower's military headquarters, and for that reason this location was called Eisenhower Platz or Little America. If anyone asked where she worked, Hedy was instructed to say she was a government employee, a secretary at the American Embassy.

In 1938, President Roosevelt had named Joseph P. Kennedy, Sr. to be the American ambassador to the United Kingdom. Kennedy's term was a short and unpopular one. He made it clear that "wars were bad for business" and was sure Britain would lose the war. He resigned his post during the German bombings of 1940.

The following year, the President made a better choice and offered the post to the former New Hampshire governor, John Gilbert Winant. When the newly appointed ambassador arrived in March of 1941, King George VI met him personally at Windsor Station and then rode with him to Windsor Castle for tea. This remarkable act underscored the need of the entire country for the support of the United States. The ambassador delivered, and by the time the war was over, the British people considered him to be a true friend.[29]

A short walk away from Ambassador Winant's office at number 1 was a heavily guarded, fairly nondescript building at 72 Grosvenor Street, the first overseas station for the Office of Strategic Services. Colonel David K. E. Bruce was head of European operations for the OSS, and this location served as a base for clandestine activities in Europe, Africa, and the Middle East.

By the time Hedy arrived, the huge buildup before D-Day was underway, and there were 3255 OSS London employees working from several locations. Only 446 were women.[30]

As a final preparation for living in London, the OSS office gave Hedy four sheets of mimeographed onionskin instructions titled "A Short Guide to Grosvenor Square."

> Civilians will be given a ration of 60 coupons per year, which is a drop in the bucket on the basis of 26 for a suit, 5 for a shirt, 3 for socks, and 5 for shoes; so don't come with the idea that you will stock up from your favorite tailor. Anyway, his clothes aren't as good as they used to be.

Almost everything was rationed—clothes, gasoline, and food. By 1944, even toilet paper supplies had run low. Soap was very hard to come by. Fresh fruit was almost nonexistent.

The ration coupons were extremely valuable. By the end of January, Hedy had to apply for supplementary clothing coupons. The ration book she was initially issued had only 24 coupons, 12 short. Without the additional coupons, she couldn't have bought a suit if she'd wanted to. If one did have the coupons, a wool suit might cost $25.

Whiskey and gin as well as wines are rare and getting rarer. Although there is usually plenty at any public bar, purchase of a bottle is possible at the rate of about one per two weeks, and even then only if you know the wine merchant of old.

Mail. There are four methods of sending mail:

- Regular sea-mail takes about a month but is roughly the same the year round; during the winter it is frequently better than air-mail.
- Regular air-mail varies from ten days to six weeks.
- Via travelers is faster, unless the traveler is held up on the way. In any event, it must all be pre-censored.
- "V" mail is far away the best and fastest.

On both mail and cables, censorship is normal; names of places are barred particularly when they reveal troop or ship movements. You can't use hotel stationery with APO address. The main thing to remember on cables is they have to make sense, or the censor will send them back.

Transport. London has excellent bus and underground services. The minimum fare by bus or subways is 3 cents, but fares vary with length of journey. On the subway ("the tube"), you buy a ticket at the start of the journey and hang on to it grimly all the way. Because of the gas shortage, buses don't run later than 10:30 and the trains stop at midnight. Taxis are becoming increasingly rare, and late at night don't be surprised if you find you have to walk all the way home.

Flats are most difficult to find and expensive. The continued flow of American officers has jacked all the prices up. If you can get a service flat for one under 8 guineas or for two under 12 guineas per week you are lucky. But then you are lucky if you can get one at all.

Hotels were jammed. The OSS guide highly recommended Claridge's, "almost an American Club." The Savoy, the Ritz, the Berkeley, the Mayfair, Grosvenor House and the Dorchester were all in the same class, it went on to say.

Hedy ended up at the Adelphi Hotel at 127 Cromwell Road. The rooms were small, but the price was right, and the location was good. Her instructions were to get a good night's sleep.

When I first arrived in London, I lived at the Adelphi Hotel with the people who came from our Washington, D.C. office. They were all college professors—and me!

It wasn't long before I moved to a lovely apartment on Park Close on the fifth floor, the highest floor around at the time. Since most people didn't want to live that high up while London was being bombed, the rent was less expensive. We got it from wealthy Londoners who had fled to the country. It was beautifully furnished with a lot of dark wood, and I got to sleep in a big four-poster bed.

Park Close was near Harrods Department Store. The night a flying bomb hit Harrods directly, we lost some windows. Our windows were covered with thick heavy drapes. London was completely blacked out every evening.

Not a glimmer of light could escape to be seen by enemy pilots. Vehicles had their headlights covered. Walking at night in the pitch black was difficult until the eyes adjusted. A small flashlight, a torch, could be used as long as it wasn't noticeable.

Park Close was in Knightsbridge near the south end of Hyde Park, the Central Park of London. Flats in Knightsbridge, near excellent shopping and restaurants, were popular with the women of the OSS. On a nice day, they could walk through Hyde Park and see an American game of baseball. This peculiar game was altogether new to most of the Londoners watching from the sidelines.

I lived with a girl who had her Ph.D. We used our stamps for one big meal a week when we invited friends over from the office. Entire families had to live on the coupons! The rest of the week, I ate out.

Again, I couldn't believe all this was happening to me. London! No. 1 Ryder Street was our office. A lot of espionage novels mention that address. At the time, I thought it a dump! We were crowded and often cold. American secretaries were treated royally, but the British employers did not give their helpers, girls, i.e., much respect. Penalized them if they came in late, etc.

The British government's foreign intelligence service is MI6, also known as the Secret Intelligence Service, or SIS. The domestic security intelligence service is MI5. In 1943, MI6, Section V, involving foreign counterintelligence, had offices in a brick and masonry building at the corner of Ryder and Bury, not far from Piccadilly. American counterintelligence, X-2, moved into the floor above. This was not by accident. The two services developed a close working relationship, and the British made available to the OSS the results of their years of intelligence activity.

The official address for the two services was 7 Ryder Street. At first the Americans had only one room, crowded with up to 17 people working with little privacy. Gradually more space was available as additional offices were completed. By February, X-2 had a staff of 75.[31] Head of X-2 Europe was Norman Holmes Pearson, a Yale English instructor.

Around the time Hedy arrived in London, her desk in the Scandinavian section moved into the building directly adjoining number 7, and she always referred to her address as number 1.[32] The rooms were heated by wood burning fireplaces, and sometimes the young women typed in their gloves. Steaming hot tea helped keep their hands warm and functioning properly.

X-2 London became the principal headquarters for American counterespionage. There were many vital sources of information, as well as the British files, and these could not be safely transmitted to Washington. In addition, most of the refugee governments now had their headquarters in London, and it was imperative to have secure cooperation with them.

One of X-2's most important assignments was to keep updated files on anyone who could possibly be an enemy agent. The British gave the Americans access to their index card system, already in use for many years. Information was gathered from many sources and collated in such a way that all data related to a single personality could be obtained quickly.[33] It was a massive undertaking to correlate the index cards with volumes of thick files and then keep the cards up to date. By the end of the war, X-2 had a collection of 300,000 cards targeting individuals who were somehow connected with German intelligence or were suspected of being collaborators.[34]

The primary enemies were the Abwehr, German military intelligence, and the Sicherheitsdienst or SD, the intelligence agency of the Nazi Party.[35] Through their Double Cross system, the British had been extremely successful in turning German spies into British agents. MI6, along with the Government Code and Cypher School, had set up shop at Bletchley Park, a mansion 50 miles from London. The codebreakers there had successfully broken the Nazi codes. With knowledge of the German messages coming through on the wireless, the British were able to use their double agents to feed misleading information back to Germany. The cooperation between MI6 and their American counterparts in X-2 proved invaluable.

From Ryder Street came some of the most highly classified intelligence of the war. Everything was hush-hush, top secret. Hedy could never tell anyone where her office was located. Each time she took a taxi to work, she gave the driver an address on Regent Street, a few blocks farther. Then she cautiously walked the rest of the way. Her route took her by St. James Square, its once lovely gardens planted with cabbages and other vegetables during the war.

London and the surrounding countryside was filling up with men and supplies. A million and a half American men and women had arrived in the United Kingdom. That number didn't include those from other Allied countries and those whose homelands had been overrun by the Germans. It also didn't include 500 journalists from the United States alone.[36] Wartime correspondent Walter Cronkite described England as the "world's largest aircraft carrier."[37]

As battles with Germany and Japan raged on, Hedy and her colleagues were caught up in an almost surreal other world, the social frenzy of London.

Britain was tired of war, but London morale was soaring as soldiers from so many countries arrived in the city. Despite the rationing, despite the blackouts and bombings, London was an exciting place for Hedy. Sidewalks were teeming with uniforms. Pubs and restaurants enjoyed a brisk business. Many offered music, dancing, and cocktails, a welcome relief from looming hostilities.

There were many more men than women in Hedy's office, and the beautiful brunette never wanted for a date. In fact, by the end of September 1944, there were 147 people working for X-2 London Headquarters. Of those, only 30 were women.

Hedy's favorite restaurants were in the fine hotels such as the Savoy and Claridge's. Most Londoners were not able to dine out in such style, but the Americans could. The bands played the same songs heard back in the States, and the liquor flowed freely. At Savoy's American bar, you could even get a mixed drink with ice, and Hedy learned to appreciate a martini served with an olive.

I went to every theater in London, did not miss a one. When we would leave the theater, it was pitch black outside. I was petrified. Hundreds of people could be rushing all around you, but in the murkiness, all I could hear was muffled footsteps. One night I watched a girl smash her flashlight on top of some fresh guy's head.

Going to the theatre was an important part of life for Londoners. When war first broke out, the government closed the theatres for fear they would be hit by the bombs. Gradually rules were relaxed. Theatres opened again and became an escape for the Londoners, a reprieve from their problems. "God Save the King" was played at the end of all London's shows.

Written on the back of the theatre programs were important announcements. "If an Air Raid warning be received during the performance the audience will be informed. The warning will not necessarily mean that a raid will take place. Those desiring to leave the Theatre may do so, but the performance will continue." The show must go on!

A lot of weekends, I went by bus to an airfield I called Great Yeldham. I traveled with the showgirls from the plays Hi de Hi *at the Stoll Theater and* Strike a New Note *at the Prince of Wales. There was this guy from Hibbing, Minnesota who was the Air Force public relations guy, and he was in charge of bringing the girls to dance and spend the weekends. Great fun! The first weekend I attended I expected to see three boys from Hibbing. Two of them went down over Germany the day before. One never came back.*

Not long after Hedy left her desk in Washington, D.C. for London, one of her former co-workers sent a verse:

While you were gone away
Someone called to say,
"Is that beautiful bombshell around?"
No, sorry, she's gone to town.

Then that Major Angleton in he flew
Wanted to know where were you?
Inquired, if on his T/R, you were working
Or, if your duty you were shirking?

But, of course, I let Angleton be.
You know that no man phases me!
After all, what a substitute am I
When it was for you that he came by!

There were two Angletons who came through the Washington office. The senior Angleton, James Hugh Angleton, had a brief career in OSS Counterespionage X-2. His son, James Jesus Angleton, graduated from Yale and attended Harvard Law School for a year before going into the army. After 12 weeks of basic training, he was offered an assignment with the OSS.[38] Angleton went to London in January of 1944 to work at the X-2 Italian desk. The notably bespectacled OSS officer arrived at Ryder Street shortly after Hedy did.

Young Jim Angleton brought a cot to his tiny office so he could sleep after working late into the night.[39] There was no central heating in the building, and since it was forbidden to open the windows, Angleton worked in a cigarette smoke-filled fog.[40]

At the end of the year, he went to Italy and was soon named Chief of X-2 in Italy. He remained there until 1947. Angleton went on to serve with the CIA and in 1954 became head of counterintelligence.

Hedy couldn't have helped but notice one good-looking MI6 officer, Harold "Kim" Philby, who roamed in and out of Angleton's office on Ryder Street. In 1944, Angleton had no idea that his friend and mentor had become a Soviet agent soon after his graduation from Cambridge University. Philby and four of his classmates, the Cambridge Five, had been sending whatever top secret information they could get their hands on—the codebreaking, the identities of agents, the Double Cross—straight to Moscow.

The Baby Blitz

More than three years earlier, in September of 1940, Hitler had unleashed his bombers on London and other cities in Britain. In the beginning, there were bombings every day and every night. Londoners fled to underground tube stations converted to bomb shelters. Countless homes and buildings were destroyed, and more than 42,000 civilians were killed. The Blitz, short for the German word *Blitzkrieg*, or "lightning war," lasted until May of 1941.

Hedy knew what awaited her in London. During the bombings, Edward R. Murrow broadcasted over the radio directly from England and described the horrific events live.

Only 10 days after Hedy arrived, the Luftwaffe resumed mass bombing of London in what was called the Baby Blitz. These raids went on for three months, up to 100 planes per night. Fortunately, the damage was not as extensive as in 1940. During the previous four years, Germany had lost too many planes and pilots to wage as severe a strike.

During those days of bombings, the tension in the Ryder Street offices was palpable whenever the piercing air raid sirens went off. Suddenly everyone could hear the rumble as German planes approached the city. In late February, the windows of the outside X-2 offices were destroyed. Everyone had to move into the inside rooms until repairs were done.

Then, just days after the Allied invasion at Normandy, Hitler began to send over the *Vergeltungswaffen*, his vengeance weapons. First to arrive were the unmanned V-1s, jet-powered airplanes that carried a one-ton bomb. These were known as buzz bombs or, as nicknamed by the RAF, doodlebugs. Lord Hee Haw, the American-born traitor who broadcast Nazi propaganda over the radio, had hinted that a new wonder weapon was coming, and Hitler's propaganda chief Goebbels bragged that it would bring Britain to its knees.[41]

The first night, 217 bombs were aimed at Britain, with 45 of those hitting London.[42] These flying bombs thundered across the Channel day and night. In July, Hedy mailed home a cartoon she had cut from the *Daily Express*. Cartoonist Carl Giles had drawn a busy London street scene. Everyone sported one normal ear and one huge ear. A man remarked to his companion, "It's ridiculous to say these flying bombs have affected people in ANY way."

Children were evacuated from the city, as they had been during the 1940 Blitz. Their train was called the Doodlebug Express. These robot planes ravaged the city until the end of August.

At night, we watched the bombings by the German planes and the ack-ack of the British artillery attempting their destruction. This was exciting, but when the buzz bombs (V-1s) started, that was different. The bombs flew over, and when the motor stopped, that was it. You knew it was going to hit. You had to either hide or pray. They started every evening, all night long, and I could hardly sleep.

In 1944, new underground shelters opened, each able to accommodate 8000 people who could sleep in tiered bunks. There were dormitories for the babies and canteens for refreshments. People arrived immediately after work and sat around chatting and reading the newspaper before trying to sleep. Hedy went to a bomb shelter once. She never went back.

Later on, we had daytime treats also. I spent my evenings in underground nightclubs and my boss, Bill Carlson, got me an ankle bracelet he insisted I wear because he knew I would be found dead somewhere with no identification.

When I went home in the evenings, I would see long lines of mothers with their children waiting to get into the underground shelters. If I'd had children I would have been right in line with them.

During the bombings, OSS staff members were assigned to fire guard duty on the roof of their building to watch for incendiary bombs. Looking out over London, with a protective steel helmet on her head, Hedy watched buildings ablaze, some not far away. Sparks and smoke filled the sky. One night Hedy was scheduled alongside the English author Graham Greene, who also worked at Ryder Street as a deputy under MI6 officer and Soviet spy Kim Philby. In order to pass the time, Hedy and the already-famous author talked all night long.

What I remember is how thrilled the fire watchers were with the breakfast the next morning. Fish, boiled potatoes, porridge, and coffee (half hot milk, half strong coffee—good!)

All in all, the Germans sent 2000 V-1 bombs that killed some 6000 Londoners and wounded many more. The RAF had some success in intercepting and destroying the bombs. The antiaircraft guns and the barrage balloons were an additional line of defense.

The BBC newsreels stressed, "London can take it!" The Germans were not allowed to know what was really happening. "The British people suffered so," Hedy always remembered.

During the early months of 1944, activity in the OSS offices focused on the impending Allied invasion of Europe. Each morning, an information sheet from headquarters gave updates. As the day of the landings approached, the personnel felt both excitement and concern.

William Donovan arrived in London on May 14 to oversee last-minute details. Special operations commandos were moved secretly into France to gather vital information and to aid the Resistance in their sabotage efforts.

Even though military commanders were dead set against the idea, Donovan and David Bruce, head of London OSS, went aboard the heavy cruiser *USS Tuscaloosa* to wait out the final days before the invasion. They watched as 6000 ships gathered for the largest military mission ever. On D-Day plus one, they found their way to Utah Beach, dodging enemy fire before they found a safe spot.[43] Fortunately for the world of American intelligence, they weren't at Omaha Beach, site of the bloodiest fighting.

The invasion had been a complete surprise, and although the war would not be over for nearly another year, the Allies had crossed Hitler's impregnable front.

William T. Carlson

Hedy's boss in London was William Theodor "Bill" Carlson. He was born in Portland, Connecticut, on May 15, 1907, to parents who had emigrated from Sweden. Because Hedy's parents were Swedish-Finns, Hedy's and Bill's common heritage gave them an immediate connection.

Carlson was 5'10 ¾" and weighed 178 pounds. He had blue eyes, brown hair, and a stocky build. An accomplished pianist and organist, he sang in his college glee club. He enjoyed the outdoors, especially tennis, swimming, hunting, and fishing.

After graduating from Wesleyan University, Carlson went to work for the cosmetics firm Elizabeth Arden, first as an export manager and then as general sales manager. In his own words on his application to work for the OSS, he "started from the bottom and worked up."[44] Company business took him all over Europe. He lived in Berlin for two years (1930–1932) and then in London for eight years (1932–1940.)

In 1932, Bill married Valerie Georgette Klee in Frankfurt, Germany. Six years later, the couple separated because of "incompatibility and wife's pro-German proclivities."[45] Valerie had been born in Ohio to parents of German descent, and by wartime she was in Munich working as an artist. She and Carlson had no children.

Carlson left Elizabeth Arden to join the army in July of 1941. He graduated from Officer Candidate School at Fort Benning, Georgia, in December 1942 as a second lieutenant.

He was fluent in German and Swedish and could converse fairly well in French and somewhat in Spanish. In short, Carlson was the perfect candidate to work in counterintelligence for the army, and by 1942 he was doing exactly that.

Carlson's abilities were duly noted by economist Dr. Calvin B. Hoover. Following his service during World War I, Hoover had worked in the Soviet

William T. Carlson in the 1940s.

Union, Germany, Poland and other European countries. After Pearl Harbor, he joined the OSS to organize operations in Northern Europe and Poland with the goal of penetrating Germany from those areas. He quickly realized the benefit of setting up shop inside Sweden, a neutral country near to Germany.[46] At the beginning of 1943, Hoover requested Carlson be transferred to work for the OSS in the Secret Intelligence (SI) section. Because Carlson had lived in Europe for some 15 years, Hoover noted, he was excellently qualified for this work.

Originally, the War Department turned down Hoover's request. Carlson's commanding officer didn't want to release him, but the determined Hoover issued a new and stronger plea. In a March 26 letter, Hoover stressed that "an exceedingly responsible foreign post has opened up for which Lt. Carlson is better fitted than any other available to us." On April 30, Hoover's request was approved, and Carlson was assigned to the OSS in Washington, D.C.

Carlson first met Hedvig Johnson in Washington, and they liked each other immediately. Their 14-year age difference was probably the primary reason Hedy never let the relationship grow beyond a close friendship. Before Carlson left for Europe, he recommended Hedy be sent there too.

Carlson arrived at OSS London in July of 1943 and was initially in charge of the German desk of SI. By January, he was executive officer under the head of X-2 counterintelligence at Ryder Street, in charge of the Scandinavian Section.[47]

When Hedy arrived in London, she immediately began to work for Carlson at the Scandinavian desk, side by side with his other secretary, Edith Rising. In preparation for his imminent transfer to Sweden, Carlson asked that all exit permits from the United Kingdom to Scandinavia be submitted to X-2. He also began to order necessary materials for upcoming special projects in Stockholm. These items included two cameras, a case of American cigarettes, a 25-pound bag of coffee, two cases with concealed compartments, an invisible ink set with developer, a letter opening set and a one-pound tin of Edgewood tobacco. Bill Carlson loved to smoke a pipe.

During the first quarter of 1944, hurried arrangements were being made to send Carlson on to Stockholm to work for X-2 under diplomatic cover. Originally, it was planned to have him designated as an assistant military attaché, and approval had been given by officials in Stockholm. However, MIS (Military Intelligence Service) in Washington rejected this plan. The State Department finally approved Carlson's designation as a commercial attaché.[48]

Since military personnel were not acceptable to Sweden's American Ambassador in any office other than military attaché, Carlson resigned his commission, and on April 12, 1944, left for Stockholm. He was followed on April 26 by Edith Rising.

Hedy had been in London not even a month when she entered the Berlitz School of Languages to brush up on her Swedish. A move to Sweden was on her agenda, too.

The X-2 London Scandinavian desk was greatly handicapped during early April by the departure of Carlson and Rising. For the next few months, the search to find a satisfactory substitute for Carlson and adequate desk staff was not productive. When the first candidate arrived, Carlson was already gone, and there was little or no training available. Candidate number one was sent back out into the field. Carlson's second replacement was "temperamentally unsuited for X-2 work." His secretary, Miss Hedvig Johnson, heartily agreed. He soon went back to the States.

To further complicate matters, Carlson continued to urgently request the transfer of Hedvig Johnson to Stockholm.[49] But she could not leave until a suitable replacement arrived from Washington.

In the meantime, Hedvig worked feverishly to update all active cases related to Stockholm. Photographs of each card made in London were sent to Stockholm without delay. Reports titled "Axis Intelligence Activities in Sweden," with lists of known and suspected German agents, were scrutinized for necessary revisions to the all-important card files.

Finally, secretary Sophie Egloff arrived, and candidate number three for Carlson's position was on his way to London. On August 11, 1944, Hedvig Johnson left for Stockholm.[50]

When the offer to go to Stockholm, Sweden came, I took it. We had to fly over Norway which was occupied by the Germans, so we waited for two weeks before the weather was foggy enough to fly late at night.

My first day in the Swedish office, I was introduced to Herman Allen. And that is another story!

Chapter 3

Herman's Story

In 2005, Herman landed in the hospital when his behavior became so erratic that Hedy insisted something terrible must be wrong. His doctor admitted him to the psychiatric floor of Baptist Hospital for a week. One evening, Hedy, Kathy and her two children, Bill, and I were in his room playing cards when the doctor walked in and asked, "Herman, how are you?"

Herman, always in charge, answered, "I am fine and ready to go home."

The doctor replied, "Let me ask you some questions, Herman. What year is it?"

"2005."

"Who is our President?"

"Bush."

"Who are these people?"

Herman panned the room. "I have no idea who they are."

We were used to our father's antics, but we weren't sure the doctor got the joke. Hedy laughed so hard, she cried.

Israel Nathan Aharon

Herman's father, Israel Nathan Aharon, was born August 15, 1886, in the village of Rimshan, Lithuania, about 90 from Vilna, the country's capital and largest city.

Lithuania, positioned between Poland and Russia, has a long history of occupation by both those countries. In the years before World War II, small villages known as shtetls, each with a high percentage of Jews, could be found all over Lithuania. There were 30 or so Jewish families living in Rimshan.

Israel came from a large family. His parents, Avraham and Sara Esther, had 18 children. Four died before the age of two. Their home was 17 miles from a lake where Avraham owned a fishery with several boats. He supervised more than 100 people. The men who worked for him would catch the fish, crate them aboard wagons, and then take the fish into the cities for the fish auction. One of his sons later wrote, "Avraham Aharon was respected by all."

Avraham also owned a little store in town. Always working, he didn't have much time to spend with his children.

Sara worked in the fishery business too. She kept her new babies in the house for five months and then gave them over to a wet nurse. Until he was two years old, Israel spent little or no time with his mother. When Israel was a school boy, he went to a rabbi to study Hebrew and Polish. He was a good student and excelled in languages. When he was older, Israel got up early each day to work with the fishermen and the drivers, helping in various parts of the fishing operation. He loved the horses and in the winter raced them on the ice.

In 1907, 21-year-old Israel was called into the army. For the Jews of Lithuania, the anti-Semitic military was a well-known nightmare, almost surely a death sentence. The Jews were beaten, humiliated, and often forced to abandon their religion.

After Israel received his official notice to join the army, he took the physical examination and passed. He had two days off before reporting for service. In those two days, his mother bought him a ticket for the city today known as Kaunas, Lithuania, more than a hundred miles away. From there, he traveled by train all the way to Bremen, Germany, where he boarded the ship *Barbarossa*, headed for America.

When Israel arrived in New York City on October 16, his first stop was to see a relative. This man had a brother in Nova Scotia, Canada, and suggested Israel might find better opportunities there. He even paid for Israel's train ticket.

At the border crossing into Canada, the official had trouble understanding the pronunciation of Israel's Yiddish last name, so he simply wrote "Allen" on the form. Thus, Israel Nathan Aharon became I.N. Allen, and American history for the Allen family began.

Glace Bay, Nova Scotia, was a small but thriving coal mining town. When the mine opened some years earlier, the company advertised in European newspapers for workers. Jewish families from shtetls in Poland and Russia came to Canada, all searching for a better life. I.N. found this to be a community of people he could relate to, and Glace Bay is where he settled.

The young man had no professional skills and didn't speak English. He had to earn a living, but it would not be in the coal mines. I.N. borrowed a package of writing paper from a friend. He put the paper in a peddler's pack and called on the households around town, selling stationery.

Thus, I.N. became a paper peddler. With the coins he got, he bought more paper and worked hard to sell it. Finally he had enough money to open a small store, and he sold his goods to the mining families.

One day, a road show from the United States came to town. The outgoing and sociable I.N. made a date with one of the girls. She told him, "I'd like a fur coat." He must have liked her a lot because he gave her a nice coat from his stock. The next morning she left town by train without a word. I.N. took off in an automobile and raced after the train. He caught up with it at the first station, went aboard, and forcibly removed the coat from the young lady.[51]

I.N. wrote a letter to his mother and offered to pay for anyone in the family who wanted to come to America. In these efforts to bring more people to his new homeland, I.N. joined a local group that wanted to assist European Jews by bringing them to Glace Bay. He became an active member and traveled to Minneapolis for a big meeting. At a social gathering there, he was introduced to a pretty young woman named Emma.

Emma Greenberg

Emma Greenberg was born on November 20, 1889, in Wisconsin. Her father's name in Russia had been Chaim Avrum Minalow, the eldest child of an affluent Jewish family living in a region then known as Bessarabia. Employed by a grain broker, Chaim went out into the country to buy wheat from the large landowners. He traveled to beautiful cities—Kiev, Vilna, Odessa—and the noblemen on their huge estates often invited him to dine. After his wife, with whom he had a daughter, died, Chaim wed a girl named Hannah Sherman.

Anti-Jewish pogroms began to increase in Russia, and Chaim was afraid he would be forced into the Russian Army to suffer the horrific treatment given to Jews. He decided he and his family must leave the country. Chaim, Hannah, along with his daughter Bertha, arrived in

New York City around 1886. A family named Greenberg befriended them. Worried that the Russian czar could trace him even in America, Chaim took the name of Charles Abraham Greenberg.

To eke out a living, Charles became a peddler selling needles, thread, and other small household goods. The housewives he sold to identified each item and helped him learn English.

The Greenberg family moved to the small town of Necedah, Wisconsin, probably because Charles thought living there would be easier and less expensive than in New York. Six more children were born. With his two brothers, who had also come to the United States, Charles opened what became Greenberg's Big Store. He drove into the countryside peddling wares from his wagon while his brothers ran the store.

Then newspapers publicized a gold rush in Republic, Washington, a town almost at the Canadian border. Land was free to be homesteaded, and prospectors rushed in to stake their claims. In 1902, Charles traveled west to Republic by stagecoach. The primary industry there was iron ore mining, but there was excitement over the discovery of gold. Prospectors set up tents, and families built log cabins. Charles opened a store and sold blankets, shoes, and outerwear. The miners passed by his store on their way to and from work, and business was good.

Two years later, when a passenger train began to run to Republic, Charles sent for his wife and seven children. The Greenbergs were the first Jewish family in town. As the settlement prospered, so did they. Charles built a large five-bedroom home with porches in front and along the side, and he and Hannah had three more children.

As time went on, Charles learned to type and wrote in a daily Yiddish newspaper, the *Tageblatt*, describing the opportunities available in the West. It was a dream come true when he established a small Jewish settlement similar to the kibbutz communities in Israel. After the hardships these Jews had experienced in Europe, they longed to find a home where they could live in peace.[52]

In 1910, Hannah died of a streptococcus infection. Emma, now 20 years old, took over primary care for the younger children. She also continued her education and taught school. Each morning, Emma rode to the schoolhouse in a two-wheel sulky pulled by a white horse. It was a sight to see. The publisher of the local newspaper fell in love with her, but marriage was out of the question. The young man wasn't Jewish.

Emma's mother's family had emigrated from Russia to Minnesota. During a visit to her grandmother, Sura Sherman, in Minneapolis, Emma met I.N. Allen, a tall, handsome gentleman from Nova Scotia. Known to be a successful business owner, he had come to the city as a delegate from an organization trying to recruit European Jews to Canada.

After her holiday, Emma returned home, and I.N. went back to Canada. Four years later, he read about the Jewish settlement that Charles Greenberg had founded. I.N. decided to travel to Republic to investigate the settlement, as well as to renew his acquaintance with fair Emma.

The good-looking young man created quite a splash in town. The local newspaper even printed a picture of him, the visitor from afar, dressed in a formal black swallowtail suit. Emma's father and I.N. were similar in many ways. Each man spoke several languages, was a good writer, and had a passion for building a Jewish community.

I.N. invited Emma to go on a romantic sleigh ride in the snow. She was thrilled when the horses began to run fast, and she fell over into his arms. The couple was married under a canopy on November 30, 1915, at the Greenberg family home. The marriage certificate described Emma as a 23-year-old schoolteacher and her groom as a merchant. Rabbi Jacob Abramovitz, originally from Nova Scotia and a friend of the groom, officiated.

After the ceremony, a sumptuous five-course dinner was served. Toasts were offered, and guests enjoyed a short musical program. The Republic newspaper carried a front-page story, no doubt written by Emma's former beau, the newspaper publisher. He had attended the newsworthy event with his wife.

To be honest, Emma had just turned 26, but she assumed a younger age from that day forward. She had been taking care of her brothers and sisters for years, and the prospect of leaving town with this dashing fellow was very appealing. It was also a relief for her father, who had married once more. His new wife could care for the children, and he no longer had to worry that his daughter might become a spinster.

After a honeymoon in San Francisco, the newlyweds traveled by train more than 3500 miles east to Glace Bay. When they arrived, Emma was dismayed to see that her new home, described so proudly by her husband, was only a small apartment attached to his store on McKeen Street, a few doors down from the Town Hall.

After what I.N. had been through, this apartment meant everything to him. He had work, he had a home, and he had his freedom. Now he had a wife. Life was good.

Two baby boys arrived almost immediately, both born in the tiny apartment. Herman came in 1916. Louis was born the next year.

Glace Bay was scenic and lush with wildflowers in the summertime, but winters lasted from October to May when temperatures got down to ten or twenty degrees below zero. Horse and sleigh was the primary means of transport. Year round, the town was quiet and slow-moving.

While I.N. was active and energetic, the former schoolteacher Emma was shy and reserved. Much like his father had done, I.N. spent most of his time at work. He spoke Yiddish and Russian well and also some German and French.

Emma was determined to teach her new husband to read and write in English. She found a first-grade primer. On one page, it said CAT, on the next, DOG, and so forth. Her husband was an impatient student. One day, he grabbed the book from her, tore it up and said, "To hell with the cat. To hell with the dog." Most of the English he eventually learned he picked up in the course of his everyday life. He communicated with his family only when necessary.

I.N.'s business continued to grow until he had a number of stores selling clothing, furniture, and groceries in Glace Bay and nearby towns. Finally, he could afford to move his family across the street into a nice 12-room house. There was a white picket fence in the front and a large back yard with apple trees.

Emma kept her new home immaculate. The front rooms were locked and saved for company, the furniture covered with sheets. A young lady from Newfoundland was Emma's live-in maid and helped make sure everything was perfect. The family ate dinner in shifts, first the children and then, last of all when he got home from work, I.N. ate alone.

Behind their new home, a garage housed an old touring car, the first automobile in Glace Bay. A stable sheltered Sissy the cow and three horses named Crown Jay, Aubrey, and LaBee. When I.N. came home in the evening, he liked to harness a horse to pull his two-wheeled single-seat wagon. Then he raced back and forth on a mile-long lane, pacing and practicing the drive and the turns. Everyone in town took notice.

Daughter Dorothy was born to Emma and I.N. on July 3, 1919. Several years later, another daughter, Adeline, died of crib death at the age of three months. Emma was devastated. Fortunately, their third son Isadore was born in 1923. Izzy, as he was called, rescued Emma from her depression. She doted on the little fellow and put him in a small bed in her room. I.N. was already sleeping elsewhere in their large house.

The icy winter weather caused the children to suffer from many illnesses. If the ailment was contagious, quarantine signs were placed on the fence and on the front door. The affected child stayed all alone in the sickroom, and Emma hired a nurse to come in. In those days before penicillin, someone was always sick.

Fruits and vegetables were scarce during the harsh weather. When Herman was just shy of three years old he came down with what was probably rickets as a result of lack of sunshine and vitamin D. He could hardly walk and had to delay starting kindergarten and first grade. As a result, he and Lou, one year younger, were always in the same grade.

Mother Emma tutored Herman to help him keep up with the other children. In order to get Herman to class, Lou carted him in a wagon or on a sled. As time went by, Herman walked without support. By the time he was in high school, he played on the football team, but for the rest of his life he had a slight case of bowlegs.

In the summertime, I.N. rented a cabin for the family 20 miles away at Mira Gut, and he'd come out for weekends. Mira Gut was the children's place to build sandcastles and collect seashells, one of the few holidays they enjoyed.

A small Jewish community thrived in Glace Bay and the other small towns nearby. I.N. was active in the local synagogue. Herman and Lou went to the Hebrew school every day after their regular classes and became bar mitzvah. Emma rarely attended services, and when she did go, she sat in the balcony with the other women. There was little religion observed in the home.

In their classroom in the concrete block schoolhouse, Herman and Lou sat together in the back right corner next to their Jewish friends. Of all the students, only 25 were Jewish. The day began with everyone singing "God Save the King" followed by Christian hymns. In later years, Lou remarked he could still sing "Onward Christian Soldiers" in his sleep.

After school, Herman and Lou walked home along the train tracks, the fastest route. Almost every day, a group of boys from the miners' families would pick a fight, hollering "Jew boys" and accusing them of being "Christ killers." These confrontations became real battles. The attackers lobbed bricks and stones, and Herman and Lou hurled the same projectiles back.[53]

A group of the Jewish boys bought boxing gloves and practiced a few times a week at Herman and Lou's house on the third floor, where they set up a boxing ring. Finally, the boys were able to better defend themselves against the bullies. Lou was so good that when he went to college, he was awarded a boxing scholarship.

Everyone in the area knew I.N. Allen through his businesses. He let the families of the miners buy on credit, 50 cents down and 50 cents a week. Then he would get in his touring car and make collections from everyone who hadn't come in on Saturday to pay their bills. In the winter, he used a horse and sleigh. Everyone recognized this handsome friendly fellow when he came knocking at their door.

Because he couldn't write well in English, I.N. enlisted the help of his boys to send a letter to the editor of the newspaper describing the hardships he, as a local businessman, saw among the townspeople. He beseeched the mine owners to correct deficiencies and urged the miners to fight for a better life.

In 1929 came the Great Depression, and everything changed. I.N.'s prosperous businesses went broke. The bank nailed signs on the front of his stores stating, "Bankruptcy Proceedings." He sold everything and paid off what debts he could.

Desperate to make a living, I.N. traveled west, all the way to the other side of Canada. Vancouver, British Columbia, was a much larger city than Glace Bay and had an international port. The weather was warmer, and I.N. saw the potential for business. Off he went, prepared to start over again with the same pattern as when he first came to North America.

The family sold their lovely home on McKeen Street for $2500, which served as I.N.'s seed money. The new owner of the house immediately remodeled it into apartments and allowed Emma and the four children to live temporarily in one of the suites.

Six weeks later, the family boarded a train on the Canadian Pacific Railway. The ride west was a welcome respite for Emma and an adventure for the children. This was the first time they had ever dined out. Herman and Lou were intrigued by the little pats of butter, something they had never seen before. The waiter had to stop the mischievous boys from taking the butter from all the other place settings in the dining car.

When Emma and the children arrived in Vancouver six days later, their money was gone. The adventure was over. Until I.N. was able to catch up with them, they wandered up and down the streets, not sure what to do next. Herman, now 13 years old, and Lou, 12, wanted to help but weren't sure how. Neither of them ever forgot the desperation they felt. Finally, I.N. found them and brought them to the small stucco house he had rented.

I.N. purchased an old Graham-Paige car and some carpets. He went door to door and sold them to the housewives. More and more jobless people from all over Canada were coming to Vancouver looking for work, and in those hard times, no matter how hard he tried, I.N. still couldn't earn enough to take care of his large family.

Once again I.N. moved, this time about a hundred miles north to Powell River, the site of the largest newsprint mill in the world. He opened a grocery and butcher shop in the Cranberry community, and soon the family joined him. For the children, this was an exciting journey. The only means of transportation between Vancouver and Powell River was an overnight boat ride. Since money was limited, I.N. rented one cabin for Emma and the two younger children. Herman and Lou slept in chairs on the deck.

The Allens were the only Jewish family in Powell River, and people were friendlier. I.N. bought beef, lamb, and chickens from the local farmers. His was not a kosher shop. Everyone in the family learned how to butcher the meat and cut up steaks and roasts. The chickens arrived live. One boy tied a cord around the chicken's neck and stretched it over a chopping block, and the other boy whacked off the head with an axe. Emma taught them how to pluck off the feathers and prepare the chickens for sale.

Allen's Meat Market advertised in the *Powell River News* and sold T-bone steaks for 25 cents a pound. A three and a half pound chicken was 20 cents a pound. Theirs was a family business, open from 8:00 a.m. until 8:00 p.m. On weekends, I.N. peddled the meat door to door in the nearby towns while the children minded the store. When those efforts still didn't bring in enough money, I.N. sold ladies' dresses right from the car.

Herman and Lou, in high school now, loaded crates of fruits and vegetables onto a beat-up truck and peddled them from house to house asking, "Any fruit or vegetables today?"

The house in Cranberry didn't have water faucets or an indoor bathroom. The family used the outside pump and an outhouse. Furniture was fashioned from large wooden apple crates. It was a far cry from the lovely home in Glace Bay. The one thing Emma demanded was a real store-bought bed for each of them, and there were six in all.

The stove in the kitchen was used for cooking and heating the house. Herman and Lou cut down trees for firewood and brought home sawdust bits and pieces for cooking. The small icebox kept the milk cold. When the ice truck drove down the street, the boys ran behind it to grab any chunks falling off. Other children were doing the same thing. These were the Depression years, and many families in town were faced with similar issues.

I.N. was still involved in politics. He couldn't run for office because of his language difficulties, so he supported the contender for a top government position. When he was called on to write a speech for the candidate, he dictated his words to one of his children. This became the speech that the political dignitary delivered in the next few days.[54]

Everyone pitched in to bring money home to Emma. Herman and Lou picked apples. All the children gathered wild berries and then the store owners paid a penny per pound for them. Herman and Lou picked 50 pounds in an afternoon, and Dorothy and Isadore picked 20. Blackberries, huckleberries, salmonberries, black currants and wild strawberries all ripened at different times and made for a long picking season and more money for the family.

Once a year, school classes were invited to visit the paper mill. Each student came home with generous supplies of scratch pads, more than they ever could have afforded to buy. Powell River is where Herman and Lou were introduced to the Boy Scouts. The Scouts who achieved the most were able to win awards that paid the fees for attending summer camp.

Despite their poverty, everyday life in Powell River was good for the Allens. As hard as every single one of them tried, however, the family still could not succeed financially.

Emma finally wrote to her father in Republic to see if the family could live with him. Charles Greenberg was delighted and worked tirelessly to get them all into the United States, even getting his congressman involved. He had to guarantee income for his son-in-law. It took almost a year, until September of 1933, before the Allen family was finally able to join him.

The years in Republic were easier. Herman and Lou, both good-looking boys, participated on athletic teams and got into debating and class plays. In 1935, they graduated from Republic High School. Lou was valedictorian. Herman had good grades too, but he spent more time organizing social outings and looking for a good time.

Most of the time, I.N. was gone from home, trying his luck in other cities. Instead of counting on her husband, Emma leaned on Herman and Lou for support.

Both boys started college in Washington State, but money for tuition was a problem. Always looking for that next big opportunity, I.N. had gone to Florida. After their freshman year, Herman and Lou drove to Daytona Beach where I.N. was opening ladies' ready-to-wear stores. Once again, he sold dresses on credit, so Herman and Lou went door to door to collect money, calling "Dress man, dress man!" It was tough work.

Herman and Lou soon decided they had to finish college "come hell or high water." They advertised in the newspaper for passengers who would help pay for gas and then drove their Model T back north to Washington. The year was 1937. Herman attended Eastern Washington College of Education in Cheney near Spokane. To support himself, he delivered newspapers in the mornings and worked at a shoe store in the afternoons.[55]

On the 16th day of September in 1938, Herman was naturalized as an American citizen in Spokane, Washington. He was five feet, nine and a half inches tall and weighed 158 pounds. While his taller

Herman in 1938. On the back he wrote, "One of those street cameras caught me ..."

brother Lou was serious and reserved, Herman was more outgoing, often approaching hilarity with his actions and conversations.

By this time, Dorothy was graduating from Daytona Beach High School. Pretty, with brown hair like her brothers, Dorothy was determined to get an education despite the fact that her father thought she should marry. He proposed a shidduch, an arranged marriage as was customary in Lithuania. When Dorothy realized what was happening, she wrote her brothers in a panic. Herman again advertised for travelers to pay for the gas. He and Lou jumped into Herman's 1938 Chevrolet and drove all the way to Daytona to rescue Dorothy. Somehow the brothers found the money to pay her $200 tuition to St. Luke's School of Nursing in Spokane.

Herman wrote constantly and put together collections of stories, poems, and original quotations. *A good woman is like a cool drink, sip to be appreciated.* There was always a girlfriend in his life. When he met someone he liked, Herman quit the kidding around and delved into conversation. It wouldn't take a young lady long to appreciate his serious side. *How many friendships have been choked because of the lack of a word to bridge the gap of time?*

A serious relationship with a young lady named Patricia led to an engagement. Then tragedy struck. When Herman's love died of a sinus infection, he practically had a nervous breakdown. He took a leave from college and went back to Daytona Beach to recover.

Herman wrote about his depression, *"I stood on the edge of a bottomless vast and vainly sought to pierce the gloom of the pit, but with no success. It seemed the harder I stared, the denser became the void… It was like coming up against a stone wall and blindly searching for a secret door to pass through. I knew once it was found, on the other side would spread a valley of sunshine, but the task is to find the door."*

Finally, Herman returned to Cheney and, in June of 1941, graduated with a Bachelor of Arts in Education degree. His goal was to go on for his master

I.N. and Emma's children, bound together by hardship, inherited the best traits of each of their parents. Their mother inspired them to get the finest education they could. She taught them to be loving and supportive toward each other, no matter what. Their Dad passed on the drive to work hard and venture toward new opportunities. Herman and Lou had grown up quickly, taking onto their shoulders the responsibility for keeping the family together.

By 1941, Herman and Lou were both in college. Dorothy was in nursing school, and Isadore was graduating from high school. They had survived the long years of the Depression, but their parents' marriage had not. Emma and I.N. divorced in 1944. Their differences had only grown wider. I.N. had been adventurous in too many ways. They would never sit in the same room again.

Chapter 4

The War Book of Herman Allen

In 1940, as Hitler marched across Europe conquering one country after another, President Roosevelt signed the Selective Training and Service Act. All young men were required to register with their local draft boards and then were conscripted by a national lottery.

Most Americans still believed it best to stay out of another European war. Then, on Sunday, December 7, 1941, the Japanese attacked the American fleet at Pearl Harbor, Hawaii. The next day President Roosevelt asked Congress to declare war on Japan. Congress did, and three days later Japan's two closest allies, Germany and Italy, declared war on the United States. Now it was official, the Axis powers versus the United States, Great Britain, and their allies.

The mood of the country changed. It was almost impossible not to get caught up in the groundswell of anger, duty, and excitement. Herman had begun graduate studies at Washington State College in Pullman. The number one topic of conversation among the students was the war and what choice each would make. Herman was ready for the battle, and he wanted to choose his area of service rather than be drafted. His school advisers assured him that if he enlisted, he could come back later and pick up where he left off.

Both Herman and Lou decided to join the Air Corps. Years later Lou told us, "The general feeling was these monsters must be eliminated as quickly as possible. There was a great feeling of solidarity, and there was absolutely no question this was something we had to do." Lou enlisted in January, and Herman followed on March 18, 1942.

Why did Herman choose the Air Corps? If he had watched *Winning Your Wings*, the recruiting film released that year, he would have heard actor Jimmy Stewart explain exactly why they should. "Right now the greatest mass mobilization in the history of the world is taking place," Stewart said. "And this war we're fighting today and tomorrow and the next day until we win is a war of the air. The whole world knows that."[56]

What Herman didn't realize, and most likely neither did Jimmy Stewart, was that he was volunteering for one of the most dangerous jobs of the war.

The Eighth Air Force

In later years, when Herman talked about his branch of service, he always said "Air Corps," the name of the aviation arm of the United States Army since 1926. By the spring of 1942, at about the same time that Herman joined its ranks, the Army Air Forces (AAF) became a separate U.S. Army Command.[57] In essence, the term Air Corps had been replaced, even though that name is still used today by veterans and their families.

Long before the United States was officially at war, a lot was going on behind the scenes. Ever since World War I, aviation scholars and planners had written and studied about how, in upcoming conflicts, air power could replace trench warfare. The future would belong to the bomber, and as said in 1932 by British politician and later Prime Minister Stanley Baldwin, "The bomber will always get through."

The concept of daylight precision bombing was born in the 1930s at the Air Corps Tactical School at Maxwell Field in Montgomery, Alabama. During the same decade, Dutch engineer Carl Norden developed a bombsight so accurate that it became a highly guarded military secret. The theory was, with this new technology, American bombers could destroy critical enemy war industries from on high.[58] This theory would soon be put to the test.

The Army Air Forces was organized into numbered divisions. Fifty-three days after the attack on Pearl Harbor, the Eighth Air Force was activated at the National Guard Armory in Savannah, Georgia. Almost immediately its strategic bomber arm, VIII Bomber Command, was on its way to England with Gen. Ira C. Eaker in charge.

Lou, Dorothy, and Herman Allen in 1943.

The Eighth Air Force was made up almost entirely of volunteers, men from every part of America, with wide-ranging economic, religious, and social backgrounds. Due to official Air Force policy, however, no African Americans were enrolled in the combat units.[59] Most of the men who would operate the bombers were 20 years old or younger and had never seen the inside of an airplane.

By mid-1940, President Roosevelt, confident that the country would be pulled into the war, pushed for a dramatic increase in the production of combat aircraft. America's factories went to work. As hundreds of thousands of planes rolled off the production lines, the United States needed to recruit and train men to fly them.

The Bombardier

After Herman enlisted at Geiger Field in Spokane, his first destination was Fort Lewis, Washington, a 300 mile train ride south. Fort Lewis, a huge army post dating back to World War I, was a reception center where young men entering the army, both infantry and air corps, were processed. New recruits underwent medical exams, shots, and testing. They were interviewed about preferences in job assignment and then went through even more physical and psychological testing if they wanted to be on an air crew.

Because he had gone to Washington State College, Herman was quickly nicknamed Cougar, short for college mascot Butch T. Cougar. Years later Herman recalled, "I received $21 a month, and they kept $3 for laundry. I had more money to spend than I have now. You could take gals out and mess around and do everything with that kind of money." Herman went out with Betty, Mary, and Julie, always trying to forget his lost love Patricia and perhaps trying to find someone like her again.

Private Allen was at Fort Lewis for three months. He ran, did push-ups and chin-ups, and learned to march. "You had to wait your turn to get into training camp," he wrote. "Next I went down to Santa Ana and became an Air Corps Cadet."

Santa Ana Army Air Base (SAAAB) was a large classification and preflight center on the California coast where new aviation recruits were indoctrinated into military life. Herman arrived in July of 1942. In spite of his rigorous schedule, he began to play poker, a profitable diversion that lasted for the rest of his active duty career.

Los Angeles was about 40 miles away, and in one of his letters Herman described the many weekends he spent there. The Hollywood Palladium, America's largest ballroom, was a favorite stop. Big bands entertained huge crowds. Herman never missed a party, so more than likely he danced to the sounds of Glenn Miller, Tommy Dorsey or Frank Sinatra. "The stars were always there," he wrote, "and they loved to talk to us because we were new cadets."

Cadets took rigorous medical exams and numerous aptitude and physical tests to determine whether they were best suited to be pilots, navigators or bombardiers. Once their classifications had been determined, they entered nine weeks of preflight training. They received instruction in such subjects as maps and charts, Morse code, naval and aircraft identification, and safeguarding of military information.

Herman wanted to be a bombardier, but the tests indicated that he was a good pilot candidate. According to Herman, "This was in the early part of the war when they needed pilots like mad over in Europe, so they were taking everybody they could into the pilot programs."

From Santa Anna, the cadets went to other bases for further training in their specialties. In September, Herman was sent to Sequoia Field in Visalia, California, a little more than halfway between San Francisco and Los Angeles. New arrivals were immediately labeled "dodos" by the upperclassmen. The day after coming on base, dodos met their flight instructors and had their first lessons in the air. For many of them, including Herman, it was their first plane ride. While half the school was flying, the other half was studying flight-related courses such as meteorology, navigation, and engines.

At Sequoia, true to form, Herman was on the dance committee, but he washed out as a pilot. For *Propwash*, the Class of 43-C yearbook, Herman wrote a poem and dedicated it to "E," shorthand for his flight instructor.

Ode to "E"

I was musing, gently musing,
On the bench on the Line,
The planes were flying, flying,
The hour was around ten or nine.

I heard a murmur, gentle murmur,
From in beside the door.
Eagerly I began to wonder, wonder,
Would it be my name as before.

The plane flew higher, gently higher,
As I climbed for a spin.
Could it be I blundered, blundered -
I brought her sadly in.

Presently I heard a whisper, whisper,
A voice close to my ear,
It was quietly saying, saying,
Things I didn't want to hear.

"When the Board asked what I wanted to do, I said I would still like to be a bombardier," Herman said. "They pulled out my file, looked at it and said, 'You're going to Victorville!' "

The bombardier training school Herman went to was at Victorville Army Air Field, California. Pilot school wash-outs were common candidates to be bombardiers as long as they had the advanced math proficiency and motor skills required.

In Victorville, Herman was formally introduced to the top-secret Norden bombsight. In an effort to move away from bombing broad areas with the inherent danger of civilian casualties, the Army Air Forces began to use the more accurate Norden to identify their targets. Student bombardiers had to take an oath to guard the secrecy of the bombsight "if need be, with my life itself." The Air Force was afraid to print textbooks about this secret weapon, so students had to learn by copying diagrams from the blackboard. At the end of class, all drawings were gathered up and destroyed.

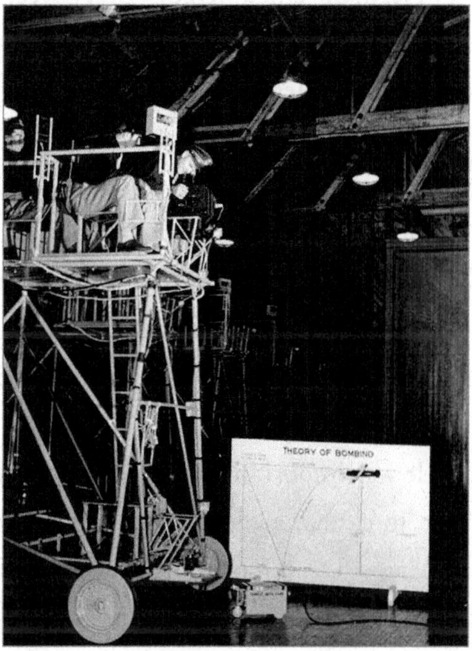

Bombardier trainer. (Air Force Historical Research Agency)

The Norden bombsight was an early computer that controlled the downward path of the bomb after taking into consideration factors such as wind direction, air speed, and drift. The bombardier made precise calculations by turning a series of knobs. The Norden was connected to the B-17's autopilot and, during the bomb run, the bombardier actually controlled the plane until "bombs away!"

The cadets practiced on an A-2 bombing trainer, a 12-foot high steel scaffold mounted on wheels. On the top a bombsight was mounted. Perched on top of the trainer, the bombardier aimed at a moving "bug" operated by another student down below. The experience must have felt something like a giant arcade game.

The degree of bombing accuracy with the Norden bombsight could not be matched by any device used by any other nation. Bombardiers liked to brag that with the Norden, they could drop a bomb into a pickle barrel from 20,000 feet. It would be more than six months before Herman had the opportunity to test this theory for himself.

Herman remembered, "Every weekend we'd go into Los Angeles, and we stayed at the Gaylord Hotel. It's gone now, but we used to call it the 'Happy Jesus.' "

On Saturday afternoon, May 8, 1943, Herman was graduated from the Victorville Army Flying School, Class 43-7. His mother and sister Dorothy came down from Washington to watch as he received his wings and was commissioned as a second lieutenant. It had been more than 14 months since he had enlisted, and he wasn't through yet. The next stop was Carlsbad, New Mexico for a special intensified course in dead reckoning navigation.

It was important for a bombardier to be schooled in navigation so that, in case of a crisis, he could take over and perform the job of the navigator. Dead reckoning was a method the navigator used to know the exact position of the plane and to determine the direction of the flight. With the wind direction (determined from a wind meter), air speed, ground speed, and compass heading corrected for distortion of

The officers: pilot Charles W. Smith, co-pilot Merle P. Brown, navigator Charles L. Stevenson, bombardier Herman F. Allen

the plane, the navigator plotted the airplane's position. The process was complicated but critical.

After a trip to Salt Lake City for crew assignment, the next stop was Moses Lake, Washington, closer to Herman's family home. Combat crews were assembled here and given their initial flight and gunnery training. Most importantly, Moses Lake is where Herman met the other nine men who would be his crew. Herman wrote:

> The Crew. We've had so many identification numbers thrown at us that, as a signpost, they are insignificant. The Crew. Not because they are the

outstanding crew of the Air Force do I write of them. Their happiness, their grief, their laughs, their luck. No, it is because I am one of them, and because of this I know them best. The Crew.

There is Smithy, our pilot extraordinary. MP in the right seat. Steve, beside me in the nose. Tiny, a touch of Brooklyn wherever he flew, our engineer. Vic, number one static chaser, whose fear of the water was as strong as his desire to see the Statue of Liberty. Tom, silent Tom, throwing the ball turret around as if it were an inanimate thing. Don, with all the traces of the Rebel still intact, at left waist. Howard, never a foot from the escape door, at right waist. RB, flak happy Gremlins running amuck while he sat in solitary confinement at the tail position. And I, the Bombardier.

From Moses Lake, the crew moved east to Kearney Army Air Field in Nebraska for B-17 training. Kearney was a heavy bombardment processing center where bomber crews prepared further for their eventual overseas duty.

The plane for Herman's crew was the legendary B-17 designed by the Boeing Aircraft Company. In the 1930s, the Air Corps invited Boeing, along with other airplane manufacturers, to design a long-range bomber, "a multi-engine aircraft capable of carrying a ton of bombs at more than 200 miles an hour over a distance of two thousand miles."[60]

Boeing completed its plane, Model 299, by July of 1935. At the time, it was the largest landplane ever built in the country. When it was unveiled

B-17 "Flying Fortress." (U.S. Air Force)

at Boeing Field in Seattle, 69-feet long with five gun emplacements, a newspaperman described it as a "Flying Fortress." The name stuck.

In spite of a tragic accident during a demonstration flight, the Air Corps recommended the purchase of what would eventually be called B-17s.[61] The idea was to have an aircraft so tough and with so much defensive power it could fly into enemy territory without an escort, drop its bombs, and fight its way back home again.

Although this theory would be revised as the bomber crews experienced combat over Germany, it didn't stop the B-17 from becoming an enduring symbol for World War II. By the end of the war, the United States had produced more than 12,000 B-17s. The men and women at Boeing were churning out one every 40 minutes.

On the B-17, each crew member had his own assigned station. Pilot 2nd Lt. Charles W. Smith not only flew the plane, he was its commander, primarily responsible for its safety and that of the crew. His was the final word. Early on, Smithy and Herman became close friends, almost like brothers. Because Herman referred to Smith as Smithy until the day he died, it is how I will refer to him also.

Co-pilot 2nd Lt. Merle P. Brown was Smithy's right-hand man. He sat in the seat next to the pilot and had to be ready to take over the commander's job at any time. How each of these two men became pilots was eerily similar.

In September of 1940, while London was being pummeled and the world was speculating whether or not the United States would enter the war, Smithy enlisted in the armed forces. Like Herman, he wanted to select his branch of military service. Growing up in Westchester County, New York, Smithy learned from his father how to fix anything mechanical. It only made sense that he should become an aircraft mechanic.

A year later, this enterprising enlistee was at Bangor Army Air Base in Maine. On the 7th day of December, he and some friends hitched a ride into town to watch a movie. Suddenly the show stopped. A voice announced, "All military personnel return to base immediately!" Pearl Harbor had been attacked. A week later, Smithy achieved two milestones. He celebrated his 25th birthday, and he qualified for pilot training.

Merle P. Brown, sometimes called M.P., was born in West Virginia. Merle also enlisted so he could be part of the Army Air Corps. Like Smithy, he told the recruiting officer he wanted to be an aircraft mechanic. He signed on the dotted line but, by some mysterious mishap, ended up in an infantry battalion. Merle was furious and worked hard to become the worst soldier ever. One day he was ordered to see the captain, who barked, "What's the matter with you, soldier?"

Merle replied, "Sir, I'll tell you what's the matter. I volunteered to join the Army Air Corps to become a mechanic, and I ended up in the infantry. That's what's the matter, sir."

The captain said, "Well, there are only two ways you can get out of here. You can take the test for Officer Candidate School or take the test for the Aviation Cadet School."

Merle replied without hesitation, "I'll take the test for the Aviation Cadet School, sir." Brown soon graduated as a pilot in the class of 43G.

The third of the four officers on Crew 60-14 was the navigator. Born in Pennsylvania on May 23, 1920, 2nd Lt. Charles L. Stevenson, known as "Steve," was the youngest of three boys, and they had a baby sister. By the time he was three, the family had moved to New Jersey. Because of his prowess in baseball, Steve was nicknamed "Babe" after his hero, Babe Ruth. In 1943, he was attending the Drexel Institute School of Engineering in Philadelphia when he enlisted. Shortly before going overseas, Steve married his sweetheart, Gracie Lohring.[62]

Steve's engineering background was perfect training for the technical job of navigator. His job was to know the exact position of the plane at all times. He sat at a wooden desk in the nose of the B-17 right behind the bombardier. The navigator was probably the busiest man on the crew while preparing for and during a mission. He had to know where the plane was going, what track they were to follow to get there, and what track they should follow coming back. During the mission, he had to be aware of where the concentrations of enemy antiaircraft batteries were, where German fighter airfields were located, what planes were reported to be there and how many, and what the weather was like on the way in and out. He had to make note of every unusual activity, how heavy and where the flak was, from what directions fighter planes came and how they attacked, casualties in their group or others in the wing when he could see them, and when necessary, he had to man one of the two machine guns called the cheek guns.

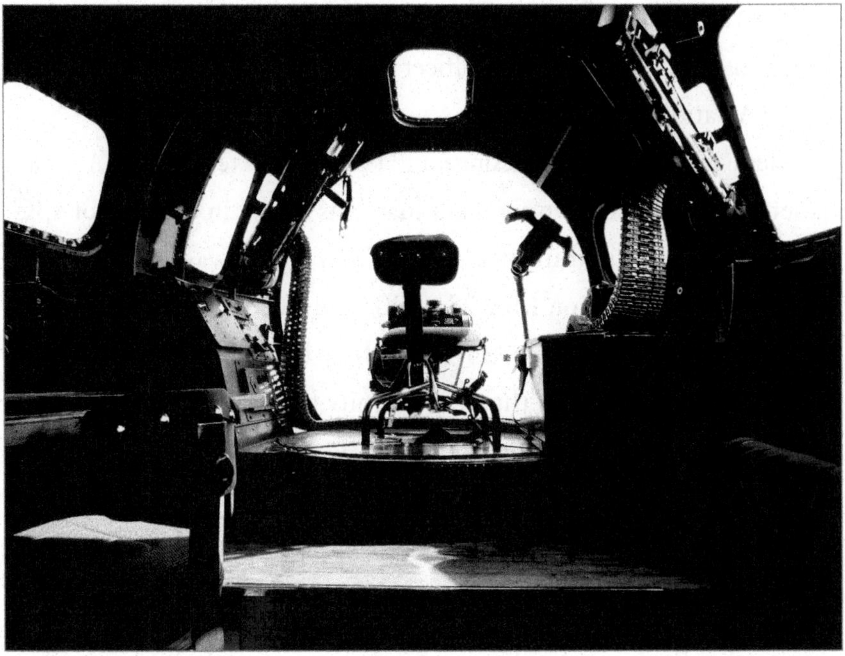

The Nose where both the bombardier and the navigator sat. (photo by John DiGeorge in the Aluminum Overcast B-17, 2010)

Herman, the bombardier and fourth officer, flew up front in the Plexiglas nose of the B-17. His seat was an arm's length from the navigator's. Herman and Steve affectionately called themselves "The Nose." Their area was right under where the pilots sat. To get there, the bombardier and the navigator crouched and slid down through a small opening. It would not have been possible for an overweight crew member to enter the nose.

Herman had a panoramic view of everything out there, good and bad. B-17 crew member Sgt. William Sapp Dixon, waist gunner of a B-17 crew with the 100th Bomb Group, described it best. "The view from the bombardier's position was probably the scariest of all. He could see all the flak ahead, and he got a head-on view of all the winking lights from those little planes attacking from the front. For the uninitiated, those winking lights were 20mm cannon fire. In addition to manning the bombsight, the bombardier manned the chin turret. During the bomb run, the bombardier, through the bombsight, controlled the plane, and his full attention was devoted to the task of dropping the bombs exactly where they were supposed to go. A difficult task when you know you are being attacked but necessary because that was the whole purpose of the mission."[63]

Yes, the bombardier had the best seat in the house. The Plexiglas surrounding him was not bulletproof, so it could be the most frightening seat as well.

Whenever on base, military protocol required the four officers to sleep in different quarters and eat in separate mess halls from the six enlisted men. However, all ten knew the camaraderie and mutual respect of a shared responsibility and a desire to survive. They became a tight-knit group.

Smithy was also known as Pappy. He wasn't the oldest member of the crew; the nickname was given out of respect. Herman, the oldest, had just turned twenty-seven. Smithy would be twenty-seven soon. Merle was twenty-six, and Steve was twenty-three.

The rest of the crew were younger. Although the enlisted men hadn't had the additional training required to become officers, they all went through extensive technical instruction to learn how to do their jobs on the aircraft.

The engineer, Sgt. Carl A. Heuser, was nicknamed "Tiny" because he wasn't. Carl was born in Germany. When he was only three years old, his parents brought him to the United States on the *SS Resolute* sailing out of Hamburg. They settled in New York where Carl's father became a butcher. Carl had two years of high school when he enlisted at the age of 21.

The engineer had to know the airplane inside and out. He worked closely with the pilots and the bombardier to make sure all equipment was working correctly. He also manned double machine guns in the top turret, a Plexiglas dome at the top of the airplane.

Between the front of the plane where the officers and the engineer worked and the back of the plane where the primary gunners were positioned was a narrow catwalk over the bomb bay where the bombs were held. In the bomb bay area, there was no oxygen nor were there any plug-ins for the electrically heated suits. No one wanted to be there for long.

In the early segment of each bombing mission, the bombardier left the nose and traveled back over the narrow catwalk to the bomb bay to manually arm the bombs. Hanging onto the bomb racks, he pulled a tagged pin from the nose of each bomb. The pins were there to prevent the bombs from going off prematurely.

If one or more of the bombs didn't drop when they should have, the bombardier had to walk back to the bombs. From his designated spot in the nose, he unhooked his oxygen supply and grabbed a walk-around oxygen bottle. Then he climbed back to the bomb bay while the plane was being assaulted by flak or enemy fighters or both. The bomb bay doors were wide open with a frigid gale blowing through while he tried to steady himself enough to shimmy across the 18-inch-wide catwalk. There was a safety belt to prevent him from falling out of the airplane, a fortunate arrangement since now he had to lean over and manually release the bombs to drop through the open doors.

Radio operator Sgt. Victor R. Marcotte, all by himself in the center of the plane, huddled over a wooden ledge in a small compartment between the waist area and the bomb bay. Next to the radio was a Morse code key used to send and receive coded transmissions. Marcotte was the communications link with headquarters and other planes in the squadron.

On the way to and from the target, radio silence was the norm, so Marcotte was primarily a listener. Anything meant for his ship had to be written in his log. The radio operator also served as photographer and was the crew member trained in first aid.

The other four crew members were gunners. They operated .50-caliber machine guns and protected the bomber on its precarious journeys. During gunnery school training, the gunners practiced with shotguns and clay pigeons. Eventually, these men became so familiar with their weapons that they could take them apart and put them back together blindfolded.

The left waist gunner was Sgt. Donald S. Courson from Winborn, Mississippi. His father owned a farm and worked in the local sawmill. Don had finished one year of college when he got his draft notice and went into the army.

Sgt. Howard C. Granger from Strong City, Kansas, was the waist gunner on the right side of the bomber. The waist gunners were stationed in the largest space in the plane, but it wasn't large enough when the two of them were frantically working their weapons. After a couple of missions, a waist gunner could sense where the other gunner was and where he was likely to move, so they were able to avoid bump-butt encounters.

The crew had to deal with two deadly hazards on every mission. When the B-17 flew at 10,000 feet or higher, crew members had to put on their oxygen masks. If his mask failed, an airman had no warning. His crewmates had to detect the threat quickly enough to revive him.

Just as dangerous, the temperature of the unpressurized interior of the aircraft was the same as the air temperature outside. The higher the plane flew, the colder it got, as biting cold as forty, fifty, sixty degrees below zero. The crew wore layers and layers of clothing as well as temperamental electrically-heated suits that had to be plugged in at each station.

In some of the B-17s, the waist windows were enclosed, but when the Smith crew later flew in the *Liberty Lady,* the area was wide open to the elements. At the frigid temperatures, it was a monumental task for the gunners to operate the machine guns deftly enough to shoot down enemy fighters. In spite of their bulky clothing, the men would sometimes sweat. For these young men in combat, frostbite could be an even worse enemy than the enemy.[64] The waist gunners incurred more casualties than any of the other crew members of the B-17.[65]

It's hard to say which of the final two gunners had the loneliest position. At the very rear of the plane was the tail gunner. Sgt. R.B. Trumble, previously a machinist, had enlisted from Kalamazoo, Michigan. Each time he entered the plane, R.B. had to crawl back to his bicycle-type seat where he knelt in order to operate the two machine guns that protected the aircraft from attacks coming from behind. R.B. was the most comical crew member, always cracking a joke and having a good time.

The other contender for the loneliest position was in the most claustrophobic one. Sgt. Thomas E. Stillson, "Tom," was the quietest man on the crew, probably a good trait for the ball turret gunner. The only person who could defend the plane from below, he hung beneath it all by himself in a permanently fixed sphere.

The ball turret gunner sat in a fetal position, swiveling around in a glass bubble while working his two machine guns. Tom entered the turret only after the plane was airborne because the guns had to be pointed straight down for him to fit in. Then he had to be up and out before landing.

All in all, this Flying Fortress was a formidable airplane. Speaking of the B-17, German ace Adolph Galland warned Hermann Göring, head of the Luftwaffe, "unless we immediately reinforce our fighter units, unless we are given new tactics for the attack, these birds will one day fly all the way to Berlin."[66]

While the newly formed crew was in Kearney, they flew practice flights all over the country. This is when the ten men discovered each other's strengths and weaknesses and learned to work together as a team. At this point, they didn't grasp the horrors yet to come.

In October, the crew got their overseas orders and headed for Camp Kilmer, New Jersey, the point of embarkation for shipment overseas. They had hoped to be able to fly to England on a B-17, but during winter months the airmen sailed across the Atlantic on one of the ocean liners converted to a troop ship.

A few days in New York City gave the boys a chance to let off steam. Finally, on the 24th of October, 1943, they set sail on the *Queen Mary*, the largest and fastest liner from the Cunard-White Star shipping company. Stretching over 1000 feet in length, the mammoth ship was twice the size of the *Titanic.*

In September of 1939, when war broke out in Europe, the *Queen Mary* became the *Gray Ghost* with her exterior painted camouflage gray. All luxurious interiors were removed and stored in warehouses so that wooden bunks and hammocks could be installed. The gymnasium, squash court, and sports deck slept nearly 200. Even the swimming pool was converted to a sleeping hall of more than 100 bunks.[67]

On each voyage, the *Queen Mary* was teeming with troops, as many as 16,000 at a time. She sailed alone and unescorted for most of her treacherous trip. Like the *Aquitania,* which would transport Hedy across the Atlantic at the end of the same year, the *Queen Mary* sailed in a zigzag pattern, changing direction every eight minutes to evade German U-Boats. This avoidance maneuver, as well as her speed, made it almost impossible to predict her course. Adolph Hitler was so frustrated by her success that he offered a $250,000 reward and the Iron Cross to any submarine captain who could sink the ship.

Officers stayed in first class staterooms, while the enlisted men were in the tourist sections. William Dixon remembered, "After first entering the ship, we walked as far forward as it was possible to go and then descended as far down as it was possible to descend. We reached a room with a sign over the door that read 'Max. Occupants 13.' We entered, all 63 of us, and found hammocks slung in every available inch of the room. Our pilot said the officers were griping about their abode with bunks four high, until he saw where we were and made the officers come take a look."

For much of the trip it was freezing cold on deck. The men spent their days playing cards or watching films. Sometimes during craps games, American money, British money, and Canadian money were on the deck. No doubt Herman gravitated toward the poker games. Most men had no idea what the exchange rates were. Likely the winners did.

Sometimes nearly half the passengers were seasick, and even a moment of privacy was impossible. Dining and sleeping schedules were rotated in order to accommodate everyone. Meals were served mess style day and night in the grand dining room and included chipped beef on toast, kidney stew and stewed apricots. None of the crew members had experienced standard British fare, but they quickly learned to adapt.

The ship landed in Gourock, Scotland, on November 2, her tenth day at sea. The crew was immediately put on a troop train for a destination unknown. They were handed sack lunches with pork pies. Each man was also given a small book that explained how to treat the reserved, but not unfriendly, British people. "The British don't know how to make a good cup of coffee," the booklet said. "You don't know how to make a good cup of tea. It's an even swap."

The train took Crew 60-14 to the replacement depot north of London where they were ordered to proceed to an airfield called Thurleigh. Assignments were made as current needs dictated—in other words, a group where a crew had been lost and needed to be replaced. Sixty miles north of London, Thurleigh was the home of the 306th Bombardment Group (BG) of the Eighth Air Force. The Smith crew would join its 368th Squadron, nicknamed the "Eager Beavers."

Gunners were sent first to The Wash, a gunnery school for refresher training. It was on the English coast, and the men fired their guns out over the water.

Except for Carl Heuser, who had come to the United States from Germany as a three-year-old, none of these young men had been this far from home. By November of 1943, it had been more than a year, perhaps nearly two, since they began their training. All the training in the world could never have prepared them for what they were about to experience.

Thurleigh

The bombers of Great Britain's Royal Air Force (RAF) had been hammering German cities since 1940. Originally, the RAF tried daytime bombing, but the results were so poor and they were losing so many planes, they began to bomb German targets at night.

In July of 1940, a civil engineering company began to build a bomber base for the RAF in rural Bedfordshire County near Thurleigh. This was one of many picturesque English villages in the area, others nearby being Bedford, Keysoe, and Milton Ernest. With their thatched roof cottages, old churches, and numerous pubs, any one of them could have been a movie set.

RAF Thurleigh opened the following year. When the United States officially joined the war, the British agreed to hand over the use of RAF bases. Most had to be improved and enlarged. It was a huge logistical operation, considering the limited amount of time required to finish the job.

The majority of the airfields, close to a hundred in all, were in the southeastern area of England known as East Anglia. Suddenly military vehicles, construction crews and heavy equipment arrived to build runways, hangers, and Quonset huts. The tranquil English countryside was transformed almost overnight.

Meanwhile, back in the States, the country was rapidly gearing up to take the air war to Europe. The 306th BG was activated in March of 1942 at Salt Lake City Air Base. One month later the group moved by train to Wendover Army Air Field in Utah under the command of dark-haired, mustached Col. Charles B. "Chips" Overacker. After a period of intense training, the 306th was assigned to serve with the Eighth Air Force in England. Officers from the RAF visited Wendover and explained British procedures. The Brits were gracious, but there was no doubt they considered the idea of daylight precision bombing to be unrealistic.[68]

The 306th in England

Finally it was time for this initial group of the 306th BG to go abroad. Much of the workforce sailed to England from New York on the *Queen Elizabeth* and the *Queen Mary* troop carriers. Both ships crossed the Atlantic safely. When Radio Berlin reported the 306th had gone to its grave at the bottom of the sea, the men on board had a nervous laugh.

They were extremely happy to see dry land again when they finally docked in Scotland in early September, 1942.

Squadrons of new B-17s, 33 planes in all, were flown over and arrived that same month. The final destination for the group and their heavy bombers: Station 111, Thurleigh. Military units were identified with a station number for security reasons so as not to pinpoint their exact location.

The crews who flew over were surprised to hear over the radio a welcome greeting from Lord Haw Haw, broadcasting his propaganda messages from Berlin.[69] Obviously the enemy had been following up on them as well as on the men coming over on the ocean liners.

On the day the airmen arrived at the base, they watched the RAF shoot down a lone German plane. In spite of the quaint and tranquil setting, war was nearby.[70]

When the personnel began moving in, the airfield was far from ready. Runways needed immediate repair. Initially, the more than 800 men lived in tents. Conditions were crowded and muddy, while everyone focused on construction, training, and making preparations for the missions ahead.

A new mess hall was christened by the group with a beer party, the first of many. In the beginning, the crews ate British rations. The food was monotonous, and the men complained. Finally, American cooks arrived and served a variety of vegetables, as well as lots of Spam. The army newspaper *Stars and Stripes* even had a contest with prizes for the mess sergeants who could come up with the best way to disguise the prolific pork product.

Because of a shortage of dairy products, eggs were usually powdered. On the morning of a mission when the men sat down to real eggs, they knew the operation was going to be a tough one.

One airman remembered with not much affection an oversupply of Brussels sprouts. All kidding aside, beans, cabbage, Brussels sprouts, always plentiful, could cause gas in the airmen's intestines. This intensified at high altitudes, leading to extreme discomfort. A favorite bit of advice was, "If you must make a forced landing, do it in a Brussels sprouts patch."[71]

The 306th Bomb Group was organized into four bombardment squadrons: the 367th, the 368th, the 369th, and the 423rd. The men continued to train, and finally came the day they had been waiting for—their first raid. It was October 9, 1942.

Led by group commander Overacker, who piloted a 369th Squadron plane, 24 bombers left the base for the steel and locomotive works of Lille, France. All in all, with many injuries and damaged airplanes, the mission was a baptism of fire. The dismal weather over winter-time England delayed a resumption of missions until November 7.

The English weather was always a factor in whatever the airmen did. In fact, one British meteorologist claimed perfect precision bombing weather existed for only 12 days a year.[72] Needless to say, there were few days perfect enough, so the mission planners had to make tough decisions, weighing the demands from their superiors against the safety of the crews.

The first months of combat operations were extremely difficult. After the Spanish Civil War and the Nazi takeover of much of Europe, the German Luftwaffe was superior in numbers and experience. The German pilots were close to home and knew the territory.

Early high-priority targets were the well-defended submarine bases in Germany and France. The U-boats, short for the German word *Unterseeboot*, were wreaking havoc, sinking ships delivering critical food and supplies to Great Britain. In 1942 alone, the wolf packs of U-boats sank more than a thousand ships in the North Atlantic.[73]

After one particularly costly mission to the submarine pens at St. Nazaire, three 306th bombers were lost. The remaining crews were forced to land their battered planes at Portreath, an RAF base located on the lower tip of England. When the traumatized crews hit the mess hall, they expressed their fractured emotions in a boisterous way. The Americans pulled the officers' club chandelier down from the ceiling and broke their glassware. The English were appalled. Colonel Overacker sent an apology and a check for 200 pounds.[74]

Fortunately, in November of 1942 came a welcome morale booster. Several famous movie stars arrived at the airfield for the production of the movie *Four Jills in a Jeep* starring Carole Landis, Mitzi Mayfair, Kay Francis, and Martha Raye.

A Polish Air Squadron flying out of Thurleigh before the Americans arrived had inscribed on a mess hall ceiling the names of the targets they had bombed. The 306th continued this tradition, and after each mission, the men would take a candle and smoke the ceiling of the officers' club with the date and target for the day's mission. After a big party one night, squeezed in between the mission

Smoking the ceiling. (306th Bomb Group Historical Association, Dr. Thurman Shuller collection)

data, there appeared a cartoon of a nude young lady. The image was ordered to be blotted out.

When the movie stars visited the officers' club, Carole Landis noticed this ceiling immediately. She was thrilled to see the officers select the airman they thought had done the best job that day and hoist him up, pyramid style, to memorialize the name of his mission.[75]

In January of 1943, President Roosevelt and Prime Minister Winston Churchill met in Casablanca, Morocco, to plan for a Combined Bomber Offensive, the strategy of round-the-clock bombing. The RAF would bomb critical enemy targets during the night, the Eighth Air Force by day. The goal was twofold: wipe out the Luftwaffe and annihilate German military production. The pressure on the air crews intensified.

That same month, General Eaker, now commander of the Eighth Air Force, made a visit to Thurleigh accompanied by Col. Frank A. Armstrong, Jr. and Lt. Col. Beirne Lay, Jr. At the main gate, their staff car was casually waved through by a sentry. By the time the tour of the base was over, the general was fuming about the low levels of military propriety.

The 306th had lost nine planes on its last three missions. The general thought Commander Overacker was too closely attached to the men. Eaker's solution was to immediately replace Overacker with Colonel Armstrong who would transfer from the 97th Bombardment Group where the disciplinarian's nickname had been "Butcher."[76]

Not long after the war was over, this event was immortalized in the novel *Twelve O'Clock High,* co-written by Beirne Lay, Jr. In the 1949 film that followed, actor Gregory Peck played a fictitious Gen. Frank Savage who similarly assumed command of a bombardment group the scriptwriters named the 918th. (918 equals 306 times 3.)

At the end of the movie, General Savage has a nervous breakdown. This was fabricated and never happened to Colonel Armstrong who worked hard to improve morale. On the 27th of January 1943, Armstrong personally led the 306th in the first American bombing raid into Germany, and his group was thereafter known as the "First Over Germany." On February 17, Armstrong became a brigadier general and relinquished command of the 306th to Lt. Col. Claude Putnam. Armstrong had been at Thurleigh only six weeks.

Just as in the movie *Twelve O'Clock High,* morale at Thurleigh had plummeted. By early 1943, the 306th had lost nearly 80 percent of its original crews. There were long lines at sick bay. A 306th flight engineer wrote, "We were getting killed, and no one was doing anything about it."

On Sunday, February 21, group surgeon Maj. Thurman Shuller wrote in his diary, "I think some of these fellows who meet death so often do a lot more thinking than they once did. … In the nearly six months we have been over here, it is striking that some of the young officers have aged ten years or so. When they first came, they stayed out as late as possible as often as possible, but earlier in the week I went to a movie in Bedford, and to my amazement about eight of the most notorious playboys caught the 10:15 bus back to the field."

Since its first mission, the 306th had lost 21 planes in combat. In April, 14 more were added to this list. Major Shuller wrote a passionate letter to Commander Putnam about the declining morale. No crew member thought he could possibly survive.[77] Shuller declared there should be a maximum number of missions set for the air crews, and he suggested 20.[78]

Soon afterward, General Eaker announced that after a tour of 25 missions, crew members could go back to the States. The crews were thrilled. On April 5, Sgt. Michael J. Roskovich, son of Russian immigrants and known around Thurleigh as "The Mad Russian" was the first flier in the Eighth Air Force to hit the 25 mission mark. The handsome Russian wore a tall furry Cossack hat. If an officer dared enter his plane wearing a tie, the rascally Rosky pulled out a pair of scissors and cut it off.

In June of 1943, after Roskovich was commissioned as a second lieutenant, he returned to Thurleigh as a gunnery officer. On February 4, 1944, he was killed in a non-combat plane crash. Michael J. Roskovich became a great legend of the 306th, known not only for his antics but for his bravery and service.

A crew from the 91st BG based out of nearby Bassingbourn reaped the most publicity when in May of 1943, their B-17 *Memphis Belle* completed its quota of 25 missions. Capt. Robert K. Morgan and crew went back to the United States for a whirlwind publicity tour. Their story gave courage and motivation to other air crews and to their families as well. Everyone was counting off to 25.

During the month of May 1943, Commander Putnam, in a commendation to the group, summed up the reality of the circumstances. "Warmest congratulations to every member of the 306th Bomb Group for outstanding accomplishments achieved during the first fifteen days of May. During this period, we have continued to deliver our full quota of heavy blows to the enemy, both in occupied territory and in his homeland… This feat is all the more remarkable when it is considered that well over one-half of all crews who have been lost in action in this theatre were lost before they completed their first five missions."[79]

The rest of 1943 continued to be brutal. Two missions to bomb the ball bearing works at Schweinfurt, Germany, led to devastating losses. The second of these was on October 14, a day forever remembered as Black Thursday. The 306th sent 18 crews. Only five returned.

The fliers who did return to Thurleigh were physically and emotionally exhausted. Major Shuller reported that, although morale was low, he hoped an influx of replacements might rejuvenate the devastated men. The 306th was temporarily grounded in order to return the group to full combat status.

Replacements began to arrive. Two days after Black Thursday, seven new crews checked in. The massive training program back in the States was paying off. New arrivals had the benefit of better preparation, often by combat-experienced instructors who had entered the war zone early on. Soon 12 new B-17s flew in, and the 306th was back in action.

Despite the great number of losses during this period, Air Force leadership in Washington demanded more, more, more, "more planes over the target on more days of the month."[80] In response, General Eaker begged for additional long-range fighter escorts. The unescorted attacks flying deeper and deeper into Germany were resulting in devastating and unacceptable losses.

By the end of 1943, Gen. James H. Doolittle was moving into the position of commander of the Eighth Air Force. General Eaker, not one bit happy to be forced from the command he had nurtured, was moved to the Mediterranean where he took charge of both the Twelfth and the Fifteenth Air Forces.

General Doolittle had become a popular American hero after he led the daring Tokyo Raid in April of 1942. The Eighth Air Force he took over was a lot different than it had been in 1942. Hundreds of planes, even close to a thousand, could go out on a single mission. Losses were still staggering, and Air Force statisticians predicted that only 26 percent of crews would complete their goal of 25 missions.[81]

Doolittle's assignment was to decimate the Luftwaffe before the scheduled invasion of Europe. He had less than six months.

The Smith Crew at Thurleigh

When the Smith crew moved into Thurleigh in November of 1943, they discovered a small city with many conveniences on base, including a gymnasium, a cinema, a library, and a laundry and dry cleaning establishment to take care of uniforms. At any one time, there were approximately 3000 men and a small number of women. Most of these personnel never flew in a combat plane. Ground officers performed executive staff and technical functions, often behind a desk. A large number of the ground personnel stayed until the end of the war or even afterward.

Critical services were provided by the ground crews, mechanics and technicians who worked on the planes. They knew that the condition of the engines might determine whether or not a B-17 would make it back. If there was to be a mission, no matter what the weather was like,

The control tower at Thurleigh (306th Bomb Group Historical Association)

the ground crews were up several hours before the flight crews to get their planes ready for combat.

By afternoon, nearly everyone on base gathered near the control tower, sweating out the return of the B-17s, counting each one as it appeared on the horizon. The ground crews watched for their specific planes, ready to make any and all necessary repairs. If a plane came back with wounded men on board, the ground crews cleaned up the blood. When a straggler didn't return at all, it was a sad day. Back at the barracks, the ground support staff had to pack up and mail home the belongings of each missing crew member.

A young British boy named Ralph Franklin lived on his family's farm less than a mile from the runway at Thurleigh. Ralph, his brother, and their friends often awakened to the sounds of B-17s taking off. The boys watched the bombers fly overhead on their way to the enemy targets.

After school, the youngsters tallied the number of bombers that made it back. If the planes were flying low, the boys could see what damage had been done, such as gaping holes in the fuselage or propellers no longer turning. A flare shot from a plane indicated wounded on board. "We got a pretty good idea, in our own tiny minds, just how painful the mission had been by the number of flares that came up from the respective aircraft," Ralph remembers.[82]

Planes were parked alongside the country roads, near enough that the young boys on any given day had a close-up view of what was going on. Sometimes the crews threw used ammunition into the nearby hedges, and the children scampered to bring the shells home as souvenirs. On special occasions and when it was safe and quiet enough to do so, an airman would lift Ralph up over the fence and let him climb into a B-17.

Ralph now owns and lovingly nurtures the 306th Bombardment Group Museum on the site of the old airbase. He delights in giving

Gathering around the potbelly stove. (306th Bomb Group Historical Association)

visitors a glimpse of what it was like when hundreds of bombers roared overhead, a sight never to be seen again.

During the winter months that Herman and his fellow crew members were at Thurleigh, the average lows hovered around 2 degrees Celsius (mid-30s Fahrenheit.) Compared to Glace Bay, Nova Scotia, this temperature was familiar to Herman, but for Don Courson from Mississippi, every minute was plain cold.

Living quarters at Thurleigh were metal Quonset huts heated by potbelly coal stoves. The concrete floors were cold and damp. Coal was rationed, so stealing coal became a popular pastime. Newcomers got the less desirable bunks, those farther from the one heat source. When a crew didn't come back, other men quickly moved closer to the stove.

There was no indoor running water. Using the toilet meant a walk outdoors. During the summertime, the stroll wasn't so bad, but in the wintertime walking to the latrines offered a frosty shock. The water in the group shower building was heated by coal. Often there was only cold water, so winter showers were few and far between. Some airmen went into Bedford, the largest nearby town, for a shower and a shave.

For security reasons, the barracks were scattered about on the outskirts of the base. Blackout hours were posted in the daily bulletin. All windows had to be draped so not a speck of light showed on the outside. As a precaution against enemy raids, bomb shelters were built into the farmers' fields near the sleeping quarters.

Protestant and Catholic chaplains assigned to the 306th led regularly scheduled Sunday services at the base chapel, a large Quonset hut with a small steeple erected on the front. In the beginning, the Jewish men went to services in town, probably Bedford, but eventually Saturday morning services were held at the base chapel and were conducted by a visiting rabbi from division headquarters.

The base chaplains attended mission briefings with the airmen. Afterward, Father Adrian Poletti gave Holy Communion to the Catholics. The men who were Jewish were on their own.

The Smith crew logged hours in trainers or fired practice rounds on the skeet range. They attended ground school classes, sometimes all day long, to study British flying procedures and radio practices. They learned what to do in case they had to ditch their plane while over water or if they were forced to use their parachutes. Airmen who had landed in German-occupied territories and made it back with the help of established underground organizations coached them on how to proceed. Some airmen even took classes to learn French. Many of these students found that their few key phrases proved to be lifesaving after they had to bail out over France.

The young men had serious sex hygiene lectures, too. Condoms were readily available, and the American Red Cross operated prophylactic stations in their clubs. Years later, 306th medic William H. "Bill" Houlihan described a special flag flown over the airfield with the highest incidence of venereal disease the previous month. His base held this dubious honor four months in a row.

When the crews weren't flying, working or training, they had plenty of distractions. On days when there wasn't a mission, the men had early morning calisthenics. Those who wanted more physical activity could play baseball, football, basketball, and handball as team sports became organized. At the officers' club or the enlisted men's club, the airmen could buy a drink and shoot the breeze.

The men's first purchase was often a bicycle. In fact, selling bicycles became a lucrative trade for local shopkeepers. Suddenly Yanks were cycling through all the nearby villages. Before long they welded two bicycles and then two tandems together. The locals were delighted to see four men pedaling all together down the country roads.

One of the nearby pubs. (306th Bomb Group Historical Association)

As soon as the airmen had wheels, they explored the surrounding countryside and villages, and they found the pubs, the center of local social life. The Falcon, the Jackal, and the Queen's Head were a few of the favorite nearby destinations. The pubs thrived once the Americans arrived. Even though beer was served warm, the men often stayed until it was gone.

On days of major parties, the more inventive men scheduled training flights. They brought containers of water into the waist area of the B-17s and let ice form at 30,000 feet. This ensured they had cold drinks to enjoy later in the evening. The British liaison officers on base were amazed.[83]

Certain establishments were occasionally restricted to the airmen as out of bounds for security reasons. When Herman's crew arrived in England, the Allies were frantically preparing for D-Day. So was the enemy. Whenever the English-speaking Lord Haw Haw reviewed the day's mission over German radio, the men were reminded how easy it was for someone to overhear them talking amongst themselves about where they might be going. Area signposts had already been removed from the streets to confuse any spies who might be wandering about.

Almost everyone smoked cigarettes, an important part of the airmen's rations. No one knew or cared about consequences. Even if an airman didn't smoke, he quickly found the robust American brands—Chesterfields, Camels, or Lucky Strikes—to be valuable gifts for local girls and their families. Ralph Franklin remembers that "some locals thought the Americans were noisy and had too much money, but on the whole we were friendly to the young men so far from home."

Another important taste of home came from remodeled London buses, the American Red Cross Clubmobiles. These were driven to the airfields, each with three American girls on board, along with coffee and a doughnut-machine, cigarettes, chewing gum, stationery, and newspapers, all free to the servicemen. A record player with loudspeakers played the latest American tunes.[84]

The airmen enjoyed the American girls, but they liked the locals too. The British Women's Land Army consisted of women who worked the farms so men could serve in the armed forces. On Red Cross dance nights, the post orchestra performed in one of the mess halls. The base sent a lorry around to the villages and to the Land Army camps to pick up the girls who liked to dance. The Land Girls loved to jitterbug and looked at the Yanks as movie stars, so dashing in their uniforms.[85]

Inevitably there were requests for weddings. After the war, one of the commanders remembered, "The chaplains and I had an agreement. All applications for marriage to English girls were turned down on the first submission. We felt this helped some men who found themselves in an untenable position."[86] Despite this tactic, there were many marriages. Several hundred from the 306th were among the 50,000 Americans, primarily from the Eighth Air Force, who married British girls.[87]

A nearby concert venue was the Bedford Corn Exchange, an ornate building constructed in 1874. The most famous American musician to play there was band leader Glenn Miller, already well known when he joined the army in October of 1942. Right after D-Day, Captain Miller arrived in England with his Army Air Forces Band. The musicians were originally housed in London, but once the V-1 buzz bombs began arriving, they realized the need to find a safer home. The BBC Orchestra was already broadcasting from Bedford for the same reason, so in July of 1944 Miller and his band moved there, too.

Miller's first performance was at Thurleigh on July 14, 1944. A makeshift stage was built inside one of the four hangars on base. Around 3500 people sat on the floor, perched on the wings of the planes, and literally hung from the rafters.[88] The place was almost too crowded to dance. It was fabulous.

Occasionally Glenn Miller and his band could be heard practicing at Thurleigh in the enlisted men's mess during the noon hour. On September 8, Miller returned to Thurleigh to perform with his swing sextet.

It wasn't only the Americans who loved the distinct Miller sounds. As German Luftwaffe pilots flew over London to drop their bombs, they adjusted their radios to catch a few bars. Back home, the Nazis censored jazz. It was too American.

Miller often stayed near Thurleigh at Milton Ernest Hall, the Eighth Air Force Service Command Headquarters. This is where he spent the night on December 14, 1944. Even though the weather was foggy and cold, the next day he took off in a small single-engine plane from a nearby RAF Airfield at Twinwood Farm. His destination was Paris where he was scheduled to play for Allied troops. The plane never arrived. With the temperature at freezing, a current explanation is that a defective carburetor iced up, preventing fuel from getting to the engine. Glenn Miller, along with the pilot and another passenger, crashed into the sea.[89]

Another well-known name closely associated with Thurleigh was war correspondent Andy Rooney. As a young reporter for the army newspaper, *The Stars and Stripes*, Rooney visited many airfields, but he was most comfortable with the 306th.[90] In February of 1943, Rooney flew with the group on their first bombing raid to Nazi Germany. Years later, Rooney attended a 306th reunion held at Thurleigh and afterward wrote a newspaper article filled with 40-year-old memories. Andy admitted that he was not much for reunions, but "as reunions go, the 306th Bomb Group is special."[91]

The Missions

Herman kept a journal of his missions, one through eleven, as letters to his brother Lou. He named these accounts *The War Book of Herman Allen*. Airmen were discouraged from keeping diaries. Herman's letters were never mailed. The censors would never have allowed such detail. Lou didn't see them until after the war.

The *War Book* opened with a poem, a tribute to all the lost airmen whose bunks his crew had taken over. On the day he wrote it, barely ten days after arriving at Thurleigh, he had no idea when he would fly his first mission.

ONLY THE BRAVE

Only the brave will be there to meet you.
They will wave as you come on in.
Only the brave will be there to greet you
Above the roar of the engine's din.

Only the brave will be there all cheering
As the brakes squeal for a stop.
A checkered jeep will lead you to the clearing.
The pilot will cut the prop.

Only the brave will come to the hangar
To bring you to their Boss.
Then you will know the Great Commander
From Orion to the Cross.

Only the brave will be there around you
As He welcomes you to His Base.
You will know this the final rendezvous
As you see many a familiar face.

Only the brave will be there to meet you
Each time you come on in.
Only the brave will be there to greet you
Above the roar of the engine's din.

Somewheres in England, Herman F. Allen, 11-30-43

Mission 1 – 1 December 1943

The target for December 1 was Leverkusen, an industrial town in western Germany. Because the objective was completely overcast, the 281 heavy bombers that flew from the Eighth Air Force hit secondary targets, industries at nearby Solingen that made aircraft components and machine tools.[92]

As the bombers flew into enemy territory, their two most dangerous threats were the enemy fighters and the flak. The word flak comes from *Fliegerabwehrkanone*, the German word meaning antiaircraft cannon. The Germans had an organized defense system of antiaircraft guns that shot lethal 88 mm or larger shells toward the Allied aircraft. Each weighing more than 20 pounds, the flak shells exploded at predetermined altitudes, creating a black smoke cloud and breaking into fragments of razor sharp pieces of metal. If the flak hit the aircraft, the metal could cause great damage to plane and crew.

When the guns on the ground spit up the shells, there was a deafening noise, but the roar of the bomber engines muffled the sound. The black smoke clouds alerted crews they were about to fly straight into a highly defended flak zone. Bombardier Bill Runnels remembered, "When flak was close enough to be heard, it was too close. The sound was like a muted thud."

Particularly toward the end of the war, more air crews and planes were downed by flak than by enemy aircraft. The airmen could see a fighter coming and shoot back, but the flak was just there. Their only option if they were in formation was to fly through it.

Not all casualties were from flak or fighters. On this raid, there was much crowding at the target. Bombs dropped from a B-17 overhead destroyed one of the bombers flying directly underneath it.

LETTERS TO MY BROTHER LOU

Somewheres in England, December 1, 1943

Today saw my first baptism under fire. Believe me, it's an experience one can't really appreciate nor fully understand until he himself sits in on the show. Words aren't mine to describe the thoughts, the feelings, the puzzlement endured under such circumstances, but I shall endeavor to convey these to you the best I know how.

The groups were alerted last night, but I hadn't planned on going out, for I was still regarded as a fledgling, having just recently arrived on the field. You can imagine my surprise this morning when the

CQ[93] came through and called my name amongst those to go. I guess I was still too sleepy to grasp the full import, for it was more or less a mechanical reaction to pile out of bed, dress, and report to operations, not even considering breakfast.

I was told one of the Bombardiers was grounded, so I was to go along with Kelly's[94] crew. There it was, what I had been looking forward to, training for, anticipating all these months. Now I was to find out just how much I had digested. Now I had to look grim reality in the face.

As yet my flying equipment hadn't arrived, so by dint of begging, borrowing, and stealing, I managed to get outfitted, picked up my maps and forms, then was driven out to the ship.

It was a beastly morning, dark, cold, damp. I wondered how the Hell we could bomb under such conditions, but the weatherman said it would be 3/10 undercast[95] over the target, and that, with God at our wing tips, the powers that be must have figured would be a reasonable percentage of chance on our side.

Lieutenant Boswell[96], the Bombardier I was replacing, helped me check the bombs, the oxygen equipment, the guns, saw that all the crew was present, their equipment OK, then waited for the take-off. Boswell really checked me out in great fashion, for this was my first mission, and doubtlessly without his assistance I would probably be there in the stew.

Frankly my thoughts until this moment were nil, for I was too damn busy rushing around to consider what the score was. All in all, thus it was throughout the entire mission—flashes here and there, nothing more.

We hit the ramp at 0800, and at 0805 the planes began to roll. As we came down the runway I looked out the side window, and there lined along both sides of the strip were the ground crews, the men not on the mission and all the rest who could come, waving. They were cheering too, for in the early light you could see, though you couldn't hear them. That was a great show. Do you remember, Lou, at a football game, when the home team came on the field, how the crowds used to stand and bleat out their lungs. Well, that's how this was, except the gathering wasn't near as large, but it more than made up in sincerity. For some this was the final send off, their last glimpse of the field, and all they held dear. For some, when this game was over, there would be no hot showers, no hearty meals. Somehow there's a grim finale to death. Each ship as it came past received its share, and so we hit the blue.

Soon as we reached 3000 feet, I went back to the bombay, removed the pins from our donation for the day, gave the men a final once over, then returned to the nose. By this time we were at 10,000 feet, so I called over the interphone for the crew to go on oxygen. They checked in all OK. We headed for our rendezvous near the channel.

It was still hazy outside, visibility damn poor. I could just make out the other ships in the squadron formation, seven of us. Leveling at 15,000 feet, I checked the crew again, which incidentally is one of the duties of the Bombardier. Call the crew and have each station check in at regular intervals to be sure all was well. It only takes six seconds for something to go haywire, and when things start popping up there, things pop plenty damn fast.

We rendezvoused. Ships—the sky was dark with them. Above, below, on either side, about as far as the eye could reach. Hundreds of them, all there for the common cause. Each with its deadly load. Jerry would receive a just tribute today, a payment on account.

At the Channel, we were at 26,000 feet. This was bombing altitude, so the leader leveled off. We were in the lead wing, flying high in the tail position. A damn good spot, for by the time Jerry brought a degree of accuracy into his flak, we'd be out of reach, at least in theory. The poor devils behind us would have the headache. It's a dog eat dog proposition, Lou. Each man is chiefly concerned with his own ship first, then the others. If the one next in line gets it, they put on a good show, tried, but whatever or whoever it is decides who returns and who doesn't, well, the decision was made, and that's 30.[97]

My first glimpse of the Fatherland was a break through the undercast soon after we reached the enemy coastline. Hell, there was nothing there but more land, a lot like what we just passed over in England. I felt a cold chill in my back. Not that I was scared, but this was Germany, Jerry, the enemy. This was war in the clouds. Looking back, I reckon I was too busy to even think of being frightened. A sharp eye for enemy ships, testing the guns, checking the crew, and the many small things that crop up. I probably was full of goose pimples, but I don't remember.

Up until now I had read about flak, heard about it in the lecture room, seen it on the screen, but a few minutes from the Channel I saw it, visibly with the naked eye, for the first time. It looked harmless enough coming up through the clouds at 11 o'clock. Black puffs, the smoke cleared away, and once again nothing but vapor trails and a slight haze. Hell, I thought, if that's flak there should be little to worry about. Soon, too damn soon, I was to see how badly I erred.

About 30 minutes before the target, off in the distance, I saw the first of our fighter support. Those 47s looked like angels, Lou, and I'll wager every man aboard heaved a sigh of relief, for by this time several Fw 190s and Me 109s had been sighted, and those babies meant business.

When we reached the I.P., Mike[98], our navigator, told me we were about to turn, so I left my guns and prepared for the bombing run. The Plexiglas in the nose, by the way, was continually frosting, so I scraped a clear spot and watched the lead ship of the squadron. We were briefed to drop on the group leader, but the visibility, due to contrails and the continued weaving of the ship, made that impossible, so the next resource was our squadron leader.

The flak was coming up, fighters continually looking for a hole, the damn windows frosting. All in all, it was a sweat. The bomb run, my first release in combat, suddenly I saw the bombs leave the lead ship, then from the others in front. I flicked my toggle switch, glanced at the lights on the panel board, saw them flicker out, then I hit the salvo lever and called through the interphone "Bombs Away". There they were beneath me, just about to enter the undercast, demos and incendiaries, a hot seat below, believe me.

The radio operator called that the bombays were clear. Just then the co-pilot called "Me 109 at 1 o'clock coming on high," so I jumped for the right side gun and began pumping shells. He continued to come in only a short distance then turned off. I hardly think I touched him, but the sight of the tracers must have given him cause for thought.

In the excitement, I evidently forgot to close the bombay doors, for the ball turret gunner called and said they were still open. I remedied this in short order though I could still swear I hit the door switch before I went for the ME. That goes to show, perhaps, how unconscious one's reactions are to a reflex.

After we dumped our load, we were on the way back, and that was cheering, for our main objective had been successfully completed. Now all that remained was to return to the field intact.

Jerry had some good fuse cutters on duty, for the flak began to pop up too close for comfort. We must have been about five minutes on our new heading when a 17 in the forward squadron on the left caught a burst of flak in its second engine. It immediately caught on fire and soon parts of the wing and fuselage tore apart and flew off. The pilot kept in formation for about 3 minutes, evidently believing he could control the ship. Finally, he gave ground. As he pulled off to the left I saw the bombays open and a man jump. Then the plane exploded and pieces flew in all directions. Imagine a toy plane flying around above you, Lou, then suddenly it tears apart. That's the way it was from the nose. A cold sweat broke out all over me. For a moment, I forgot everything, except for the final pieces of that plane and the chute, still unopened, disappearing into the undercast, as if a giant hand was reaching up to claim its own. Even after the last particle had gone, I still stared at the place where but seconds before a plane like ours, with ten men aboard, had been.

It's not a pleasant thought, Lou, to sit there and know that but for the grace of God went you. It was only a matter of seconds, but it could have been a lifetime too.

The co-pilot's voice over the interphone sharply brought me back to the present. Four Jerries had decided to make a pass, they were coming in at 10 o'clock. By some twist of fate, two of them collided on the way in, but the other two kept coming. It's hard to realize as I write that this was happening faster than I can put it down, for the rate of closure is terrific. Before the navigator could bring his guns to bear on the FWs they had passed by and were rolling out at our tail, where the gunner managed a burst into their bellies. They had been so close, coming in just beneath our left wing, I could see the oxygen mask on the pilot's face.

I should tell you at this point the left waist gun was frozen, the ball turret guns were out due to a malfunction. Only one of the tail guns and one of the top turret guns were operating. You can see we were returning on a prayer indeed.

We were now almost to the Coast, our Spit escort was in sight, so we began to feel reasonably safe.

At the Channel, Kelly began to let down, for our oxygen was getting low, and the gas was beginning to run out. About mid channel, we left our group and headed for home alone by the most direct route. Mike was on the ball, and without any further difficulty, we landed at 1520 o'clock with about 150 gallons of gas. But the ship was OK and no casualties, something to be thankful for.

It was quite a journey, Lou, into Happy Valley, the term given to the Ruhr Valley, our target for today. Twenty-seven ships from the entire formation did not return, but all from our group did. Some the worse for wear, perhaps, nevertheless they all either landed at the field or somewheres in England.

Looking back, perhaps the major incident was the ship hit by flak and its reaction. Wherever they are, those men and the others, whatever they are doing, in Germany or at His base, may they have the peace they so valiantly fought for, and know the cause for which they died was right and just. That they died in the line of duty, in the face of the enemy, unflinching and unafraid. They, like others, will probably receive no medals, no fanfare to recall their glory, but as long as we live, and those who come after, they will be remembered. If, in the course of events to be, that is to be my fate, I shall ask for no greater epitaph.

I only wish several personages in the States had been along, I'm sure they would change their tune in a hurry.

I flew with a damn good crew. Each man was best at his job. I can say no man alone brought us back, but each contributed his share, and that, with God at our wing tips, is in the main why I am here this evening to scribe these words.

Twenty-four more to go. Twenty-four more missions. I do not dare attempt a thought so far ahead. All I can do is to go on each, sublime in the faith of God and know that each of you, Dad, Mom, Dora, Ace, and yourself are with me.

Take care of yourself, Lou, and should it be that these words come via the War Department, know wherever I am, it's

Always the Best, Brother
S/ Herman

In his diary, Herman mentioned the names of several fighter planes, the smaller acrobatic one-pilot aircraft. Throughout the war, faster and better fighters were being developed by both the Allies and the Axis, each side seeking air superiority.

Originally, the theory of the Air Force strategists was that the bombers could fly to their targets and back without fighter escorts. The Air Force considered it impossible to build a fighter plane fast enough to keep up with the fortresses. Extra gas tanks would hamper the escort planes' performance, the strategists believed.[99] But when American bombers were being clobbered by the German fighters, opinions began to change.

Four American fighter groups were established, and bombing missions began to have limited fighter cover. The B-17s flew across the English Channel with the small armed planes by their side. The crews called them their "little friends." Just inside the French coast, the escorts turned around, not having the fuel necessary to venture deeper into France or Germany.

The two Luftwaffe fighter planes Herman saw for the first time on December 1 were the Fw 190 (Focke-Wulf 190) and the Me 109 (Messerschmitt 109.) Like the American fighter planes, the German fighters had short range because of their small fuel capacity. The Germans would show up, fight it out, and then go back to their bases to refuel. The Americans didn't have the luxury of finding a nearby base. They had to fly all the way back across the Channel to England.

When Herman's first mission was over, the debriefing officer questioned the Kelly crew about fighter support. The men reported there was "not much support coming in—good going out for Spits and P-47s, no P-38s."

The Submarine Spitfire was a British aircraft, legendary for its role during the Battle of Britain. This nimble short-range plane was used by American and other Allied fighter groups. The Republic P-47 Thunderbolts were larger than the Spitfires and, when equipped with belly gas tanks, could go farther. The plane reported as not seen by the Kelly crew was the Lockheed P-38 Lightning, faster and with even greater range than the P-47s.

By the time the Smith crew arrived at Thurleigh, fighter escorts equipped with larger drop tanks could escort the bombers into Germany. In the fight for air supremacy, heavy pressure was on to build a fighter that could fly even deeper into enemy territory. The long-range North American P-51 Mustangs began to appear at the end of 1943. Soon, equipped with two 75-gallon drop tanks, these fast, maneuverable fighters would fly alongside the bombers all the way to Berlin and back.[100]

Mission 2 – 5 December 1943

Four days after his first mission, Herman flew his second, this time with several of his regular crew members in a B-17 called *The Great Patriarch,* piloted by 1st Lt. Willard D. Reed.

Around 550 heavy bombers were dispatched from the Eighth to attack Axis airfields at Bordeaux, Cognac, La Rochelle, and Saint Jean d'Angely, as well as industries at Paris. Nine aircraft were lost on the mission but none from the 306th.[101]

When Herman's crew first arrived at Thurleigh, they were met by Maj. John M. Regan, the 368th Squadron Commander. Even though he was four years younger than either Smithy or Merle, Regan was an experienced combat pilot who welcomed each new crew with a pep talk.

Years later, Smithy still remembered the words Regan said. "Imagine you are a Luftwaffe fighter pilot. You are flying several thousand feet above the bomber formations, and you are looking around to see who you want to shoot down. Would you attack a tightly packed formation, or would you attack a group of airplanes more or less going in the same direction, strung out all over the sky?"

Smithy said it was the easiest question anyone ever asked pilots. From the beginning, whenever they were flying in formation, Lieutenants Smith and Brown snuggled up close to the other planes. Smithy claimed that Regan's words helped save their lives.[102]

After the planes took off 30 seconds apart, the first step was for them all to assemble into proper formation. Each mission was planned with bombers from different airfields meeting at a predetermined point. It might take the planes an hour or more to get there and find the proper spot. Eighteen to 21 planes, even more, were staggered side by side and top to bottom in a precise layout called the combat box, each plane positioned where its guns could do the most damage. The planes had to stay together all the way to the target, even after "bombs away." This tight formation was their best chance of survival. A straggler on its own was easy prey for German fighters. Studies carried out in 1943 showed that nearly half the B-17s lost in combat had left the safety of the formation.

Flying so close had its own perils. Sometimes the airmen in one could look out their windows and see the facial expressions of the crew in the bomber beside them. If one B-17 got a direct hit and blew up, all nearby planes were in jeopardy.

B-17s in formation. (U.S. Air Force)

When you factor in the thick clouds, the weather, enemy fighters, and flak, collisions were easy to understand. A pilot who suddenly lost his focus or became injured could spell doom for his entire crew and possibly another.[103]

Somewheres in England, December 5, 1943

The CQ came through the barrack this morning at 0230, put on the lights, and read off the list; amongst the roll was "Allen" so I dressed for my second mission. I was wiser this morning for I stopped by the mess hall for breakfast.

At 0500 the briefing started. The major introduced the target by saying it would be a milk run. This immediately put us on the alert, for these so-called milk runs sometimes prove to be anything but.

The target for today was the factories at the airport near La Rochelle, deep in France, southwest of Paris.

Lts. Smith, Stevenson, Sgts. Heuser, Courson, and Marcotte were the members of our crew, along with the addition of experienced men at the tail, left waist, ball turret, and pilot's seat to round it out. Lt. Reed was our pilot with Smithy flying in the right cockpit.

We were out at the ship, The Great Patriarch, at 0700, and saw it was in readiness for the mission—guns, oxygen, bombs, and so forth.

At 0815 we were on the strip ready to take off, with twelve 500 pounders in the bombay, each tuned for its spot below. Just think, Lou, six thousand pounds of fury unleashed.

The weather wasn't too bad considering England. Foggy in places, with haze in others, and a few clouds to iron out the visibility. We rendezvoused over the field with the remainder of the group, then, headed towards the Channel and France, we were off.

En route to the Coast, we were joined by three wings of 17s and two of 24s. Those 24s were a welcome sight, for somehow whenever they were along, Jerry makes his first bid for them. After watching their formation and flub-dubbing all over the sky, I could readily understand why.

At the Channel, we started to climb, and at 20,000 we were above the undercast. I can still hear the weatherman saying "You'll have little trouble once you cross the Channel, about 2 or 3 tenths undercast". He wasn't along to see how far off his prediction was.

Our heading was directly in the sun, and all due credit is due Lt. Reed and Smithy for doing such a damn good job of formation work. They sure had a Hell of a time.

It was a beautiful day up there at 20,000. The clouds below, stretched out like a vast lay of white sand, with its knolls and dunes scattered all around. Planes, planes, planes. Those in the distance appeared like giant specks on a white board.

You would have enjoyed this trip, Lou. We were flying in the hole of the lead squadron in the lead group, so it was ringside.

Soon as we hit the French coast, P-38s and P-47s joined us. They maneuvered around in the outskirts and ahead of the formation. You could see their vapor trails as they jockeyed about. They sure looked good, damn good.

The deeper we flew into enemy territory the more apparent it was our target was going to be obscured, for the clouds were bellowing heavier. Off in the distance was another cloud bank, rising above the ones we were going over.

We were due at our IP at 1111 o'clock, but by 1100 hours we were at 26,000 trying to climb over. Major Regan, the lead pilot, decided it was a no-go, and it would be suicide to attempt a break below, so at 1110 hours the formation turned, and we set a course for home.

That was a Hell of a feeling, here we had come so far, about 40 miles from our target, yet we couldn't dump our load. However, it's all in the game.

Soon after the turn, the tail gunner reported about 20 bursts of flak at 7 o'clock low, just above the undercast. Doubtless a shot by Jerry to let us know he knew we were around. At this point, one of our 17s dropped from the formation and hit for the clouds. Probably engine trouble, but they'll make out OK, for France is a damn sight better spot to land than Germany.

The return was merely a ride. At the Channel we let down to 10,000, came off oxygen, and at 1400 we were back on the field.

Truly a milk run, but there was always that possibility, and the flak made it a mission. Through it all, always the constant check, the constant watch. Reading this, Lou, may make it sound rather drab and routine, but believe me it was no picnic.

I should say the entire gathering did not all turn back. At a point in southern France, the force divided. The 24s went after another target, and some of the 17s did the same. Most of those found the target obscured also and returned, but five 17s did drops on Bordeaux and others at other spots. Nine of our ships did not return. You can easily determine from this fact that conditions vary for each plane. What might have been a milk run for us was completely the opposite for others. Thus the way of battle.

So Lou, my second mission. Twenty-three to go. This one indeed was a far cry from the first effort, and, believe me, I won't shed a tear if the remainder are of the same caliber; however, that is a wishful hope. But God constantly at the wing tips, with the crew continually working as a unit, each succeeding return will prove itself.

Take care of yourself, Lou, and I shall do the same.

Always the best,
S/ Herman

Mission 3 – 13 December 1943

U-boats continued to ravage the Allied convoys. A total of 649 B-17s and B-24s bombed port areas of Bremen and Hamburg and U-boat yards at Kiel,[104] a port city with a major naval base in the north of Germany.

This was the first Eighth Air Force mission in which more than 600 heavy bombers attacked targets. The English people looked up to see a sky of planes thundering overhead. "We knew there would be peace one day," one observer remembered.

Thurleigh sent 22 aircraft, of which 19 completed the mission, and all but one aircraft returned. Herman and most of his regular crew again flew in the *Rationed Passion* piloted by Lieutenant Reed. They were assigned to the Purple Heart Corner of the formation, the lowest, rearmost, and, many thought, most exposed position. It was an omen of things to come.

England, December 13, 1943

Am gradually becoming an experienced combat crewman, especially after today's mission.

Went through the usual routine prior to take off–checked the bombs, the oxygen, the ammo, the guns, the crew and so forth. At 0837 we were off and on our way. The ship, Rationed Passion, flew lead of second element, with Lt. Reed as pilot, a chaplain from 40th Wing as co-pilot, and the remainder of the crew from the old bunch—Steve, Tiny, Vic, Don, Howard, Tom, RB, and I.

The target for today was Kiel, and that in itself should have been a warning, but ignorance is bliss at times, and this was one of them. I wised up in a hurry, a damn hurry.

We left the coast, flying low squadron in the low group of our wing, which is well termed Purple Heart Corner. Three wings, I believe, were to hit Kiel, and six wings Bremen, with two wings of B24s along as escort. It was a well-planned campaign, but in an instance the best-laid plans of men and mice... The Bremen contingent was over their target OK, and the majority of our division hit Kiel, but a few, like Rationed Passion, came within shouting distance, and that's all.

About 30 minutes before the target, we hit flak. Lou, that confounded flak meant business. It came up at all altitudes, all over the sky. Our evasive action was like a line through a maze of dots when the bursts hit. We really began to know what "flak happy" means. Someone was watching out for us, for as far as I could see no ships were hit in our immediate vicinity.

There were no Jerry fighters about, probably due to the concentration at Bremen. P-38s and P-51s were very much in evidence. They make Jerry think twice any time.

There was a 10/10 undercast, which, incidentally, is where the weatherman messed up again. He said the most would be 3/10. I'll bet he has a red face when the first of the month rolls around, and he goes to collect his pay.

The whole formation made a 360 degree turn somewheres near the IP. It was a damn good thing Jerry was not around, for he would have had a picnic the way the 17s were scattered. As the 360 degree straightened out, our 4th engine started to play up. A second later it started to windmill, the cowling flew off, and poof—there we were by our lonesome. The formation flew on. Rationed Passion lost altitude fast. It is a funny feeling to find yourself there all alone, with the whole sky around you empty. You remember a lot of things in the flash of seconds and suddenly appreciate a lot more. Perhaps some of the people who figure this war will be over in a day or so should be placed in the position we were. They'd change their minds mighty fast.

At 1235, I dropped the bombs. Steve figured we were somewheres near the target, but not on it. At least I personally believe they did some good. The ship was steadily losing altitude, and about 1310 we came out of the undercast on the deck right above a Danish island. The name escapes me at the moment.

Looking around, I saw we were right over a German convoy. Simultaneously a Ju 88 hopped us. It was quite a fight. All stations had a crack at the fighter. At the same time, the convoy started throwing flak and lead. It was a hot spot. Lt. Reed did some fast evasive action through a mist just off the water and finally lost the Ju 88. By this time an engine caught on fire, so the pilot and co-pilot decided to turn around and land in Denmark.

As we came in sight of the Danish coast, the fire went out, so we turned for the North Sea and England. Steve was really on the ball, and too much credit can't be given to him for his navigation. He gave Reed a heading of 200 degrees. We were on the deck, about 200 feet above the water.

Ten minutes on this heading, the Ju 88 came back in for another play. We were fast approaching a six-ship Jerry convoy. The Jerry started to come in on us at our level at 3 o'clock. Just as he broke to point his nose, Reed turned into his direction. The Ju 88 continued to come. As he passed us at 12 o'clock, Tiny in the top turret and I in the nose started pumping lead. He was only around 50-75 yards. As he came at 11 o'clock, our tracers were bouncing off his ship, and black smoke started trailing him. It was a hit from both our guns. He continued on around, and Courson at the left waist gave him a good burst. The last we saw of the ship, it was disappearing into the mist at

7 o'clock, engine burning and smoke bellowing like Hell—one Ju 88 less.

All this time, the convoy was sending .50 calibers our way with 20mm bursts and flak to add to their fire. We were pumping lead at them in return, and I know we did land a few good bursts in their midst. It was indeed Hell for a while. Empty shells and links, powder smoke in the nose, and constant conversation on the interphone. A real dogfight and battle. Fortunately, none of us were hit. And as far as we could determine, our ship undamaged.

We soon left the convoy behind and continued on our course. Reed was having trouble holding the small altitude we had. He called for all spare ammo and extra equipment to be thrown out to lighten the load. Oxygen bottles, flak suits, ammo, and what not hit the drink. That helped, and skimming the waves we flew.

Thirty minutes later, we intercepted another convoy. It began to throw lead our way, and we reciprocated. Reed altered course to go around it, and soon we saw it in the distance. By this time, Steve was able to get a radio bearing on the English coast so we knew we were comparatively safe and headed in the right direction. Half hour later he managed a GI fix,[105] and all breathed a sigh of relief. It was home boys, home.

It seemed a helluva long time to sight the Coast. One of the fellows came in over the interphone, "They must have pulled down the balloon barrage and the Island sunk." We had damn good spirit aboard, Lou, which helped tremendously to bridge the time of flight.

Finally we came in over the Coast at 1554 and landed at 1627. Exactly an hour later than the briefed ETA.

As I sat down to mess this evening, frankly, a few hours before I never expected I would. There was a time when I actually wondered when I would be writing you again, and from where.

So, Lou, my third mission, twenty-two to go. We can only look to the next one, and each succeeding one in turn, with the sincere faith of God constantly at our wing tips, the crew continuing to function as in the past, and the knowledge that you all are in there pitching.

Take care of yourself, shall do the same, and know

Always the best,
S/ Herman

In the 368th Squadron Diary, the historian reported, "Lt. W. Dale Reed and his crew drew all the excitement. A Ju 88 engaged them in a rare duel which forced them to dive to cloud cover at 4,000 feet with one engine on fire. The enemy found them again, only to be outmaneuvered and raked by the bombardier, Lt. Herman F. Allen, the top turret, Sgt. Carl Heuser, and the left waist gunner, Sgt. Donald Courson, as the 88 crossed 782's nose and down her left side. Having thus disposed of the Ju 88 by setting both her engines on fire, our crew next took on a convoy single-handed at deck level. Then, finding no further opposition, the boys threw guns, ammunition, and everything handy overboard to lighten the ship and turned up cooly at base without a single injury."

Herman now had a short break for Christmas. Before the war had even begun, the British government began to evacuate children from the urban centers to more rural areas. The men on base contributed candy from their weekly PX rations for Christmas parties for local children. Even though Herman was Jewish, he enthusiastically participated in the festivities. On December 27, Thurleigh hosted a party at the Empire Theatre in Bedford for orphans and evacuees. The men drove their trucks around the villages to pick up the children. In all, there were six Christmas parties conducted in Bedford, Kettering, and nearby areas.

Mission 4 – 30 December 1943

From the Eighth Air Force, 658 heavy bombers, escorted by P-51s and P-38s, attacked the oil plant at Ludwigshafen. Twenty-three bombers were lost.[106]

The Nazi-controlled IG Farbenindustrie chemical plant at Ludwigshafen was vital to Germany because of its production of raw materials such as synthetic oil and rubber. In order to maintain its essential output, the company was relying on concentration camp inmates and slave laborers from conquered countries. Incidentally, IG Farben, the shortened name of the company, held the patent for the cyanide-based pesticide Zyklon B, used in Nazi Germany gas chambers.

England, December 30, 1943

Isn't there a saying "deep in the sleep of peace?" Suddenly I felt a light upon my eyes and a voice saying, "Sirs, are all officers awake"? I glanced at the clock then looked for the voice. 0345 and the CQ. "Breakfast at 0415, briefing at 0515." He then read off the list: "Ship 767, Smith, Keilt, Stevenson, and Allen."

The briefing took the regular form—target, routing, weather, escort, and so forth. It was to be a long haul, deep into the Fatherland. We were flying as a spare, to fill in the position of the first abortion in the group. A tough spot, for it meant flub-dubbing behind the formation until a ship left and returned to the field due to engine or personnel failure. As a rule, there were generally two or three on each trip.

For the first time, we were to fly with Smithy as our pilot, and that was strictly OK. The crew was complete except for the co-pilot and the ball turret, who was in the hospital.

Checked the ship for its bomb load, oxygen, guns, ammo. Saw the crew was present and set. The take-off was at 0830.

We rendezvoused over the field at 0939 at 16,000, then headed south for the target, stooging on the outskirts waiting for a plane. Just before we hit the channel, the ship flying in the hole of the lead squadron pulled out and turned for home. Smithy saw the opening. We were it.

All in all, it was a quiet trip compared to some of the others. The fighter escort was excellent all the way. We hit our first flak just before the target and waded through the stuff for about twenty or thirty minutes.

This was a Pathfinder raid which meant we couldn't see our target but bombed through the clouds. We dropped our bombs on the lead ship at 1207.

The weather was fair. We flew above 10/10 undercast practically all the way from the English coast and return. Temperature ranged from -30°C to 35°C at altitude of 24,000 feet.

Coming back, our #4 engine began to act up and by the time we hit the Channel it was out. On the last leg it was a three engine job. Smithy played her close, and at 1602 we were home.

Thus Lou, my fourth mission racked up. Ludwigshafen was our target. Twenty-one to go, but now to sweat out my fifth.

Take care of yourself, Lou, and know at this end, all is OK. God flies at our wing tips, and the prayers of you all hold fast.

As always the best,
S/ Herman

The day after this raid, a confession was made by German and neutral sources that the big "gas" town had been crippled. The 368th combat diary gave much credit to the "best friends a B-17 could have: a P-38 escort which outdid itself."

Mission 5 – 31 December 1943

Almost 500 heavy bombers attacked targets inside France and off the French coast. Twenty-five airplanes were lost to antiaircraft fire and fighters.[107] Although Herman and his squadron had been briefed to bomb the airdrome at Bordeaux, because of visibility issues the 368th Eager Beavers bombed their alternate target of Cognac.

> Seems I was no sooner asleep when the lights came on this morning. My aching back, this was Air Medal mission with a vengeance. Seven hours yesterday of combat, five on oxygen, and now up and at 'em again.
>
> Breakfast at 0400, briefing at 0500. Again, Smithy and the crew, which might lead to the assumption that from here on out we fly together.
>
> I guess Bomber Command decided to finish up 1943 in style. At briefing we learned this was to be one of the largest fleets of planes to be sent across in one mission. We were given the target, the routing, the fighter support, the weather, and the complete dope prior to takeoff. It was to be another long haul, just what length I really did not appreciate until night.
>
> Checking the crew and ship as usual went off like clockwork, and at 0810 we were on the ramp ready to take off. Had a full bomb load aboard, twelve five hundred G.P. bombs, and around 3000 gallons of gas.
>
> In the half light of early morning, I watched the crowd along the runway as we roared down the

strip, and so we hit the air. Once again we went along as a spare. However, this time, in case of no abortion we were given a definite spot to fly.

We rendezvoused at 6000 feet over the field then headed toward France. We were just outside the formation. After we reached the channel, no ship turned. Smithy took his spot with the high squadron, flying right wing with the third element.

As we crossed the Brest peninsula, I looked around and there on all sides, behind and in front, flew the Forts. Frankly, so damn many I couldn't count them. It was a beautiful sight. Flying might all out for the purpose of a common goal. All loaded with instruments of destruction and death, if need be, to see that it was so. I have no qualms, Lou, for it is now either we or they. There are no regrets.

Right on the southern tip of the Brest coast, we hit our first flak barrage. It was inaccurate and way off to the left. Overhead a few P-47s flub-dubbed around and then we hit the broad Atlantic, turned south, on course for our next turning point.

Below it was 10/10 undercast with the visibility at our altitude about 17,000 feet. Sure some view. The clouds were like a vast snow drift on the water with an occasional mound to break the monotony of vision. As we flew south, the undercast broke until about 6/10.

Presently Steve and I figured our position and decided the lead navigator had messed up somewheres.

The time was fast approaching to start our turns and make the bomb run. No evidence of such a move was noticed. The briefed IP time passed, still we flew on. What the Hell was going on? Gas was being burned, and we only had so much.

Finally, around noon we took a heading almost due west, flew that for about twenty, then flew north.

This was supposed to be a usual bomb run. Looking down and ahead, where was the ground? It was there in patches. Suddenly we broke over clear ground for about a fifty-mile area with only scattered clouds. There off to the left was Bordeaux, completely covered with a smoke screen. Our primary target was an airfield about six miles west of the city. Evidently the lead Bombardier reasoned it would be covered, so we flew on. For the life of me, I don't understand his method of figuring, for from where we flew it looked plenty clear over that area. Flying north was the secondary target.

Jerry worked his flak guns overtime and too damn close for comfort. We were glad to leave that spot.

About 1300 hours we came in sight of our secondary target, and it was really in the clear. My aching back, I thought there was flak at Bordeaux, but here the sky was heavy with it, especially around the target, the airfield at Cognac.

The 305th Bomb Group led our Wing so they made their run first, then we turned. I called the crew and told them to be damn sure they had their flak suits on. I switched on my racks and was all set.

The bombing run—this is the first time I had been on a visual target. There we were, 23 ships in bomb formation spread out for the best concentration. It was a tough go to sit up there and ride through that damn flak. It burst all around. The red flash, the black smoke, pop, boom, pop.

Suddenly a dark line from the lead ship hit the clear. I touched my toggle switch, threw the salvo knob, "Bombs Away." Looking down, Christ! Bombs from all the ships seemed to hit with one helluva thud. A direct hit.

As we left the target, I glanced out the side window, saw the flak, old splashes and new. A cold sweat broke out all over me. "Out of the Valley of Death" we rode. One burst of that stuff upon our ship, and it would be "so long". God surely rode at our wingtips today.

France is a scenic country, especially from the air. It looked so damn beautiful down below, it was hard to believe war existed. But there we were, and Jerry surely knew something hit him.

On the way back we skirted by several more flak areas. Jerry fighters pointed their noses several times, but I guess they saw our might and turned tail for other fields. However, there were several stragglers. The tail gunner reported over the telephone that they were being attacked, but they proved too much for Jerry and came along OK.

At the channel, we began the letdown and, by the time we were at the English coast, were at 6000 feet.

Now our troubles really started. The weather began to close in. After going through all that Hell, now this. About 40 miles from the field, it was so bad all Smithy could do was to see the ship ahead. We all worried about our gas which was running low. We were an hour overdue on flight time already, darkness closing in, and rain. Believe me, Lou, we all had our fingers crossed.

Finally, it became so bad we couldn't see the wing tips of our own plane. There we were, flub-dubbing around at 1000 feet sweating out a field, any field. Suddenly through the haze, Steve picked up a perimeter track of lights which meant a field nearby. He called up Smithy, and he followed them in. Man, that runaway looked good. It was the 305th at Chelveston, about 14 miles from our field.

My fifth mission is now behind me. Twenty to go, with the sixth on the horizon to sweat out. There are really no words to describe what one goes through each time he hits the air. It leaves its mark, its sear, and only God Himself knows the price eventually to be paid. All that matters is to have faith in Him, and in the end it will prove itself. I still remember what we once said, to the effect that as long as we do our best to the utmost of our ability that is the most that can be expected. It is our own mind, our own conscience we have to live with, and there lies the story.

Take care of yourself, shall do the same, and know,

Always the best,
S/ Herman

After a 5:12 p.m. landing at Chelveston, home of the 305th Bomb Group, the crew traveled by truck back to Thurleigh in time to celebrate New Year's Eve. The 306th had been in combat for a year and three months and had sent out planes on 97 missions.

Andy Rooney reported in the magazine *Stars and Stripes* that the 368th Eager Beavers was "the first squadron in the USAAF to drop 1,000 tons of bombs on the Germans—or on anybody. They passed that mark the last day of 1943."[108]

Losses were still high, but Herman's squadron celebrated with raised glasses to toast their hope that Hitler's Europe would be no more by the end of 1944.

Mission 6 – 7 January 1944

The winter weather kept Thurleigh quiet for the first three days of 1944 and allowed everyone to recover from their New Year celebrations.[109] Herman had a few more days, as he wasn't assigned to fly again until the 7th.

On January 2, 1944, bombardier Herman F. Allen, pilot Charles W. Smith, co-pilot Merle P. Brown and navigator Charles Stevenson were promoted to first lieutenant. For sure there were drinks all around.

Five days later on January 7, 420 heavy bombers from the Eighth Air Force returned to the IG Farbenindustrie chemical plant at Ludwigshafen. Twelve aircraft total were lost on the mission.[110] From the 306th at Thurleigh, there were no losses, but more than half the aircraft suffered damage from heavy flak.

A newspaper headline the next day read, "Reich Gas Center Is Wiped Out." The paper went on, "Ludwigshafen, heart of Germany's war chemical and poison gas industry, was completely flattened by the massed American heavy bomber raid in daylight Friday ... one of the largest formations ever to strike the Reich."

Herman wrote only a paragraph after this mission. Immediately afterward, he went to the base hospital. B-17 crew members were prone to develop aerotitis media, inflammation of the middle ear caused by the ear's inability to adjust to changes in atmospheric pressure. This happened most often during the multiple descents at high altitudes. Their unpressurized cabins were freezing cold. If an airman had a respiratory infection that blocked his Eustachian tube, his eardrum could rupture. A cure was never found for this condition, which accounted for two-thirds of the instances of crew members being grounded.[111]

England, January 7, 1944

This is going to be brief and to the point, for as a result of this mission have cracked an eardrum and have to report to the hospital for a sojourn there, nothing serious.

Target—Ludwigshafen

Mission—#6

Crew—OK

```
Comment—MP's first ride
To go—19

As always,
S/ Herman
```

The flight surgeon removed Herman from flying status for a month. Although removal guaranteed his safety, being grounded was a big disappointment. The bomber boys were primarily concerned with one thing—reaching their goal of 25 missions.

Whenever the men were lucky enough to get a three-day pass, they hopped on a train for London. During the month he was grounded, Herman had his chance. The London that the airmen saw was scarred, with entire blocks leveled by the night after night bombings which began in September of 1940 and ended eight months later.

During the month of January 1944, Hitler's Little Blitz raged, and once again London was experiencing the piercing sirens and the intermittent air strikes. None of these attacks hampered the visiting servicemen. London was the center of the world to them.

When Allied soldiers began to arrive in droves, for the most part Londoners were happy to see them. If at first the British were standoffish, they warmed quickly. The Yanks had money to spend and spend they did. London's nightclubs, theatres, and pubs were packed. Only after the Normandy invasion did business let up.

The airmen came to London to drink and have fun. One of Herman's and his crewmates' favorite pubs was The Lamb and the Flag. The barmaids learned to recognize them when they came in and would give them a special shot of whiskey.

Herman saw all the familiar sights—Big Ben, Westminster Abbey, Buckingham Palace, St. Paul's Cathedral, and especially Piccadilly Circus. At night, the blackouts slowed things down, but the men managed.

Piccadilly Circus was the place to be and be seen, reminiscent of a small Times Square with its oversized signage, crowded sidewalks, double-decker buses, uniforms everywhere. At night, the area was pitch black, and the men carried flashlights to get around.

This was the venue for the hookers known as the Piccadilly Commandoes, ready to take care of the men's physical needs. Antics in London surely helped Thurleigh earn its reputation as the airfield with the highest rate of venereal disease four months in a row.

During the daytime, Herman and his pals walked down the street side by side with their arms clasped around each other's backs. They moved in perfect unison to capture the young ladies as they came toward the men from the opposite direction.

Herman's other trick was just as mischievous. Because nylon stockings were so scarce, women often painted a fake seam down the backs of their bare legs. When Herman saw a hand-drawn seam, he licked his finger, wiped it across the painted line, and howled with delight.

During his short visit to London in January of 1944, Herman may well have passed a good-looking brunette on the street. He would definitely have noticed her. She was seeing London for the first time too, having recently arrived from Washington, D.C., to work for the "oh so secret" OSS.

Chapter 5

11 January 1944

As of January 11, 1944, the 306th at Thurleigh was leading the Eighth Air Force in number of missions flown—100. The group had lost 87 planes.[112] Because he was grounded, Herman did not fly on the 11th of January. Even so, this mission haunted him for as many years as he could remember.

According to records of the Eighth Air Force, on this date over 570 B-17s and B-24s bombed German industrial targets and targets of opportunity in Oschersleben, Halberstadt, and near Brunswick. The attackers encountered fierce opposition, estimated at 500 German fighters, and 60 American bombers were lost.[113]

For that day, Air Force meteorologists had predicted only a few hours of clear weather over Germany. Unable to find the bombers in the dense clouds, some of the fighter escorts returned to their bases. When the Germans thought the bombers might be headed straight for Berlin, they sent out every fighter plane available.[114]

On both his second and third missions, Herman had flown with pilot Lt. Willard D. Reed. On this day, while Herman recuperated from his ruptured eardrum, Reed and his crew were again in the B-17 *Rationed*

Passion. While flying back from Halberstadt, the plane was hit hard by flak. The extensive damage caused the plane to catch fire and go into a spin. As the plane broke up, eight of the ten crew members bailed out, landing in Nazi-occupied Netherlands. The co-pilot died when he hit the ground.

Pilot Reed was captured by the Germans and sent to the Stalag Luft 1 camp at Barth in northern Germany. The bombardier, after landing near a small Dutch town, also became a POW. The navigator and the tail gunner managed to evade capture, and with the help of the Dutch resistance were able to reach Paris where the French Underground safely brought them back to England.

Three members of the *Rationed Passion* crew spent more than three months moving from place to place with the help of the Underground. By April 22, those three men had made it to Saint Rémy, a heavily wooded Belgian village near the French border. Sympathetic farmers housed and fed them along with five other American airmen who were also trying to avoid capture.

As they were finishing breakfast, the men heard the sounds of automatic weapons being fired. They, along with two farmers who had helped them, were taken prisoner by men in German uniforms. At the same time, 30 Belgian citizens from the nearby town were arrested, and many were sent to concentration camps.

The airmen were undressed and searched. Because of their dog tags they could never have been mistaken for freedom fighters. That afternoon, the Americans, hands tied behind their backs, were taken into the woods, each accompanied by two armed men in German uniform. The eight airmen were separated, and on a signal, each was shot several times in the back.

This heinous crime is remembered as The Massacre at Saint Rémy, and after the war, Belgian military authorities arrested many of those responsible.[115] Unfortunately, several of the perpetrators escaped. Only a few served jail time, and only one was sentenced to death.[116]

At the time, Herman only knew that his friend Lieutenant Reed and the crew were missing in action. The 368th Bombardment Squadron Diary reported on the day, "This is one of those missions when IT happens. Ground personnel as well as crews on the mission will long remember the activities of this day. Their target was a new one for them, an aircraft component plant at Halberstadt, Germany.

"About an hour and ten minutes after leaving, 30 to 35 Fw 190s made desperate attacks on the 306th Group, now flying alone [without fighter escorts.] Enemy aircraft repeatedly attacked in waves of four. At the start of the attack, there were nineteen aircraft in formation. 7 1/2 minutes later, only 11 were visible."

Smithy flew the B-17 *Weary Bones* along with most of his regular crew and later wrote about the mission to Halberstadt.

> The 306th Group reached the enemy coast at 1044 hours. The term enemy coast is somewhat misleading. Yes, the land is occupied by the Nazis, but the group has just passed 20 miles northwest of Amsterdam, Netherlands. The flight crews know if they have to bail out or crash land, they will have a chance to be picked up by friendly people.
>
> The German border is only 105 air miles from Amsterdam. According to the navigator, Weary Bones has a groundspeed over the earth of 230 miles per hour, and that includes 10 miles per hour of help

from the wind, so the word is that Weary Bones will reach the true German border in 26 minutes.

When the 26 minutes are up, the land below will suddenly seem darker, more forbidding and dangerous to the crew. They know this is mostly psychological, but the same thoughts arrived when on other missions they flew from over France into German airspace. After getting a good visual check of when Weary Bones crossed the true border between Germany and the Netherlands, the navigator told the crew his ETA for the target was 11:53. The rest of the crew was interested in this news because the run in was for God and country, the way home was for the crew.

There was no enemy opposition on the way to the target from either flak or fighter aircraft. The bomb run lasted 60 seconds. … Six minutes later, at 12:00 hours the group was attacked by twin engine fighters. One fighter circled around the group and attacked within 200 yards. These attacks lasted for 1 1/2 hours; none of the group's B-17s was shot down. During this period, our crews saw a lone B-17 from another group fight the twins for half an hour. The crew finally started bailing out; seven or eight parachutes were seen. The pilot of another ship stayed at his post while all the crew bailed out except the tail gunner who stuck to his guns fighting off the attacks. Neither pilot nor gunner made an attempt to bail out. Tail guns were still firing when the ship exploded.

... During these attacks, the nose section of Weary Bones was struck by shell fire. Almost immediately the bombardier called on the intercom, "The navigator has been hit!" The only crew member close enough to render aid was the bombardier who was just inches away, so the pilot asked the bombardier to give what aid he could to his wounded comrade. The navigator had suffered a massive head wound which must have killed him instantly. The horror of those few seconds still remains to haunt the surviving crew members of Weary Bones.

The crew of Weary Bones and the crews of seven other B-17s of the 306th managed to find a bomber base at Hethel near the coast and land there just before darkness fell and the fog closed in. Before landing, the Weary Bones crew fired double red flares to signify wounded aboard so Weary Bones would be met by the medics. As a cold damp wind blew in from the North Sea, the medics lowered the body of 1st Lt. Charles L. Stevenson, navigator, out of the nose hatch of Weary Bones. The nine tired crewmen watched and silently wept.[117]

Thurleigh was fogged in, so communication about the fates of the crews was delayed. By the end of the day, five 306th planes had gone down. Fifty airmen were lost.

Herman with navigator Charles Stevenson. Scrapbook photo is labeled "The Nose."

When Herman learned that Steve had died on this mission, he was devastated and always regretted not being there for Steve's final flight. A few days later, Herman wrote a heartfelt tribute to his good friend.

WE WILL REMEMBER. And we shall say to him when we meet once again "over there." There were no tears, we bowed our heads, each with a silent prayer, each with a personal thought. Through each flight you were with us, in spirit, in guidance, as it always was.

We will remember with each bomb dropped, each mile flown, each letter written. Yes, Steve, we will remember".

In memory of Charles Stevenson, Navigator, killed in action January 11, 1944, Halberstadt Mission.

Herman Allen
January 15, 1944

Chapter 6

Big Week

Finally on February 11, Herman was allowed to fly. February was the beginning of Operation Argument, code name for the Eighth Air Force's campaign to finally destroy the Luftwaffe. Planners projected if they sent in enough bombers to Germany's aircraft industry targets, the enemy fighters would come out full force and could be destroyed. This tactic was a critical factor in preparation for an Allied invasion of Europe, to prevent the land forces coming on shore from being decimated by the Luftwaffe.

In order to accomplish this goal, the Eighth Air Force needed to put out a mass of both bombers and fighters. By February, they were finally ready to do so on a large enough scale.[118]

Mission 7 – 11 February 1944

Industrial targets at Frankfurt/Main and a V-weapon site at Saint-Pol/Siracourt were attacked by 187 heavy bombers. A further 130 heavy bombers bombed Ludwigshafen and other targets of opportunity when failure of blind-bombing equipment caused diversion from primary targets.[119]

England, February 11, 1944

Since January 7, a lot of water has flown beneath the bridge. As a result of my broken eardrum, the flight surgeon grounded me for a month. January 11, somewheres over Germany, Steve was hit by a 30-30 caliber and is now buried at Cambridge. Smithy and the crew put in quite a few missions, seven to be exact, so now they are really up on me.

It was good to be back in harness. This morning the CQ pulled his usual routine at 0230—break out at 0300, briefing at 0400. It was sure cold. The thermometer played tag at 0"F, a few clouds, and a full moon.

I was the only one of the crew scheduled to fly today, with Kelly in the lead position of the squadron.

Went through the usual procedure of preflight, and by 0730 we were airborne, headed for the Fatherland. It was still dark as we rendezvoused, but slowly the sun rose, and above the undercast it was the beginning of a beautiful day.

This was but a small foray in relation to others I've flown. Two other wings, and at the coast we joined up and headed for Frankfurt. By this time, we had been on oxygen for about an hour, and the effects were already beginning to tell.

Occasionally, as we crossed the Channel, we could see the water through breaks in the undercast. At the enemy coast I called the radio operator for pictures. The clouds were now about 6/10-8/10, and here and there the navigator and I could pick up a landmark. Snow lay thick in the fields below, and it was really chilly at 26,000 feet, 48 degrees C below.

We passed only spotted flak bursts until Frankfurt, and Lou, those lads down there were really sharp today. It was barrage type mostly and covered the damn sky. The wing in front of us passed over the target without dropping their load, so we followed suit. Still don't know the exact reason.

About twenty minutes later, I noticed the lead ship was opening his doors, so while opening mine I looked ahead and there saw the secondary target, a German town. We came in on the bomb run, and about a minute before the bombs were away a dense blackness hit the front of us. At first I thought I was seeing things or having spots. Christ! The flak we had passed was child's play compared to what we were about to go through. There was no escape, no avenue. Those bastards down below were tracking us, sending every damn thing they could muster. Scared, that's putting it mildly, but I grabbed the salvo handle, kept an eye on the lead ship, and prayed. God was at our wing tips I know, for no mortal could fly through that Hell alone.

It was "Bombs Away." I leaned over the sight to watch the drop when suddenly, above the roar of the engines, I heard a sickening pop. I jerked my head up, glanced around at the navigator, and asked over the phone, "What the Hell"? It was a long ten seconds as we sweated out a flak hit to know whether or not it was serious. Life is sweet. Nothing happened, so I guessed it was a glancing hit, and so it proved later.

Well Lou, we came through that Valley of Hell, and once again turned on the homeward course.

The fighter support was excellent. Above, below, and all around. P-47s, 38s, and 51s. Saw one Jerry from a distance, looked like a Me 210. At the coast we hit another flak area to our right, skirted it, and at mid-channel started to let down. That was sure a relief. Six hours of oxygen is no fun.

Arrived back at the base at 1526.

And so Lou, I look back on mission seven and forward to number eight. Take care of yourself, Lou, shall do the same.

Best always,
S/ Herman

The day following this mission, the newspapers reported, "Forts Blast Frankfurt. Yesterday's operation included the greatest number of fighter sorties ever made by U.S. fighters from bases in England."

This was Herman's last mission before what has come to be known as Big Week. A few days later, a film titled *Target, Germany* was shown at the Post Theatre. The men of the 306th had to know something big was coming.

The Plane

On the 18th of January, a new B-17G, serial number 4-240006, arrived at Thurleigh and was assigned to the Charles W. Smith crew. The first time Herman flew in it was February 20.

The system for marking the planes began in December 1942 and kept changing until August of 1944. When the Smith crew first caught sight of their new plane, they would have noted triangles on either side of the vertical stabilizers. These indicated it belonged in the First division. The letter H inside each triangle meant the B-17 was from the 306th. Under each triangle was the serial number: 240006, and beneath that was a large G for the model.[120] There was another triangle H under the left wing and again, one on top of the right wing.

It was common practice for the air crews to christen their planes with creative names and eye-catching artwork, often a pinup girl, the sexier the better, or a cartoon character such as Little Audrey or Donald Duck with bombs. One hopeful crew named their plane *25 or BUST.*

A pilot sometimes painted the name of his girlfriend near where he sat. So, under his window, Smithy lettered "Helen B" in honor of a young lady he had met back home on a double date. He also began to sketch a picture of Helen, but before the paint could dry, the crew had to take the fortress up on a mission. When the wet paint met the slipstream, it created long streaks behind the half-finished image. Helen B looked like she was a ghost running into the wind. On the same side of the plane under the waist window were written the words "Memphis Belle," purely for good luck. They all wanted to finish their 25 missions and go home.

The final name the Smith crew chose was neither Helen B nor Memphis Belle. The day they christened their beautiful new plane, two men hoisted fellow crew members onto the horizontal stabilizer, the part of the plane by the tail that resembled a small wing. Gunner

Don Courson hung out the waist window, brandishing a machine gun. Someone snapped a picture, and the name was official: *Liberty Lady.*

There was one more customization by the two pilots. Smithy and Merle had earlier visited the Thurleigh salvage yard on a special quest. After the sergeant in charge understood what they needed, he took his cutting torch to a crashed B-17 and created two perfectly sized armor plates to fit under their seat cushions. This extra protection, they were convinced, would better protect their "family jewels." *Liberty Lady* was ready to fly.[121]

The period of February 20 through February 24 was a continuation of Operation Argument. The winter weather delays had allowed a buildup of the U.S. fighter force, but in February, weather was still a huge factor. It was urgent that the German fighters be knocked out, so even though forecasts were bleak, the strike force was ordered to go.

Herman's diary included detailed reports of his missions 1 through 7 but practically nothing for the next four. It was Big Week.

The Smith crew explores the *Liberty Lady.*

Missions 8, 9, 10 and 11

February 20, 1944: This mission, the first in which the Eighth dispatched over 1000 planes, launched Big Week attacks on central German aircraft plants and airfields.[122] The 368th historian described their squadron's foray to Leipzig, Germany best. "No more satisfactory target could be imagined for a bomber crew than a Me 109 factory. … All (from the 368th) came home safely, assisted by the biggest fighter escort ever yet put up."[123] Other squadron crews fared less well, and losses rose dramatically during the rest of the week.

February 21, 1944: The target for the 306th was near Lippstadt, Hopsten airfield. The 306th suffered no losses, but 17 out of 21 planes were damaged.

February 22, 1944: The 306th went to Bernburg airfield where Ju 88 fighters were being constructed. It was the bomb group's most costly mission. Seven planes were lost.

February 24, 1944: From the Eighth Air Force, 231 B-17s bombed Schweinfurt ball bearing plant while 238 B-24s hit factory and airfield at Gotha. Herman's squadron, the 368th, led the entire mission.

England, February 26, 1944

These past four raids have all been of the same caliber so feel justified in writing of them in the same light. Tough, rough, long in hours and touching on the very brim of Hell.

Up until now I thought I knew what the score was, but frankly I found out how much I erred.

Give the Jerry credit, he's endowed with guts. On each of these missions, he came at us full head on, not once or twice, but queued up after each pass and came through again. Forts were hit by the score and dropped down in flames, in bits like flies. It's a fascinating feeling to watch them. First they are there, flying like a giant eagle beside you, then a '20 or a burst of flak finds its mark, and another ship fills in the empty position. The Leipzig mission hardened me, but by the time we were through Schweinfurt it meant merely a call over the interphone to the navigator to make a note, if time could be taken out between the fighter passes to do so.

We had good fighter escort, but if a Jerry makes up his mind he is coming through, then it is pretty near impossible to stop him. Fw 190s, Me 109s, Ju 88s. Christ, the Luftwaffe sprouted fangs. Must have been a desperate attempt to bolster German morale, for it was practically the pilot's own ticket in blood. True, many of them weaved through the formation, but just as many didn't. An Fw 190 found himself square in my sights at Schweinfurt, headed on at 12 o'clock level. Net result, one confirmed Jerry to my credit.

Was one tired lad this week. I didn't think it so much the ride as the length of time on oxygen, the strain of continually being on the alert, and the ever-present fear of being afraid.

Over the route home from Bernburg, the lead navigator messed up and took us directly over a concentrated flak area near Happy Valley. Sincerely I thought that was it. I couldn't possibly see how any ship could ride through that and come out whole. Somehow we did, though the Lady was a sieve. God must have been there, Lou, at our wing tips. Fact is, I know He was. Then again at Schweinfurt, we had an engine knocked out directly over the target. Confusion for a moment, but Smithy had her. We pulled out of the formation, dropped our bombs, fell in with another Group and managed the trip home. Frankly, a trip to Kiel would now seem like a milk run.

I could write a volume on these missions yet not express the mark they left. Words are inadequate. My score now is eleven. Fourteen more to sweat out. The twelfth and each other in turn. All that is left now is to take every possible precaution against human fault and place a supreme trust in God, know He will be there each time to see us through. Destiny will write its own history.

Take care of yourself, Lou, and know it's always

The best,
S/ Herman

On February 25, the Smith crew, all except for Herman, flew on a mission to Augsburg in southern Germany to bomb Hitler's leading Me 410 factory. Three planes from the 306th were lost. Although she was sporting many flak holes, the *Liberty Lady* came back safely.

On February 28, the *Liberty Lady* flew with another crew to V-weapon sites in Pas de Calais, France. There was no damage to the *Lady* on this day.

After the pressures of Big Week, the crews were exhausted. Now they faced their most perilous target yet.

Chapter 7

Mission 12 – 6 March 1944

The airmen knew that their ultimate target would be Berlin, the prize. They called it the "Big B." The center of Germany's war machine with factories, rail centers, and military headquarters, Berlin was also the most heavily defended city in all of Europe, ringed with tens of thousands of antiaircraft guns.

In 1939, Hermann Göring arrogantly promised the German people, "No enemy bomber can reach the Ruhr…" However, by 1940, the RAF was already sending night bombers to Berlin. These raids continued but did not do enough to halt war production.

The Eighth Air Force made an effort to send bombers to Berlin in late November and again in December of 1943, about the time the Smith crew was arriving at Thurleigh. Both missions were recalled. Weather was lousy, there wasn't enough daylight, nor was there enough long-range fighter support.[124]

By the first week in March, the planners decided it was time to make another go for Berlin. More long-range P-51 Mustangs had arrived. When Doolittle took over as commander of the Eighth, he changed the role of the fighter escorts.[125] Instead of sticking close to the bombers as they headed toward the targets, the fighters would aggressively go after the enemy fighters, even if it meant leaving the bomber formations unprotected. General Doolittle's objective: the bombers would act as bait, bringing out the Luftwaffe that had survived Big Week to be destroyed by the Americans.

The first Berlin mission was scheduled for the 2nd of March. Doolittle cancelled it because of heavy clouds over the target. Instead, the 306th bombed railroad marshalling yards in Frankfurt. The Smith crew, flying the *Liberty Lady*, took off but never got there, turning back at 1048 hours because of internal engine trouble. They had been in the air for just under four hours, and for them the Frankfurt mission was labeled an abortion.

The crew was up predawn the next morning for yet another Berlin effort. The *Liberty Lady* was being repaired, so the Smith crew flew a different plane. Once the formation reached the German coast, the weather was once again so bad that the bombers had to go back. The substitute B-17 developed engine problems, and this mission was also an abortion.

On March 4, one more attempt to get to Berlin was called back for the same reason, but three squadrons didn't get the signal and made it through. Five bombers were lost, but March 4 was actually the first American attack on Berlin.[126] The Smith crew, flying in yet another B-17, returned to base with all their bombs, and this time their mission was noted as abandoned.

To everyone's chagrin, about this same time, General Doolittle extended the tours of duty from 25 to 30 missions. Abortions and abandonments did not count as one of the required numbers.

The weather on March 5 was not suitable at all, but on March 6, conditions had improved. Orders from headquarters came by teleprinter the evening before saying that, yes, there would be the all-out maximum effort which the crew of the *Liberty Lady* was anticipating with more than a little trepidation. The men had been up early and in the air for three of the last four days. They were physically and mentally exhausted, but their *Lady* was ready for what would come.

Herman wrote,

> Damn, it was cold. Sleepily I opened my eyes and wondered who the Hell had turned on all the lights. Out of the murky fog of drowsiness, I could faintly hear someone speaking, "breakfast at three, briefing at four." Must be one of those confounded nightmares I had been troubled with lately. I began to roll over to find relief from the bright glare when a hand began to shake me, and a faraway voice said, "Lieutenant, are you awake? Breakfast at three, briefing at four, your ship is 006." I must have mumbled something, for the hand and voice left, and soon that blessed solace only brought by the first pangs of sleep began to creep over me. I must have fallen into a slight nod, for the next thing I knew, someone was yelling, "Hold that truck, hold that God damn truck."
>
> It suddenly dawned just what that meant. This was the preparation for a mission, the weather must have cleared, good old freakish English weather, unstable as everything else.
>
> As I jumped out of bed and stood shivering from the sudden change of bed warmth to the early

morning cold, I looked around and saw that most of the fellows who had been called had left, whilst the others were about ready to leave. The lucky devils who had not been alerted slumbered on. I envied them, yet there was nothing personal in that envy. Other mornings they had stood there shivering, glancing at my sleeping form, simply a vicious circle, like a matter of having your name placed in a huge hat, a matter of luck, call it that if you will.

I dressed hurriedly, making sure I had everything I needed, flashlight, extra handkerchief, cigarettes, matches, pictures, pencil, paper. Being the last to leave the barracks, I switched off the lights, quietly closed the doors, then a brief spurt and I made the tailboard of the truck as it was leaving the site.

As we rode to the mess hall, I glanced up at the sky and saw that a complete changeover had occurred in the last few hours. Just before hitting the sack, I had come out to give a quick look at the Heavens as was my habit, and saw they were completely overcast, not a twinkle in sight. In fact it was gradually growing cold enough that I would not have been in the least surprised to have awoken in the morning to find a blanket of white. And now as I looked there was scarce a cloud to be seen, the stars were full and bright. Crazy English weather is right.

Smithy was about to enter the mess hall as I came into the Club foyer. Upon seeing me, he waited until I hung up my coat, and we entered together. The tables were crowded. This morning's deal must be a maximum effort and meant a long haul, probably somewhere deep in the Fatherland. Smithy's thoughts must have been running neck and neck with mine, for he broke in my meanderings, "Looks like it might be Big B."

"Well, there's the Colonel." Looking around to where Smithy nodded, I saw Colonel John deep in a pile of hotcakes, talking between mouthfuls to those around him. As we passed in the aisle, Sig waved, and we stopped to ask him what the score was: "Don't know for sure, we're leading the wing, Colonel John and Nally will be in the lead ship, with Logan as Bombardier, and Samaway as Navigator. See you fellows after briefing."

We found two vacant spots at the next table, the orderly brought our coffee and hotcakes, and we ate in silence, each of us deep in our own thoughts.

It's odd what strange channels you go into when you stop and think, perhaps this will be the last breakfast you'll have. When things happen up there, it takes only a moment, then "poof" you've had it. One misstep and it's all over. I was pleased I had written the folks last night and also sent off a few other outstanding letters. It was three-thirty, hell, the people in the States were beginning to crawl into bed. They'd wake up in the morning, tune in on the early news, and hear some dry, crackling voice, "American heavies are out in force this morning. Indications are their target is somewhere in Germany."

And Smithy, his mind was a thousand miles away as I saw a dreamy look in his eyes. Indiana, perhaps, and Helen. Whatever the thoughts, they must have been pleasant, for I watched a silent chuckle sneak about the corners of his mouth, then spread from ear to ear.

"Come on, Smithy, snap out of it, and let's get rolling, there's work to be done."

"What the Hell is the hurry, can't I even eat in peace without your hounding; we'll be there soon enough."

At this, he pushed away his chair and rose mumbling something about "damn Bombardiers."

On the way out we picked up MP and started for briefing. It was one of those mornings in late winter when the stars were out in all their brightness and added a pleasant exhilaration to the nippy, frosty air. We didn't say much on the way. I know Smithy and MP were going over what was needed for the mission and figuring the pros and cons for the crew. We were short two men, right waist and navigator. Who in Hell were we going to draw? It isn't that new men were not capable, but they had never flown with the Crew before, and, in the pinch, that smooth, unthinkable reaction as a unit is what counted.

The briefing room was practically deserted, for we were early. We had a few minutes to light up and have a few drags before the business of the day started. We knew once the word was given, there would be little time for a cigarette until the return. We took three seats toward the front of the room, next to Buck, navigator on Kelly's crew. As we sat down I turned to him and asked, "What the Hell you doing here?"

"Sig rolled me out to fly with 006, seems they are short a navigator."

"006, that's our Lady, and we are still short a navigator." At that, I turned to Smithy, who was next to me and told him the cheerful news.

"All I can say," Smithy replied, "is that I hope to Hell it's a short haul and we don't wander from the group, Navigator." It was all said in good, clean fun, for we knew we had one of the best men aboard.

"Gentlemen," and briefing was on. The Colonel was up front, waiting for attention. Instantly the room quietened, and he began with the usual pre-target introduction. "Gentlemen, we made several starts, but this time, it's the long haul. There will be plenty of flak, and Jerry will not be sitting on the ground. Yes, there will be trouble encountered, plenty of it, so be on your toes, keep your eyes peeled, and good luck."

As the Colonel took his seat, dead silence throughout the room. The intelligence officer began to pull up the curtain over the map. As it rose higher and higher, tense faces expressed the feeling of all. A murmured hubbub as sounds of "Nice knowing you," "This is it," and so forth filled the room. Silence once more as the Major raised his stick for attention.

"Gentlemen, you have waited for it, and now you have it. Berlin. The first big daylight raid on the nerve center of the Nazis. Heretofore the Germans have only heard of the Eighth Air Force. Today they will see the might and size of one of the largest-scale operations to date. You will not be out there alone. Fighter cover is assured for the route and over the target area. There will be Forts and Libs, hundreds of them. Now here is the briefed route."

He took us along the route we were to fly in and out, step by step, showed us where we were to bypass flak areas, where we were to expect fighters, number of flak guns at certain areas, where the fighters would pick us up and leave us. Showed us our specific target, the IP, and in case of necessity, our secondary and last resort targets.

Next came the weather. Indications were there would be about 3/10 cloud cover part of the way, with the target clear, most of the route would be CAVU (ceiling and visibility unlimited.) The temperatures at the target would range from 55 to 60 degrees at altitude.

After the weather, radio gave us the call signs, colors of the day, and the many other details so necessary for a successful mission. Yes, it was indeed a big show.

Then the time tick, and the operations officer with his poop. After they completed, we rose and went to individual briefing. Pilots and co-pilots, navigators, bombardiers, radio operators, and gunners.

"See you lugs at the ship," and we parted.

Yes, all systems were go, and every available B-17 crew would participate. By 5:00 a.m., crew members jumped on the trucks to be taken to their planes. Pilots Smithy and Merle briefed the crew on the day's mission. The captain introduced the two airmen who were filling in. Howard Granger was sick, so Sgt. Joe Paul would fly as right waist gunner. Lt. Stan Buck would be navigator as replacement for Charles Stevenson, who had died on January 11.

At 28 years old, Stan Buck was the eldest by one year of the *Liberty Lady* Berlin crew members. He had been born in Canada, and at one time his father was a member of the Canadian Mounted Police. By the time war broke out, the family had moved to Portland, Oregon. Stan attended the University of Oregon for three years before enlisting. He had taken private flying lessons in Portland before the war and wanted to be a pilot, but as so often happened, for one reason or another the army decided he should be a navigator. Fortunately, Stan Buck was an excellent one.

Joe Paul, the youngest of the crew at 19, enlisted after graduating from Aquinas Catholic High School in La Crosse, Wisconsin. There he was involved in football and boxing as well as dramatic productions. He arrived in England on the 10th of February and on March 6 was assigned to fly with the Smith crew. This would be his first mission.

Everyone recognized the significance of Berlin. They knew all too well that the capital would be defended with everything the Germans could throw at them, both antiaircraft guns and Luftwaffe fighters.

After the briefing and a little pep talk, each crew member went about checking his area. Smithy entered the plane from the right rear door near the tail. He preferred entering the plane at this location so he could greet each member of the crew as he worked his way to the pilot's seat. The tail gunner, the right and left waist gunners, and the ball turret gunner were first. Then came the radio operator or "Static Chaser" as they liked to call him. From there Smithy walked across the bomb bay's six-inch wide catwalk to the cockpit. The navigator and the bombardier were already at their places in the nose underneath.[127]

A green flare fired from the control tower meant "start your engines." At 7:45 a.m. the first heavy bombers took off from the English airfields. There would be more than 800 in all. It took about an hour for them to assemble into their formations. Even before the hour was over, German radar picked up something big heading their way, and fighter and flak units were alerted.

In the 40th Combat Wing of the 1st Bomb Division, the 306th at Thurleigh flew 27 B-17s. Their primary target was VKF Ball Bearing Works at Erkner, a German suburb on the eastern border of Berlin, seven miles from the city center.

VKF is short for Vereinigte Kugellagerfabriken AG or United Ball Bearing Company. It was a subsidiary of the Swedish company SKF,

Svenska Kullagerfabriken AB. The first factory was built in Göteborg, Sweden. Business was so good that the company had expanded into other countries, including Germany.

Ball bearings were critical to the production of war materials such as planes, tanks, other vehicles, guns, and submarine engines. The bearings reduced friction and wear in the machinery being produced at breakneck speed.

In less than three hours, the sun was shining, and the *Liberty Lady* reached Cromer on the northern coast of England. She then flew over the North Sea through stronger than expected headwinds toward the Dutch Coast where the first groups of the fighter escorts joined them.

At 11:30 a.m., the Luftwaffe reported that the bomber stream, now one hundred miles long, had crossed into Germany. They didn't know exactly where the bombers were going, but they would be ready.

By this time, a navigational error by the lead navigator caused the bombers to drift off course. The 1st Bomb Division flew over flak zones at Zwolle, a city east northeast of Amsterdam. One of the bombers, also of the 40th combat wing, was badly damaged and the crew had to bail out.[128] Too close for comfort to the *Liberty Lady.*

By 12:00 noon, the Americans were well into Germany. In Berlin, a warning was issued to the military, police, hospitals, and potential targets that the enemy was within 30 minutes flying time of the city.[129] The antiaircraft batteries and fighter groups were put on alert. Some were ordered to the southern parts of the country in order to attack the American planes on their way back home.

As the bombers drew closer to the capital, German fighters were already brutally attacking. The air battle has been described as the biggest ever fought in the history of military aviation. Gunner Don Courson remembered seeing planes as far as the eye could see, many on fire. Parachutes were everywhere. Planes were going down, but the other crews had to focus on how to keep theirs up. There were lots of prayers.

Shortly after 1:00 p.m., the 1st Combat Wing leader headed for the assigned target, the ball bearing plant. At a critical moment, clouds obscured the target. The leader ordered the groups behind him to call off the run on Erkner and drop their bombs on other targets.[130] The 306th flew into an area near the center of the city to drop their bombs. While the *Liberty Lady* was moving toward the new site, the angry flak batteries seriously damaged even more bombers.

As the crew of the *Liberty Lady* saw the city of Berlin spread out before them, they suddenly felt a fierce impact. The number 2 engine was on fire. The plane had also been hit in the fuel tank. Immediately, the plane slowed and began to lose altitude. As the pilots were forced to abandon the formation, the *Lady* became easy prey for enemy fighters. Bombardier Herman Allen quickly salvoed the bombs.

At one point, someone hollered out that the plane was in a spin, but tail gunner Trumble always kept a bolt tied to a string fastened to the fuselage so he could tell what was happening to the plane. He called, "No, we're not spinning. The bolt is steady."

The son of pilot Charles Smith recalled his father's account: "The critical problem was, not only did the round take out the engine, it drained the oil, so they couldn't feather the prop. Thus, the flat surface of the propeller was presented to the slipstream, markedly increasing the drag and slowing the plane. Dad estimated it was the equivalent of losing one and a half engines." The fate of the *Liberty Lady* was now uncertain.

The mission on March 6, 1944, came to be known as Black Monday to the Americans. Sixty-nine bombers did not return to their bases. The primary target, the ball bearing plant at Erkner, was unscathed.

At the end of the afternoon, on the 368th Squadron mission loading list there was but one word, underlined and scrawled in large black letters over the names of the crew of A/C Number 42-40006: MISSING. It was the only aircraft lost to the 306th.

This would be the Eighth Air Force's 250th and most costly combat mission. It was Herman's 12th mission, the *Liberty Lady*'s 13th, and the final mission for each.

Chapter 8

Liberty Lady

It was impossible for the wounded fortress to stay in the safety of the formation, and the pilots agreed the crippled aircraft could never reach England. Just north of Berlin, a horde of enemy fighters spotted them. Smithy quickly flew into a sharp dive and slipped into the cover of thick clouds.

Up to this point, the *Liberty Lady* gunners had been furiously shooting back at enemy fighters, but once the plane was in the clouds, it was disconcertingly quiet. Waist gunner Don Courson explained, "If you're ever flown in a cloud in a big airplane, you have no idea what's out there. There could be another plane in the same cloud, and you can't see it." To make matters even worse, the *Liberty Lady* lost a second engine.

At one point, the plane flew too close to a town. German antiaircraft gunners caught the *Liberty Lady* on radar and began to shoot. The plane was vibrating fiercely. Pilots Smithy and Merle struggled together to keep it flying straight in any direction.

The navigator had no maps for countries outside the areas of combat. Merle Brown remembered someone saying, "Let's go to Russia." The pilots initially flew in that general direction, but then another crew member spoke out, "Sweden is closer. Let's try to get there." So they changed course toward where neutral Sweden should be. The risk, they knew, was the proximity of the neighboring German-occupied countries of Denmark and Norway.

Knowing they were losing fuel, in order to lighten the load the crew began to throw some of the heavy equipment out the window. They kept the guns, just in case.

All they could see was water, and they were afraid they would have to ditch in the sea, never a safe option but particularly dangerous when they were near enemy territories. To Herman, the idea of being taken prisoner by the Germans was especially frightening. He thought of the dog tag around his neck marked "H" for Hebrew, as was customary for the Jewish airmen. The tags of the Catholics were marked "RC," and the Protestants were marked "P." Herman had heard stories about Jewish prisoners being separated from other Americans for various degrees of brutal treatment.

Flying blindly away from Germany, they had no time to dwell on anything but getting to safety. Finally, they caught sight of land through an opening in the clouds. The navigator was unsure of their position and told Herman, "That could be Denmark. If it is, we're in trouble." Even so, the pilots had little choice but to get the airplane down. They had 15 minutes of fuel.

The countryside below appeared to be sparsely populated. They flew over a village and saw, among the rooftops below them, the spire of a church. Fortunately, the weather was good, with a slight breeze. Stan and Herman, with their panoramic view from the nose, picked out a nearby expanse of land that might work for an emergency landing.

Captain Smith agreed. He called over the intercom and queried the crew, "Do you want to bail out, or do you want us to try to land?"

The consensus was a definite, "Land the plane!" Don Courson thought, "We know we have good pilots, and if it can be done, they can do it."

Before they could land, they had to dispose of the top-secret Norden bombsight. The pilots flew the plane a short way back to the water so Herman could drop the equipment into the sea.

Guided by the tall spire of the church, the pilots flew the *Liberty Lady* back to the area they had spotted, to what looked like a farmer's field. On closer inspection, they noticed fences made from piled rocks. The pilots were afraid that if they hit the fences with their landing gear down, they might flip the plane. The decision was made to land with wheels up, a belly landing.

Smith ordered the crew to gather in the radio room with Marcotte and assume crash positions with their heads down between their knees. The eight young men filled the tiny room. Herman said a silent prayer.

The pilots skillfully guided the crippled B-17 as it slid hard for 2500 feet through stone walls and a barbed-wire fence. "We tore that farmer's field all to hell and crashed through two of his fences before the plane stopped," ball turret gunner Tom Stillson wrote home. "I shouldn't have been so worried. Lieutenant Smith has pulled us out of a lot of tight spots."

On the Ground

When the *Liberty Lady* came to a stop, only one engine was running. The crew members were stunned but unhurt. They had been up in the earsplitting noise of the bomber for hours. Now, it was eerily quiet. Looking out their windows, they saw no one and assumed they were most likely in German-occupied Denmark. As a standard precaution, Smithy ordered navigator Buck to set off an incendiary in the radio room. The plane must not be allowed to be taken intact by the enemy.

The ten men left the *Liberty Lady* quickly as a column of black smoke rose from the airplane. They were fully dressed, with coveralls over their electric suits, along with silk gloves, heated gloves, fleece-lined boots, and helmets. Trying to get far enough away before the ammunition in the plane exploded, they hurried through patches of snow and jumped over a narrow creek toward a nearby thicket of trees. At least for the moment, they were safe.

From the pine thicket, they were considering their next move when they spotted a car coming down a dirt road. When it stopped, out stepped a uniformed man armed with a German-made Mauser rifle, a bayonet attached to the end of it.

The man spotted them and, gesturing with his arms, hollered out in a foreign language. Carl Heuser, born in Germany, knew that language well. When he heard the words, he whispered, "Okay boys, the jig is up. He's German!" To make matters worse, more and more men began to arrive, some in uniform, some not.

The Americans put their hands in the air. One still had his gun and handed it to the officer who seemed to be in command. Back in training, they had been warned that if they landed in Germany and were found hiding a gun, they would be shot.

The ten men, assuming themselves prisoners, were in a state of total confusion. Shaken, hungry, exhausted, and frightened, they were surrounded by foreign soldiers and people talking back and forth in words no one understood.

Suddenly, without warning, the flares and the ammunition from the machine guns in the burning plane began to explode. The startled crowd, including the crew, dove for cover, and there was bedlam until the ammunition explosion had run its course. Anyone who wanted to approach the area had to crawl along the ground.

Safe

Unbeknownst to the *Liberty Lady* crew, their plane had entered Swedish airspace at 1503 o'clock. Sweden had small outlook towers around the country, each reporting to a central source so they could collect all the facts about any observed aircraft. When people on the ground heard or saw a plane, they called in a report.

As soon as the lost B-17 reached the southeast corner of the Swedish mainland, the aircraft warning service began relaying details of the bomber's altitude and flight path. One of the lookouts was on the tiny island of Hanö, near the country's southern tip. According to the airplane spotters, the *amerikansk* plane flew north and then slightly east until it was out over the water again.

At this point, *Liberty Lady*'s mapless navigator had no idea where they were. Still in thick clouds, they may not even have known when they were over land and when they were over water. At 1606, they were sighted above a larger but very narrow island, Öland, flying east, at a height estimated to be about 2000 meters (just over 6500 feet.)[131]

At 1630, the plane was seen over Gotland, the largest island in the Baltic Sea. The B-17 had come in from the western coast toward the village of Hablingbo. It was flying lower now, perhaps 500 meters (about 1600 feet) while the crew searched in all directions for an emergency landing field. Gotland's terrain is rich with gravel, stone, and limestone rocks, so any landing was a potentially hazardous one.

That afternoon, 17-year-old Lasse Svensson happened to be relaxing in his home on the main street of the village of Hemse. The minute he heard the deafening noise of a plane in flight, he ran to the window, and there it was, right over the rooftops! Because his father owned a photo shop, there was always a camera loaded with film within reach. Lasse grabbed it, ran out onto the second-floor balcony and snapped a remarkable picture of the lost *Lady*. Then he took off on his bicycle, camera in hand.

At the time the *Liberty Lady* was photographed, it was headed east in the direction of the Baltic Sea so that bombardier Allen could dump the Norden bombsight. The spotters on the ground noted an object thrown into the sea at 1640. Then, Smithy and Merle turned back to the church spire and the nearby field to set down the plane.

Photo of the B-17 *Liberty Lady* by Lasse Svensson. March 6, 1944.

The chosen landing spot, just west of the tiny village of Hemse, was actually an old tested emergency landing field on the Oxarve farm,[132] a boggy expanse located in an area known as Mästermyr. In the autumn of 1936, a farmer plowing his rich wet soil had uncovered a wooden chest with old blacksmith and carpenter tools dating back over a thousand years to the Viking era. The location is well known for this important archeological find.

Liberty Lady was not the first bomber to land there. Four years earlier, on the 21st of April, 1940, a Heinkel 111 German bomber named *Jumbo* belly-landed on the Mästermyr a little farther west. The crew of four was unhurt and was interned in Sweden.[133]

Moments after the *Liberty Lady* hit the ground, two nearby farmers ran out in time to see the crew leave the plane as it began to catch fire.

They noticed a couple of the men throw handguns into the icy water as they jumped over a narrow channel, running for the trees.

The official who had first driven to the scene was Albin Larsson, workshop owner and member of the Gotland Home Guard. Larsson was indeed armed with a German rifle, a type widely used in Sweden during World War II. He spoke no English, and German was the second language taught in the Swedish schools at the time.

When Larsson saw the plane in the air, he jumped into his car and rode down the one lane road as close to the crash site as possible. The two farmers who had been first on the scene pointed toward the copse of trees. Larsson hollered out to the crew and frightened Carl Heuser.

Defense units known as the Home Guard had been formed in order to protect the country's localities. Members of these units were men exempt from the draft, including former professional soldiers who were generally well known and respected within their communities.[134] They were literally on guard to protect their island. Sweden had declared neutrality, but a potential invasion by Nazi Germany or Russia was always a threat. The Swedes were very concerned about violations of their airspace, as evidenced by the careful tracking of the B-17 as she flew over the edge of Sweden, across the sea, and then to this island.

By this time, everyone in Hemse had seen and heard the huge bomber flying low and loud over their quiet village. It was so low that some people feared it might strike the new fire station's hose tower. After the aircraft landed, the tall spiral of black smoke was easy to spot.

Young Lars Björkander had received a day off from school to visit the dentist in Hemse. On his way home, he was amazed to see the giant plane overhead. At least two of the engines were stopped, he remembered, with only one of the inner propellers spinning. Lars watched the bomber turn west toward the large plain of old marshland bordering his community. All at once everyone in town seemed to be heading toward the Mästermyr in cars and on bicycles, walking and running. Lars found a bike and followed the crowd. When the road ended, he threw his bike into a ditch and continued walking, following the stream of people.[135]

Thirteen-year old Arne Gahm was working at another farm on the edge of the Mästermyr. He first heard the roar of the B-17 and a few seconds later watched it pass right over him. Like most of those who lived in the village, he had never seen such a plane. He watched as it disappeared behind some trees. Then he and a friend grabbed their bikes and pedaled less than half a mile to reach the spot. By the time they got there, the plane was already on fire.

In the local school, the students immediately picked up on all the excitement. Their teacher, Gunnar Jonsson, taught in the folkhögskola, translated "peoples' high school." The folkhögskola is a special form of school peculiar to Denmark and Sweden, meant for the adult youth to receive a good all-around education.[136]

The schoolteacher spoke English and may have been the only person in the village who did. He later wrote to Smithy, "At the humming of your engines, we all looked out and saw the big eagle sweeping down from the sky. 'That isn't a Swedish plane!' one of my boys called out."

When Jonsson saw the bomber flying overhead, he didn't immediately recognize it as an American plane. "Sorry," he wrote, "but your plane looked so dirty in the clear sky. Your color was quite new to us, and it looked dusky and strange. At the moment, we didn't remember that the Russian star is red. We were agreeably surprised when we found you to be Yankees."

When the young men in his class cried out, "He will land in the marshland," the students all set off running, and their teacher followed on his bicycle.

Soon half the town was at the site or on the way toward it. Troops had arrived from a nearby military camp. Members of the Home Guard were trying to keep the growing crowd of curious villagers back out of the way.

The teacher recalled, "When we got there, we at first saw a gigantic smoke ring and a rather tall column of smoke. When we reached the field behind the bushes, I went as near as I dared, but it wasn't so very near due to the exploding ammunition! The ricochets piped and whined over us, so we had to take cover."

When the explosions were over, and everyone understood what had happened, Albin Larsson noticed the arrival of the schoolteacher. Larsson beckoned him over so Jonsson could explain to the frightened young airmen, in English, that they had landed on an island in Sweden and were on neutral soil.

First the teacher asked them some basic questions. "What happened? Is anyone wounded? Are there any bombs on board the plane?" Smithy spoke for the crew. He didn't want to volunteer any information and even initially denied they had set fire to the plane.

Jonsson wrote, "I remember you all looked a little doubtful at first, but I also remember your demonstration of joy by spontaneously giving me several thumps on the back!"

Yes, although some members of the crew continued to be skeptical, the men were safe at last. There were cheers and high fives. Someone in the crowd offered the crew cigarettes. The airmen replied, "Thank you, but no. Not now." Not yet.

A military flatbed truck arrived to transport them into town. Captain Smith motioned for the men to go back to their plane to retrieve any personal belongings.

Out came the silk parachutes. While his crew gathered around, some bearing smiles, others still dazed, Smithy opened one wide, examining

Captain Smith and crew examine the parachute. March 6, 1944. Herman F. Allen is on the far right.

it as though confirming it was not burned. The parachutes were distributed to the local women, who made garments with the valuable fabric.

The ten airmen, along with the teacher, climbed onto the truck and were driven away under armed guard. Herman wrote about their last sight of the *Lady*.

> The last time we saw her, a giant smoke ring was wafting its way slowly upwards towards the blue Heavens above, as if the very soul of the Lady was free at last to seek its own undeniable place amongst those other queens now so proudly in the service of the Great Commander. To dwell for evermore up there amongst the high scattered clouds where she had so gracefully roamed in the days

```
when she had brought us so gloriously through the
very fires of Hell, of flak, and evaded the mur-
derous snub nose of the Jerry fighters. Liberty
Lady. Our Ship.
```

An hour and a half after the crash landing, the Hemse fire department arrived to put out the fire. The plane had run out of gas before it hit the ground, so only the cabin and the nose were destroyed. The engines were intact.

As the military truck left the crash site, Smithy asked Jonsson if the church they passed was the one the plane had circled around while searching for a safe place to land. The reply was affirmative. This was one of 92 such medieval churches on the island, all built prior to 1350.

The truck soon came to a stop in front of a complex of one-story buildings. Five years earlier, at the beginning of European hostilities, a military hospital had been established on the grounds of the folkhögskola.

The *Liberty Lady* at about 1710 hours.

Each man was given a medical examination and declared unhurt. When questioned by the Swedish military, they gave only basic information. The reason they had to land so urgently, they explained, was engine failure.

Their first meal in the safety of Sweden was pork and beans, served on long tables, barracks style. A reporter who arrived on the scene wrote in the local newspaper that the new arrivals were in a great mood. He was surprised to see such excellent camaraderie among them.

To the Americans, it was a shock to see the electric lights on at night. In England, they were used to the strict blackouts. Although Gotland had originally had similar restrictions, they were more relaxed by 1944.

The crew spent two nights under guard in this war hospital, two to a room. Late on the evening of Wednesday, March 8, accompanied by members of the Swedish military, they were loaded into taxi cabs and transported to the medieval city of Visby, a distance of about 30 miles. Although the men weren't able to explore Visby, perhaps they noticed the ancient wall surrounding the coastal town. Its harbor had been used by the Vikings when Visby was an important trade locale.

Two ships, the *Hansa* and the *Drotten,* regularly took passengers back and forth between Visby and the Swedish mainland. More than likely, the crew traveled across on one of them.

After they were on board, the Captain of the ship sent for the crew to gather up on deck. He told them he had traveled everywhere one could go on a ship and had been all over America. They were now headed for the Swedish mainland. Because German submarines might be searching for them, they had to travel at night. Their route from Visby was north to the coastal town of Nynäshamn, 60 kilometers (37 miles) south of Stockholm, a three-or four-hour boat ride through the brackish Baltic Sea.

Later in the year, on November 24, a Russian submarine torpedoed the *Hansa* on its trip between Nynäshamn and Visby. Of the 86 passengers and crew on board, only two survived.

Fortunately, the crew of ten reached the Swedish mainland intact and enjoyed a good breakfast. Once in Stockholm, they were met by a representative from the American Legation who was able to convince everyone, even Carl Heuser, that they were safe and headed for the Land of the Midnight Sun, where darkness is banished and the sun shines all night long.

Chapter 9

Sweden and World War II

At the time of World War II, more than 6 million people lived in Sweden, a country about the size of the state of California. It was the largest of the three countries generally known as Scandinavia, the other two being their neighbors Norway and Denmark. Just east of Sweden was the country of Finland, which until 1809 had been a part of the Swedish kingdom. All four countries were close, not only by geography, but by common traditions and relationships.[137]

As it had since the early 1800s during times of war, Sweden affirmed its policy of neutrality when World War II became a certainty. In the beginning, 19 other European states had done the same thing, including Norway and Denmark. By the end of 1944, however, there were only six neutrals left: Sweden, Switzerland, Turkey, Spain, Portugal, and the Irish Republic.[138]

According to the Hague Conventions, the international treaties that outlined the laws of war, neutral Sweden was required to be impartial toward all belligerent countries. To emphasize Sweden's intention, in 1939 Prime Minister Per Albin Hansson stated, "Friendly with all other nations and strongly linked to our neighbors, we look on no one as our enemy."[139]

Maintaining a policy of impartiality would not be easy. By 1940, the neighboring Scandinavian countries of Norway and Denmark were occupied by Nazi Germany. To the east, Finland was dealing hard and fast with both the Soviet Union and Germany. Bruce C. Hopper, the Eighth Air Force historian who served with the OSS, described Sweden as "an oasis of neutrality encircled by war."

Sweden knew it had to maintain a strong defense in order to protect its borders and maintain its independence. Following World War I, Sweden had radically disarmed.[140] Then with war suddenly breaking out all around them again, the country dramatically increased its military budget. Nearly every young man was drafted into the army.

During the 1930s, Hitler's successes in reducing unemployment in Nazi Germany looked good to many Swedes. Ties with Germany ran deep, especially since the latter years of the 18th century. By the time the war of 1914 arrived, German was the primary foreign language taught in the Swedish schools. German music, art and books permeated Sweden's culture.[141]

Pro-German sentiments were deeply rooted. Swedes, including members of the Swedish royal family, married Germans. The reigning Swedish king, Gustav V, was married to Victoria, the German granddaughter of Kaiser Wilhelm I. The king's grandson, Gustav Adolf, was married to the daughter of the German duke of Saxe-Coburg, a member of Hitler's Nazi party.

But when Germany invaded Norway and Denmark in April of 1940, Swedes were horrified. Would freedom-loving Sweden be next? Suddenly the news coming out of Germany began to give that country a sinister aura. Anyone who didn't step in line with the Nazi Party could be tortured and either sent to a concentration camp or murdered.

The question is often asked, "Why didn't Germany invade Sweden too?" The threat of German invasion was always there. Sweden wanted Germany to believe it could be a more valuable asset as a neutral.

Sweden had a long record of lively trading with many foreign countries, but historically Germany was its most important provider of imported goods.[142] Though a small country, Sweden was rich in natural resources, valuable minerals, and metals. It was one of, if not the, world's largest exporter of iron ore largely because of its mining district north of the Arctic Circle.[143] When war broke out, for obvious financial reasons, Sweden needed to continue its import and export business. Such imports as petroleum, coal, food items, and cotton, to name a few, were critical in order to keep the country operating and to prevent its citizens from starving. Exports of iron ore to Germany were increased. Similarly, Sweden's ball bearing manufacturing industry had become indispensable to the German wartime production of tanks and airplanes.

The laws of neutrality specified that a neutral country could continue diplomatic relationships with all belligerents. Swedish diplomats and businessmen could travel to and from Germany, with oversight.[144]

While Sweden was permitted to continue its trade arrangements, the neutral country was not supposed to allow belligerent armies to transport troops or supplies across its borders. Germany put on the pressure for concessions to be made, and Sweden found itself in a difficult dilemma. Finally, the Swedish government bowed to increasing demands from Germany. A transit agreement was signed in July of 1940, allowing Germany to transport supposedly unarmed troops and their supplies through Sweden to Norway and Finland. This continued for three years until, after pressure from the Allies, Sweden's exports to Germany were reduced to nearly zero, and Sweden agreed to no longer allow German military transports of war materials and troops.

Sweden was one of the few European countries to have a free press during World War II. The German minister complained almost daily to the Swedish Foreign Office about news stories, editorials, even advertisements criticizing the Nazis. His premise was that a country could not be neutral unless its public opinion was neutral. Early in the war, this pressure was effective.

One of the most ardent critics of Hitler and National Socialism was Torgny Segerstedt, editor of a liberal newspaper in Göteborg. When Hitler became chancellor of Germany in 1933, Segerstedt wrote, "Hitler is an insult." By 1940, even King Gustav V pleaded with this unswerving editor to end his attacks on Hitler. No matter how much pressure was applied, Segerstedt persevered in his warnings of the evils of Fascism. Often, his toxic sarcasm was written so masterfully that it was difficult to call it offensive.[145] Rumors raged that the Nazis threatened to have a Swedish ship sunk without warning for every one of Segerstedt's sensational stories.[146]

Another motivation for Sweden to maintain the best possible relations with Germany was Sweden's past history with the Russians. At one time, Sweden had been a foremost power in Europe. The country's preeminence came to an end in the early 1800s during the Russo-Swedish war when Russia attacked and forced the Swedes to give up Finland. In 1922, the massive country of Russia reorganized as the Soviet Union. When the Soviets attacked Finland in November of 1939, Sweden's adversary had once again come much too close.[147]

Berlin radio raised a Red scare by proclaiming Sweden as "the principal stronghold of Bolshevism in Europe." Swedish Nazis talked incessantly about the necessity of saving Sweden from the Communists.[148] The Swedes were "caught between the devil and the deep blue sea."

Stockholm

Although nearly everyone in the cities of Sweden, especially those located on the seacoasts or near the borders, was busily involved in wartime activities, the spotlight was on the country's hub, the capital city of Stockholm.

Often described as "The Venice of the North," this magnificently picturesque city lies at the influx of Lake Mälaren and the Baltic Sea. It spans 14 different larger islands along with thousands of small islands in what is known as the Stockholm archipelago.

Stockholm was established around the year 1255 by a Swede named Birger Jarl. The site of his original settlement was repeatedly destroyed by pirates and hostile tribes. Jarl fortified three of the islands with towers and walls in an effort to protect his dominion from invaders. For a long time, the city didn't extend beyond the island known as Staden, along with the two adjacent islets of Helgeandsholmen and Riddarholmen.[149] Today the three islands together are known as Gamla Stan or simply "Old Town."

Dominating the island of Staden is the massive Royal Palace, Kungliga slottet. This was the official residence of King Gustav V who had ruled Sweden since 1907, first through World War I and then into World War II. In 1944, the king was already 86 years old. He would rule for seven more years and become the oldest monarch of Sweden.

Compared to the bombed and blacked-out cities throughout Europe, Stockholm looked like a bright and beautiful paradise. By 1944, there were over half a million inhabitants. When the sun went down, the bright lights were turned on. Well-dressed citizens strolled along the avenues, stepping into shops filled with luxury items, an amazing contrast to London and Berlin.

Because of wartime shortages, coffee had become a luxury in this heavy coffee-drinking country. More than 50 kinds of ersatz coffee were certified safe.

Neither grain nor potatoes could be used to make alcoholic beverages. Liquor was government controlled, rationed, and heavily taxed. Men were allowed a larger portion of liquor than women. If you wanted to drink alcohol in public, you had to order a meal.

In August of 1944, U.S. labor attorney Isaiah S. Dorfman came to Stockholm to join the OSS staff. Upon arrival, he reported back to OSS London, "I write you from the country beautiful, a country bright and gay, flooded with sunlight, abounding in waterways, forests and gorgeous flowers of every kind and description. The streets of Stockholm are immaculate, the buildings tastefully modern (except for the quaint old section) and the men and women healthy in appearance and well dressed. Blonde is the prevailing color."[150]

Dorfman's apartment was in the district known as Kungsholmen, west of the Old Town. East of there was the section known as Norrmalm. It was here and in the Östermalm district adjacent to it that most of the action took place for the Americans who worked in the city.

In Östermalm, right on Stockholm's Nybroviken Bay, was the magnificent avenue Strandvägen, translated appropriately "Beach Street." Elaborate, palatial structures lined one side of the street and, on the other, passenger steamships pulled in and tied up. Seagulls graced the sky.

A short walk from Strandvägen toward Staden was the Grand Hôtel, one of the finest in Europe with its turrets and towers and a magnificent view of busy quays and harbor. In the late 1800s, French chef Régis Cadier led the project to build this first class hotel as a neighbor to the Royal Palace. Through the years, there were expansions and modernizations of the original structure. After World War I, an illuminated crown was installed on the hotel roof. This addition supposedly did not please King Gustav V who may have thought visitors would mistake the crowned hotel for the royal residence.[151]

Two grand ballrooms of the hotel, Spegelsalen (Hall of Mirrors) and Vinterträdgården (Winter Garden) offered popular jazz music and became popular Stockholm destinations for the Americans.

The Rotary Club of Stockholm, a branch of the international service organization of businessmen, met every Tuesday at 12:45 upstairs in the Grand Hôtel. Membership of the club was at 140 and included representatives of science, art, and literature. Crown Prince Gustaf Adolf was the honorary governor of Sweden's Rotary District 78 and attended most meetings.

Hitler had abolished Rotary Clubs in Norway. At least one club there had changed its name to the Friday Club.[152] Rotary was never abolished in Denmark, but in 1944, most meetings were abandoned. The members thought it unwise to hold gatherings with more than a hundred men together in one place.

The Nazis had already forced Rotary out of Germany, as well as Austria and Italy, as they were opposed to any organization not 100 percent theirs. Also, the international aspect of Rotary, particularly the fact that the organization started in America, was the death knell until hostilities were over.

The term "Land of the Midnight Sun" describes any of the Scandinavian countries in the areas above the Arctic Circle where the sun never sets from May until mid-July. During the winter in the more southern city of Stockholm, sunset was as early as three or four o'clock in the afternoon. In the summertime, it could be light outside until as late as ten in the evening.

During the darker winter months, Stockholmers relied on the opera and theater for entertainment. Concert halls showcased talent such as Ulla Sallert, Julie Bernby, and Rosita Serrano, known as the Chilean nightingale.

When the summer season approached, two large amusement parks, Tivoli and Nojesfaltet, presented open air circus-vaudeville programs. *Billboard* magazine reported that Stockholm's recreation activities were functioning normally in 1944, "the chief aches stemming from inability to book foreign talent for cirks, parks and vaude spots."[153]

Winter or summer, going to the movies was one of Sweden's popular pastimes. Newspapers printed two or three full pages of movie ads every day, and most of the films were straight from Hollywood, with captions in Swedish. The audience cheered during the scene in *Casablanca* when the French voices drowned out the Germans with the "Marseillaise," a response that prompted protests from Berlin as being un-neutral.[154]

The American Legation would privately show anti-Nazi films, such as Billy Wilder's *Five Graves to Cairo* with its wacky view of Germany's General Rommel. The most notorious anti-Nazi film might have been Charlie Chaplin's *The Great Dictator*, an unsubtle parody of Hitler. It was banned from Stockholm public theaters, but because of his attaché status, the OSS director of secret intelligence, R. Taylor Cole, was able to show the film to large Swedish trade union audiences.[155]

Dancing was forbidden as frivolous in Germany and Finland. In Stockholm, establishments such as the Grand Hôtel and Cecil's had orchestras, and dancing continued until midnight. As *Time* magazine reported, Swedish youths in Stockholm were introduced to the jitterbug by a group of American aviators, the military internees.

Interned Airmen

By the time World War II was over, more than 300 aircraft from various countries had force-landed or crashed in neutral Sweden.[156] As the pilots of battle-damaged planes determined there was little or no chance to return to their home bases, growing numbers began to head toward Sweden as a safe refuge in order to avoid bailing out over enemy territory or ditching in the sea.

Initially, the Swedish military issued orders that when aircraft of a belligerent power arrived in Swedish airspace, the planes were to be fired upon for effect. The goal was to make the alien aircraft go away.

As war progressed, more and more aircraft, obviously in distress, were flying into Sweden to make emergency landings. Regulations were revised. Warning shots would first be fired, and then in many cases Swedish fighters flew up to guide the foreigners to a nearby airport. Swedish historian Torbjörn Olausson illustrated with this story,

> The Swedish anti-aircraft battery would radio the intruding plane: "You're violating Swedish airspace!" To which the pilot would reply: "We know!" The anti-aircraft unit would fire a warning shot. Whereupon the pilot would radio the fire-control officer on the ground: "You're shooting too low!" Reply from the ground: "We know!"[157]

Sweden's declaration of neutrality included the condition that aircraft and crew members landing in their country be interned until the war was over. Sweden would take care of them at the expense of the home country of the plane and crew.

The first two aircraft to divert to Sweden arrived in 1939. One was from Poland and contained refugees. The second was from Germany, and during the following year most arriving aircraft were from that country. By the end of the war, 126 German planes had entered Sweden. German crews were interned at various camps throughout the countryside. Rarely were they housed with Allied airmen. In one of the camps, the Germans were booed by local citizens as they marched through town to the bathhouse. The German internees were never given the freedom of movement allowed to the British or the Americans.[158]

In 1940, an Allied expeditionary force was sent to Norway in an effort to prevent Germany from taking control of the country along with its shipping routes that allowed valuable raw materials to come out of Sweden. When the Germans prevailed, a large number of British army personnel escaped into Sweden. A camp was set up for them in Främby, outside the mining city of Falun. In July of that same year, 125 of these British Army officers and men were repatriated.[159]

The camp at Främby was surrounded by a 16-foot-high barbed wire fence, and there were guard towers every 200 yards around the perimeter. Housing consisted of tar paper huts whose windows and doors were covered with burlap cloth. Inside were bunk beds with straw mattresses. There was also a headquarters building with an office and a meeting room.[160] Even though the facility was basic, by all accounts living conditions were satisfactory.

When the first British airplanes began to arrive, the crews were interned in Främby. The men were free to visit the tiny town to look around and go shopping. Inevitably they made friends with the locals. The British airmen did receive a per diem from the British Legation, but it was deducted from their pay after they were repatriated.[161]

As the daylight air battles intensified, the Eighth Air Force was flying deeper and deeper into enemy territories that were powerfully defended with fighter planes and antiaircraft batteries. The first American crew to arrive in Sweden came on July 24, 1943. After bombing an industrial factory in Norway, the *Georgia Rebel*, a B-17 from the 381st Bomb Group, lost two engines and was leaking fuel because of damage from heavy flak. Rather than risk an emergency landing in German-occupied territory, the crew headed for Sweden over Norway's western border.

What happened next was much like the story of the *Liberty Lady*'s final landing. Flying low, the crew of the *Georgia Rebel* searched hard and fast for a suitable landing spot. They finally found a long field and prepared for a belly landing, necessary because they didn't know the condition of the ground. As they came down onto the field, the boggy earth helped stop the plane. A farmer and then the Swedish military arrived quickly and took control. The crew was sent to Främby, joining other Allied airmen being housed there. The nearby guest house Humlebacken was opened to make room for them.[162]

A total of seven American crews arrived in 1943. Initially, crew members were reported to their next of kin as "missing in action," and in many cases this statement is what was published in their hometown newspapers. Families feared the worst until they received a letter such as this from the War Department in Washington, D.C.

> A report has been received that the above-captioned individual is safe and interned in a neutral country. The term "interned in a neutral country" is used to designate the status of a member of our armed forces who has been apprehended within the borders of a country not engaged in the war and has there been detained by authorities of that country. The rights and privileges of such a person and the duties and obligations of a neutral country to that person are governed

by The Hague Convention No. V of 1907 and by general principles of international law.

American diplomatic officials in neutral countries take a serious interest in the welfare of Americans interned there. Special attention is given to seeing that our internees are well cared for and that they receive pay, clothes, food, shelter, medical care, recreation, and freedom of movement.

You are urgently requested not to disclose this information to anyone outside your immediate family, as public knowledge is not considered to be in the best interest of the country and may hinder efforts toward the ultimate release of the internee.

At the present time the name of the country in which he is interned cannot be revealed; however, should it become appropriate to release that information in the future, it will be communicated to you.

Members of his immediate family may send him mail (letters and packages) when addressed as follows: [a Washington, D.C. address given].

It is believed that the internee will be able to communicate with you, but it is to be expected that his letters may be delayed somewhat due to factors incident to the war.

It is hoped you will find comfort in the realization that your son is not in unfriendly hands and that he enjoys many advantages not available to those held in enemy territory as prisoners of war.

Sincerely yours … The Adjutant General

The day anxious families received these letters, they were no doubt relieved beyond belief. They were not told where their sons were interned, but the families finally knew that they were alive and safe.

When, on March 6, 1944, the *Liberty Lady* landed on Gotland, she was only the sixth American plane that year to force-land on Swedish soil. She was also one of four Flying Fortresses to arrive that same day. All had been bombing areas around Berlin. Two aircraft landed at Bulltofta airfield in Malmö near the southern coast of Sweden. The other set down at an airfield called Rinkaby, nearly 60 miles northeast of Malmö. As the weeks progressed and weather improved, the dangerous missions from the English airbases increased, and American planes started coming to Sweden in greater numbers.

Standard USAAF directives were in place for forced landings in a neutral country. During training, the airmen were taught to immediately request communication with the nearest representative of the U.S. government. If classified maps, documents, and papers could not be safeguarded until they could be turned over to the U.S. officials, they must be destroyed. Guards hired for the safeguarding of the plane and equipment were to be viewed with suspicion until absolute proof of their reliability was established.

Emergency landings were taking place in every neutral, and conditions for the internees varied from country to country. Even the Soviet Union, a neutral in regard to Japan, dealt with internees.

Sweden housed thousands of men who entered their country in ways other than via an airplane in distress. Crews from a number of Soviet vessels from the Baltic countries sought asylum. A camp was set up for those men in Mariefred, more than 30 miles west of Stockholm. The Soviet Legation did not want its internees to mix with the Swedish population for fear they might discover that life in Sweden was better than in the workers' paradise.[163]

The Americans were facing a different set of circumstances. As soon as it became clear that more and more pilots of crippled aircraft would be flying to Sweden searching for a safe place to land, secret memos flew back and forth from Stockholm to Washington in an effort to establish specific procedures.

Immediately after a crew arrived on Swedish soil, the first authorities on the scene were either the local police or armed soldiers on duty in the general area. Often, the first greeting the airmen heard was something like, *"Välkomna till Sverige. Nu är ert krig över."* "Welcome to Sweden. Now your war is over!"

First of all, any dead or injured were taken off the plane. Wounded fliers went to nearby hospitals. By the end of the war, there would be 60 U.S. airmen listed as KIA, or "killed in action." Three bodies washed up on the Swedish coast, their aircraft lost in the Baltic. Others were found in the sea after their planes crashed near the coast. The rest were dead when their aircraft arrived, or died during a crash landing, or died later from their wounds. Twenty airmen from these crews were MIA, or "missing in action," their fates unknown.[164]

When the crews were on the ground, local officials searched the airmen for weapons, and any weapons found were confiscated. The plane was sealed with all equipment intact until representatives of the Swedish Air Force and the American Legation arrived to inspect conditions and make a complete inventory. Immediately, a guard was posted around the aircraft to prevent tampering or theft of classified equipment.[165]

Uninjured crew members were moved to temporary quarters. To the personnel of the neutral country they were to give, besides name, rank and serial number, only their aircraft number, name of the pilot, time and place of landing, number of personnel, any injuries, and damage to the aircraft. Their reason for coming to Sweden should be something like, "We were on an air-sea rescue mission and got lost."

The airmen often found that the members of the Swedish military who took care of them before the Americans arrived were extremely curious. They might ask questions about the equipment and the guns on the plane. Perhaps they asked, "How many raids have you been on in Germany?" or "How long was your training period in the United States?"

In nearly every case, the well-trained men simply replied that they weren't allowed to talk about such things. This level of vigilance was necessary. Despite a strong spirit of cooperation between the governments of both the United States and Sweden, there were known to be members of the Swedish police and military who were sympathetic to the Germans.

Responsibility for the downed airmen fell upon the American military air attaché's office in Stockholm in coordination with the Swedish government and the Swedish Air Force. Military air attachés were the commanding officers of all U.S. Army personnel interned in a neutral country and had the authority to issue orders and make necessary financial arrangements for the welfare and repatriation of interned personnel.

In February of 1944, Lt. Col. Felix M. Hardison arrived in Sweden as the new American air attaché. Highly respected and experienced, Hardison had been pilot of the B-17 *Susy Q*, described in *Life* magazine as "the fightingest Flying Fortress." In an article in January of 1943, *Life* reported that the *Suzy-Q* had run more long-range bombing missions against the Japanese than any other plane. Before coming to Sweden, Hardison had been commanding officer of the 93rd Bomb Squadron, first in the Philippines, and then in Australia.[166]

Lt. Col. Felix Hardison on the right with Dr. Floyd A. Potter

Hardison had support personnel in Stockholm at the American Legation, the diplomatic offices similar to an embassy. His staff had the responsibility of overseeing what happened to the U.S. internees from day to day. As soon as possible after landing, crews were met by his representatives. The airmen were thoroughly debriefed regarding their mission and what caused them to have to come to Sweden. Detailed records were kept.

The legation representative proceeded to explain to the men the rules of internment. The internees were again ordered not to divulge details of their flight to anyone, including the press or the police. Unlike conventional prisoners of war captured in enemy territory, internees had to agree that they would not try to escape from Sweden.

Since the beginning of the war, the Americans had been watching closely as military personnel from other countries were interned in

Sweden. They made a careful study of their treatment and conditions in the inevitable event of U.S. crews landing there. Whenever the Americans approached the Swedish Foreign Office in this matter, they dealt primarily with one military officer who was in charge of all interned personnel.

Count Folke Bernadotte

The Swedish government designated Count Folke Bernadotte, the nephew of reigning King Gustav V, as chief of the Internment Section of the Swedish General Staff. As such, Bernadotte was responsible for all interned airmen who force-landed in his country.[167]

Folke Bernadotte was born in 1895. His father, Prince Oscar, was the second son of King Oscar II who ruled from 1872 until 1907. When Prince Oscar married a lady-in-waiting, he gave up his right of succession to the throne. Folke's biographer, British correspondent Ralph Hewins, compared this 1888 sensational event to the 1936 abdication of the duke of Windsor in England.[168] Upon the death of King Oscar in 1907, Folke's uncle became King Gustav V, who reigned until his death in 1950.

Folke's parents made sure that the youngest of their five children had a strict upbringing with an emphasis on doing good works. When he was 21 years old and an officer in the Royal Horse Guards, Folke was diagnosed with bleeding stomach ulcers, a condition from which he suffered for the rest of his life.[169]

In 1928, Folke married Estelle Manville, a 23-year-old American from a wealthy New York family. They met at a party in the south of France and liked each other right away. She was beautiful, tall and dark haired. The handsome couple wed the same year in Pleasantville, New York, and the *New York Times* reported that this was the first royal wedding to take place in the United States. The couple moved to Sweden and settled into a Stockholm apartment owned by Folke's parents.

A few years later, the couple converted Folke's former regimental mess into their residence, named Dragongården. Their first party was a crayfish feast for the builders and decorators who had worked so hard to create a real home for them.[170]

Located near the lower shoreline of Ostermalm, the Dragongården estate is actually part of the royal island of Djurgårdern. Less than two miles east of the American Legation on Strandvägen, the lovely home was convenient to many of the offices that Bernadotte visited during the war. In fact, he often rode his bicycle to work, as did many Stockholmers.[171] Folke and Estelle had four children together. Tragically, two died at an early age.

Determined to live a life devoted to humanitarian service, in the 1930s Bernadotte worked with the Swedish Scout Union and developed a lifelong interest in scouting. A few years later he applied that same dedication to the Swedish Red Cross.

In 1939, Folke Bernadotte was in New York at the World's Fair. He had completed a huge job, overseeing the construction of the Swedish Pavilion. His team designed the Swedish Square to be a replica of a market square back home.[172] The Three Crowns restaurant featured a revolving snack bar called the "Smörgåsbord," an instant hit with visitors. When the fair was over, the restaurant moved to midtown New York, complete with the popular revolving Smörgåsbord.

Bernadotte and his wife were still in New York when Great Britain and France declared war on Germany. When he returned home, he accepted responsibility for caring for the military personnel of belligerent countries who would end up in his country.[173]

Aircraft Internment

Soon after March 1944, it became evident that larger storage and repair facilities were needed for the growing numbers of interned aircraft. Military Air Attaché Hardison discovered the Swedes had no experience with the four-engine aircraft, nor did they have adequate personnel available to repair or maintain such a large number of planes.

The Swedish government and Air Force authorized the use of Västerås and Såtenäs airfields for bomber storage. The field used for fighter storage was the military airport of Stockholm, located on the outskirts of the city of Barkarby. The Bulltofta airfield in Malmö was designated for repairs and salvage, after which the planes were moved to one of the other fields.

Hardison, in conference with the commander in chief of the Royal Swedish Air Force, General Bengt Nordenskiöld, developed an agreement that repairs on the interned aircraft would be made under the supervision of interned Americans placed on detached service from the American air attaché's office. The result was an atmosphere of cooperation and camaraderie between the Swedes and the Americans who worked together at the various locations.

If an aircraft needed to be salvaged, usable parts were removed, and the remaining scrap was collected and sold to local companies. Salvaged parts were tagged, stored, and maintained by the Swedish Air Force. Classified equipment was sealed and shipped to Stockholm, taking precautionary measures to prevent their compromise.

When the airmen arriving in Sweden were initially interviewed by the American authorities, they were asked to describe their skills and previous assignments. Those qualified to do so were assigned to work on the planes.[174]

Back in the States, *Liberty Lady* gunner Donald Courson had attended an engine school as well as a mechanics school. After being in Sweden for a month, both Courson and crewmate R.B. Trumble were sent to Bulltofta to perform repair and salvage.

During the war, Bulltofta was the home of the Swedish Air Force Fighter Wing F10. Their pilots patrolled the coastline of southern Sweden. Since the airfield was no more than 250 to 300 miles from the German coast, it was an opportune spot for damaged bombers to land. When they were seen approaching, the Swedish fighters flew over to escort them.

Auxiliary internee camps for the working internees were set up at the various bases. While Don Courson was at Bulltofta, he stayed at Malmö's Grand Hotel. Some Americans even stayed in homes of local families.

Courson remembered there were about twenty internees on the job five and a half days each week. Because of lack of hangar space, the planes were all out in the open. If it rained, the men worked on engines under a tent. After a while, outdoor heaters were supplied. Until then, Don from Mississippi recalled, "It got mighty cold."

He added, "New crews coming in with their damaged planes might crash land. Some ran out of fuel and hit the ground hard. Or the brakes ran out, and they smashed into planes already parked on the field. Sometimes the planes landed in other areas out in the country, in wheat fields or pastures, and we had to travel there to get them ready to fly. One plane ran out of fuel and landed within sight of one of the royal residences. We spent the night nearby, got the plane ready, and flew it back to Malmö the next day. When we took off, I remember there was a big crowd of the local people watching us."

Many of the early forced-landing crews, like that of the *Liberty Lady*, intentionally destroyed their planes with an incendiary device. These ruins became dangerous obstacles in the way of other aircraft trying to land. In early 1944, an agreement was made between the American and the Swedish military that crews would no longer attempt to destroy their aircraft. In exchange, the Americans were given sketches and detailed instructions for airfields most suitable for landings.[175]

On July 14, 1944, Hardison sent Gen. Carl Spaatz, commander of Strategic Air Forces in Europe, a set of detailed instructions for the guidance of American crews landing in Sweden. The airmen could continue to land at Rinkaby or Göteborg. Another possibility for forced landings was Sövdeborg, a grassy field north of Ystad with more than 5000 feet of unobstructed landing ground. When possible, Swedish fighters would intercept and escort the bombers there. Bulltofta, being enlarged to about 4000 feet, was recommended for planes bearing wounded airmen.[176]

On the 20th and 21st of June, no fewer than 25 bombers landed at Bulltofta after large bombing raids over Germany. The activity was intense with landings coming in from all directions. In fact, in the space of just over an hour, 16 B-24s landed or crashed on the grassy field. Locals in the area were asked to stay inside because of the risk of injury from falling pieces of damaged aircraft. The Swedish personnel had a hard time keeping up with so many incoming planes but, in spite of the chaos, most crews managed to land safely.[177]

The historical report from the Office of the Military Air Attaché concluded that the cooperation of the Swedish government, Swedish Air Force, and the Swedish Airline AB Aerotransport was of the highest standard in maintaining American aircraft. Both aircraft and equipment were cared for by the Swedish authorities in the same manner they cared for their own.[178]

In August, the *Vestmanlands Läns Tidning*, a newspaper in Västerås, reported on the creative artwork decorating the planes being stored there. "The first things that strike the eye of the layman, and the only things he is permitted to write about, are the funny emblems, the nicknames, and the bombs painted on the ships to indicate the number of attacks. The most recent arrivals show neither emblems nor painting; apparently there was no time for decoration before the invasion."

Bernt Balchen

The Stockholm airport Bromma, some five miles west of downtown, was inaugurated as a city airport by King Gustav V in 1936. During the war, tourist traffic came to a halt. However, since both Allied and German planes were flying out of the airfield, the area was swarming with spies, all trying to figure out what their enemies were doing.

From Bromma, Allied planes flew to and from Britain, not easy trips because they involved flying over Nazi-fortified territories. The person most responsible for these American flights to Britain was Norwegian-born Bernt Balchen.

By the 1940s, Bernt Balchen, muscular and handsome with wavy blonde hair, was a legendary polar pilot. When he was only 12 years old, he met Captain Roald Amundsen, the Norwegian explorer who, in 1911, had led the first expedition to reach the South Pole. Young Bernt told Amundsen, "I want to be an explorer and go on an expedition with you!"[179] Twelve years later they met again, and Amundsen remembered the boy who had idolized him so. The following year, Balchen was part of Amundsen's team, assisting with preparations for a historic flight across the North Pole.

Not long after, Balchen joined the crew of Commander Richard E. Byrd and steered his boat into New York Harbor. It was a thrilling first trip to America for Balchen. In 1929, he piloted Byrd for the first ever flight over the South Pole. After he returned with Byrd for the resulting

Bernt Balchen, Felix Hardison, Robert Robb, 1944
Stockholm (family of Stan Buck)

celebrations, a special bill was passed by Congress to make Bernt Balchen an American citizen.[180]

Balchen's polar experiences and airplane expertise would prove to be invaluable during World War II. In July of 1941, he was recruited by Gen. Henry H. "Hap" Arnold, chief of the Army Air Forces. Arnold sent Balchen to Gen. Carl Spaatz to be briefed on his first assignment, establishing a base on the western coast of Greenland as a staging field for planes flying from the U.S. to Europe. When Balchen remarked to Spaatz that the United States wasn't even in the war, the response was, "It will be."[181]

Two days after the Japanese attack on Pearl Harbor, Balchen and his men stationed in Greenland learned that the United States was indeed at war. Now, they would not only have to battle the intense weather, they would also have to be combat-ready. Balchen led hazardous rescues of air crews who landed on the ice, but there were also times when the unforgiving Arctic conditions prevailed, making rescues impossible.

Balchen met General Arnold again in September of 1943. He told the general what he wanted to do next was to somehow to help the Norwegian resistance movement. After the German invasion of Norway in 1940, underground forces were growing in number and needed outside assistance. Balchen's next trip was to Washington to meet with William Donovan of the OSS.

Donovan directed Balchen to neutral Sweden to set up an air transport service, code-named Operation Sonnie. Ever since the beginning of the war, Norwegians had been streaming into Sweden, many of them eager to fight against the Nazis. The first Sonnie mission was to fly 2000 Norwegians trainees from Stockholm to England. From there they could be sent on for naval or flight training.

Under cover of the Air Force's Air Transport Command, Balchen was given five worn B-24 Liberators and personnel, called the Carpetbaggers, from a special services group associated with the OSS. Balchen asked for B-17s, but they were too much in demand that near the time of the Normandy offensive.

In preparation for their missions, the crews shopped at Selfridge's in London for civilian suits. They also had civilian passports. The unarmed B-24s were painted dark green, almost black, with military insignia removed.

The Liberators flew at night out of the RAF airbase at Leuchars in eastern Scotland. Ideal weather for take-off was solid overcast so they could evade the German night fighters as they sped over Nazi-occupied Norway and then on into Sweden.

The initial Sonnie flight, piloted by Balchen himself, was on March 31, 1944. The weather was bad enough for their covert journey. In fact, the fog was so thick that the plane had to circle for two hours before landing at Bromma. As Balchen climbed out of the camouflaged B-24, the first person he saw was a German, supposedly a press attaché. Balchen recognized him immediately and knew this man to be head of the Gestapo in Sweden. The stunned German smiled tentatively and then walked away.

Balchen and his crew went straight to the luxurious Grand Hôtel for hot baths and a breakfast more scrumptious than anything they could have found in London. Nazi undercover agents at Bromma had also noticed the nine civilians disembarking from the unmarked Liberator. They were immediately suspicious and followed the group to the hotel. With interest, Balchen noticed the wide array of guests from every belligerent country. Allied, Japanese, and high-ranking Nazi officers all ate in the elegant dining rooms and roamed the same hallways.[182]

After the first flight with the Norwegian trainees, Sonnie operated as a courier and transportation service for the internees, the American Legation, and the OSS. The OSS exit permits to Sweden were being processed in London by Hedvig Johnson, X-2, with notifications to Bill Carlson, code named Limit, in Stockholm.

The Rockets

In January of 1944, Berlin dispatches to the Swedish press disclosed that Nazi Germany was ready to test a liquid air rocket. Preliminary tests had been made in Austria, and an eyewitness noted, "It was as if bushes, trees, and everything had been smashed to atoms by the blast." Weeks earlier, Berlin radio announced, "Mankind is not far from the point where it can, at will, blow up half the globe."[183]

Then on May 22, *Time* magazine reported, "Swedes got an unscheduled preview of a new German weapon last week. A pilotless, rocket-driven aircraft crashed near Bertilstorp in southern Sweden. Apparently it had strayed, out of control of its radio beam. Observers who studied the wreckage said the craft had no wings, tail, or landing gear."[184]

Actually seven German missiles found their way to Sweden during the war. The one reported by *Time* landed on May 11, 1944. It was a V-1 rocket, one of the buzz bombs soon to terrorize Hedy and the rest of London.

The most important missile find arrived on the 13th of June, 1944, when a rocket exploded in the air with its debris and metal parts showering down over Bäckebo, in southern Sweden. The authorities knew immediately that it was not a V-1, but they were not sure what it was.

The rocket had been launched on a test run from Peenemünde, the site of Hitler's top-secret rocket base, some 335 kilometers (just over 200 miles) south on the northern coast of Germany. Wernher von Braun, the German rocket engineer who would eventually work in the United States for NASA, was responsible for the design of this new weapon. The Swedes immediately brought the parts to the FFA (Military Aeronautical Research Institute) in Stockholm.

News got out quickly, with articles and photographs in the Swedish newspapers the next day. The Grand Hôtel was abuzz, as was the German Legation in Stockholm.

Felix Hardison saw a small news article about the strange object. Although he didn't speak Swedish, he had studied German in college and could pick out important words. He asked his secretary, Susie Gyllenskiöld, to translate for him. Hardison immediately went to General Nordenskiöld, commander of the Swedish Air Force, for permission to visit the site. Arrangements were made for Hardison to travel by plane. He did not wear his uniform, as this was not an official trip. Forced to sit near German passengers, Hardison did not utter a word.[185]

After a few weeks of careful study, the Swedes allowed the remains to be taken to Great Britain for further analysis, and Hardison was able to assist with the logistics of getting them there. On July 30, wooden crates of parts and debris weighing about two and a half tons were transported from Bromma Airport by Lt. Col. Keith N. Allen, one of the pilots who flew with Bernt Balchen. The boxes were too large to get through an opening in one of Balchen's Liberators, so an old C-47 was used. The secret cargo arrived at the Royal Aircraft Establishment at Farnborough Airfield the next day.[186]

What was unearthed was brand new technology. The German vengeance weapons program had taken years of research and used a workforce of slave laborers from nearby concentration camps. By September, what was known as the V-2 would be unleashed on London, southern England, and Belgium. Hitler's goal was to pound these countries into submission and turn the war around.

Unlike the V-1 buzz bomb, the V-2 gave no warning. It was the world's first intermediate range ballistic missile, and there was no defense for it. In Britain alone 2,500 people were killed by the V-2.[187] Fortunately, the V-2 was developed as late as it was and thus did not have a material effect on the outcome of the war. In addition, the Eighth Air Force was sending heavy bomber raids to the rocket construction and landing sites. Eventually, some of the airmen who flew over these heavily defended locations would be forced to land their badly damaged planes in Sweden.

The Americans in Sweden

Of the more than 300 planes that crashed or force-landed in Sweden during the war, 140 were from the United States.[188] All in all, there were 1218 U.S. crew members who were interned in 1943, 1944, and 1945.[189]

When these tired young men first set foot on Swedish soil, their emotions were high. The landings were traumatic endings to a long, horrific day, and their planes often carried men who were injured or dead. Crew members might even have been forced to parachute from their badly damaged aircraft.

Many times, as happened with the *Liberty Lady* crew, because of the foreign languages spoken around them, the men had no idea where they had landed. Had they found Norway? Denmark? Sweden? One officer remembered that after landing, he and his crew were taken to a hotel room. Two foreigners asked him to go with them. He thought he was being taken outside to be shot, but they only escorted him to a toilet. As the highest-ranking officer, he was politely offered the facilities first.

With more and more airmen arriving, Sweden had to scramble to find housing for them. The Swedes began to convert boarding houses, health spas, and even ski resorts located all over the country into internment camps. Over the next year, camps opened at Falun, Rättvik, Loka Brunn, Gränna, and Mullsjö. Almost without exception, the Americans were treated warmly by the Swedish people who took care of them.

In command at each camp was a Swedish officer assisted by a staff of two or three, all answerable to Count Bernadotte. An assistant to Bernadotte was the popular Capt. Leo Sager, in charge of camps at Granna, Mullsjö, and Loka Brunn. These Swedish officers spoke English and had either lived in the United States or had connections that made them familiar with Americans and their customs.

Also at each camp, working in coordination with the Swedes, was an equally large staff of U.S. officials. The senior officer's authority covered passes, leaves, travel, discipline and general policy, only when pre-coordinated with the Swedish commanding officer for approval.

Count Bernadotte inspects the American internees in Rättvik. 1944.

For example, permission for a three-day pass to Stockholm was obtained by making a request to the American C.O., who in turn furnished the information to the American staff in Stockholm. This information went to the office of Count Bernadotte who transmitted his decision back to the Swedish C.O. of the camp. All this red tape resulted in tight control over the movements and action of every internee.[190]

Serious disciplinary issues were rare. In one instance, an airman got into a bar fight with a Swede and had to be confined to the security section of the Främby camp. He was one of a few to be demoted.

The interned airmen had the freedom to explore their camps and nearby towns within two or three miles in each direction. For recreation, they enjoyed Sweden's great outdoors. The men hiked, rode bikes, boated on the lakes, and in the winter, they skied. At the various camps they organized baseball teams and in some cases, football or soccer.

On June 21, 1944, a Swedish newspaper reported on a football game in Loka Brunn. The Swedes won the game 6–2, but one of the Swedish players broke his leg. The newspaper reporter wrote that in spite of some unfavorable reports written about these "fat cats," the American boys behaved like gentlemen.

The following Monday, an American delegation from Loka arrived at the hospital to visit the injured Swedish football player. The patient was thrilled when the visitors presented him with 200 Swedish crowns. The Americans then told the doctor to put the patient in a private room and send them the bill. "Even though the Americans have plenty of money, we think the episode is indicative of a pretty warm heart on the part of the fliers," the reporter concluded.

The internees were paid their usual salaries plus a per diem of at least $7 per day for being away from their home base. This payment added up to $400 a month or more, producing a higher income than airmen from the other countries received and much more than the earnings of the Swedes who lived in the towns. The monthly income of an average Swede was somewhere around $60 at that time.[191]

Smithy in Vikarbyn, exploring the area around Rättvik.

Each internee was responsible for paying a flat rate for food and lodgings to the owner of his accommodations, whether it was a hotel, a boarding house, or a private home. After those bills were paid, the Americans had plenty of money left over to go shopping.

Wearing military uniforms was not permitted, so immediately the airmen were given ration coupons and cash to buy civilian clothing. They purchased bikes, ski equipment, and canoes. Local shopkeepers had more business than ever. The men also bought gifts for the pretty girls in town, and because most of the local young men were away in the Swedish Army, there wasn't much competition for the attentions of the ladies.

The press took notice. In July 1944 a pro-Nazi newspaper published an article about the (translated) "American Dollar Charmers" who had fallen from the skies into Sweden and were giving many different localities the pleasure of their presence. Every weekend, the article read, crowds of young ladies poured in, dying to see the heroes, swill champagne and perhaps be given the honor of a dance or two.

It was no secret that the local girls were enthusiastic about the young, energetic airmen. They were handsome and fun and had money to spend. In fact, everyone was noticing them. Soon, the Nazis were trying to figure out how they could use the popularity and the loquaciousness of the Americans to their own advantage.

First Stop, Falun

Two days after their emergency landing, the *Liberty Lady* crew sailed from Gotland to the mainland port of Nynäshamn. From there they were escorted 60 kilometers (37 miles) north to Stockholm.

From Stockholm, the crew caught a train to Falun, about 150 miles northwest. Falun is the capital of Dalarna County in the mid part of Sweden. A city historically known for copper mining, Falun once provided this ore to countries all over Europe. In 1687, parts of the underground mine collapsed, leaving a huge crater and bringing a gradual end to Falun's copper production.

A byproduct of the copper processing was a red pigment historically used to make paint known as Falun red. Throughout the countryside and beyond could be spotted homes colored by the distinctive deep red hue.

Because of Falun's prosperity, it had developed into one of the larger cities in Sweden with a population around 19,000. In 1944 there was an established business district with stores, restaurants, and even four movie theatres. The arrival of the internees brought lots of new customers and a welcomed period of prosperity.

Most crews were taken first to Falun to be processed at Främby, the camp encircled with a barbed-wire fence. The men were officially questioned, if they hadn't been already, and were scheduled for a physical exam. The period of time for this temporary assignment varied depending on, for one thing, the availability of permanent housing.

As time went on, and more and more crews arrived, additional accommodations in Falun were rented out by the Americans. A few internees stayed at the local Grand Hotel. Alcohol wasn't available in pubs as it was in England, but in the hotels an airman could order a drink with his meal. Cold beer was a newfound luxury. These refreshments made Falun's Grand Hotel a popular spot.

One of the earliest American bombers arrived in Sweden on October 9, 1943. The crew of B-17 *Sack-Time Susy* flew with the 96th Bomb Group out of Snetterton Heath. Their target was shipyards on the northern coast of Poland, on the Baltic Sea. Attacked by enemy fighters south of Copenhagen, the crew flew their damaged plane north and landed at Bulltofta airport. After being processed, the crew was housed at Solliden, a comfortable pension a few miles from the city of Falun. Both American and British airmen were interned at Solliden throughout the war. In all, the pension could accommodate about 25 airmen at one time.

It was uncommon for British and American crews to be housed together. Once the Americans came, their salaries were much higher than the salaries of the British crews, and airmen from the two countries had to be separated. In most cases they were kept so until the end of the war.

The right waist gunner of *Sack-Time Susy,* Sgt. James T. Degnan, quickly settled in to life at Solliden. He began to write letters home, and over the next few months kept his family up to date on his new adventures. Degnan reported that each man received two cartons of American cigarettes a month. After that, they needed to buy the local brands, a "good substitute."

Degnan had also met a blond Swedish girl who spoke English fairly well. "All the Yanks here have a girl," he wrote. "We are worse than sailors."[192]

At the time the *Liberty Lady* crew arrived in Falun, there were fewer than 75 American airmen in Sweden. The men were briefed as to the regulations under which they would be living and were told how they needed to conduct themselves.

After the required paperwork and interviews, the representative of the Military Air Attaché's office gave the men money and ration cards and led them to the local bath house. Internee 2nd Lt. George L. Winans described his Falun bath experience: "We were herded into a room, told to disrobe, and hustled into a large steam room to be greeted by three old women (probably in their 50s) who handed us soap. We were told to scrub up, all this in sign language. We were totally embarrassed, trying to cover up with what bath towels we had. They were pushing us down onto some long benches, attempting to wash us.

Finally, we were made to jump into a swimming pool of next-to-frozen water. Then they proceeded to come in and dry us. Laughable now but not then."[193]

More than likely this was the same routine experienced by the *Liberty Lady* crew. After they had their bath and a shave, they walked down the street to a large department store. Their escort instructed them to buy a suit, overcoat, extra pants, shoes, and shirts, whatever they needed. As Don Courson remembered, "I had the surprise of my life seeing those men. They cleaned up good, they really did."

One of the *Liberty Lady* crew members in his flight jacket.

In no time, crews had their first exposure to what they began to describe as the "Swedish flickas." Tall, dark, and handsome with an Errol Flynn mustache, radio operator Vic Marcotte, was immediately swept off his feet by a young lady who worked in the dime store. Even after the crew moved on to their next stop, Marcotte regularly packed his bag and returned to Falun for a tryst.

Ebba Lindblad, whose family owned the Solliden pension, was 19 years old when the airmen arrived. Ebba recalled, "The whole town of Falun woke up. It was very exciting. The Englishmen, they were men, well-behaved. The Americans, they were like boys. They were so much fun."[194]

Rättvik

After a few days at Främby, the Smith crew took the train about 30 miles west to the small resort town of Rättvik. On the shore of majestic Lake Siljan, Rättvik had a population of about 900 people. As the Americans began to arrive in greater numbers, it became one of the main locations for housing them.

For years, the area had been a popular vacation destination for wealthy Swedes and other Europeans. Steamboats brought travelers to the Långbryggan, a long bridge stretching nearly 700 yards out into the lake. The bridge terminated at a tiny artificial island, complete with a bathhouse where swimmers could change into their suits.

In the late 1800s, after the train came to Rättvik, a deluxe hotel was built next to the train station to cater to affluent guests who traveled there to enjoy both winter and summer attractions, most of them centering on Lake Siljan. The new hotel was named Turisthotellet, the "Tourist Hotel." Outside and in, it was splendid. The exterior had lots of what can be described as gingerbread, with many ornate architectural details. By 1944, the Turisthotellet may have lost some of its early grandeur, but the interned airmen assigned to live there didn't care one bit.

When the *Liberty Lady* crew arrived at the Rättvik station, they climbed into one of the coal-burning taxis and drove down Storgatan, the main street, to a destination less than half a mile away. The first Americans had come to town only two months earlier. Compared to the hustle and bustle soon to descend on the village, it was quiet. Up a fairly steep hill, the taxi drove and pulled in front of a small hotel.

The year before, Sten Hagberg had borrowed money so he could buy a guest house known as Pensionat Lerdalshöjden. Three weeks later, the Americans leased the entire establishment. Soon Sten was able to buy neighboring land, giving him about 12 acres in all.

Sten Hagberg at the Pensionat Lerdalshöjden. 1944.

His first internee guests arrived on March 11, 1944. The hotel started out with only 20 beds, but Sten had plans to expand and began construction in May[195] with the help of the men he referred to as "my boys."[196]

Sited high above Lake Siljan, the Lerdalshöjden provided guests with magnificent views all the way to the pier and beyond. In March, Lake Siljan was covered with thick ice that didn't melt until May.

Just out the door was excellent snowy terrain with a ski slope, a winter wonderland that probably hadn't changed much since the beginning of the century. Snow was plentiful, and for a couple of months the men were able to ski, most of them for the first time. Behind the hotel is where Herman learned how to master small hills before taking to the actual slopes.

The first Swedish officer in charge of the Rättvik internees, Capt. Carl Rosenblad, had competed as an equestrian in the 1912 Summer Olympics. During his military career, Rosenblad served with the Royal Life Regiment Dragoons and the Royal Life Regiment on horseback.[197] Later in 1944, Lt. Torkel Tistrand replaced Rosenblad as camp commander. Tistrand had been a captain in the Swedish Army Maintenance Corps and had served on the *Gripsholm*, one of two Swedish ships used for prisoner of war exchanges and repatriation voyages. Known as "Jimmy," Tistrand was popular with the Americans and treated them as guests of Sweden. He had spent time in their country and spoke perfect English.[198]

Every morning a roll call was held at each of the hotels, followed by an hour of exercise before breakfast. Then the men wandered into town to see what was going on.

Local action centered on Klingberg's Konditori, a coffee and bakery shop on Storgatan. Bikes were always parked out front. Once the weather warmed, customers gathered on an upstairs deck to watch the action down on the street. It wasn't unusual for the same young men to go in two or three times a day for a *fika*—coffee and pastry—and to talk to the attractive young waitresses who were all too happy to see the *utsocknes*, the handsome foreigners who looked like movie stars.

In fact, girls came from as far away as Stockholm to meet these fun, good-looking young men. Some evenings, Herman's crew socialized right up until the nine o'clock curfew. Smithy kept his eyes peeled for Engra, reminding the boys, "My girl in Indiana has everything, but she doesn't have it here." Marcotte, Heuser, and Stillson took on as a personal challenge the young gunner, Joe Paul, whom they nicknamed "Virgin," and introduced him to all the girls. Just like Falun, Rättvik came alive when the Americans moved in.

Herman and Smithy. In scrapbook, photo is labeled "A bottle, a friend."

A group of internees built a bobsled and, to the delight of the townspeople, raced down the hill and onto Main Street. By the time their wild rides were over, the men estimated they were flying at 50 miles per hour. A Swedish airman in town on a training exercise was watching all the fun and asked to take a ride. The sled was soon airborne and came to an abrupt landing. The Swede flew off and ended up with a broken bone. After that mishap, the police put an end to bobsled rides in town.

The Crew in Rättvik. Seated left to right: Charles W. Smith, Carl A. Heuser, Merle P. Brown, Stanley N. Buck. Standing: Victor R. Marcotte, Joseph R. Paul, Thomas E. Stillson, Donald S. Courson, R.B. Trumble, Herman F. Allen.

Once settled in, Herman immediately found a typewriter and began to write a two-column newsletter he named "THE BEAVER'S SPUR," the title inspired by his 368th squadron at Thurleigh, the Eager Beavers. In his newsletters, Herman emphasized the importance of keeping quiet and not talking about "business" to anyone. "Herr Goebbels is still to be reckoned with," he wrote, "so keep the dope under the well-known bonnet." The warning was timely. Official alerts from OSS Stockholm cautioned about pro-Nazi sympathizers, including women who were "very easy with their morals," moving into the area. The risks would escalate as more and more Americans arrived.

A large map hung on one of the walls so the men could follow what was happening in the rest of Europe and so Herman could report on the world news. His primary objective, however, was to describe in witty detail the exploits of his crew.

By a twist of fate, these young men had been magically transported from the months of terror in the skies over Europe to an extended leave of absence.

THE BEAVER'S SPUR

WORLD NEWS

The Eighth AF is still on the move giving the Fatherland its own particular kind of Hell. The Finns have definitely thrown the peace offerings of the Soviets into the wastebasket. Evidently they figure Herr Schicklgruber can offer them a loaf. A conservative estimate by Mr. Churchill is that the European conflict will not be finished by 1944. Roosevelt echoes with a firm amen.

LEFT WAIST KEEPS SLATE CLEAN

The Axis tried, without success, to bring S/Sgt Don Courson under their sphere of influence. The Rebel, in his best drawl, said "Not interested." The frau will be back however for another try.

NAVIGATOR NEWS

Stan Buck left for Stockholm on March 23rd to assume new duties as the assistant to the assistant to the assistant at the American Legation in Stockholm. The well wishes of his fellow crewmen are sincere in the hope that he will discover a more fertile pasture in his new surroundings than ever dreamt of amongst the flickas hereabouts.

Working under Military Air Attaché Hardison, Stan Buck was placed in charge of the Scandinavian Air Fields section — maps, files and pertinent data regarding Scandinavian countries. While there, he worked with Bernt Balchen who was initiating the courier service between Sweden and the RAF airbase at Leuchars in Scotland. Balchen also led his B-24 crews on clandestine operations aiding the Norwegian resistance. It was critical for his team to have detailed maps and information on the Scandinavian countries.

One of Stan's more entertaining responsibilities was to attend evening social functions. The August 26, 1944, issue of *Collier's* magazine included an article titled, "Swedish Stopover" with photographs of interned airmen, and the photo in prime position was of Stan Buck.

For most of the families back home, the *Collier's* story was their first glimpse of the internees. The men were shown bicycling, skiing, swimming, and hanging out with the ladies. In short, they were safe and sound. Stan returned to Rättvik in July and resumed the life of a regular internee.

> HAPPY ANNIVERSARY
>
> STO, April 6. It was a beautiful day in Chicago the afternoon of March 6, 1944, but it held no twilight to the waning light in Sweden. A tired and thankful crew looked back on the Liberty Lady as the flames licked their chops around her gallant body. A man broke out of the nearby woods at a trot with his gun cocked, shouting some foreign tongue. Sgt. Heuser, drawing on his smattering of German, turned to the tense white faces, and said, "Lads, we've had it." A sigh of relief as the Home Guard drew closer and we found a case of mistaken identity ... praise the Lord for terra firma and Sweden.
>
> It has been a full month, a good month. There have been no tears. Happy Anniversary, Eager Beavers.

The summer of 1944 was warmer than usual, so the lake was a magnet for swimmers, boaters, and sunbathers. There were more sailboats and canoes than ever before.

One of the most popular destinations for the internees was Rättviks folkpark, a little over a mile from downtown. When dances were held on Saturday nights, rows of bicycles were parked outside the front gate. The folkpark was the perfect spot to meet up with local girls and practice the jitterbug.

Internees in Sweden during the summer of 1944 (family of Stan Buck)

One Saturday evening, William S. Dixon introduced *Liberty Lady* co-pilot Merle Brown to Maj Britt, a beautiful Swedish girl. Merle could not speak Swedish, and the young lady could not speak English. The language barrier didn't seem to matter one bit. In fact, a local newspaper described the match as "the most talked about romance in Sweden."

Not every story had a happy ending. When the war ended and the Americans had all gone, there were some broken promises and even babies left behind.

Andy was another internee who lived at the Pensionat Lerdalshöjden. One day when he was at the folkpark, he became infatuated with a lovely young Swedish girl who worked at a shop in a nearby town. She thought he was the most beautiful man she had ever seen. He didn't want to dance, so they just drank coffee together and tried to converse, a few words here and a few words there. As the months went by, they talked often, and their relationship became more and more serious.

Late one afternoon Andy received notice that he would be leaving Rättvik the next day. In a panic because he had no idea where he was headed, he grabbed a taxi without permission and went to the young lady's home, a little over ten miles south. He left all his extra belongings with her and promised to return. The next day, Andy was taken to Bromma airport and left Sweden. He never got to meet his daughter who was born in Stockholm. This was but one of the long-remembered stories to come out of the "American invasion."[199]

Even with all the diversions, Herman wrote to his sister Dorothy that he was restless and tired of the inactivity.

Somewheres...

March 23, 1944

And so, the days succeed each other as we sweat out this period of internship. Frankly, it isn't so bad, except the ugly demon inactivity is beginning to rear its ugly head, especially after those hectic months just past. However, the rest is beginning to show its good points. Have lost the greatest part of a few dark circles and acquired an addition of seven pounds to the weight I normally pack around. From these facts, you can easily see the surroundings are conducive to good health. Have good accommodations, considering a few of the places I've been. The food is plentiful and well prepared, though slightly monotonous in its fare. So all in all the complaints are few and far between. Can say, with a hearty amen, we are indeed fortunate to come out as well as we did.

The entire crew is here together. Enclosed you will find a group picture. Smithy and I have a room together as in the days of old. Radio, heater, spring beds are amongst the conveniences offered. The evenings are filled with either reading, writing, gab fests, an occasional movie when the local cinema house rates an English film, or simply hitting the sack early to catch up on all those hours of sleep lost somewhere along the line these past two years. Most of the day is spent outdoor enjoying the spots offered. So goes our time.

Mail from your end takes about three months to reach here, and from here to you is a mute question, so under the circumstances write as regularly as you can, at least once a week, and shall do the same.

Have patience, faith, for someday I shall drop in on you all, unexpectedly as usual, and things which I am not allowed to write of now will be forthcoming.

Love always, brother Herman

Yes, Herman was bored. Years later, he recounted what happened next.

"The commander of the internee camp announced they were looking for a typist in Stockholm. They needed more help down there, and they wanted to know if anyone could type.

"Right away, I put up my hand. I don't know how well I could type, but somehow to get out of there, well enough! I looked around,

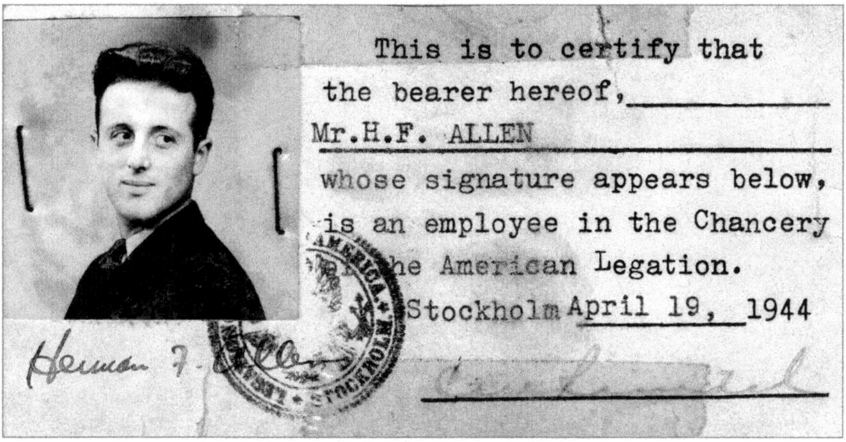
This is to certify that
the bearer hereof,
Mr.H.F. ALLEN
whose signature appears below,
is an employee in the Chancery
the American Legation.
Stockholm April 19, 1944
Herman F. Allen

Herman's ID Card.

and I was the only one who raised his hand. There were about forty of us in the room.

"So he said, 'Allen, you're it. You're going to Stockholm!' I got orders from the Swedish Air Force that I could go to work for the military air attaché in the Internee Section."

Thus the typist left Rättvik and set off for Stockholm. Herman's first official day at the American Legation, according to his ID card, was April 19, 1944.

He had just begun what would be the finest adventure of his life.

Chapter 10

November 20, 2007, Providence Hospital

On Tuesday I spent the night at the hospital in Mother's room. There was only a hard chair to sit on, and since I knew I wasn't supposed to stay past nine o'clock, I didn't ask for anything more comfortable. I plugged in my laptop, hooked it up to the wireless, and settled in to work while Mother dozed.

A few hours earlier, the surgeon had come to Mother's bedside. As he spoke to her, I instantly recognized the same sober expression on his face as I had seen on the cardiologist's. "Mrs. Allen," he explained, "doing open heart surgery now will be a lot more complicated than the surgery you had ten years ago. If you were my mother, I wouldn't recommend it."

Hedy had smiled, nodded her head, and said, ever so graciously, "Thank you, Doctor."

The first thing I did when I turned on my computer was to google "aortic dissection." I learned more than I wanted to know. The condition is usually fatal instantly. It is what killed both Lucille Ball and John Ritter. Lucille Ball had undergone an excruciating open heart surgical repair and two weeks later her aorta ruptured.

Mother and I talked off and on most of the night. I didn't breathe a word of what I had read. We never mentioned that she might die at any moment, but we did talk about a future without her. Mother said Daddy would definitely need to be in an environment with other people around him. He needed company. He would want female company. He would never be happy at home all alone. That evening Kathy sent an email to her friends and co-workers.

"You know I said my Mom has been so uncomfortable. It has been her back. It was what brought her to the hospital, and the pain has not stopped. Her doctor decided to do a CAT scan tonight because he could not figure out why. It is bad news. Her aorta has a tear, and she is bleeding internally. It happened because she has an eighty-six year old body with an unhealthy heart. The doctor said people usually die instantly. He is not sure why she is still alive.

"If she stays stable, she wants to come home. My whole family is on the way. Wouldn't it be great if she can make it to Thanksgiving? Not ours to decide.

"I am doing okay. In January, I asked God to please give us more time. He did."

Chapter 11

Spies, Spies, Spies

Because of its neutrality, wartime Sweden had quickly become a natural spot for clandestine activities. Many countries maintained legations there including the United States, Great Britain, France, Germany, Russia, Poland, Norway, Italy, China, and Japan. In addition to these diplomatic centers, most countries set up covert intelligence operations, all trying to learn each other's secrets.

Representatives from the belligerent nations traveled back and forth, stayed in the same hotels and ate side by side in the restaurants. Wartime Stockholm has been described as the "Casablanca of the North," with a social scene right out of Rick's Café in the legendary 1943 movie. Discreet conversations, off-the-cuff questions, eavesdropping—all had the same purpose, to gather useful information and pass it along.

In March of 1943, a pro-Nazi newspaper wrote an article declaring the Swedish capital to be the center of international espionage. In Sweden, the paper concluded, spies didn't have to go to much trouble to collect information. It was provided free of charge.[200]

The Swedes

As the threat of war intensified and then became a reality in Europe and around the world, in order to protect their neutrality and their national security, the Swedes had to beef up their intelligence services. Just as in the United States with the overlapping FBI, OSS, and military intelligence services, in Sweden various security organizations were operating.

A Military Security Service headed by Colonel Carlos Adlercreutz was set up in 1937. Then by 1938, a Civilian Security Service was officially launched. The latter was a secret organization responsible to the government and the military. Suspicious people were followed and photographed. Communications of all types, including mail, telegrams, and telephone calls were scrutinized and censored.[201] There were seven districts across the country. The regional controller of the largest one, the Stockholm bureau, was Martin Lundqvist, and he headed what was generally known as the secret police. The Civilian Security Service, mockingly called the Svestapo, was so secret that it was unknown to the Swedish public until 1943.[202]

Another branch, established in 1939, was a Swedish Secret Intelligence Service known as C-byrån (C bureau). The "C" was in honor of its leader, Major Carl Petersén. Second in command was intelligence agent Hellmuth Ternberg. This organization was very independent, and the other services knew little about its activities.

The actions of foreigners who traveled into Sweden were carefully monitored. Visa requirements were stiffened, and aliens were prohibited from entering certain railway, harbor, and factory areas. Hotels and anyone providing sleeping quarters were required to supply the police with pertinent information about their guests.

More attention was paid to those who were particularly sympathetic to the Communists or to Germany's Nazi Party.[203] In order to keep track of both Swedish citizens and visitors, a blacklist was kept of people suspected of espionage or related activities.

After the German occupation of Denmark and Norway, the Germans leased Swedish telegraph lines for their coded communications with these countries as well as with Finland. These lines were tapped by the Swedish Signal Intelligence, and the German code was cracked by mathematics professor Arne Beurling.

As Swedish historian Tommy Jonason explained, it is still not clear how Beurling managed to decipher the code with a pencil and paper while at Bletchley Park in Britain code breakers had to build a huge computer to achieve the same goal. More than 300,000 telegrams were read by the Swedes, giving them much important information about the plans of Nazi-Germany.

As for the Americans, the Swedish secret police knew in a general way what they were doing. Telephones were tapped, and conversations were recorded. There was no official censorship of either foreign or domestic mail in Sweden, but the police were known to steam open envelopes and read the contents.[204]

When war broke out in 1939, members of the international press began to set up headquarters at Stockholm's Grand Hôtel.[205] There were news agencies and correspondents from so many different countries that this location became one of the principal news sources of the war.

The section of the Grand Hôtel that housed many of the American, British and French foreign correspondents was known as "Fleet Street."[206] In the hotel barbershop, an American news correspondent might sit side by side with a member of the German Legation. It was from there or from the popular hotel bar that stories developed.

The major Swedish newspapers had correspondents working in Berlin. Reports were rushed out to all parts of the globe from the Stockholm rumor factories. "Germany won't last until Christmas." "Hitler may still invade England." "The Nazis are nearly ready to send a whole barrage of rockets over the Channel." Certainly, any news coming to Stockholm directly from Berlin was reviewed with caution by the Allies.

As *Time* magazine admitted in 1944, most of their news from inside Germany came from Stockholm. "Sweden is so close to the heart of Hitler's Europe that, when the wind is from the south, people there can sometimes smell the smoke of burning Berlin."

The magazine posted one of its most experienced foreign correspondents in Stockholm. John Scott spoke Russian, German, Spanish and French, and had also picked up Swedish. Sixteen thousand copies of the first Scandinavian issue of *Time* sold out within a few hours.[207]

Not only was the Grand Hôtel the center for wartime news, it was Stockholm's most exclusive—though not the most clandestine—gathering spot. American intelligence agents arriving in Stockholm were warned immediately not to use this hub of German espionage as a meeting place.

Many of the hotel employees worked secretly for the Swedish counterespionage unit. Rooms were routinely searched by the Swedish police and by the Gestapo. The Americans did their share of information gathering too. Wilho Tikander, OSS mission chief, kept a suite at the Grand Hôtel. For a while, Tikander had an agent deliver to his suite the ink blotters from all the rooms as well as the names of the occupants, and the OSS routinely checked the contents of hotel wastebaskets.[208]

At lunch one day, Herman was dining with a few of his buddies at the Grand Hôtel. They spotted two Germans at the next table and decided to play a familiar prank. The airmen began an animated discussion about some elaborate military plan. While they talked, Herman drew a map on a napkin in order to demonstrate his point. When the airmen had finished their lunch, he casually crumpled up the napkin and threw it on the table. As they walked away, Herman glanced back and watched one of the Germans grab the napkin and put it in his pocket.

When Herman arrived in Stockholm, he was fortunate to find an apartment with another of the internees. Their street was a short walk to the boulevard Strandvägen and the main offices of the American Legation. "We enjoyed the Swedish smörgåsbord, the light wines and the dark wines," Herman said. "It was incredible to be there. I'd sometimes close my eyes and wonder if I'd made it to heaven."

The Americans

The United States' diplomatic offices in Stockholm were known as the Legation of the United States of America or, in short, the American Legation. Today a similar function is fulfilled by the U.S. Embassy in Sweden.

Diplomat Herschel V. Johnson served as the American Minister to Sweden from December 12, 1941, until April 28, 1946. In this position, he was the official representative of the U.S. government. The chancery, or main office of the American Legation, was located on the magnificent boulevard Strandvägen at address 7A.

Count Folke Bernadotte and American Minister Herschel V. Johnson. 1944, Stockholm.

In the mid-1800s, this location was a swampy slum lined with shacks. The dirt paths were so impassable that it was often difficult to get from one point to another. Garbage thrown out in the streets emanated a foul stench.

Local visionaries imagined a grand tree-lined boulevard built along the waterfront. The hovels would have to be demolished. There was opposition, but plans were finally approved, and work began. The first houses were built during the early 1880s, and in 1907 construction began on the last, those at number 7.[209]

Designed by a leading architectural firm, Strandvägen 7 consists of three unified buildings known as A, B, and C. Rising seven-stories high, they are arranged in a U shape with 7B at the center rear behind a courtyard. Ornate corner towers straddle each side of 7A and one edge of 7C. Still standing today in the inner square is Eko, a large-as-life statue of a Roman nymph, sculpted by Gusten Lindberg.

The exterior façades of 7 were made of light plaster with elaborate limestone ornamentations around the windows, doors, and balconies, typical of the architect's favored Art Nouveau style. The interior was just as ornate. Craftsmen decorated the stairways with stained glass windows

Strandvägen 7 in 1944. (from the collection of Nicholas B. Kehoe, Jr.)

and bas-relief sculptures of draped young women adorned with fruit and flora. Even the elevator was a work of art, fashioned of polished wood and ornamental wrought iron.

Strandvägen 7 turned out to be perhaps the finest structure on one of the most popular streets in Stockholm. From the front, one could look out over the water toward the islands of Skeppsholmen and Djurgården. Boats pulled up to the edge of the promenade.

At this prime location, the American Legation established its home, with the chancery on an upper floor of building 7A. The office of Minister Johnson was in the corner tower, its view being the dome of Skeppsholmskyrkan, the 100-year-old church on the next islet. Behind Johnson's desk hung a framed image of Gilbert Stuart's unfinished portrait of George Washington.

The offices of the U.S. Military Air Attaché were next door in 7B. Housed just across the courtyard in 7C was the German Military Attaché. The German Legation was a ten-minute walk away, closer to the Grand Hôtel. The legations of other countries were nearby also. The Japanese Legation was at Strandvägen 25, and Britain's was farther on Strandvägen at number 82. Eventually, as the war progressed, Stockholm housed the only American diplomatic station in Northern Europe.[210]

From 1939 until the end of the war, the number of personnel at the American Legation grew from eight to over 400, although not all worked at the chancery. There were several annexes scattered throughout the same area of Östermalm, all within walking distance.

- Annex A at Nobelgatan 2 housed the Press Section and the Naval Attaché's office.
- Annex B at Bibliotecksgatan 26 was the Foreign Countries Division.

- Annex C at Kommendöragatan 16 was the Swedish Division with the Politico-Economic Division, Press Telegram Section, and Commercial Section.
- The Military Attaché's Finance office and the Military Air Attaché's Internee Section, Annex D, was nearby at Smålandagatan 2.
- Annex E was also on Strandvägen at number 63 and was the Financial Attaché's Office as well as the War Refugee Board.

The Kibre Section was at Strandvägen 59.[211] Dr. Adele Kibre headed the unit that collected written material from the Axis countries. By 1943, 20,000 pages per week were being sent to Washington, D.C.[212]

So it was at Strandvägen 7A, within the confines of the American Legation, the OSS set up their primary top-secret offices. In March of 1942, there was one Coordinator of Information agent assigned there. By fall, the COI had become the Office of Strategic Services, and Harvard Professor Bruce Hopper came to Stockholm as the first chief of station, OSS Sweden.[213]

Wilho "Ty" Tikander, a Finnish-American attorney, arrived in September to work as deputy under Hopper. Tikander's official cover was special assistant to Minister Johnson. Then during 1943, Tikander replaced Hopper as chief of the OSS mission, a position he held until the end of the war.[214] Bruce Hopper went on to become historian for the Eighth Air Force.

The main objective of the OSS Mission in Sweden was to disrupt its enemies, discover what they were doing and who was doing it, and wherever possible, sabotage their efforts. Because of Sweden's neutrality, it was important for the OSS to maintain anonymity for reasons of diplomacy and security.

Most OSS personnel worked under the cover of diplomatic positions. The Office of War Information, or OWI, was a U.S. government agency functioning out of the American Legation, its purpose being to create and deliver propaganda. Their efforts included printed materials, radio broadcasts, and movies supportive of the Allies. The OWI provided a convenient cover for several of the OSS personnel.

In the beginning, not everyone was happy about having "snoops" in their midst. Years later, Tikander wrote about the reception he received from Minister Johnson the first morning the two men met. Johnson warned Tikander that if anything should happen to reflect negatively on the integrity of the legation, he "would make it a point of going to the Swedish Foreign Office and request that Ty be declared persona non grata."

A calmer Johnson invited Tikander to be his guest at a dinner party where Ty was introduced to other officers of the legation. Military Attaché Col. Hugh Waddell asked Tikander, "What is the purpose of OSS sending special agents to Sweden? Aren't the American military authorities satisfied with the flow of information from the MA's office? What more do they want?"

Eventually, conditions improved. Col. Charles Rayens, who came to Sweden in early 1943, became American Military

Col. Charles E. Rayens, Stockholm 1944

Attaché and, according to Tikander, established good working relations between the OSS and his office.[215]

When Bernt Balchen arrived in Stockholm to set up his mission to fly 2000 Norwegian trainees from Stockholm to England, he was also subjected to the American minister's suspicions of anything that appeared clandestine. After Balchen explained his evacuation plans, the protective Johnson sternly warned him not to make any contacts that would embarrass the State Department. "As the highest American official here in Sweden, I want to know what is going on all at times. If I ever catch you doing anything illegal here, I'll have you deported."

"Don't worry, Mr. Minister," Balchen assured him. "You'll never catch me."[216]

One of the first secret agents was Roy V. Peel, who arrived in August 1942 and stayed until February of 1944. Peel had been a former visiting scholar in Sweden during the 1930s and re-established himself, renewing old contacts and making new ones. After he left Stockholm, Peel wrote detailed reports on field conditions of the OSS in Sweden, including his concerns about security and secrecy.

Keeping the outside world from knowing who was working for the OSS was a constant challenge. One of the concerns Peel expressed was the risk taken by the men and women who came to Sweden without diplomatic cover. They were under suspicion, he said, the minute they landed. Short-time visitors were followed wherever they went, perhaps by the Swedish police, perhaps by an operative from another country.[217]

In April of 1944, William "Bill" Carlson arrived to create the OSS counterespionage division X-2. His cover was commercial attaché, and he brought one secretary with him, Edith Rising. His other secretary, Hedvig Johnson, was still in London, working with Carlson's replacement at the Scandinavian desk. The first two candidates for his former job had been unsuitable, and until an acceptable replacement for him could be found, London refused to allow Hedvig to leave.

Carlson set up his offices in the legation's most remote corner. When he or Edith needed to send a memo to London or to Washington, one of them walked down the hall to the State Department code room. When a message came in for X-2, only Carlson or Edith would decode it. In the evenings, Edith came out into the main reception area to burn sensitive papers in the fireplace.

As commercial attaché, Carlson would be presumed to be in Sweden to promote the business interests of the United States. His international business background with the Elizabeth Arden cosmetic company gave his cover credibility.

In order to maintain at least some semblance of his cover, Carlson had to enter fully into legation social life. Even though he had an outgoing personality and loved to party, he was concerned about the amount of time socializing took away from his official duties. A second secretary to ease his workload was essential, and he sent another urgent request for the transfer of Hedvig Johnson from London to Stockholm.[218]

The counterintelligence unit X-2 was responsible for identifying enemy agents and their ties to subversive activities. Back in London, Hedvig had been compiling watch lists for some time. X-2 processed visas for Americans entering Sweden and also vetted non-American employees of the various U.S. installations.

The Swedes provided the OSS with photos and personal information of anyone coming into the country so they could be screened to identify Axis agents. This process included every German citizen who crossed the border in either direction. The Swedes also gave X-2 their blacklist of local citizens suspected of being pro-Nazi. By the end of the war, with Carlson's team adding names to the list, the number reached 3000. Up to 1000 visa applications per month were investigated, and anyone on the blacklist was denied legal entry to the country.[219]

One of Carlson's first directives was to evaluate the physical security of the legation offices. A detailed report indicated that, as Carlson had suspected, the guarding of the offices was not done properly. People were walking in and out with no effective control.

Furthermore, everyone had to assume that someone was listening in on their phone calls, most likely the Swedish Civilian Security Service.

German Legation flag at half-staff after Hitler's death in 1945.
(by Lennart af Petersens. Stockholm City Museum.)

In fact, by the end of the war, the Swedes claimed they had listened to over 11 million telephone conversations.[220]

Carlson hadn't been in Sweden long when he wrote a memo to X-2 London detailing that a reliable source had explained how the listening system worked in Göteborg and most likely in Stockholm too. Certain phones were controlled. At the main Telephone and Telegraph office on Kungsgatan, a controller picked up when a monitored phone was called. If the controller was busy when the phone rang, he caused it to be busy temporarily until he had time to listen in on the conversation.[221]

Because there were shops, businesses and residential apartments underneath and above the American Legation, each office was thoroughly searched for hidden microphones. None were found,[222] but at the time no special instruments were available for detecting listening devices hidden behind the walls or under the floors.

In agent Peel's field report, he disclosed suspicions that legation employees, with few exceptions, could be paid to pass along secrets. Carlson began to gather information on the 50 Swedish nationals working in the legation offices. Even though it was commonplace for Swedes to have business and family connections with Germany, some of the individuals were obvious security threats, and he had to dismiss them.

One employee, for example, until 1937 had been a member of a fascist organization in Norway. He had gone to Germany in 1941 to buy products for his business. After the Germans ordered him to work for a Third Reich military engineering organization, he fled to Sweden. One Saturday after his shift on guard duty, he took home a key to the legation annex at Kommendörsgatan 16. When he was telephoned about it, he said he couldn't immediately return to the legation because he was expecting guests. The key found its way back the following Monday morning.

To make matters even worse, the man had a relationship with a young lady whose uncle had once been married to the deceased first wife of Nazi leader Hermann Göring. This employee was the first to go.[223]

The Germans

The most obvious early player in the espionage game was Germany. Because of the country's long-standing business and social connections in Sweden, a percentage of Swedish citizens favored Germany, especially at the beginning of the war. Pro-German Swedes could be found in the armed forces, in the clergy, and in the police corps. Being pro-German wasn't the same as being pro-Nazi. Most Swedes were not Nazis, but the door to Nazi infiltration was wide open.

Long before war broke out, the Nazis began to set up fifth column networks in most countries, including Sweden. These were organized efforts to strengthen the doctrine of the Nazi regime while weakening the morale of the Swedish people to object to it.[224] According to one estimate, in the mid-1930s, there were approximately 30,000 members of various Nazi organizations in Sweden.[225]

No other country maintained as many offices in Sweden as did the Germans. The German Legation in Stockholm was one of the best staffed of any the Germans maintained.[226] It was housed in the Edelstamska huset at Hovslagargatan 2, a prime waterfront location near the Grand Hôtel. Until February of 1943, the German minister was Victor Prince zu Wied, an ardent Nazi. He was later replaced by tall and handsome Hans Thomsen, who had most recently been Germany's acting ambassador in Washington, D.C.

While in the United States, Thomsen received word that COI Director William Donovan had a proposition for him. Donovan proposed that the

German be paid $1 million to publicly renounce the Nazi government. Thomsen didn't take the bait.[227] The German diplomat's last official duty before leaving Washington was to deliver to the State Department his country's official declaration of war.[228]

The OSS reported that, once on duty in Stockholm, Thomsen could hardly keep up with the ever-expanding network of German intelligence agents coming into the country. He claimed they were hampering his official political work.[229]

Later, an American journalist wrote that Minister Thomsen complained that the interned Luftwaffe airmen, mostly fighter pilots, were not provided with the same comforts as the Allied crews.

Most of Germany's numerous offices were within walking distance of their legation. These included:

- Karlavägen 59 was German RadioCentral where the legation teleprinter was located.
- Karlavägen 99 housed the German Air Attaché.
- At Kaptensgatan 8 was German Information, Propaganda Minister Goebbels's local branch.
- Nybrogatan 27 is where the Abwehr, German counterintelligence offices were found.
- Across the courtyard from the American Legation at Strandvägen 7C, was the German Military Attaché.

One person on the German payroll was likely to have rubbed shoulders with Herman and Hedvig during the years of 1944 and 1945. All three dined in the same restaurants, walked the same streets and lived in the same neighborhoods. By the time the war was over, this young lady would interact with the Americans in a remarkable way.

Erika Wendt

The young lady was Erika Wendt, only a few years older than Hedvig when she came to work at the German Legation in Stockholm. Pretty and slender with dark eyes and light brown hair reaching to her shoulders, she looked even younger than her age. Her last name was the name of her ex-husband Jochen, a painter and art teacher. Their marriage had lasted only three years.

Erika's father had been editor-in-chief of a local newspaper in Germany. In 1933, the Nazis closed the newspaper down for appearing to be unsympathetic toward Hitler, and the family moved to a city on the south side of the Baltic Sea, across from Sweden. Erika could speak several languages besides her native tongue of German—Norwegian, Swedish, English, even some French and Spanish. Like Hedvig, the fact that she could speak these languages was an important reason she was hired by her government to work in Oslo, Norway, doing letter censorship.[230]

Erika and Hedvig would soon became counterparts in the Stockholm intelligence world, each working for a different side.

After a year in Oslo, Erika was ordered back to Berlin. There she was sworn in by Admiral Canaris, head of the German Abwehr, the group responsible for military intelligence gathering. In January of 1942, she was ordered to Stockholm to work for Dr. Hans Wagner, head of the German counterespionage organization known as Büro Wagner.

Wagner was housed in the German Legation under diplomatic cover and with approval from the Swedes.[231] It is easy to understand why the Swedish security services wanted to stay as close as they could to the Germans working in their country. It was to their advantage to know as much as possible about what the Germans were doing. When Wagner originally arrived at the legation, his charge was to "cooperate with the Swedish military intelligence in the neutralization of hostile intelligence organizations operating on the Swedish territory."[232] In other words, Wagner's job was to uncover enemy spies. He would never run out of potential suspects.

Erika did typing and shorthand, although she admitted that, particularly in the beginning, she was not good at either. Her supervisor was Dr. Wagner's secretary, the middle-aged Fräulein Alice Fischer. Before long, as seemed to be standard in her new office, Erika was calling Wagner "Papi" and his second in command, Captain Utermark, "Uncle Albert."

The diplomatic staff at the German Legation was not at all happy about the Abwehr sharing their building. In October of 1942, Erika moved with Dr. Wagner and company from the beautiful location on the water to an 1870s building at Nybrogatan 27. Their new office was a ten-minute walk away through Berzelii Park and down a busy road filled with shops, restaurants and apartments, the same streets where the American Legation employees walked each day.

Across the street, the congenial owner of a tobacco shop was hired by the Swedish secret police to keep an eye on things.[233] Since at the time most people used his products, he had a steady stream of customers. Many stopped in either before or after visiting the office at number 27.

Erika loved Sweden at once, a free country with no blackouts and no bombs. On her first day at work, she encountered Captain Hellmuth Ternberg,[234] a Swede she had previously met in Berlin. He was the intelligence officer who was second in command in Sweden's C-byrån.

Ternberg stopped by the German offices often and recognized the potential value of having a friend inside Büro Wagner. When the handsome and charming man invited Erika to dinner, even though she knew "Papi" would not approve, she accepted.

Before the year was over, Erika and Ternberg had developed a clandestine relationship, one of friendship and secrets. When Ternberg, or "Teddy" as he wanted her to call him, asked for snippets of information from the Abwehr folders, she complied. Erika had access to the names of German agents, the "V-men" who brought information about resistance activities in Poland, Norway, and Denmark. Many were Swedish businessmen, trusted in their communities.

She gave Teddy the name of Dr. August Finke, head of the Gestapo in Sweden, acting as assistant commercial attaché. Erika didn't understand why the Gestapo wanted to be in a neutral country. The Gestapo are dangerous here too, Teddy explained. They want to keep track of refugees, anyone who might be working against them. From then on, the Swedes kept Finke under surveillance.[235]

One of Ternberg's associates in the Swedish Security Police asked Erika to give him words and sentences copied from the coded telegrams coming to her office. He explained that these fragments could help the Swedes break the German code. Despite the great risk, she complied. Erika's love for Germany did not extend to any affection for the Nazi party.

The Swedes gave Erika a code name. "Onkel" they called her, or "Uncle." The name was, she learned, for her protection.[236]

The Office of the Military Air Attaché

When Herman arrived to work at the American Legation in April of 1944, he was assigned to the office of Lt. Col. Felix Hardison, military air attaché. Until trained personnel could be sent over from the U.K., all administrative work for the American airmen was done by internees themselves. Most were officers who, like Herman, were recruited from their respective camps and brought to Stockholm. This was all done with the approval of the Swedish government.

Eventually, a primary team of four internees worked together to take care of the needs of the American men spread out in camps all over the country. One of the four was Thaddeus C. "Ted" Borek, a navigator whose B-17 force-landed at Bulltofta airport on May 13, 1944. Borek was sent to Stockholm for a similar reason as Herman. Shortly after he settled in at the camp in Loka Brunn, he discovered a typewriter and a mimeograph machine. Ted began to put out a newsletter. The major in charge of the camp came to him one day and said, "I see you type."

"Yes sir," Ted replied, "and I also take shorthand."

The major asked Ted to type up a sensitive report to be sent to Stockholm. A couple of pilots had bailed out and left the crew behind in the bomber. Some of the crew did survive when the plane crashed. After the military air attaché got the report, he asked Ted to come work with Herman.

As Borek explained, he and Herman rarely came in contact with Hardison. The assistant military air attaché Maj. Arthur Conradi, Jr. was technically in charge of their small group, but "it was Herman Allen who ran the show," Borek said. Because of the extensive travel involved, Herman and Ted received extra diplomatic protection so they could travel all over Sweden, even into zones normally prohibited to foreigners.

Whenever an American crew made an emergency landing, one or two of the internee affairs team traveled to the crash site. They interviewed the crew and gathered the official details of what had happened. They oriented the newly arrived airmen to the rules of internship and directed them on to their next destination in one of the camps set up for the Americans.

The internee affairs team made a determination as to whether the detour to Sweden was absolutely necessary. Years later, Herman said,

Herman Allen at his desk.
Stockholm, 1944.

"More often than not these men were terrified. A couple times, we had to get them out of jail, where the Swedish military had put them for safekeeping."

In May, Herman was off on another assignment. Along with Capt. George Kelley, a navigator who force-landed in Sweden in November of 1943, Herman met with Swedish representatives about conditions at the internee camp Loka Brunn. Herman maintained there weren't only one or two complaints about the food, but 50 or 60. The Swedish report on this meeting stated that Lieutenant Allen found it outrageous that camp standards had not improved. The Swedes promised to improve the situation even if doing so would be costly. They were determined to demonstrate their value and good will in the matter.[237] Everyone he worked with was impressed at how assertive Herman was when it came to fulfilling the needs of the interned airmen.

One item extremely important to the Americans was cigarettes. Tobacco products were strictly rationed. The cigarettes that the legation managed to get were carefully allocated, and in some cases, the OSS personnel voluntarily gave up their rations to the agents in the field who could distribute them judiciously, especially if they were working in enemy territory. In one example, a Norwegian OSS agent skied into Norway on a secret mission. On his way back to Sweden, he was apprehended by a German border guard. The agent's life was saved with a package of Chesterfields offered as a gift to his captor.

In order for Swedish tobacco taxes not to apply, the Swedish Red Cross agreed to act as agent for the American cigarettes coming in from the U.S. or the U.K. One day, so many cigarettes arrived at the airfield that the customs official called OSS Mission Chief Tikander to inquire whether the American Legation was about to go into the tobacco business. As Tikander explained, the cigarettes were for the internees. One million cigarettes were not at all excessive, for there were over a thousand internees, adding up to five cartons per man.[238] Herman's responsibilities included carefully keeping track of the cigarettes and making sure they were distributed fairly.

At the end of the war, a military report detailed, "In charge of the Internee Section in general was Internee Adjutant 1st Lt. Herman F. Allen, a bombardier who, over a period of several months, succeeded in completely organizing a system capable of handling all problems. At the time of his appointment, Lt. Allen with his staff of selected internees promptly began the organization and development of sufficient administration to allow for the payment, discipline and health of every internee. His work in this respect is worthy of the highest commendation."

Escape and Evasion

In addition to the crews landing in Sweden, Allied airmen were slipping into the neutral country from the neighboring occupied countries of Denmark and Norway. Most of these airmen had barely avoided capture by the Germans after their crippled planes were forced to land, or worse yet, their crews had to parachute out. All in all, 50 Americans arrived in Sweden from Denmark, nine from Norway. Many local citizens risked their lives helping these men escape. In turn, the British and Americans in Stockholm provided much support to the underground resistance forces.

Whenever American airmen who had escaped or evaded capture arrived in Sweden, they were taken to Stockholm to be questioned by Herman Allen or another of the men working under Hardison. The first evader Herman questioned was 2nd Lt. Robert R. Kerr who flew out of Molesworth with the 303rd Bomb Group. He was co-pilot of the Howard J. Bohle crew, and on April 19, 1944, their target was Berlin.

Over the target, heavy flak knocked out an engine of their B-17, *Spirit of Wanette.* There was a severe gas leak in the number three tank. Pilot Bohle feathered the engine, but the gas remaining was insufficient to take them back to England. He asked the navigator, 2nd Lt. John K. Brown, for a heading to Sweden.

When the *Spirit of Wanette* crossed the Baltic Sea, the crew spotted land through a hole in the clouds. At the same time, an Me 120 attacked the plane. The enemy fighter was shot down by the tail gunner but must have radioed the ship's position to the antiaircraft batteries because a barrage of flak shot up. The plane was hit square, knocking out another engine. The flight control cables were severed. The pilot could not recover control, so he ordered the crew to bail out.

Co-pilot Kerr drifted away from the water and was able to land in an open field. He noticed a young boy watching him, and asked if this was "Svenske." The boy replied, no, it was "Danske," and warned that the Germans were close.

For the next several days, Kerr was assisted by members of the Danish Underground. He was taken to a harbor near Copenhagen where he joined nine Danes who were also on the run. One was a young man of 21 who had been condemned to death but then escaped from a prison near the city. The ten men boarded a small fishing boat and waited until 0620 hours when they proceeded cautiously from the harbor, avoiding German patrol boats in the vicinity.

At 1000 hours, once they were in international waters within sight of Malmö, a Swedish fishing boat took them to shore. The group was taken to the police station where Kerr was separated from the Danes, interrogated, and given a medical examination and ration coupons. He was then taken to the American Consulate office.

Kerr departed for Stockholm the next night and arrived around eight in the morning of May 11, 1944. Lt. Herman Allen met him at Central Station. Their first stop before heading to the American Legation was the Continental Hotel where the two men had a good breakfast.[239]

One of Kerr's first ventures was to go shopping for clothes, paid for by the American Legation. Herman generally took his business to the large Nordiska Kompaniet (NK) Department store. Before long, he was on a first name basis with the store manager.

When Herman formally questioned Kerr, the first thing he asked for was a recounting of the crew's mission, or as Herman put it, "Describe everything that happened in the plane before the jump." Kerr had learned from the locals in Denmark that four members of his crew were captured by the Germans, and three others had landed in the water and drowned.[240]

When Herman heard Kerr's story, he couldn't help but realize how easily his own crew could have suffered a similar fate. Both the *Liberty Lady* and the *Spirit of Wanette* had been hit by heavy flak over Berlin.

With engines knocked out, both flew over water trying to get to Sweden. When the *Liberty Lady* landed, Herman and his crew thought they were likely in occupied Denmark. What a close call it had been!

Robert Kerr was back in England on May 28. According to Article 13 of The Hague Convention (V) of 1907, "A neutral Power which receives escaped prisoners of war shall leave them at liberty." Those who escaped or evaded capture were not interned but were sent back to their bases as quickly as practically possible.

It was imperative the airmen who avoided capture in the occupied countries not talk with anyone about their experiences. Such talk furnished useful information to the enemy and could jeopardize future escapes, evasions, and releases. Those who helped airmen leave the occupied countries were in danger of being sent to prison or worse.

A resistance newspaper in Denmark carried a detailed story about an American crew that was forced to land in Denmark and then, with the aid of local citizens, escaped to Sweden. In the article, not only were the names of the airmen printed, there were also two photographs. The U.S. Military Intelligence Service was alarmed. The personnel at the legation, all officers, enlisted men, and civilian clerks, had to sign a certificate swearing to "maintain complete secrecy and refrain from publishing any article or book violating these orders, nor will I give to others any information which might be used by them for such purpose."[241] On the list was Internee Adjutant 1st Lt. Herman F. Allen.

The critical nature of this diligence would be confirmed by the fate of three Danes who helped Americans reach Sweden. One of the Danes was shot down and killed by the Gestapo on the City Hall Square of Copenhagen in May 1944. Another was executed in Copenhagen in February 1945. The third man, an important leader in a resistance movement, was executed in March of 1945.

Enemy Penetration

Internees from the various camps were routinely given three-day passes to go into Stockholm. Their headquarters while there was the Continental Hotel, across the street from the Central Station. The men were warned not to leave out any papers in their rooms. Hotel workers who were loyal to the Germans passed on anything they thought might be important.

The OSS kept detailed watch lists of suspected pro-Nazi meeting places and persons. They kept tabs on waitresses in key restaurants. Many such restaurants were in the same hotels the Americans tended to frequent—the Grand Hôtel, the Strand Hotel, the Castle, the Eden.[242] In his 1944 field reports, OSS agent Roy V. Peel emphasized, "No restaurant is safe."

One of the most notorious establishments was Regnbågen, near the public square Stureplan. A report from OSS files stated Gestapo agents had long been meeting there and were also regularly spotted at the popular confectioners shop OGO.[243] Both hangouts were a 15-minute walk north of the American and German Legations.

Herman reported that the owner of the Continental Hotel was known to have been an employee of "the Hitler organization."[244] Another report sent to OSS London and to Washington exposed the head maid at the Continental. The woman in question "formerly worked in the Tempo Store in Falun as a sales clerk, then she acted as cook at a hotel in Falun. She went on to Rättvik, where she taught the fliers Swedish."[245]

The internees, who always had money, frequented these nightspots, and the Germans were well aware of the weekend passes. Hungry for any information about the American Air Force, the Germans recruited women to frequent the most popular places and befriend these young men.

Before the Americans returned to their camps, Herman had the job of questioning them, recording who they had been with and what they talked about. After carefully compiling records of each debriefing, Herman soon discovered which names came up again and again. One such debriefing came from Sgt. George Dolan, an internee who arrived in Sweden three days after the *Liberty Lady.*

> SUBJECT: Suspect German Agent
>
> Subject has tried to pump Source about the following things.
>
> What job did Source have on his plane?
> How many U.S. planes are in Sweden?
> What condition are the planes in?
> How many U.S. fliers are there in Sweden?
> Are they ready for action?
> Do the U.S. planes bring much ammunition with them when they land in Sweden?
>
> It is to be noted that these questions are in direct line with instructions we know to have been given to other German agents who have been sent to Sweden.[246]

The number of instances of what the OSS called Airmen Penetration was increasing. Herman went to Bill Carlson, who confirmed that the suspects were likely German agents. From then on, at the beginning of their weekends in town, certain airman were instructed to pass on false or misleading information. Sometimes, Herman gave the airmen cameras so that, if appropriate, they could take pictures.

In a memo, June 17, 1944, Bill Carlson wrote to the head of OSS counterespionage in London:

SUBJECT: USAAF Internees in Sweden - Security

There are at present 520 interned U.S.A. flyers in Sweden...The U.S.A. airmen are naturally a good source of information for the enemy Air Intelligence. There is evidence of attempts on the part of certain suspicious persons to befriend the airmen. In order to be able to control the security of our interned airmen, we have arranged with the Air Attaché to have a security officer appointed for each group of airmen. Major CONRADI has been appointed Security Officer for Stockholm airmen, and the other appointments will be arranged shortly.

It will be the task of the Air Security Officers to continuously impress on the internees the absolute necessity for their observance of security at all times. Further, the Air Security Officers will obtain from the individual airmen the names and particulars of persons with whom they come in contact, together with any suspicious activities they may observe.[247]

1st Lt. Charles R. Huntoon had been a chemical engineer before he became a pilot with the 453rd Bomb Group at Old Buckingham airfield in England. On August 25, 1944, Huntoon and his crew flew the B-24 *Hoo Jive* to bomb a Focke-Wulf engine plant near Wismar,

Germany. After flak took out their number four engine, the B-24 fell out of formation and then another engine failed. Realizing they had become a prime target for enemy fighters, Huntoon headed for refuge in Sweden and made a perfect landing at Bulltofta.

Almost immediately, after learning about Huntoon's engineering background, the military air attaché recruited him to help with maintenance of the bombers stored at Såtenäs airfield. Huntoon became the air security officer assigned to process weekend passes for the men working with him. If Huntoon discovered an internee had been questioned about military matters, he forwarded a detailed statement to the legation. If there was anything particularly significant, Charles took the train to Stockholm and gave the report directly to Herman Allen.[248]

Herman and Folke Bernadotte

In his position as internee adjutant, Herman worked closely with Count Folke Bernadotte, the Swede primarily responsible for all interned airmen. Bernadotte asked Herman to call him "Folke," in Swedish pronounced with two syllables, "Folk-e." He preferred not to be addressed as "Count."

The two men quickly developed a professional rapport. Each was orderly and organized in his business affairs. A marked difference between the two was that Bernadotte drank sparingly because of his ulcer. Herman, on the other hand, rarely passed by the opportunity for what he called a "short snort."

Early in their relationship, Bernadotte suggested that Herman not mention he was Jewish to the Swedes and other foreigners he came across in his dealings. Because it would have been considered impolite for a Swede to directly question Herman about his religion,[249] it is likely that

Count Folke Bernadotte with Maj. Harley Robertson and Capt. Robert Robb, Stockholm 1945.

Herman brought up the subject during one of his early, and certainly private, conversations with Bernadotte.

Bernadotte's friendship with Herman, as well as his many humanitarian efforts to help the Jews, is evidence that this advice was not based on anti-Semitism. He knew about Herman's activities all over the country, and he anticipated that there could be prejudice.

At the time, Sweden's Jewish population was relatively small. All citizens were required to register with a church, and atheism was not an option. In the late 1930s, approximately 7000 Swedes called themselves Jews.

Anti-Semitism existed in Sweden just as it did almost everywhere. It was not unusual to find blatant anti-Semitic remarks in the writings and speeches of certain politicians and other well-educated upper-class Swedes.[250]

Yet, anti-Semitic feeling was not the case overall, and some Swedes began to protest Hitler's policies. In 1933, despite his lifetime of traditional pro-German sentiments, King Gustav V traveled to Germany to meet with President Hindenburg and to complain about the increasingly severe treatment of the Jews.

After 1938, as Hitler's persecution of Jews became unbearable, more and more Jews wanted to come to Sweden. As a neutral country, Sweden was a natural refuge, but because Sweden's immigration laws were so strict, few were allowed to enter.

Some of the practical reasons for the government to restrict immigration sound familiar today. How could the refugees be taken care of? Wouldn't they compete with an already difficult job market? Even physicians objected to competition from Jewish doctors coming into their country.

Then in October of 1942, Swedes were horrified when more than 700 Norwegian Jews were arrested and sent to their death in Poland. Over the following year, Sweden provided refuge to most of Norway's remaining Jews.

In late 1943, Jews from Denmark were able to escape to Sweden in a dramatic rescue effort. Hours before the Germans were scheduled to round up the Jews and ship them off to concentration camps, the Danish resistance went into action. Hidden by their fellow Danes and helped across the water, most of Denmark's 8000 Jews were saved. Amazingly, many German officials in the occupied country looked the other way.

Even though sentiments regarding the Jews may have officially softened in Sweden by 1944, in some parts of the population anti-Semitism was bubbling under the surface. It was a hard time to be a Jew in Europe. Herman took Bernadotte's advice. Had he ignored the counsel of his new friend he would have had a very different experience during the next several months.

Social Shadows

An important activity for the members of the OSS, under the supposed protection of their cover identities, was to go out in the evenings and socialize. Depending on the assignment, a covert engagement might take place in a trendy Stockholm restaurant or in a more clandestine meeting place.

Herman and Swedish colleague at front door of the Military Air Attaché's Internee Section, Annex D, Smålandagatan 2.

Swedes purchased alcohol by using a rationing system. Each person was given a motbok, a booklet to be stamped each time a purchase was made in the official store, the Systembolaget. This arrangement had been going on since 1917, the Swedish government trying to limit the harmful effects of alcoholism as much as possible.

The Americans were always looking for ways to get around the system. Shortly before D-Day, General Eisenhower issued an Order of the Day forbidding officers in the European Theater of Operations from importing hard liquor.

For the Americans in Sweden, however, whiskey flowed freely. Technically, neutral Sweden was not part of the European Theater. Bottles were either shipped or flown in and, years later, Mission Chief Tikander explained how difficult it was to keep track of all the alcohol. "Considering the fact that many of the meetings with agents or cut-outs (intermediaries in clandestine operations) occurred at night and that it was necessary to consume varying amounts of liquor, there were bound to develop accounting deficiencies."[251] Liquor was a significant element of the secret intelligence work. A jigger or two of whiskey helped the OSS agents relax their subjects who might otherwise have no intention of revealing secrets.

Shortly before the end of the war, a warning was issued to the commissioned and clerical members of the staff, signed by the legation consul Christian M. Ravndal, who had arrived in Stockholm in 1943. He had a rich Foreign Service career and worked well with the members of the OSS.

> You will shortly be informed that you may place another two months liquor order through the Commissary. In this connection I regret to advise you that the Foreign Office has complained about the excessive liquor orders, that it has implied that legation personnel have ordered liquor for their friends who are not entitled to the free entry privilege, and that it has warned all legations that if the liquor orders are not substantially reduced the Swedish Government will have to stop approving them. The reason for this is that there is very little liquor left in Sweden, and under existing conditions there is no possibility of Sweden's replenishing its stocks.
>
> It creates bad feeling when our consumption is obviously out of proportion to that of the Swedes. Please, therefore, make your order small, keeping in mind the possibilities of your Motbok; and remember if we do not get teamwork in this matter we shall be put on Motbok rations.[252]

Soon after Herman arrived in Stockholm, he eased into the legation's social circuit of evenings out, parties in hotels, and readily available liquor. He made friends quickly and was at his best when working the crowd.

It was common knowledge which restaurants and hotels were hangouts for the Nazis or had staff sympathetic to them. Erika Wendt and her German associates frequented all the same watering holes as Herman and his American friends. The most popular were Berns, the Strand, Bellsmanro, and the Grand Hôtel.

When members of the legation were out on the town, everyone knew the rules: Listen a lot, and don't talk about anything sensitive. If you are with someone who may be sympathetic to one of our enemies, remember what they say, what questions they ask, and write it up later to add to their file. Don't ever give them anything they can add to their file on you.

When Felix Hardison came to Stockholm as military air attaché, he rented a flat at Karlaplan 10, half a mile from the legation. The building, ornate with arched windows and a corner tower, faced a popular park featuring a circular pool with a fountain in the center.

Hardison's flat had previously been sublet to the Chilean singer named Rosita Serrano. Amelia, the resident maid, had been her maid, and the two women continued to speak on the phone.

Amelia mentioned to Rosita that Hardison was making plans to host a large cocktail party at his apartment in honor of the new assistant military air attaché, Major Conradi. Rosita begged her former maid to find a way to get her into the party.[253]

Born in Chile in 1914 as Maria Martha Esther Aldunate Del Campo, Rosita Serrano was a beautiful brunette singer and an actress. Her mother was a well-known Chilean opera singer, and her father was a diplomat. In the early 1930s, Rosita moved to Europe, getting work here and there. In 1936 she settled in Germany where she became well known, popular not only with the soldiers on the front but also with many of the high-ranking Nazis. Her German record company marketed her as the "Chilenische Nachtigall," the Chilean Nightingale, for the clear soprano timbre of her voice accented by distinctive whistles and trills.

According to OSS reports, Rosita had once been Hitler's guest for dinner. On April 1, 1943, she sang at the home of Hermann Göring, head of the Luftwaffe, and received an exceptional diamond bracelet as a gift. Göring assured her that in all personal and political matters she would receive his private protection.[254]

Later in 1943, Rosita traveled to Sweden with her mother on tour. She sang in a concert, the proceeds of which were used to benefit Jewish refugees who had been persecuted by the Nazi regime. Because of her support for the Jews, the Germans accused her of being a spy and banned her music and her films. Heinrich Himmler, head of the Gestapo, issued a warrant for her arrest, and she was unable to return to Germany until years later.[255]

In an April 1945 letter to the Ministry of Foreign Affairs in Santiago, Chile, Rosita wrote that she could speak and sing in Swedish, Finnish, and Russian. She owned a country house 20 minutes out of Stockholm, surrounded by a big park on the banks of the river Mellan. Obviously, the Swedes were reading her mail; this letter was postmarked from the Grand Hôtel.

Sure enough, Rosita showed up at Hardison's party along with her manager, Gustav Wally. Wally's real name was Gustav Axelsson Wallenberg of the prominent Swedish banking family. Wally didn't go into the family banking business, instead choosing the field of entertainment. In 1944, he was manager of the Oscarsteaterns, the "Academy Award Theater" in Stockholm.[256]

Before they left Hardison's apartment, Rosita and Wally invited the host to attend an after-party at Bellmansro restaurant on Djurgården, the park-like island east of Old Town. Like so many other establishments,

Rosita Serrano and Gustav Wally. 1945. (Author unknown. Source Nycop, Carl-Adam.)

it was popular with both the Americans and with Stockholm's pro-Nazi crowd.

Hardison wisely declined the invitation, but others at his party did not. They hurried to comply. In attendance at the party hosted by Rosita were none other than Herman Allen and Charles W. Smith.

Herman made a beeline for the most beautiful woman in the room, Miss Serrano. When he finally introduced her to Smithy, they talked about her music, in particular *Estrellita*, the Mexican ballad she had recorded in Berlin. Most likely, she did not confide to the two Americans that this was a song she sang during a tour of the Wehrmacht as she entertained the German soldiers.

Afterward, Allen typed a report for the OSS.

SUMMARY OF EVENTS OF THE EVENING OF THE 20TH OF MAY 1944

I arrived at Col. Hardison's cocktail party at 10 Karlaplan the 20th of May 1944 at approximately 18:30 hours. Along with other guests, I was introduced to Miss Rosita Serrano and her manager, Mr. Gustav Wally. During the course of the conversation, she suggested to Wally that Lt. Smith, who was also at the same party, and I be invited to a dinner party at Bellmansro later in the evening. We arrived at Bellmansro at approximately 20:00 hours where we were joined by Mr. Geo Axelson of the New York Times, Consul Lönnegren and his wife. Champagne, Schnapps, and wine were distributed freely along with an excellent dinner. The conversation was general throughout the evening except for a few instances. At one time, I found myself alone with Miss Rosita Serrano, about half-way through the evening.

She motioned me to sit closer, then started to talk about nothing in particular, finally leading up to the following questions (as close as I can remember) "How long have you been in Sweden?" I remember replying that I was here yesterday, I am now, and I expect to be here tomorrow. She laughed and made some remark about my being clever. She then wanted to know the type of a plane I flew in. I told her it was a big job which dropped "eggs" on the "Jerry." She then started talking about her music and forthcoming opening of her show.

The subject was brought around to my home in the states. She wanted to know where I lived there, and how long since I had been home. I told her I came from Washington, and it had been quite a while since I had been there. We started talking about the relative merits of Washington State and Washington, D.C. As I recall, soon after this she wanted to know how many missions I had participated in and over what occupied countries. I told her I was not supposed to discuss such matters, and before we could continue further, Mr. Lönnegren and his wife returned to the table. He asked Rosita to dance, which terminated our two-some conversation.

The party concluded about 23:00 hours at which time we were invited for a drink at the home of George Levin, Strandvägen 59. As I remember, Mr. Levin approached Wally just as we were leaving the restaurant with this invitation. Consul Lönnegren and his wife and Axelson begged off due to the lateness of the hour, so Lt. Smith, Rosita, Wally, Levin and myself proceeded by taxi to the Levin residence.

We met several other people at the house, but nothing unusual occurred except liquor flowed freely and everybody was in a jovial mood. Above information is what occurred on the evening mentioned to the best of my memory.

Signed,
Herman F. Allen
1st Lt. A.C.
Internee Section[257]

True to form, Herman was proving to those in the OSS that he was at home in the Stockholm social scene and was capable of easily conversing with, charming, and earning the trust of those around him.

Because of Rosita Serrano's reported history with the Nazi leadership, she was already on the OSS watch list. Bill Carlson was interested in the fact that she questioned Herman about military matters and wanted to develop the case further. Carlson's primary focus, however, was on another guest at Rosita's Bellmansro party, and that person was Consul Lönnegren.

Dr. John Lönnegren

John Alexander Lönnegren, at 65 years old, was known as an independent Swedish businessman. Because he had obtained his doctorate degree, he was occasionally referred to as "Dr. John Lönnegren," and that is what his business card read.

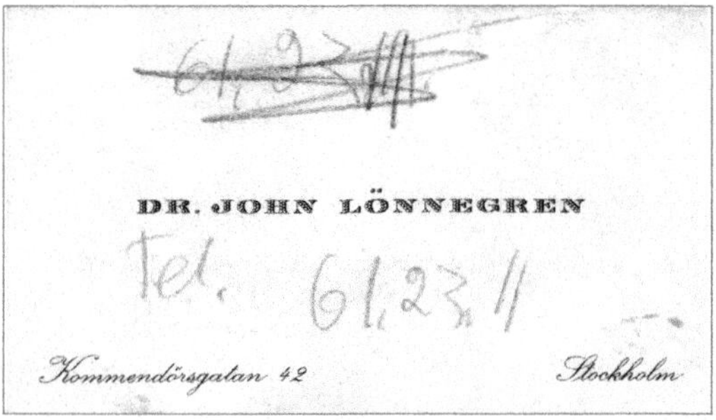

Lönnegren's business card.

Lönnegren was a nice-looking older gentleman, five feet, nine inches tall. His hair had grayed, and because he often wore a hat, his receding hairline may not have been obvious to those he passed on the street. His double chin and corpulent frame were indications of how much he enjoyed cocktails and fine dining in the Stockholm restaurants. He resembled the famous American comedian W.C. Fields when he let go with a big belly laugh. Like Herman, Lönnegren liked to work the crowd. He was easy to talk to and enjoyed sitting down with strangers for schnapps and a chat.

From 1910 to 1913, Lönnegren was Berlin Correspondent of *Svenska Dagbladet*, a daily newspaper in business since 1884. While he lived in Germany, he obtained his doctorate degree in law and political science at the University of Greifswald. In 1916, Lönnegren took a position on the editorial staff of *Aftonbladet*,[258] a Swedish evening paper with German connections. It was at the top of the OSS list of pro-Nazi Swedish newspapers.

For a time, Lönnegren was the owner of an import firm in Stockholm and traveled to Asia, Africa and America on business. In 1924, Lönnegren was named Brazilian vice-consul. From 1931 until 1942, he was publicity agent for the Brazilian Consulate.

In 1938, the Scandinavian Telegram Bureau (S.T.B.), a Swedish news agency with ties to Berlin, was established in Stockholm and supplied German propaganda. From 1938 to January 1941 Dr. Lönnegren was its man in charge.[259]

According to an OSS report, the S.T.B. supplied the press with news at a cheap rate. Its subsidiary in Amsterdam became the only news agency able to function after German occupation there. "It has no compunction in falsifying a London or New York dateline whenever convenient," the report read.[260]

The British Secret Intelligence Service (whose cover was Passport Control Office) revealed in 1941 that Lönnegren was involved in a scheme for making money through arranging faked marriages for German Jewish women in order to obtain Swedish nationality for them.

Then in 1943, Lönnegren's name came up in a Michigan Grand Jury report about a U.S. spy ring sending war information to Germany. The head of this ring was Grace Buchanan-Dineen, an attractive 34-year old Canadian woman descended from French nobility. FBI Director

J. Edgar Hoover disclosed that she had been carefully trained by the Germans in espionage work. On August 24, 1943, the Associated Press reported that Dineen obtained information on the "capacity of the Ford Motor Co. in manufacturing war material, the safety of construction of such plants against sabotage, the safety of construction of the plants against airplane attack and bombing and the operation plans of the United States by which military airplanes departed from this country for battle fronts."

Lönnegren was named in the report as one of several co-conspirators intending to commit offenses against the United States by establishing and maintaining addresses for the purpose of receiving material and information to be forwarded to the government of the German Reich.[261]

In 1944, despite the fact that Lönnegren was no longer officially and legitimately working, he was often referred to by his former titles such as "Press Officer of the Brazilian Legation" or "Brazilian Consul."

Bill Carlson asked Hedvig Johnson, who was still working in London, to send him information on the cover addresses used by Grace Buchanan-Dineen. One was Kommendörsgatan 42, the alleged home of Dr. John Lönnegren.[262] To no one's surprise, Lönnegren was high on Carlson's watch list of those suspected of having close connections with the Nazis. Lönnegren was also being closely watched by the Swedish police.

Carlson alerted Herman to be on the lookout for Lönnegren, frequently seen in the popular Stockholm restaurants, and to report any interactions the Swede might have with interned airmen. Lönnegren had been seen in the company of Robert Paulsson (also spelled Paulson[263]), a Swede who held an important position in the government department that kept track of foreigners coming into and out of the country.[264]

Early in 1944, John Lönnegren visited the Abwehr office at Nybrogatan 27. He was introduced by "Uncle Albert" Utermark to Erika Wendt, and before he left their office, Lönnegren asked Erika to have dinner with him. She accepted reluctantly when she learned that he wanted her to come to his apartment on Kommendörsgatan. He reassured her that his housekeeper would be there all evening.[265]

She did go to the apartment on Kommendörsgatan, only a ten-minute walk from her office at Nybrogatan 27. After a pleasant meal, Erika was dismayed to see the housekeeper leave the premises. Sensing that his guest was uneasy, Lönnegren at first kept the conversation going with small talk, but then he began to ask more personal questions. At this point, the young lady politely excused herself, explaining she needed to be up early the next morning. When her Swedish officer friend Ternberg heard about this dinner, he made her promise never to see Lönnegren again.[266]

All this time, Erika was continuing to give bits of information to the Swedes. One of the most inflammatory was the name of a Swedish official in the Aliens Commission, the agency responsible for registering all foreigners, issuing visas and work permits.[267] This person, Robert Paulsson, was providing the Germans with lists of refugees in Sweden.

As an added measure of protection, Ternberg informed the Swedish police chief about Erika's tenuous situation. When she had inevitable pangs of guilt, Erika only had to remind herself that the Third Reich was not her Germany.

As spring arrived, Erika became ill, coughing and sweating at night. She feared that the cause was tuberculosis, the same condition that had killed her father the year before. Soon her fear was confirmed by x-ray. When he heard the news, "Papi" Wagner immediately made arrangements for her to go back to Germany for treatment.

As soon as Ternberg discovered what was happening, he warned Erika that she would be going straight into the arms of the Gestapo.

He was correct. What Erika did not realize was that Dr. Wagner had become suspicious of her activities.

The Swedes devised a plan. She would suddenly become too ill to travel and be forced to enter a local hospital. It was the third day of June, 1944.[268]

Overlord

The Allies were finally ready to face Hitler on the beaches of France. In numbers, their ground forces were severely outmanned by the Germans, nearly ten to one. The Allies' advantage was their almost total air superiority.

The Germans knew an invasion was coming and were focused on uncovering exactly where and when. The Allies were just as focused on misleading them. The code name for the invasion was Overlord, and the code name for the deception plan was Fortitude.

The foundation for this complex ruse was already in place. German spies who had infiltrated Great Britain had been captured and turned into double agents by the British Secret Service. Working under creative code names such as Zigzag, Garbo, Chopin, and Tricycle, some of the double agents had been feeding misinformation back to the Germans for years, always under direct supervision of the British. As a follow-up and unknown to the enemy, the British code breakers at Bletchley Park were able to intercept and read German communications.

One false notion transmitted to the Germans was that the Allies would first send forces to Norway, and then the main attack would come later at Pas-de-Calais, the shortest route across the English Channel. This location was where most of the German high command thought the invasion would take place.

As part of the Allies' deception plan, dummy landing craft were installed in southern England to confirm the reports of the double agents. Phantom wireless radio traffic created an entire American Army group in southeast England preparing to cross over to Pas-de-Calais. The actual destination of its commander, the notable Gen. George Patton, was Normandy.

The British built a fake oil dock across the Channel from Pas-de-Calais, and even the king inspected it. An actor who looked like Field Marshall Bernard Montgomery was sent off to Gibraltar. When word got back to the Germans that the commander in charge of all the Allied ground forces was away from England, they were confident the invasion would not be anytime soon.[269]

There was even a German agent in Sweden, Carl Heinz Krämer, whose faulty intelligence corroborated the Pas-de-Calais story. Known by the code names Josephine and Hektor, he was a member of the Abwehr, posted in Stockholm since November of 1942. Fortunately, the Germans had faith in his reports.[270]

As the day of the invasion neared, arms and ammunition were parachuted into France. Specially trained three-man teams, code-named Jedburgh, were dropped behind enemy lines two days ahead of the projected invasion date. These teams were generally comprised of one man from the OSS, one from Britain's Special Operations Executive (SOE) and one French officer. Their mission was to link up with the local Resistance, the Maquis, to wreak havoc on the Germans. The Jedburgh teams blew up railway lines and bridges, sabotaged communications, and cut telephone lines. As a result, German headquarters had to communicate with their radios, giving the codebreakers in England a much easier way to intercept and translate the German's military plans.

There were close calls. In case they heard Germans with dogs, the Jedburghs were taught to urinate around the trunk of a tree to throw off the scent and then climb the tree. The operation was a huge risk because these fighters knew the final plans for the invasion, and their capture would be catastrophic. It was critical that Hitler believe the landings would come farther north so that he would keep his best divisions one hundred miles away.[271] Operation Jedburgh was a success, and the Germans were stalled. These heroic men were predecessors to today's U.S. Army Special Forces.

On June 6, 1944, American internees in Rättvik listened to the invasion news on their radio stations. William S. Dixon from the Turisthemmet Hotel heard a German announcer erroneously describe how Allied troops were being repulsed and thrown back into the English Channel.

The international press correspondents at the Grand Hôtel in Stockholm were at the bar, scrambling for news bits. Hedvig Johnson, at London's OSS office on Ryder Street, waited impatiently along with everyone else as the official reports began to come in. Overlord was the beginning of the end for Germany's Third Reich.

Hedvig E. Johnson

Herman spent his first few months in Stockholm traveling back and forth to sites where the American air crews were making emergency landings. As the crews' missions were taking them deeper and deeper into Germany, the numbers of badly damaged planes forced to divert to Sweden were increasing.

By the time August arrived, Herman was working overtime to get all his reports written and typed. Fellow internee Ted Borek helped as much as he could, but between the forced-landing reports and the weekend espionage reports, neither man could keep up. Herman told

Bill Carlson he desperately needed a secretary, preferably one who could speak Swedish, since Herman could not. Carlson reassured him that help was on the way.

Finally, a replacement for Carlson at X-2 London was in place, as well as one for Hedy. As soon as she got the go ahead for Stockholm, Hedy had to spend two weeks in Scotland waiting for the weather, the foggier the better, to be suitable for a trip over the German-patrolled skies of Norway. Finally, on August 11, she left for Sweden.

Hedy traveled with a gentleman whose name was coincidentally John J. Johnson, American-born of Danish descent, on "official business for the U.S. government." On the OSS memo noting approval of their exit visas, the name of Hedy's hometown was circled. "Highly suspected as a hotbed of activity" were the words scribbled over "Hibbing, Minnesota."

Many of the iron ore workers in Hibbing, having endured often dangerous working conditions during the terrible Depression, were ripe candidates for radical political parties to recruit. The immigrants supported socialist and communist groups they believed would end injustices.

The notation would have been no surprise to Hedy. Her Uncle Charlie was a member of the Communist Party. Perhaps the OSS knew that too.

But Hibbing politics were far from Hedy's thoughts. After the months at Ryder Street

William C. Carlson, Stockholm 1944.

and after enduring the bombings in London, Hedy was ecstatic to be going to Sweden. It would be wonderful to be working for Bill Carlson again.

She flew to Stockholm in one of Bernt Balchen's unarmed B-24s. Bench-type seats had been installed lengthwise along both sides of the waist area. The route over Norway was not direct but would avoid the antiaircraft guns and fighter planes. When the plane landed at Bromma, the airport on the west side of Stockholm, Hedy and her traveling companion were met by a man from the American Legation.

As their taxi drove to the center of town, Hedy was amazed to see a city intact. There were no bombed-out buildings, no balloon barrages. As in London, few cars were on the road. Instead, she saw hundreds of bicycles. Along the grassy strips up and down the streets were towering stacks of firewood. As Hedy soon learned, wood was a precious commodity and was strictly rationed.

Grateful that she had taken the Berlitz Swedish language course while in London, she encouraged the taxi driver to talk about the neighborhoods and the elaborate buildings they passed. Listening to him speak was much like listening to her parents, whom she hadn't seen for well over a year. They had no idea she was no longer in England.

The driver came to a stop at Strandvägen 7, in front of the beautiful waterfront buildings. Their escort jumped out and opened the door for her and gestured toward the boats pulled right up to the road.

The three walked through a tall iron gate marked with a round sign, "Legation United States of America." They climbed up the ornate curved staircase to the door of the chancery. The receptionist, upon hearing their names, immediately called Bill Carlson to the main lobby. He gave Hedy a big hug. She reciprocated enthusiastically, saying "I can't believe I'm finally here!"

As they walked back to his office, Bill introduced Hedy to everyone they passed. When they stepped into the smaller office next to his, Hedy was thrilled to see Edith Rising again. The two made plans for Hedy to stay temporarily in Edith's apartment, a short bus ride north of the legation.

Bill, eager to orient Hedy to Stockholm and its environs, took her on one of the city's steamboat tours. He told her about the Stockholm archipelago, the cluster of many thousands of islands to the east of the city where he hoped he could live someday.

Hedy bought a Stockholm guidebook and began to mark with her pencil all the locations she found significant. The apartment she shared with Edith, Stureparken 3, faced a small city park. Hedy realized she needed a place of her own, but in the meantime this spot was wonderful.

South of Stureparken was Stureplan, a city square with its restaurants, shops, and cinemas. At night, the area was brightly lit with dazzling neon signs. After being in blacked-out London for months, walking through Stureplan was a spectacular experience.

In the square was "Svampen," a ten-foot-tall sculpture that looked like a mushroom. Everyone knew exactly where it was, so it was customary to tell a friend to meet "under the mushroom."

Also near the mushroom was Sturebadet, the palatial public bathhouse where Hedy could enjoy a Turkish bath and get a massage. Since apartments didn't typically have bathing facilities, it was a popular destination for Swedes and visitors alike.

It didn't take long for Hedy to adapt to the whirlwind of activity at the legation. There were so many people to meet. Several clerks who worked in the office were Swedes, and she was able to converse easily with them. She enjoyed talking to Wilho Tikander, the head of the OSS. Both their families were from Finland. Furthermore, Ty, as she learned to call him, had grown up in the iron ore ranges of northern Minnesota. His father had operated a country store in a town 25 miles from Hibbing.

One unforgettable person Hedy on met her first day was an American internee named Herman Allen. Bill introduced her, "Herman, this is the person you've been waiting for. She can understand, speak, and write Swedish, and she can help you with your typing."

According to Herman, he took one look at this beautiful brunette and thought to himself, "You're for me!"

Hedy liked the handsome outgoing American officer at once, but Edith quickly filled her in on Herman's reputation with the ladies. "Herman is a lot of fun," Edith said, "but watch out. He flirts with everybody."

So Herman did the debriefing of the internees, and Hedy did the typing. As Herman admitted later, "The only bad thing—well, maybe the good thing—was in order to test these German girls, the men might have to go all the way with them, if you know what I mean. And I had to write it up when they came back. The code was 'will shack' or 'won't shack.' Hedy had to type up whatever it was."

Plots Thicken

A few days after Hedy arrived in Stockholm, Herman was working in his office at Annex D, the Military Air Attaché's Internee Section located at Smålandsgatan 2. Wally Olsen, a legation employee, walked in and asked for a private interview. Herman detailed the conversation in his report for Carlson, X-2.

Wednesday, August 16, 1944

… After passing the time of day for a few minutes, Wally Olsen brought up the subject of LÖNNEGREN in the following manner.

He had a slip of paper with LÖNNEGREN'S name on it, and he asked me if I recognized it. I told him no. Then he said, "Are you in a position to contact each internee as they come into Stockholm on a pass?" I replied that all internees had definite orders to sign in at this office immediately upon arrival in Stockholm.

He said he wanted me to warn each man of LÖNNEGREN. He was a Nazi sympathizer and went around making friends with the internees, later taking them up to his apartment, filling them with liquor and pumping any information he could out of them. At this point, I asked him where he obtained this knowledge. He hemmed and hawed for a few seconds and then as he was fidgeting with the slip of paper he had in his hand, I noticed the name of Eldon Posey on the other side. I immediately asked him what connection POSEY had with LÖNNEGREN. He replied that POSEY had been invited to LÖNNEGREN'S apartment and had left his raincoat there. I asked Wally, "How do you think I could manage to see this man so I could recognize him to warn the internees in case they see him?" He suggested I go to LÖNNEGREN and request POSEY'S raincoat and thus meet him.

I asked him again where he obtained this information. He said he didn't want it to go any further, but he had obtained it from the Swedish Police. I asked him if he knew of anyone else being at LÖNNEGREN'S apartment other than POSEY. He said he had heard of several other Americans being there. I pressed him for names, but he didn't have any.

I asked if LÖNNEGREN was married, and he replied he did not know but it was quite possible. He said LÖNNEGREN had plenty of liquor at his apartment. Where he got it, Wally did not know but LÖNNEGREN always seemed to have plenty of money to throw around. It appears that one of LÖNNEGREN'S favorite hangouts is Blanch's and it was there he approached the Americans, talked to them, and then casually invited them up to his apartment.

End of Report by Herman F. Allen[272]

Eldon E. Posey

1st Lt. Eldon E. Posey, a fighter pilot with the 9th Air Force, 354th Fighter Group, landed his P-51 Mustang *Z Hub* in Sweden on May 13, 1944. By the time he arrived in Sweden, Posey had already participated in some of the most brutal campaigns of the war in North Africa and Sicily. He had been placed on special assignment with the Navy in September 1942 to test P-40 fighter plane takeoffs from an aircraft carrier. While on service with the Navy, Posey was trained in navigation and map making.

In September 1943, Posey went to the 56th Fighter Squadron, 54th Fighter Group in Bartow, Florida. A special photo-reconnaissance unit was put together there to train fighter pilots to pinpoint primary targets for the Air Force bombers in Europe.

On his return to Europe, Posey's first photo-reconnaissance assignment was Peenemünde, an island in the Baltic Sea off the northeast coast of Germany. This island is where Germany was building two new powerful weapons, the V-1 and V-2 rockets, soon to ravage London.

Then on February 18, his group took photos of the military factories at Leipzig. Two days later the Eighth Air Force sent 400 four-engine bombers to attack the targets in the areas photographed. This attack happened to be Herman's eighth mission.

In April, Posey was named operations officer of his fighter group, the 354th. By this time all efforts were focused on plans for Overlord. In mid-May, the photo reconnaissance unit met to review the 1943 landings on the beaches in Italy in order to glean as much information as possible in preparation for the landings at Normandy.[273]

The book *Making for Sweden, Part 2*, which chronicles each U.S. Army Air Force crew that arrived in Sweden, specifies that at 1417 hours on May 13, 1944, Posey landed at Rinkaby Airfield, nearly 60 miles northeast of Malmö. The book notes, "The pilot declared he had landed in Sweden due to a lack of fuel."[274] In his report made to the American Military Attaché, Posey further explained that he was being chased by about 20 German Me 109s.[275]

Years later Posey wrote about his wartime experiences. His editor noted, "E.E. Posey disputed the accuracy of this article but would not elaborate, explaining he had been ordered to never discuss the experience."[276]

When he landed, Posey wasn't sure whether he was in a German-occupied country, so to be in Sweden was a huge relief.[277] His first stop was the barbed-wire enclosed Främby camp in Falun where he was processed. After a short time, he was assigned to Rinkaby to make out accident reports for American planes forced to land there. His own P-51 ended up being used by Felix Hardison as his own.[278]

On June 6, Posey was officially released from his internment and traveled to Stockholm to wait for a plane ride out of the country. He had been in Sweden only 24 days. When the Air Force discovered where Posey was, it is likely they did everything they could to get this valuable officer out of Sweden as quickly as possible.

Posey's orders for leaving were to dress in civilian clothes and fly to Leuchars, Scotland, with Bernt Balchen's Operation Sonnie courier service of B-24s. As always, he had to wait until the weather was bad enough to fly over occupied Norway unnoticed. In the meantime, Posey resided at the Continental Hotel.

Most likely, while waiting for the weather to turn, Posey and the pilot who was to fly him out went to dinner at Blanch's Café. From the time it first opened its doors in 1868, Blanch's had been a popular destination, featuring music at noon and in the evenings. By the 1940s, with new ownership, the dining and dancing still attracted a lively crowd. Located on Hamngatan at the corner of the large park, Kungsträdgården, it was a convenient location for the legation employees as well as for airmen who were staying at the Continental. It was just as popular for the Germans.

The date was Midsummer, a day of great celebration for Swedes. While Lieutenant Posey and the pilot were enjoying their drinks and dinner, they began to converse with a friendly Swedish businessman who invited them to his home for drinks. His apartment was only a 20-minute walk from the café. Why not? There were two of them, and it was a grand time to celebrate.

Spionen Börjar (The Spy Begins)

During Posey's sojourn in Stockholm, he and Herman had spent time together. It was easy for Herman to confirm the exact date of the pilot's departure. On June 27, Posey had flown out from Bromma and arrived in Scotland the next morning.[279]

Although he didn't indicate as much to Wally Olsen, Herman was aware of Lönnegren's name on the OSS watch list, and he remembered meeting the Swede a few months earlier at Hardison's apartment. After Herman took this information to Bill Carlson, the two of them made a plan for Herman to get to know Lönnegren better. Herman made a phone call to Dr. Lönnegren. Posey's raincoat gave him the perfect excuse.

SUBJECT: Dr. John Lönnegren

Wednesday afternoon, 16 August 1944, I called Dr. John Lönnegren on the phone requesting the return of Lt. Posey's raincoat which he had left there on the night of 21 June 1944. He invited me to dinner Friday night saying I could pick it up then.

I rang his doorbell at 1900 hours, 42 Kommendörsgatan, and was met by his maid Anita. As I entered the front room I met Lönnegren. I had a momentary surprise, for I thought I had met him before at a party at Bellmansro (restaurant) 20 May 1944, but I found I was mistaken.

We listened to the Swedish news, and he translated as it came over the air. The maid brought in a drink which we sipped before sitting down to an excellent meal consisting of smörgåsbord, lamb chops, raspberries, schnapps, beer, and cognac. I refrained from drinking too much with the excuse that I was duty officer at the legation starting at midnight. During the course of the dinner, we talked on many things. He appeared sympathetic to the Allied cause and made continual reference to the fact that they were making strong gains on all fronts, that he was pleased to note how good a job the bombers were doing over Germany. He said, from information he received from casual conversation with Swedes who had recently visited Berlin, the city was 90% destroyed.

He asked where I lived in the States. I told him Washington. He rambled on for about 15 minutes as to the various cities he had visited there, his experiences, and how well he liked everything American. He spoke of New York, Miami, San Francisco, and Chicago. He asked me how long I had been in Sweden. I told him I had come about 5 months ago, spending most of the time in Stockholm working at the American Legation in connection with the internees. I explained that one of my duties was to contact each force-landed aircraft as they arrived.

We talked about the war in general. He made the statement that the Germans had received orders that they were to evacuate France and hold their lines on the German border. I asked him where he had received this information; he replied it was common knowledge. We chatted about the Russian, German and Swedish situation, and he left the impression that the Swedes were constantly in fear of the Russians occupying all of Finland and thus being in position to move into Sweden should the occasion demand.

I asked him what he thought about Hitler and his organization. He didn't say much but seemed to think Hitler, Himmler, Göring, and Goebbels should be placed in a cage and toured throughout the civilized world as a first class sideshow with the proceeds going to the countries they had devastated. He was of the impression Hitler would commit suicide before he would ever allow himself to be taken prisoner.

During the course of the dinner, I noticed about a dozen photographs of good looking women on his sideboard and questioned him as to who they were and where he met them. He explained some were Greek, some were Brazilian and others Swedish. He had met them during his travels, and the pictures were presented as a bond of friendship. While on this topic he told me he knew several Swedish girls whom he would like me to meet, so I replied there was no time like the present.

He made several telephone calls and at about 2100 hours, a brunette, Brita P.[280], showed up. Soon after, two blondes, Kristina O. and Sonja B., made their appearance. They all spoke pigeon English, excellent German, some French and a little Spanish. They all admitted, during the course of the evening, as to having lived in Germany at one time or another and having spent some time in France. About 2200 hours I decided to make an evening of it, so I requested permission to use his telephone to have someone take over my duties at midnight. I talked into the telephone buzz and made arrangements for another officer to substitute.

While using the telephone, I noticed an address book on the desk. While I was casually glancing at it, he came up from behind and indifferently picked it up and put it in his pocket. I did manage to obtain one of the numbers which was Perpon 615166. Lönnegren spoke about having worked with the Brazilian Legation but quit due to not meeting eye to eye with Sampio.

He said he was very good friends with the Swedish chief of the foreign office and had dinner with him occasionally. I asked him about the name Goering which I had seen on the roster of names as I entered the apartment building. He said he only knew him by sight but did not know any details as to who he was or what he did.

When this was done, Lönnegren brought out more liquor and we settled down to an evening of small talk and a discussion about the war. Lönnegren brought up the subject of the robot bombing of London and said he did not think they were doing too much damage. I told him I did not quite agree and left the subject open for his conclusion as to exactly how much I did know. One of the girls asked if I had ever been to Paris or Berlin. I told her I had visited both places from about 20,000 feet. When I made this remark they all started talking Swedish, the gist of which I could not understand.

About 2200 hours, while we were all in the front room talking, one of the girls made the remark that someone from across the street was constantly looking into the window of the front room where we were sitting. Lönnegren arose, drew the curtains and pinned them together. Lönnegren told me someone else had taken Posey's raincoat, a friend of his from Gävle.[281] He would write to have it returned, and I could pick it up at that time.

I asked Lönnegren under what circumstances he had met Lt. Posey. He replied that a couple of months ago he had been down at Blanch's for a drink and casually started a conversation with Posey and another American, the name of whom he did not know. He did mention however that he had recently seen this other American at Blanch's and believed he was one of the boys who flew from London to Sweden regularly. I asked him where he got this impression and he said it was what he gathered on the night the two Americans had visited his apartment. He said he had nodded to the friend of Posey when he saw him recently but the American did not appear to recognize him.

He asked me where I obtained the information that he had Posey's raincoat and where Posey was at the present, wondering why Posey could not come and pick it up himself. I explained that Posey had left Sweden soon after the night of the party, and he had written me requesting I get the raincoat and send it to him.

At about 2300 hours, Sonja B. made a telephone call and left shortly after. The four of us drank a little more, talked about the differences between the various languages, and that one of the girls should help me learn Swedish if I would reciprocate by teaching her English. At 2330 hours the two girls made preparations to leave. Taking this as a cue, I thanked Lönnegren for an excellent dinner and told him I was looking forward to seeing him again in the future. He said he was leaving town for the weekend, but on Monday he would call and we would have another small party.

Upon reaching the street I found that one of the girls had a bicycle so the three of us walked to the number 4 streetcar, and Brita P. left for home. After the streetcar departed, I mentioned to Kristina O. that the evening was still young and suggested we continue at my apartment. She was agreeable so we proceeded on our way.

We arrived at the apartment around midnight, mixed some drinks, sat on the sofa and listened to the phonograph. She started to talk about the war. I told her we had had enough of that for the evening; this was no time to think of such matters.

When I first met Lönnegren I was surprised to discover he was not the individual I had expected him to be. That is, I thought he would be the person I met on the night of 20 May 1944 in company with Rosita Serrano, Gustav Wally, George Axelson, at a dinner party at Bellmansro. From pictures Lönnegren showed me and from comments he made, I believe the person I had mistaken him for was Mr. Sampio, the Brazilian minister.

Lönnegren is an excellent host, a good talker, and appears to be well educated. He gives the impression of being 100% pro-Ally and at every opportunity seemed to tear down the Nazis. Indications are this is a mere cover and further meetings should prove to be both interesting and enlightening as to the actual purpose behind the mask.

End of Report by Herman F. Allen[282]

When at 10:00 p.m. one of the girls said she noticed someone across the street looking into the window of the front room, she was absolutely right. As soon as Herman made the appointment to meet with Lönnegren, Bill Carlson notified the Swedish police authorities (namely, Chief of Police Lundquist and Sergeant Söderström, one of his assistants) that Lieutenant Allen of the U.S. Air Force Internees would be used to develop information on Lönnegren.[283] The Swedish police made certain there was a guard outside Lönnegren's apartment the evening of Herman's visit. In his statement, the lookout noted that Allen went up to the third floor. When Allen left at 2320 hours, the guard departed soon afterward.[284]

Hedy Hedy Hedy

Hedy had been at the legation barely a week when she typed up Herman's report of the evening of August 18. She likely wondered if Herman wasn't taking his new espionage job a little too seriously, along with all its perks.

By this time, internee James Degnan, right waist gunner of *Sack-Time Susy,* had come from Falun to Stockholm to work at the American Legation as a guard. He and his Swedish sweetheart, Ingegard Nilsson, were to be married on August 20 on the island of Djurgården, just south of the legation.

James and Ingegard Degnan at the Seglora Church.

Djurgården is a historic royal game park where Swedish kings hunted deer, reindeer, and elk. One of the largest attractions on the island is an open-air museum, Skansen. This exhibition was created in 1891 to show visitors what life in rural Sweden had been like through the centuries.

Also on Djurgården is an amusement park, open since 1883, called Gröna Lund. Because so many people visited the recreation destination, there were taverns and eating establishments, most of them situated along the main thoroughfare Djurgårdsvägen.

The Degnan wedding was held at the Seglora Church, inside Skansen. The old wooden church dated to the early 1700s and in 1916 was moved timber by timber to its new location. Today it is still a popular venue for weddings.

The wedding was an exciting event for the members of the legation and the internees who worked in Stockholm. Sergeant Degnan was the first interned American to marry a Swede. Herman invited Miss Johnson to accompany him to the nuptials and was looking forward to having the beautiful newcomer by his side. With Herman, Hedy knew she would get a rousing introduction to everyone. It was their first official date.

And Hedy would get to meet Dr. John Lönnegren.

SUBJECT: Night of 20 August

Sunday evening at 1700 hours, Miss Hedy Johnson and I attended the wedding of S/Sgt. Degnan at Skansen Church. After the wedding, we attended the reception at some restaurant on the outskirts of town. This lasted until 2130 hours at which time a party of us left and continued our celebration at Blanch's. We ordered drinks and settled down for the evening.

> On the way around the floor dancing, I noticed Johnny sitting at a table with a distinguished looking man. We stopped and I introduced Miss Johnson and he in turn introduced Judge Westgard.[285] We then returned to our tables. About 15 minutes later, I returned to their table, sat down, and had a drink with them. I do not know what was in the drink, but it was very powerful. The Judge could speak good English but did not have much to say. Indications were that he was not pleased to have me there; however I made a date with Johnny for the following night at 2000 hours to pick up Posey's raincoat. About a half hour later Miss Johnson and I danced by their table again. We stopped, and he offered us a drink which we accepted. Soon after, we left Blanch's and called it an evening.[286]

A coded communique from OSS London related that "36948" (William T. Carlson) had made arrangements for one of the assistants to the military air attaché to go to the apartment of "SL-11" (Lönnegren) to pick up "A's" (Posey's) raincoat. The object was to find out more about Lönnegren's interests and perhaps to obtain evidence against him. Carlson also considered this to be a suitable opportunity for "planting foodstuff," passing deceptive intelligence on to the Germans.

As the report explained, the military air attaché's assistant was "absolutely reliable but not particularly subtle."[287]

The Swedish police were alerted about Herman's second planned visit to Dr. Lönnegren's apartment and arranged for another stakeout. Bill Carlson reported back to OSS London and copied Washington that he had involved the police for the protection of the internees.[288] The Swedes also got copies of each of Herman's typed reports.

> SUBJECT: Night of the 21st of August
>
> Monday evening, 21 August 1944, at 2000 hours I visited Dr. Lönnegren presumably to pick up Lt. Posey's raincoat. Upon entering his apartment, I found a Miss Marken[289] with him. She spoke fair English and good German, and he said she was born in Brazil and had been in Sweden for several years. We drank and talked about the war in its current phase. He told me Paris had been taken over by the Allies, and indications were that the European conflict would be over by October. He said no one doubted the bravery of the German soldier, but the whole world knew of their cruelty and slave owner mentality. About 2030 hours, at my suggestion, we decided to go out for a drink and a quiet evening. He told Miss Marken to go home, and we departed for the Strand Hotel terrace where Lönnegren had reserved a table.

Directly across the water from the American Legation, at Nybrokajen 9, was the Strand Hotel.[290] It had been built in time for the 1912 Olympic Games, hosted by Stockholm. The Strand was another popular meeting place for the internees when they wanted a fine meal and cocktails. On weekends, musicians played from a balcony overlooking the main dining area.

At the Strand we ordered a drink and talked about nothing in particular for a couple of hours. Lönnegren inquired as to how long I had known Miss Johnson, where I had met her and where she worked. I told him she was employed by the legation and worked in one of the departments, that I had known her for quite a while. He asked if she was a Swedish-American and I told him yes, her folks lived in Minnesota, originating from Sweden and that was how she could talk in Swedish. While we were sitting there, he pointed out an individual who he said I was to beware of and to warn all the other Americans to this effect. He said the man was dangerous, a crook, and for all he knew might be working for the Nazis. I asked how he knew about this man, and he said he had dealings with him in the past. He had seen this man at Blanch's in the company of Americans.

He asked me if it were possible to get him a few packages of American cigarettes. I told him it would be difficult, but I would get him a few packages if at all possible. I told him if I could get some, I would take them to his apartment in the morning. He said he did not want them for himself, but his girls, when they came to visit him, preferred American cigarettes to Swedish. We talked about arranging for a party in the near future. He suggested I find three clean-cut Americans and bring a few liters of schnapps. He would arrange for women and food. He mentioned he was leaving

Wednesday for his farm in the south and would not be back until the first of next week at which time he would contact me and we would make final arrangements. Soon after this we left, walked home and said goodnight.[291]

Herman's apartment at Skeppargatan 39 was on a primarily residential street of ornate apartment buildings, many with inner courtyards. Because of its location around the corner from the legation, several other Americans lived on this street. Lönnegren's home at Kommendörsgatan 42 was a few minutes farther.

According to the Swedish police report, Lönnegren soon left his apartment again and stopped at a couple of stores to buy incidental items. He went to the Sturebadet bathhouse and then visited the Brazilian Legation at 12 Sturegatan. Shortly after midnight Lönnegren returned home.[292]

Fortunately, Herman was in charge of making sure there were always enough American cigarettes for the internees, so obtaining a supply for Lönnegren was not a problem.

SUBJECT: Afternoon 22 August

About 1500 hours I dropped by Johnny's apartment with 5 packages of cigarettes. He met me at the door and I told him I only had a minute, for a taxi was waiting. He said his trip to his farm was postponed until Friday and wondered if we could get together on Thursday night. I told him I would not know whether or not I would be free but I would call him Thursday morning and let him know.[293]

During the month of August, two Americans arrived in Stockholm, and both became fast friends with Herman. One was Capt. Robert L. Robb, assistant military air attaché. Robb came in as part of a team to handle the administrative affairs of the interned personnel in Sweden.

Before the war, Robb had worked for the Chamber of Commerce in San Jose, California. While participating in the local little theater he met Helene, a beautiful young actress whom he married before he was shipped to England. At their Newport Beach wedding, Robb's best man was the brother of film star Jean Parker.

The other newcomer was Maj. Harley L. Robertson who would serve as assistant to the military air attaché from August 1944 until January 1945. One of 11 children from a North Dakota family, Robertson graduated from Jamestown College in 1925 and went on to become a

Lt. Herman Allen, Dr. Floyd Potter, Captain Libolin, Captain Robb, Maj. Harley Robertson. Skål!

high school teacher and coach. In 1934, his basketball team won the North Dakota State Championship. Now in Sweden, he was the perfect candidate to be in charge of Special Services, i.e. physical fitness and recreational activities.

Harley, Herman, and Robb immediately connected. All three were vivacious and outgoing. They loved to party, and party they did. The Americans who worked at the legation went out on the town often. Stockholm had no shortage of restaurants and nightclubs, and because there was essentially no tourist trade at the time, the establishment owners were grateful for their business.

SUBJECT: Conversation with Wally Olsen, 25 August 1944

Soon after arriving at work this AM visited Chancery to pick up mail. Saw Wally and he motioned for me to come over. Said he understood I had visited with Johnny L. twice. Repeated that Johnny was bad medicine and for me to keep away from him. I asked Wally where he obtained his info. Said he had ways and means. Told him I would be careful.

I brought up the subject of Maja Thull[294] whom he had mentioned the previous night in the taxi on the way back from Bromma. Asked him if he could obtain any info on her for me. I knew several of the boys had gone out with her and wanted to warn them in case she was undesirable. Said he would let me know as soon as he had some dope.[295]

As it happened, Herman was unable to keep his appointment with Lönnegren. He had seen him several times the past week. It was enough for now.

Prisoner of War Exchanges

In October of 1943, a large-scale prisoner of war exchange allowed thousands of wounded prisoners being held in Germany and Great Britain to go home. Seventeen Americans were also released as well as a Dominican nun and seven Sisters of the Poor.

The initial negotiations, long and difficult, can be credited to the International Red Cross in Geneva. Neutral Sweden was the logical place for this exchange between belligerents to take place.

During the same year, Folke Bernadotte became vice-chairman of the Swedish Red Cross. His 83-year-old uncle Prince Carl Bernadotte was chairman, but Folke took on many responsibilities, including the prisoner exchange. He worked with both the British and German legations in Stockholm to firm up the details.

The Germans wanted to make sure none of the freed British soldiers would disparage the conditions they had experienced during captivity. The Allies were just as concerned about such stories for fear the Germans might take offense and keep back some of their wounded soldiers. News correspondents reporting the event were warned of the need for cooperation.

The exchange took place at the western Swedish port Göteborg. Allied and German prisoners arrived by train, ferry, and steamer. The steamships *Drottningholm* and *Gripsholm*, operating for SAL, the Swedish American Line, were painted white and marked DIPLOMAT in huge letters on their sides.

Swedish Crown Princess Louise, the British-born sister of Lord Louis Mountbatten, visited with British prisoners and then, accompanied by German Minister Hans Thomsen, greeted the Germans. Every soldier received from the Red Cross a gift of newspapers and magazines, cigarettes, matches, fruit, and chocolates.[296]

Even NBC News carried a special broadcast naming Sweden's Count Folke Bernadotte as having managed this successful operation. Bernadotte reported on the air, "These rather strenuous days have been some of the most happy days of my life."[297]

The prisoner exchange was repeated the following year in September, 1944. Although exact numbers are difficult to confirm, *Life m*agazine reported there were 234 Americans and 1700 British prisoners sent home. Pictured prominently in the article were Count Bernadotte and German Minister Thomsen in a Red Cross meeting aboard the *Drottningholm*. Prince Carl, Folke's uncle and chairman of the Swedish Red Cross, was there to speak to the wounded men as they were carried off the ships.

After the second successful prisoner exchange, Erik Wijk, managing director of SAL, and his deputy, Baron Gören von Essen, were recognized by the Red Cross for their hard work.[298]

During this period, both Wijk, and von Essen came to know Herman Allen. Bernadotte had most likely delegated to Herman some of the detail work for organizing the September 1944 exchange.

Destination Uppsala

As previously noted, after Dr. Hans Wagner's office learned that their secretary Erika Wendt was receiving treatments for tuberculosis at a Stockholm hospital, they made arrangements for her to stay only until the first of September. The Germans then planned to send her to Berlin ostensibly to continue her therapy.

When her Swedish contact Ternberg learned this, he demanded that Erika go underground and stay safely hidden until the end of the war. Two of his associates took her from the hospital at 6:00 a.m. on September 1 and headed north by car for Uppsala, a trip of less than 50 miles. Just over 41,000 people lived in Uppsala, the site of the country's oldest university.

Erika and her companions checked into an elegant old hotel, the Gillet. Eventually Erika moved to a farm in the far north of Sweden. She assumed a new identity as Ellen Berger, the widow of a Norwegian soldier.[299]

Back in Stockholm, Herman and Hedy were seeing each other often. Hedy loved the theater and occasionally convinced Herman to take her to a musical show. They particularly enjoyed the Gustav Wally productions. Rosita Serrano performed with Wally at the Cirkus concert hall on Djurgården. When his orchestra played at Berns in Berzelii Park, Hedy and Herman could dance the night away.

Earlier in the month, Herman organized a banquet for the Americans in the Military Air Attaché's office who were handling the affairs of the interned airmen and their planes. The host for the evening was American minister Herschel Johnson. The site for the September 16 dinner was the Tattersall Restaurant, upstairs in a luxurious mirrored hall. At Grev Turegatan 12, the restaurant was only a ten-minute walk from the American Legation.

That evening, Herman sat at the head table next to the honored guest, famed Swedish aviator Capt. Albin Ahrenberg. In 1931, Ahrenberg made national news when he located a missing British explorer who had been stranded on a Greenland icecap for months. The renowned pilot had a lifetime of adventure stories to share with the American airmen.

The banquet at the Tattersall Restaurant.

At the time, Captain Ahrenberg was in charge of a Swedish military division in the Stockholm archipelago. He was also head of a repair team that traveled to various American emergency landing sites to evaluate planes and determine whether they were able to return to flight. When aircraft damage was beyond repair, Ahrenberg and his crew recovered parts, which were eventually used by the Swedish company SAAB in converting to civilian status seven B-17s obtained from the U.S. government.

Captain Ahrenberg had worked for several days on Gotland at the site of the remains of the *Liberty Lady*, so during the evening at the Tattersall, he and Herman had a lot to talk about.

Three days later, Herman made arrangements for a totally different type of gathering. He had not seen Lönnegren for several weeks. Their planned party at the apartment on Kommendörsgatan would take place on September 19. As suggested by Lönnegren, Herman brought along Captain Robb and liquor. Lönnegren invited his lady friends.

SUBJECT: Evening 19 September 1944 JOHN LÖNNEGREN

Tuesday evening, 19 September 1944, Captain Robert Robb and I rang the doorbell of John Lönnegren's apartment at about 2040 hours, prepared for a small party. Upon entering the apartment, we found three girls, Greta H., Brita P., and Kristina O., with Johnny to complete the affair. Robb and I brought along a litre of gin, half litre of schnapps, and some cigarettes, thus the party started in fine style.

The conversation through the evening was general, touching on such topics as the war, the Russian situation, the possibility of Sweden entering the war, how badly beaten Germany was, the fact that they should throw in the sponge and call it quits. Between dancing and drinking, I took several photos of the gathering, which came out fairly good.

About 2245 we all went into the kitchen nook and had a light snack which the girls had prepared, along with wine and beer and schnapps. The conversation was very light.

My observation of the entire evening is that no effort was made to discuss anything pertaining to any particular subject.

During the course of the evening Lt. Posey's name was brought up, and Johnny made the remark he would like to drop him a line. I replied there was no time like the present, so we went to his reading room and pounded out a letter. While he was on the typewriter I casually glanced at the several letters, papers and so forth on his desk. Everything was pretty well covered, except for a note and a card with telephone numbers, which I managed to get—370140 and 370179.

About 2300 hours, the party broke up. We called a cab, took Greta H. home, then Robb, Brita P., Kristina O., and myself to my apartment where we consumed additional liquor, danced, played the photograph, and at about 0300 hours the girls went home, slightly the worse for wear.

Several times during the evening Johnny made mention of the fact that he was anxious for me to accompany him to Uppsala to visit friends and show me the town. We made a tentative date for sometime this weekend.

Johnny mentioned he was leaving for his farm in the south of Sweden for a couple of weeks in the near future and asked me to come spend a weekend with him. Told him I would let him know first part of the week.

Throughout the evening, Johnny made reference to his friendship with Per Albin Hanson, Swedish Prime Minister.[300]

In spite of all the liquor served to him, Herman had no problem remembering details. He discovered he could have a better evening if he drank a glass of cream to coat his stomach before he went out on the town. He could drink more and stay lucid.

One of the photos Herman snapped on the evening of the party was of Lönnegren and his three lady friends. Behind them stood Captain Robb. When the photographs were seen by the Air Attaché's office, Robb's head was quickly cut out. In a later summary report, Herman wrote that details of the party were "not available due to report being handed over to parties concerned."

John Lönnegren and friend.
Photo by Herman Allen
19 September 1944.

On September 25, only a month after Herman and Lönnegren's first meeting, the two of them took the hour train ride together to Uppsala, the site of Lönnegren's alma mater.

In his reports, Herman often referred to Lönnegren as "Johnny." Over the past month, the two men had talked for hours. Herman had majored in history in college, and Lönnegren, who had studied political science, history and philosophy, could speak on almost any subject. He confided in Herman that his dream was to live in America someday.

Herman enjoyed these intellectual conversations, so different from any he had ever had with his own father because of I.N.'s limited grasp of the English language and the fact that he didn't take the time with his eldest son.

Herman was attempting to build a close relationship with the older gentleman, ostensibly so that Lönnegren might relax and feel comfortable talking about his political activities.

The plan was working.

SUBJECT: Trip to Uppsala with Dr. John A. Lönnegren

Sunday morning September 24 at 0936 hours John Lönnegren and I took the train for Uppsala for the purpose of seeing the sights of the college town.

We arrived at Uppsala about 1045 hours and immediately set out for the campus. We visited Johnny's frat house, NORLANDA NATION, took a tour through the house, departed and went toward the Uppsala Castle. En route we stopped at the Karolina library, took several photos, visited the castle, then walked towards the administration building. We took a few more pictures, visited the Trinity Church, the Cathedral, then had lunch at the Gillet Restaurant at 1300 hours.

Johnny is an excellent guide. He explained the Swedish educational set-up, the history of various monuments, of the churches, and so forth.

About 1200 hours we came to Gropgränd Street and stopped at number 4. Johnny said he had to visit a friend, and I was to wait for him; it would only be a few minutes. We entered the courtyard and he went into one of the doors. He said this was a good friend of his, a girl, who was married, and he simply wanted to leave his card. The married name was STENSTROM.[301]

When we were about finished eating, this couple came to the restaurant, talked about nothing in particular, then we left for the train.

This couple, STENSTROM, could speak fair English, and it appears the wife and Johnny were intimate friends prior to marriage. He still has that look in his eye whenever he mentions her.

Throughout the entire day, Johnny had not hinted of anything outside the usual run of conversation. No confidential secrets were exchanged, nothing of a suspicious nature arose. Mention was made several times as to his Anti-Nazi feelings, but this is a continual reference on his part.

I noticed while waiting for Johnny at number 4 Gropgränd that a CD car was standing outside, several people were in it. Its number was C 21920.[302]

John Lönnegren and Herman Allen in Uppsala.

While in Uppsala, Herman addressed a postcard of the grand cathedral to Miss Hedy Johnson. His message was as follows: "Dearest Hedy, a souvenir of a journey so you may know if wishes were horses, then beggars would ride. Johnny and I saw the sights in a few short hours. With Love, Al." Lönnegren wrote in the lower right corner, "The same! Johnny"

Doc Potter

On September 27, 1944, Dr. Floyd A. Potter arrived from London to activate the Medical Section of the Legation of the United States of America, Stockholm, Sweden. His assignment was to give medical care to the American internees.

Dr. Potter devised a plan for both emergency and routine care of the Air Force personnel. As one of his first orders of business, he had to establish a venereal disease control program, which was critical because six current cases of gonorrhea had resisted all ordinary types of treatment available in Sweden at the time. The six infected airmen were brought to Stockholm, treated with penicillin, not readily found in Sweden, and cured.

According to Dr. Potter's final report, only one case of syphilis was found, and the man was repatriated immediately.

Authorization to write prescriptions and to admit patients into the Swedish hospitals was obtained upon application to the king of Sweden. Count Bernadotte assisted in obtaining this privilege for Dr. Potter.

Dr. Floyd A. Potter in his signature fur hat.

Sweden's medical system prevented practitioners from using the hospitals unless the practitioners were hired by the Swedish government. Thus, Dr. Potter made arrangements with the department heads of the hospitals nearest the camps to take on the internees as their private patients. Dentists were also designated to treat the interned airmen.

When a plane was forced to land in Sweden, its landing location was normally in the south, probably near Malmö. Army plasma units were supplied to the nearby hospitals for emergency use. In addition to penicillin, tetanus toxoid was supplied, as this medication was also not available in Sweden.[303]

Doc Potter's Cossack fur hat became his signature piece of apparel. He quickly fit into the legation social scene and became good friends of Hedy and Herman.

The Proposal

Even though he had known her for barely six weeks, Herman was in love with Hedy and wanted to ask her to marry him. On many afternoons, near the hour he knew she would be finishing up her work for Carlson, Herman stopped at her desk to see if she wanted to go out.

Hedy looked forward to their dinners together. He was so much fun and charmed everyone around him.

Five days after his trip to Uppsala and the "With Love" postcard, Herman asked Hedy to take the afternoon off for an outing to nearby Djurgården, just across the bridge from Strandvägen. She agreed, so they hopped onto one of the city trams[304] and got off near the Skansen open air museum.

Hedy had toured Skansen before, walking through the authentic homes set up to replicate Scandinavian life in earlier times. She showed Herman the rooms furnished with historical artifacts and the attendants in old fashioned dress.

It was a beautiful September afternoon. Herman and Hedy wandered over to the Skansen zoo. They saw the bear enclosure where white arctic polar bears named Mr. and Mrs. Stockholm, along with their offspring, reclined on huge rocks.

After an hour, Herman led Hedy on a walk outside the park and along the water. He had a definite destination in mind, a romantic setting he had discovered nearby.

Several iron benches were spaced around a lovely flower garden. In the center of the flowers was a small round fountain with a sculpture of a cherub riding on the back of a swan. There in the garden, Herman proposed.

He knew that he had a well-deserved reputation as a ladies' man. He had to convince Hedy those days and that life were over.

But asking Hedy to marry him wasn't as simple as that. For the first time, Herman had to explain to Hedy that he was Jewish. Count Bernadotte had advised him not mention it to anyone. John Lönnegren certainly didn't know. Only his former crew members were aware of his heritage, and the only one he saw on a regular basis was Smithy, his pilot.

Years later Hedy remembered, "I had no idea. I think I was a little afraid. We knew some of what was happening to the Jewish people in Europe."

Hedy's response was not a positive one. It was too soon, she thought, and her reply to Herman was, "I'm not ready for this yet, and I don't think you are either."

Stella Polaris

People from Finland regularly came through the legation. Whenever they did, Hedy was reminded of the country her parents, as Swedish-Finns, had left in the early part of the century. From the eastern coast of Sweden, across the upper portion of the Baltic Sea, was their former hometown of Närpes. Centuries ago, when Finland was under Swedish rule, many Swedes had settled there.

Positioned between Sweden on one side and Russia on the other, Finland was literally caught in the middle. The Soviets wanted control, in particular of those parts of Finland near the grand city of Leningrad, later known as St. Petersburg.

Finland experienced a civil war, a Winter War (1939–1940) against the Soviet Union, and then what the Finns called the Continuation War (1941–1944) also against the Soviets. Beginning in 1941, Finland was a co-belligerent with Germany, receiving military support from that country.

In March of 1944, President Roosevelt called on Finland to break its ties with Germany. Six months later, on September 19, 1944, the Moscow Armistice was signed between Finland on one side and the Soviet Union and Britain on the other, thereby extricating Finland from the Axis.

On September 21 and 22, four small ships secretly left Närpes and crossed to Härnösand and Gävle, two cities on Sweden's eastern coastline. On those ships were 750 refugees—the entire Finnish military intelligence service and their families. The evacuating Finns brought a huge amount of intelligence, along with the secrets to the codes of many countries including the Soviet Union. These Finns had to leave in a hurry because the Soviets were arriving to oversee the Armistice.

Once safely in Sweden with this extremely valuable information, the Finns negotiated with the various intelligence agencies, including OSS Stockholm. Mission Chief Tikander communicated to William Donovan that he had instructed OSS officials William Carlson and Dick Huber, chief of Secret Intelligence, to meet with the Finns in order to purchase the Soviet cryptographic material. The OSS Stockholm station successfully made that purchase. Carlson was ordered to personally courier the documents to Washington, D.C. as quickly as possible.

When the U.S. Secretary of State heard about the deal, he became furious and protested to the President, who ordered the code books be handed over to the Russians.

Were the codebooks copied before they were handed over? Yes, reportedly they were. What the OSS didn't realize was that the Finns had also sold various codebooks to the British as well as to the Japanese military attaché, who then gave the material to the Germans.[305] This complex exchange was another powerful example that in wartime Stockholm, anyone could be a spy, and everything was for sale.

The effects of Stella Polaris, the code name for the transfer of the intelligence documents, continued into the Cold War and beyond and today are still a topic of study and debate.

The War Refugee Board and Wallenberg

By the end of 1943, the world knew that Jews in the German-controlled countries were being sent to their deaths. The U.S. State Department claimed that the best way to help the Jews was to win the war. Frustrated by the inaction of Congress, aides to Treasury Secretary Henry Morgenthau, who was Jewish, drafted an 18-page report titled, "The Acquiescence of This Government in the Murder of the Jews." Morgenthau sent the report to President Roosevelt, and a week later the War Refugee Board (WRB), was established.[306] Its purpose was to aid the victims of the Nazi powers.

Shortly before Christmas 1943, an accountant named Iver C. Olsen arrived in Stockholm as OSS finance officer. His cover was financial attaché to the American Legation, and he was to report back to Washington on financial and economic developments in Sweden and the other Scandinavian countries. In particular, he was to keep an eye on what was happening to Axis funds. Olsen would also head the WRB in Stockholm.

Olsen met with Count Bernadotte, as vice-chairman of the Swedish Red Cross, to organize various refugee projects. One, the Baltic Fishing Fleet, smuggled Estonians, Latvians, and Lithuanians into Sweden. A side benefit of this operation was the intelligence obtained from the German-occupied territories involved.[307] However, none of these refugees was Jewish, as by this time, there were few Jews in those countries who had not already been sent to concentration camps or murdered.[308]

Hungary was the last country under Hitler's control where there had not been large-scale deportations. In 1944, Nazi Adolf Eichmann was charged with organizing the operation to rid Hungary of all its Jews. It was to be the last phase of Hitler's Final Solution.

The Swedish Legation in Hungary was already beginning to hand out protective passes to Jews in an effort to get them out of the country. King Gustav himself sent a telegram to the regent of Hungary, begging him to save those who still remained.[309]

Iver Olsen was determined to set up a rescue effort in Hungary. He discussed the idea with Kalman Lauer, a Hungarian Jew whose office was also located at Strandvägen 7a. Lauer's in-laws were trapped in Budapest, and he was desperate for them to be rescued. The two men began what would prove to be a series of fateful conversations.

Lauer's partner in his import-export foodstuff business was a 31-year-old Swede named Raoul Wallenberg, a member of the powerful banking family. The well-connected Wallenberg spoke fluent German and Russian and had traveled to Hungary in the past on business. He wanted to go to Budapest to rescue Lauer's relatives but did not yet have proper travel papers.

In June of 1944, Wallenberg met with both Olsen and Minister Johnson. The WRB officials arranged for more than $200,000 to support the rescue efforts.[310] The Swedish government officially appointed

Wallenberg to go to Hungary to do what he could to save the Jews and to augment what the Swedish Legation was already doing there.

Wallenberg arrived in Budapest on the 9th of July, 1944, on the very day that a train carried 2000 doomed Hungarian Jews to Auschwitz in Poland. This was the last transport before deportations were suspended, no doubt partially because of King Gustav's pleadings.

Remaining in Budapest on the day Wallenberg arrived were over 200,000 terrified Jews.[311] For the next months he worked, officially from the Swedish Legation, to issue protective passports, each titled "Schutz-Pass." For a while, there were no deportations, and Wallenberg even thought he might be able to return to Sweden.

Then in October, Adolf Eichmann came to Hungary, and no Jew was safe. Wallenberg opened Swedish houses to shelter Jews. Eichmann was relentless, but so was Wallenberg. Ignoring whatever personal danger he was in, Wallenberg threatened, bribed, and cajoled the Nazis as he persisted in handing out his Swedish passes.

When the Russians arrived in Budapest in January of 1945, 97,000 Jews were still living in Hungary. Per Anger, Wallenberg's colleague at the Swedish Legation, gave him credit for heroically saving these Jews from extermination.[312]

That same month, Wallenberg was arrested by the Soviets and taken to a prison in Moscow, never to return to his family. Why was he arrested? What became of him? One theory is that the Russians believed him to be a spy. They claimed he died of a heart attack in 1947, yet prisoners later released from KGB prisons insisted that Wallenberg was still alive when they were there.

Was Wallenberg a spy for the Allies? Like many well-connected and influential Swedes, he had close ties with American and British intelligence. In a 1955 CIA interview, Iver Olsen firmly denied that Raoul Wallenberg had a role with the OSS.[313] The speculation continues today.

Lönnegren Leak

On October 2, 1944, Herman called on John Lönnegren, his first meeting with the Swede since the party on September 19.

> I visited John Lönnegren's apartment at 2000 hours to give him copies of photos taken on a previous visit. He was alone and appeared to be tired. I asked him what the score was, and he said he had lain all Sunday night with a woman and was fagged out. Stated he was going to have to give up this pastime for he was getting too old.
>
> We commented on the pictures for a few minutes, then started talking about his proposed trip to his brother-in-law's farm in Skona. He said the trip was definitely on, and I could plan on a visit with him.
>
> Johnny said that on Monday he had lunch with a Mr. Paulson who was head of the Swedish Department for refugees. At this luncheon Paulson told Johnny that two high-ranking Air Corps men, one a General, were coming to Sweden to inspect the camps. Johnny wanted to know if this was true. Told him it was the first I had heard this news and accordingly didn't have any information on it.
>
> About this time the telephone rang. Johnny went to answer it in the next room, so I followed him.

He spoke in Swedish. Said it was a girl who wanted to come up and see him, but he told her "not tonight," he was too tired. While glancing over the contents of his desk, I saw the telephone number 278174 circled on a piece of paper.

We talked about the war. Johnny said he couldn't understand why the "damn Germans" didn't give up. They knew they were licked and should call it quits. He talked about being against Sweden entering the war. He couldn't possibly see any percentage; Sweden had been a refuge to date for so many people and continued to be so.

About 2130 hours I prepared to leave. He promised he would call toward the end of the week, letting me know definitely when he was going south.[314]

John Lönnegren and Herman. In Herman's scrapbook, photo is labeled, "Oh, Johnny." This same photograph can be found at the Sweden National Archives.

The Swedish police were watching when at 8:00 p.m. Herman Allen arrived in a taxi. By this time, Lönnegren's apartment was bugged. The officer reported he had a hard time understanding Lönnegren's extremely mushy speech, likely because of all the spirits the Swede had consumed. The police had no problem understanding what Allen said, however. Before Herman left at 9:35 he asked Lönnegren for the address of Miss Kristina O., a blonde he had met there during an earlier visit.

Herman had proposed marriage to Hedy just three days before, and she had not accepted. His pride was wounded. Miss Kristina might lift his spirits.

Konstnärshuset

At Smålandsgatan 7, a few minutes' walk from the Military Air Attaché's Internee Section, Annex D, was an establishment known as Konstnärshuset, the Artists' house. Built in 1897, the unusual exterior was reminiscent of Moorish style buildings in Spain, one of the countries where the architect had studied.

On the ground floor, with additional dining upstairs, was a restaurant known as KB, short for Konstnärsbaren or Artists' bar. Actors and artists flocked there, along with locals who came in for a good meal, a drink, and fine art. On most of the walls were murals painted by famous artists. The Spanish influence was evident, with an array of characters both clothed and unclothed, colored with dark earthy pigments.

This was a destination John Lönnegren frequented and wanted Herman to see. The mirrored booths in the back provided a dim quiet corner for discreet conversations.

SUBJECT: Luncheon, 6 October 1944, with Dr. John Lönnegren

At 1300 hours 6 October 1944, Johnny and I had a luncheon engagement at Konstnärs Huset. The first thing we talked about was his proposed trip south. Said he was leaving at 0725 hrs tomorrow morning (7 October 1944) and expected to remain until 17 October 1944 or thereabouts. He explained he did not think it would be advisable for me to come down at the present, for the fishing season would not start until 20 October, however he would return and on about the 19th we would go down together.

We talked about the war. He said it looked like Sweden may take up arms against Germany for the Germans were firing over Swedish territory in Northern Sweden. I asked him when, but he explained it was simply a guess on his part.

Started talking about the fliers in Sweden. At this point I told him his friend PAULSON must have some advance information, for upon checking up, I found it was true what he (PAULSON) said about two high-ranking Air Force Officers coming to Sweden. I hemmed a few seconds, trying to think of their names, finally remembered that one was General Anderson, and the other some Colonel. He said that was correct as to the information he had, one was a General and the other a Colonel. Finally, I remembered the other name, it was Colonel Bradford. He beamed all over and said that was the name Paulson had told him. Told him I couldn't understand why a man such as a General would want to come to Sweden, for there wasn't a thing here except a few internees. At this point, he interrupted and said, "There must be over a thousand fliers in Sweden." I told him I wasn't quite sure as to the exact amount but we did have a few hundred. We finally agreed that perhaps the General was going to take a holiday, and the Colonel was going to do the inspecting of the camps. He wanted to know if they were coming soon. I told him I didn't know for sure, but they were expected.

About this time the coffee was brought, and Johnny went into a rather lengthy description of how bad it was, so I told him if he had a coffee grinder I could supply him with a pound of coffee beans for his trip south. He was pleased, said he had a grinder. Remainder of luncheon was spent with small talk.

After we left Konstnars Huset we went up to my office where I gave him the coffee beans and a carton of cigarettes for his girls for good measure. He said I was too good to him, and so he left with the promise to write or phone.[315]

The General's Visit

John Lönnegren wanted to know when the general would be visiting Sweden. No American told him what day it would be, but when General Curtis and company came to Sweden, it was a grand affair indeed.

During World War I, Edward Peck Curtis was an American ace. He shot down six German planes and was awarded the Distinguished

Flying Cross. After that war, Curtis went to work for Eastman Kodak in their professional motion picture division. In 1940, he rejoined the Air Corps and served as executive assistant to Gen. Carl Spaatz, commander of the Strategic Air Forces in Europe.

General Curtis had met with Bernt Balchen in London to discuss Balchen's efforts to aid the Norwegian resistance. They also talked about the downed American airmen interned in Sweden, by then more than a thousand. This was one of the purposes of the general's visit, to confer with the Swedes about getting these pilots and their crews back.[316] Dr. Bruce Hopper, formerly chief of mission for OSS Sweden, and by 1944, Eighth Air Force historian, came to officially record the events.[317]

On Friday, October 6, 1944, General Curtis and entourage flew from Heston airfield west of London and made one interim stop, where they were met by the RAF in preparation for their flight across German-occupied Norway.

There were two complications. First, the general did not have his passport. Second, the security officers had to telephone high authority in order to get permission for him to travel to a neutral country in full uniform.

The general's Liberator arrived at Bromma airfield in Stockholm at 12:35 a.m. According to Gunnar Hägglöf, Swedish minister to Holland and a member of this group, it was the first time in history an American general had visited Sweden. Originally Gen. Frederick L. Anderson was also scheduled to take the trip, but other urgent duties prevailed.

The visitors were taken from the airport to the Grand Hôtel in Stockholm. In contrast to blacked-out, war-weary London, this neutral city was brightly lit and beautiful to behold.

The following day, Curtis made an official visit to the American Legation to see Minister Johnson. Dinner was hosted by Gunnar Hägglöf

Gen. Edward P. Curtis (center of photo) and company. Maj. Gen. Axel Ljungdahl is facing the camera on the far left.

at the Cecil Hotel, a venue popular with the young and fashionable. The general dressed in his full regalia, a variation from the norm in this neutral country. The table next to them was occupied by the Gestapo, along with their female admirers.

The Germans could hardly take their eyes away from the splendidly uniformed American and his guests. In the general's party were Count Carl Adam Moltke, a member of the Danish Resistance, and his American wife, Mab Wilson Wright. Before the war, Mab had worked in New York's world of fashion. Also in the small elegant party were Krister Aschan and his wife, lion hunters from Kenya. Dinner was Smörgåsbord, schnapps, and wine.

The Gestapo stayed late, apparently not wanting to miss a thing. General Curtis did not leave until they had departed.

Felix Hardison, Åke Stavenow, Leo Sager, Robert Robb.

The Americans were not laughing when they saw the headlines on the German newspapers soon delivered to the Grand Hôtel: "General Curtis has arrived in Sweden to bring the Swedes into the war."[318]

The next morning was Sunday, October 8, and an expedition to visit the American internees was the agenda. At 10:00 a.m., the general left his hotel, accompanied by Felix Hardison and Swedish Lt. Åke Stavenow.

Two Swedish pilots flew the group to Norrköping, south of Stockholm, to pick up Maj. Gen. Axel Ljungdahl of the Swedish Air Force. Gen. Bengt Nordenskiöld, commander in chief of the Swedish Air Force, was on the field to send them off, and they resumed their flight to a small airfield at Jönköping near Gränna, a village where American airmen were interned.

The visitors were met by Capt. Leo Sager, commandant of the internee camp, and several American officers. All proceeded to the internee camp at Mullsjö, about 18 miles to the west of Jönköping. When they arrived, the internees were lined up at attention.

General Curtis asked everyone to stand at ease and spoke to them. "I need not tell you how glad we are to see you and to know that you are so well taken care of by your Swedish hosts. You are by no means forgotten by us in England. In fact, you are very much on our minds. You are still needed. We are making every effort to get you out and back to duty."[319]

For everyone's entertainment, the internees had organized a softball game, and to their amazement, the general pitched a no-hit, no-run inning.

Afterward, the entourage headed for Margreteholm, the Sager home near Jönköping. Vera Sager was a wonderful hostess to the internees and entertained groups of them on several occasions. Also in attendance were Harley Robertson, in charge of Special Services for the internees; Floyd Potter, physician for the internees; Robert Robb, assistant military attaché; as well as other American officers concerned with the internees, including Herman Allen. Dr. Hopper asked Captain Robb to write the history of the American internees, a job he completed soon afterward.

The visitors and the American officers spent the night at Margreteholm. The next morning, General Curtis flew to Västerås to see the American planes being stored there. Lunch was hosted by Count Bernadotte at a restaurant outside Stockholm.

Dinner was with Felix Hardison at the Lidingö Hotel. Hardison had moved from his apartment in Stockholm to a beautiful home on the archipelago island of Lidingö. The estate was owned by the famed Swedish artist Einar Nerman, currently working in New York. A photographer snapped a picture of Hardison, Balchen, and Curtis looking through one of the artist's books of drawings.[320]

The entourage's final dinner was hosted by Prince Carl Johan Bernadotte, grandson of the reigning king. After a fine evening at the Grand Hôtel, Balchen piloted the group back to Scotland. General Curtis arrived in London by car and departed for France the next day.[321]

Oh Johnny

On the 18th of October, William T. Carlson, code name LIMIT, sent an account to X-2 London, with a copy to X-2 in Washington, D.C. outlining what had transpired so far in the Lönnegren case.

Carlson's secretary, Hedy Johnson, typed his report. It had been just over two weeks since Herman had proposed marriage. By this time Hedy was crazy about Herman, but he wasn't making it easy for her to believe that he was ready to settle down.

SUBJECT: John Alexander LÖNNEGREN

1. In agreement with the Swedish Police Authorities (namely Intendent LUNDQUIST, Chief of Police, and Sgt. SÖDERSTRÖM, one of his assistants) Lieutenant ALLEN of the U.S. Airforce Internees has been used to develop information on Subject. Lt. ALLEN has accepted invitations to Subject's flat, where food and willing women have been provided.

2. At all times, except one, Subject has scrupulously avoided asking any indiscreet questions, but on the contrary has bent over backward to develop the impression that he is pro-Allied and anti-Nazi. The first indication that Subject has

given so far that he is working for the Germans was on 3 October.[322]

3. On Tuesday, 3 October, Subject stated to ALLEN that he had heard from his friend PAULSON in the Swedish Passport Control that an American Air General and another high-ranking American officer were coming to Sweden. He asked ALLEN if this were true. ALLEN replied that this was the first he heard of it.

4. On Wednesday, 5 October, the U.S. Minister was informed for the first time of General CURTIS's expected arrival. The Minister notified Colonel RAYENS, the Military Attaché, but no other persons in the U.S. Legation were cognizant of the fact.

5. On Friday, 6 October, at about 1030 hours, Mr. Smith of the A.T.S. learned from Carl FLORMAN at FLORMAN's office in A.B.A.[323] that General CURTIS and some high-ranking Swedish Government official (HÄGGLOF, Swedish Minister to Belgium & Holland) were arriving that night by Liberator. At 2130 hours, A.T.S. received the message officially through the British Legation channels. The message was dispatched from Leuchars, Scotland at 1530 hours, and normally should have come over the 1600 hours broadcast and A.T.S. should normally have received it at 1630.

6. It was also learned on 6 October that it had originally been planned for General SPAATZ to

accompany General CURTIS (This information had been received at Leuchars several days before 6 October) but SPAATZ did not turn up at the last minute.

7. It has been learned that PAULSON received word on 26 September from the Swedish Legation in London to grant visas to General CURTIS and his party when they applied. The Swedish Police are investigating PAULSON, who is reported to have declared himself pro-Nazi in 1933, presumably to demonstrate his attitude towards the Communists.

8. On 6 October ALLEN had lunch with Subject, and during the conversation said that it was true that two high-ranking Airforce officers were expected, one General ANDERSON and the other some Colonel. Subject replied that this was just what he had heard, a General and a Colonel. ALLEN then said he thought the Colonel was Col. BRADFORD. LÖNNEGREN again said, yes, that was exactly the names PAULSON had told him. (General ANDERSON is expected to visit here. Colonel BRADFORD is a made-up name.)[324]

Carlson reported that this was the first indication that John Lönnegren was working for the Germans. Even before the Americans or British received notification from official sources, Paulsson leaked to Lönnegren specific details about the visit of an American general, presumably to be passed on to Lönnegren's Abwehr contacts. The fact that Lönnegren disclosed this same information with Herman was shared with the Swedes for further investigation.

Berns

A famous Stockholm pastry chef named Beinrich Robert Berns opened a restaurant in 1863 and named it after himself, Berns Salonger. He chose Berzelii Park as its location, at the time a poor area on the outskirts of town. A variety of entertainment was offered for the guests—vaudeville acts, acrobats, magic shows, and the first cancan dance to be shown in Sweden.[325]

Berns Salonger in Berzelii Park, 1940s. (by Lennart af Petersens. Stockholm City Museum.)

By 1944 the restaurant, remodeled under new ownership to be lavish inside and out, had become the place to be for festive nightlife. On pleasant days, the lawn was filled with guests dressed in their finest, sitting on benches and listening to a matinee concert.

Berns was a short walk from the American Legation. On this day, Herman rode his bicycle.

SUBJECT: Luncheon, 21 October 1944, with JOHN A LÖNNEGREN

Subject called Friday 20 October 1944 to make luncheon date for next day at 1300 hours at Berns.

Main purpose of lunch was to arrange for my proposed trip to fish with Johnny.

Johnny reported an excellent time on his trip south, his visit to his farm. (He calls it his farm, when in reality it belongs to his brother-in-law.) Said two Swedish officers were there at the same time, looking the countryside over for possible future maneuvers. They all drank quite a bit, sat, friendship in general.

Johnny wanted to know if the Generals had arrived yet, but before I had an opportunity to answer him, the waiter came for an order. By the time the order was given, the topic had been changed, and never referred to again the entire time.

Nothing in particular was said about anything. Talked a little about the war, about the ships which arrived Sweden on 7 October 1944, and about the B24 which had crashed recently on the West Coast.

Asked Johnny if I could call him Monday to let him know about this weekend.

Nothing definite was obtained.[326]

A week or so later, Lönnegren telephoned Herman to make another luncheon date. This time, Herman invited Johnny to dine at the flat he shared with Harley Robertson. The two had been fortunate to sublet the apartment at Garvargatan 5 from a gentleman temporarily away from the city. They were on the top floor of a five-story building overlooking Norr Mälarstrand, a boulevard that ran beside the water.

This prime location was just east of Stadshuset, Stockholm's picturesque city hall, sited right on the bay of Lake Mälaren. Better yet, the apartment was a couple of blocks from Hedy's on Bergsgatan. Hedy wrote home that she lived about six blocks from Stadshuset and rode the tram four times a day past it, "except when I'm lazy and hail a cab."

11 November 1944. DR. JOHN LÖNNEGREN

Mr. Lönnegren called me yesterday afternoon informing of his return. Immediately made arrangements to meet him today at lunch at GARVARGATAN 5.

Johnny showed up at 1320 hours. Major (Harley) Robertson, my roommate, was present.

Johnny spoke a good deal re his recent trip south, how much he missed my company, and wanted to be sure I was present on the next junket, probably the first part of next month.

I asked him about Paulson, when we were going to have lunch together as he once promised. He's going to call tomorrow afternoon to let me know.[327]

The Acceptance

On November 18, Herman was elected a member of the American Club of Stockholm. This club met regularly for dinner on Friday evenings at the Grand Hôtel. Its purpose was to further the spirit of American hospitality and helpfulness. On Thanksgiving Day, the American Club and the Swedish-American Society, an organization with similar aims, held a joint Thanksgiving celebration. Herman invited Hedy to accompany him to a traditional turkey banquet held in the Grand Hôtel ballroom. Minister Johnson read a proclamation from President Roosevelt, and

Count Bernadotte made a speech. After dinner the guests danced to the music of Sven Fors and his dance band.

Even with their busy calendar, the couple found time for serious conversations about a possible future together. In later years, Herman loved to give his version of the acceptance. "Hedy and I always had money. One of the things I did was play a lot of poker, and I was fortunate in the game. Hedy mentioned she wanted a fur coat. I had just had a big win, so I bought her a beautiful fur. It was expensive, about 4000 kronor.

"When I had first asked Hedy if she would marry me, her answer was, she thought she would rather wait until we went back to the States. This time I said, 'Well, either you marry me or I'll take the fur coat back.' That's all it took. We were engaged."

Herman's second proposal was more than two months after his proposal at the Rosendals garden. He and Hedy set a wedding date of February 21, 1945. Within a few days, Herman shared the news with his family.

> *Dearest Family,*
>
> *Pardon the informality of carbon, but I have news of first priority which, I hope, will be accepted with the blessings of you all. Hold your breath. Effective 9 December 1944, I am an engaged man. Prospects of the wedding are still in the offing.*
>
> *Full name Hedvig (Hedy for short) Elizabeth Johnson, age 23, citizenship American. She works here at the legation, and home town is Hibbing, Minnesota. We had our pictures taken recently and shall forward to you all for inspection and approval.*

Realize this is a refrain you have heard before, but somehow time has printed its lesson, and I know way deep down this is it. I love her, and Hedy in turn shares the same feeling. We both realize there are obstacles on the wayside but are confident that when they rear their ugly head we will have the courage and faith to meet them together.

5'3", blue eyes, brunette, a figure one dreams of but never expects to find, intelligent, can cook, and above average looks. Believe me, I know, as you all will agree.

Sugar, I know you will feel as I do when you meet and know her, which I hope will not be too long in the future. Please do not worry, for Hedy looks out for me as you always did and do. It's a great feeling, this happiness.

Take care of yourself and write. Love always, son Herman

The Arrest

On December 9, 1944, Herman was personally interviewed by the Swedish police on his dealings with John Lönnegren. The next morning at 8:45, John Lönnegren was arrested by the Swedish police and charged with rendering unlawful intelligence service to a foreign power. According to what Herman was told, when the police took Lönnegren away, the frightened man insisted, "I'm innocent. Call Herman Allen. He will tell you I am an innocent man."

There was nothing Herman could do. He had a sick feeling every time he thought about the arrest of the man with whom he had spent so many thought-provoking hours. Despite the intrigue, despite the reports, the two had become friends. The truth was that Herman had done a masterful job of gaining Johnny's confidence and thus contributing to the man's downfall.

To make matters even more interesting, one week later, on December 18, Carl August Robert Paulsson of the Swedish Aliens Commission was arrested.

The Swedish newspapers covered every detail. News bulletins quickly spread outside Sweden. There was even a small clip in the December 24 edition of the *Spokesman Review* in Spokane, Washington: "Swedes Jail Spy. Stockholm, Dec. 23. (AP) Police authorities today announced the arrest of John Alexander Lönnegren, former chief of the Scandinavian Telegram Bureau, on charges of supplying to Germany information on Norwegian refugees in Sweden."

Herman and Hedy had chosen a wedding date of February 21, 1945. However, almost immediately after Lönnegren's arrest, Herman received orders to go back to the States. The wedding would have to be rescheduled.

Herman had barely enough time to wind up his business in the military air attaché's office. He had no desire whatsoever to be involved in an upcoming trial.

The problem was that Hedy would have to stay in Stockholm until the war was over.

Christmas Holidays

On December 13 each year, Sweden observes Santa Lucia's Day in honor of a Christian Sicilian girl who was killed for her faith in AD 304. Because the name Lucia comes from the Latin word for light, the day is also known as "The Festival of Lights." Young girls put on long white dresses and wear crowns of candles and branches atop their heads.

Santa Lucia's Day is an important holiday, and in 1944 the Americans were there to partake in the festivities.

On the evening of Santa Lucia, Herman and Hedy, along with several friends, celebrated their engagement at one of the popular Stockholm restaurants. The next day, a newspaper featured a full-length photograph of Hedvig Johnson dancing with Captain Robb from the American Legation.

As a further celebration, Herman invited Hedy to take the train with him to Rättvik so the two could spend Christmas together at the resort village where he had spent his early days of internment. Reservations at a legendary hotel would be a romantic surprise.

Built in 1909 on the edge of Lake Siljan, the magnificent Hotell Siljansborg attracted affluent guests, many from other countries. In the summers of 1911 and 1912, the entire establishment was rented out by King Gustav V and his entourage. The royal family continued to visit the hotel until the 1950s and could be seen taking sleigh rides through the local villages.[328]

Possibly the most well-known non-royal personality to frequent the hotel was Swedish filmmaker Ingmar Bergman. Several of his scripts were written at the Siljansborg.[329]

Hedy was thrilled to be going with Herman to the famous hotel. The guests were exquisitely dressed, and the waitresses wore traditional Swedish attire. Views of the lake were breathtaking. Snow covered the ground and tipped the branches of the evergreen trees. Hedy could see a picture postcard in every direction she looked.

They stayed in one room and registered as Mr. and Mrs. Herman Allen. After all it was wartime, and they were in Sweden. No one's mother needed to know.

On Christmas Eve, the two enjoyed a traditional Smörgåsbord with varieties of herring and cheese. After carols by the fire and nightcaps and coffee, the night turned into Christmas morn. Then the sleigh bells rang. At 2:30 a.m., Herman helped Hedy into a sleigh adorned by lanterns with flickering candles. Hedy snuggled under blankets while Herman pushed the sleigh hard over the snow and then jumped onto the back for a few seconds' ride. They traveled about a quarter of a mile to the Rättviks kyrka, a landmark church whose oldest sections dated back to the 1200s.

Even though he was Jewish, Herman always shared in the traditions and glad tidings of Christmas. The church service lasted from 3:00 to 5:30 a.m., and Herman slept through most of it. Hedy remembered years later that it was the first time she had ever seen a grown man sleep while standing up.

They next day they dined on an elegant dinner of white fish with white wine sauce. There were more Yuletide songs with drinks and a hearty "skål" spoken from table to table. Herman slipped Hedy a poem he had written on a note-sized piece of paper.

Siljansborg Hotel, Rättvik, Sweden, 25-12-44

Dearest,
There are many things to write,
And many things to say,
But here's for you a Xmas bright,
And Happy New Year every day.
The sages thought it in ages past,
Twas old as the world is new,

Twas said on land before the mast,
The words, "I love you."
They said it then, I say it now,
The only difference be,
You are the one with whom I vow
Thus thru all eternity.

During this same week, back in the States, another family wedding was taking place. Herman's sister Dorothy married Bernard Barash, a young man she met in Chicago where she was working as a nurse and where he was studying toward an advanced degree in chemistry.

While at the University of Chicago, Barash was recruited by Italian physicist Enrico Fermi's research team to go to Oak Ridge, Tennessee. Along with Albert Einstein, Fermi had been one of the scientists who urged President Roosevelt to initiate an American nuclear research program.[330] At Oak Ridge, Barash's job was to produce heavy water isotopes. He had no idea that he was working on the Manhattan Project, only that his assignment was top secret with constant surveillance and fear of espionage.

Soon after Herman and Hedy returned to Stockholm from their romantic Rättvik interlude, New Year's Eve arrived. The merriest party of all was spent at the Grand Hôtel in the fabulous Mirror Room. This gilded hall was created in 1898, modeled after the Hall of Mirrors at Versailles. Both long walls were lined with floor-to-ceiling mirror-windows, and everything appeared to be lined with gold.[331] Dancing ended promptly at midnight.

On the last day of December, the airmen at Thurleigh were gratefully grounded after the previous day's mission to Mainz, Germany. Allied forces were engaged in the biggest battle the U.S. Army had ever fought: the Battle of the Bulge, Hitler's surprise offensive.

Most of the world was in turmoil, but the end of 1944 was magical and serene for two young lovers in Stockholm.

The New Year Explodes

On Thursday, January 4, Herman was back at work. Robert C. Goode, an internee working in Malmö, had received suspicious information. A man who claimed to be a Dane named the sites of four supposed atom bomb laboratories located in Denmark.

An atom bomb, the Dane had explained to Goode, was "able to kill all life within two miles of point of detonation with no visible signs of physical violence. As if the individual simply died from a heart attack or such." Herman wrote it up and submitted the report to Bill Carlson.

More explosive was the continuing publicity for John Lönnegren and Robert Paulsson. Bill Carlson sent to X-2 London a recap of what was showing up in the Swedish press. During the court hearings, Lönnegren acknowledged that in 1941 he befriended a German journalist who introduced him to two German agents. Before long, Lönnegren was supplying information to the duo. Details included the whereabouts, arrival and departure dates of one hundred refugees, primarily Norwegians, but also Germans and Poles. Lönnegren declared Robert Paulsson was the principal source of this information.

According to an OSS report, between November 1940 and December 1944, Paulsson sent over 500 replies to queries put to him by the German Legation. The Germans usually requested details, dates, places of birth, and other information about various persons living in Sweden or passing through the country. Paulsson's defense was that such things were authorized by the Swedish Ministry of Foreign Affairs.

The presumed reason the Germans wanted these names, newspapers reported, was so they could take reprisals against relatives of the refugees. Another motive could have been that the Germans were actively looking for individuals who had been involved in unlawful resistance activities. If these individuals were not in Sweden, then the Germans had cause to intensify a search in their homeland.

There were also discussions about British officers who arrived in Sweden after escaping from German prison camps. The prosecutor alleged that Lönnegren gave the name of one such officer to Dr. Wagner. Lönnegren declared again that he got the information from Paulsson, but Paulsson denied everything.

Lönnegren claimed he had tried to extricate himself from this work in 1942 but was threatened with exposure by the two German agents.[332]

As each article appeared in the local Stockholm newspapers, there was a storm of public indignation. Swedes became more and more outraged. Owing to the popular sympathy for their neighboring occupied countries, the activities of Paulsson, a government official no less, were viewed as particularly unsavory.

Herman could hardly bear to look at the headlines.

Although Lönnegren and Paulsson denied it, both men were charged with denouncing a certain foreigner who had been used by the Swedish Intelligence Service to unmask German agents. This foreigner was Erika Wendt, and now her secret was out in the open. In *Kodnamn Onkel,* the book Erika published in 1993, she wrote that she had no idea how they could have known what she was doing.

When the New Year had come and gone, Erika was still in hiding, moving from one safe place to another. She was sick of being on the run and yearned for an Allied victory, now seemingly her only escape from this prison-like existence.[333]

Lönnegren and Paulsson were questioned about the visit of the American generals. Lönnegren insisted he got the information that he shared with Herman Allen from Paulsson, who in turn vowed he had no memory of it. Lönnegren also maintained he couldn't remember whether or not he had disclosed any of this information to the Germans.

What with all the failing memories, Lönnegren did recall that he had eaten lunch with Allen the same day he got the alleged news from Paulsson. They had dined at the restaurant KB along with other American officers and Folke Bernadotte. "Allen knew everyone," Lönnegren testified.[334]

Another topic discussed during the trial involved the various legations' personnel lists which Lönnegren had turned over to the Germans. Named were the British, American, Russian, Polish and Norwegian legations. The lists included the names and home addresses of the military and diplomatic personnel. The typist who had prepared these lists stated that she had typed lists for all the great powers except for one, Germany.

Paulsson argued that he had no idea how Lönnegren had obtained these lists. He went so far as to say that sometimes Lönnegren had been left alone in Paulsson's office for half a minute. The trial also revealed that Paulsson was friends with one Wally Olsen, a messenger boy at the American Legation.

Lönnegren admitted that he received a monthly allowance from the Germans of 500 kronor for a sum total so far of 15,000 kronor.[335] This generous allowance permitted Lönnegren to dine out in the nice Stockholm restaurants and to buy fine things to entice pretty women to visit his apartment. Perhaps he had in mind that when the war was over, he would have enough money saved to move to America, as was his dream.

On January 14, a full-body photograph of Dr. Hans Wagner, Erika's "Papi," was featured in the newspaper *Dagens Nyheter* naming him as Lönnegren's good friend. Soon the Swedish authorities went to the German Legation and strongly suggested that Minister Thomsen arrange for the recall of certain Germans from their posts. Specifically the authorities were referring to Wagner and Uttermark, whom the prosecuting attorney had named as Lönnegren's employers.

The Swedish government also asked for the recall of Dr. August Finke, assistant to the German attaché in Stockholm and the person ostensibly in charge of Gestapo activities. Other cases of espionage had been traced back to these men.[336]

In the newspaper *Aftontidningen*, under the headline "The German Spies Must be Expelled," Thomsen called the disclosures in the Lönnegren case "a very definite hint to the German Legation in Stockholm that certain Germans, who enjoyed hospitality in Sweden because of their diplomatic positions, should take an airplane as soon as possible from Bromma to Berlin."[337]

By February however, Thomsen stated that he had not yet received orders from Berlin, and the offenders were still in Stockholm. He admitted that German-Swedish political relations were suffering from the almost daily discussions of the Lönnegren-Paulsson affair.[338] Wagner and Utermark finally did leave Sweden that month.[339]

The final day of the official Lönnegren-Paulsson hearings was filmed. The prosecutor asked for a conviction of both prisoners on a charge of espionage under Chapter 8, Paragraph 11, of the Swedish Penal Code. This chapter of the Swedish law dealt with treason and crimes which would be damaging to the realm, including the collection of or supplying of secret information which could injure neutral Sweden's relationship with another power.[340]

Paulsson spoke on his own behalf and said he did not feel that he had done anything criminal. He had not knowingly abused his position nor made any untrue statement.

The advocate for John Lönnegren read to the court a statement written by his client. Lönnegren admitted that he was deserving of punishment but urged it be understood there were mitigating circumstances. He referred to his age and his illness and said that he deeply repented his crime.

Judgment would be rendered on April 29.[341]

Chapter 12

The Wedding

Herman and Hedy hurriedly set a new wedding date for January 18. Count Bernadotte used his influence to eliminate the requirement of having the marriage bans published. Bernadotte also made arrangements for the wedding to be held at Gustav Adolfskyrkan, a beautiful red brick church just a mile from the American Legation.

No ordinary church, Gustav Adolfskyrkan was built in the late 1800s as a garrison church for the Swedish Army's Royal Life Guards, whose primary roles were to protect the Royal Palace and the heart of the Swedish Government. It was a high honor for the young American couple to be allowed to be married in this historic setting.

Herman asked Count Bernadotte to walk Hedy down the aisle and, as the Americans liked to say, give her away. Herman's good friend Captain Robb would be the best man.

Bill Carlson could not be at the wedding. He had been called to Washington, D.C., more than likely to help deliver the Stella Polaris records to William Donovan.

Gustav Adolfskyrkan on January 18, 1945. In front of the altar, from the left is Count Folke Bernadotte, Hedvig Johnson, Herman Allen, best man Robert Robb.

In preparation for the wedding, Herman and Hedy's friends at the legation had parties to celebrate and gifts to give. One of their friends expressed his tongue-in-cheek sentiment in a poetic way.

Dear Hedy:

Jag, take the man's best possession,
Long has he been free.
Many girls have so much enjoyed
Allen on a drunken spree.
If you even felt a bit guilty
Of a very obvious steal,
You'd think this all over,
And engagement vows repeal.

This man, once proud and strong,
Now brings us only dismay.
No more shall we know the drunkards tread,
Hedy will have all the say.
Accept this small gift with remorse,
And when this glorious name
Of ALLEN is taken as your own,
Think of its departed fame.

On the day of the wedding, the weather was perfect with a light snow on the ground. The full military ceremony was scheduled for two o'clock.

The entire American Legation had been given the day off to attend the wedding. In all, there were nearly 200 guests. The women were dressed in their finest outfits, complete with hats. Cameras were flashing as everyone arrived. The flashes intensified when Count Bernadotte in his full-length cape swept out of his chauffeured car onto the walk in front of the

Count Folke Bernadotte at the wedding of Herman and Hedy Allen.

church. Accompanying him was the elegantly dressed countess. Her cloche hat was worn over her forehead on one side, with a feather boa framing the side of her face.

Herman had received special permission to wear his dress uniform. Hedy wore a short aqua gown with a matching hat. Her veil was of black lace, and on her shoulder was a corsage of orchids, courtesy of Western Union. Above the altar, a rosette window reached to the ceiling and dominated their view. Pastor Svantesson performed the rites.

After the 20 minute ceremony, a reception was held a short walk away at Rigagatan 10, the apartment of Captain Robb. Thirty of the couple's closest friends, including Count and Countess Bernadotte, enjoyed an afternoon of toasts. The celebration became so noisy that the neighbors complained.

Min skål, Din skål, alla vackra flickors skål.
My toast, your toast, to all the beautiful girls toast.

Count Bernadotte presented to the newlyweds a custom-made Orrefors decanter, exactly eight inches high. Beautifully etched with a map of Sweden, the decanter was labeled with dates and cities meaningful to the couple—Stockholm, Västerås, Göteborg, Såtenäs, Malmö,

Rättvik, and Siljansborg. On the island of Gotland was an image of a B-17 and the date 6/3 1944.

To the right of the map, under the word "from" were printed the names FOLKE BERNADOTTE, GÖRAN von ESSEN, LARS HILL-LINDQUIST, LEO SAGER, CARL ROSENBLAD, ÅKE STAVENOW, BARBRO TOREN, ERIK WIJK, and OLLE ÅKERLUND.

The kiss.

Three days before the wedding, Herman had submitted a formal request to Major Conradi for a leave of absence commencing from 18 January 1945 through 25 January 1945 for the purpose of a honeymoon. The destination address was Hotell Siljansborg, Rättvik, Sweden.

The wedding gift from Count Folke Bernadotte et al. 1945 photograph.

Years later, Herman recalled his favorite memory of their Siljansborg honeymoon, "The morning of the wedding Doc Potter said to me, 'I don't have anything for a douche for you. I'll see if I can find one of

Hedy with Countess Estelle Bernadotte.

those rubber hot water bottles.' He went to the Swedish hospital and found one. It was the main contraception everyone used back then, a vinegar douche."

Hedy had written her parents as soon as she and Herman made their initial wedding plans for the 21st of February. When Hedy wrote next, she was already married. Because she thought the name Herman was too reminiscent of the Nazi Hermann Göring, Hedy liked to call her new husband "Al."

29 January 1945

Dearest Mom, Pop, and Ruby,

Married! One week, four days, and it's been wonderful! Mom, I was so sorry to have to shock you. I had written about our planned marriage on Feb. 21, but our plans fell through as Al heard he'd have to leave shortly.

We were married by a Swedish minister, in English, at Gustav Adolphskyrkan, 2:00 p.m. on the 18th. It was not a large wedding, but larger than I expected. I shook like a leaf and prayed the whole time that I'd stop shaking. Wore an aqua colored short dress (and when you see the pictures, please don't believe I looked quite that fat, really I didn't.)

Count Bernadotte gave me away! You should have seen him in his dress uniform with all the medals, ribbons, etc. all over. (Count Folke Bernadotte, nephew to the King.) I'm sure no one noticed me walking down the aisle. The pastor couldn't have been more wonderful, made all the arrangements, took care of everything. Captain Robb, who works with Al, was best man. Edith (have told you about her before, works with me and is my former roommate) stood up for me. Al in uniform.

We had a tiny reception at Captain Robb's flat, and Al and I left almost pronto on the train to Siljansborg (same place we went to at Christmas.)

We had a wonderful time, just one week, and it went so quickly, but I'll never forget it. My skiing has improved, but I still need oodles of practice. One afternoon we went to Falun, and a Swedish Captain Rosenblad entertained us. Will tell you all about everything when I get home. Al and I bought some things in Rättvik, little Swedish dolls in costume, souvenir ash trays, vases, serviettes, etc. but can't get them home until the war is over.

We came back to Stockholm late Thursday night and moved from my flat to Al's on Saturday so you can see how busy we've been. Our maid here is wonderful, two meals a day she makes, and does all laundry. The apartment is very comfortable.

You will be seeing Al before you see me. Don't know how soon and couldn't say anyway, but he'll be coming along to Hibbing. We have movies Al will show you and lots of pictures.

Oh yes, I have a fur coat! It's a honey, muskrat, and I was thrilled getting it. After all these years of trying to afford one. (It was Al who afforded it.) Can't wait till you see it.

Al's wonderful, as I've said so many times before. I'm sure we'll be so happy. By now, you must have the pictures we sent you after we were engaged. He's so considerate and good to me, and what is most important, we love each other.

Mom (I address this paragraph to you because I know it makes the difference to you, but I hope you'll get over it pronto, and I'm sure you will.) Al is Jewish. Mom, please don't think it isn't something we haven't discussed thoroughly. We have, backwards and forwards. There aren't going to be any fusses over the children, that's certain. And, I'm not going to wake Al up on Sunday mornings telling him he has to go to church with me. Al has been in the Army three years and hasn't been to the synagogue. He can't believe the things we've (Protestants) been taught to believe since childhood, but it's not easy to know what to believe, and you've said the same thing to me many times. I'm not going into religion now, but please know it is not going to be a problem.

We don't know yet what we're going to do after the war. Al was in school before the Army (he's 28 years old.) He had his Bachelors and Masters Degrees, ready to start on his Doctors, teaching history, major, physical education, minor. Whether he'll go back remains to be seen. Will probably be hard to do, but I would be willing to keep working if he should decide to. Anyway, the future is all ours, whatever we decide to do, and we'll make the best of it.

This letter is going to be too heavy I'm afraid. Will have to close now. I love you all so much and can't wait until I hear from you.

God bless you. Our love to you, Hedy

On the 12th of March, the wedding announcement appeared on the social page of *The Daily Tribune* in Hibbing, Minnesota. It gave the wedding details and mentioned the bride had worked in the State Department prior to leaving for Stockholm to be a secretary at the American Legation.

There was no mention of the Office of Strategic Services.

The newlyweds just outside *Gustav Adolphskyrkan*. Herman is holding the license.

Chapter 13

The White Buses

In mid-February of 1945, Count Bernadotte initiated a series of trips to Germany to negotiate with Nazis in top leadership positions for the release of prisoners from some of the most notorious German concentration camps.

Later that month, in deranged desperation, Hitler confirmed a rumor by then circulating all over the world. He ordered his cabinet to destroy all important cities and factories still remaining in Germany. At the same time, he demanded that prisoners in jails, labor camps, and concentration camps be put to death.[342] Hitler's longtime confidante Heinrich Himmler, head of the SS and the Gestapo, was to be the person to carry out this heinous order.

The Swedish government had already made the decision to send a rescue expedition to Germany. The request had originally come from the Norwegian minister, Niels Christian Ditleff, a personal friend of Folke Bernadotte and, like him, a man dedicated to humanitarian efforts.

As vice-chairman of the Swedish Red Cross, Bernadotte was well qualified to command this expedition. In 1943 and 1944 he had led the two successful and well-publicized prisoner of war exchanges. He spoke fluent German. He was well connected with the Germans, with the Allies, and with leaders of the Jewish community.

Beginning in 1942, the Swedish government had carried out direct measures to save Jews in Norway and Denmark. Bernadotte worked with Jewish leaders to send packages of food to Jews in concentration camps. Then Raoul Wallenberg went to Hungary in his desperate attempt to rescue as many Jews as possible.

Barely one month after Herman and Hedy's wedding, Count Bernadotte was in Germany to open discussions for the release of Scandinavian prisoners in Germany, many of them Jewish. He met with the second most powerful Nazi, Heinrich Himmler, along with Hitler's chief of foreign intelligence, Walter Schellenberg. These visits had to be kept secret from Hitler. He would never have agreed to the negotiations, particularly if Jews were to be rescued.

Schellenberg had been a frequent visitor to Sweden. He first went in 1941 to meet with Martin Lundqvist, head of the Stockholm bureau of Sweden's Civilian Security Service. It was not unusual for Nazi leaders to visit the neutral country. Intelligence officers from both sides moved about freely. After his first visit, Schellenberg began to travel to Sweden more often. The cultured German developed many important contacts there, and soon he was approached for help to free Swedes who had been captured by the Nazis. These rescue operations turned out to be largely successful.[343]

Bernadotte made several trips to Germany and had many meetings before final arrangements were made. On the 22nd of November, he was at the Swedish Legation in Berlin when the building was hit by Allied bombs. He was remarkably unshaken and more than ever determined to press forward.

The agreeable concessions by both Himmler and Schellenberg were obviously motivated by their desire to curry favor with the Allies. As Bernadotte wrote later, during his negotiations with Himmler, he asked the Nazi "if he would not admit that there were decent people among the Jews just as there were among all races. I told him that I had many Jewish friends."[344] I would like to believe Folke was thinking of Herman Allen, among others.

By March of 1945, the rescue known today as the "White Buses" was ready to proceed. This dangerous assignment would be carried out by the Swedish Red Cross with the unpublicized support of the Swedish Army. Count Bernadotte was head of the mission and received the critical assistance of many others from Sweden, Denmark, Norway, and Germany. The Swedish newspapers agreed to be quiet on the subject. It was vital that Hitler not learn about the operation.

Two convoys of trucks and buses set out from Malmö, were loaded onto ferry boats, and crossed over into Denmark. The two convoys converged into one of approximately 95 buses, trucks and ambulances as well as other vehicles carrying fuel and supplies. All vehicles were painted white and marked with a red cross so as to be clearly identified.

Their first destination was Friedrichsruh, a country estate near Hamburg owned by the Bismark family. When the entourage arrived, Count Bernadotte joined it.

The buses traveled from camp to camp within Germany and then returned through Danish territory over to Sweden. Prisoners were also transported to Sweden by ferry and by train. Many problems encountered along the way required Bernadotte's skilled intervention.

All in all, the White Buses expedition ended up being the biggest rescue effort inside Germany during the entire war. The precise number of prisoners taken out depends on the source, but the figure seems to be somewhere around 19,000 people, with just over 8000 of those being Jews.[345]

It was a foregone conclusion to nearly everyone except Hitler that Germany could never win the war. Unknown to the Führer, Himmler was already reaching out to the Allies, making inquiries about a separate peace, one excluding surrender to the Russians. During meetings with Bernadotte in Germany, Schellenberg made similar inquiries. He asked the Swede to suggest to General Eisenhower, Supreme Commander of the Allied Forces, that a German surrender on the western front might be worked out. Neither German wanted to include the Russians in their peace proposals. Certainly neither wanted Hitler to know what they were doing. Both men thought they could position themselves in a more favorable light with the Allies as Hitler's Third Reich fell apart.

Although Bernadotte refused to take the surrender offer to Eisenhower, he did send the proposal to the Swedish government. Soon the news was heard around the world. Both Roosevelt and Churchill refused to consider an option that didn't include an unconditional surrender by Germany to all the Allied powers. When he heard about this plan, Hitler was absolutely furious and threw Himmler out of the Nazi party.

By this time, the Führer's regime was as good as over. As the Russians were approaching his headquarters in Berlin, Hitler committed suicide on April 30 and took with him his bride Eva Braun. The Germans surrendered unconditionally a week later on May 7, 1945.

Walter Schellenberg reached Stockholm and was staying at Dragongården, the Bernadotte home. Estelle was not pleased, but she later explained that Folke felt indebted to the German for his help with the rescues.[346] Schellenberg used this respite to write about his fruitless efforts at peace negotiations near the end of the war. That Bernadotte had become so closely connected to this Nazi officer would come back to haunt him a few short years later.

During the White Buses operation, Col. Charles Rayens, assistant military attaché at the American Legation, followed closely the difficult negotiations between Bernadotte and the Germans. A meeting was arranged for Rayens with Schellenberg at the Bernadotte residence. Rayens' interest was to question Schellenberg on matters pertinent to the war with Japan.[347] The office of the Japanese military attaché in Stockholm was known to be active in secret intelligence operations. Stockholm eventually became Japan's most important intelligence post in Europe, with close ties to their German allies.

Schellenberg was still in Stockholm when a disguised Himmler was arrested at a British checkpoint in northern Germany. During his medical exam, the prisoner bit into a capsule of cyanide that he had hidden in his mouth. Heinrich Himmler had been a bankrupt poultry farmer who went on to order the torture and execution of millions. Unwilling to face up to his crimes, he died on May 23, 1945.

As for Schellenberg, he was tried at Nuremberg and received a sentence of six years, one of the lightest sentences given. Early in 1951, Schellenberg was released before his term was up and went to Switzerland to finish his memoirs. When the Swiss asked him to leave the country, he moved to Italy. He died there of liver disease on March 31, 1952 at the age of 42. Frau Schellenberg took his memoirs to London to be organized, edited and published.

Immediately after the war was over, Folke Bernadotte wrote his book, *Last Days of the Reich: The Diary of Count Bernadotte, October 1944–May 1945.* Readers were fascinated to read how this Swede was able to negotiate with the highest-ranked Nazis not only about a prisoner rescue but also about a German proposal of surrender. His name was now recognized all over the world.

Chapter 14

Goodbye Love

After Herman left for the States, Hedy wrote every day as she waited impatiently for news.

2 February 1945 Friday

> *Darling, Our first night apart in so long! Al, it's going to take some time to sink in. You're gone, darling! I can't grasp it.*
>
> *I couldn't go back to the office. When I saw you through the mist go down the lift, I cried like I never have before, and you old goat, on the floor were your blue silk jersey shorts and shirt where you threw them when you changed into your uniform.*
>
> *Confession, dear, and I know you're going to be horribly displeased. When the maid left, I drank over half the cocktails you had mixed in the decanter. They were no help. I felt worse, if anything. And, Al, the maid set two places at the table. Can't you see me in my place, with the phonograph playing and all those pictures? My eyes could not stay away from them.*

Now am a bit better (8:30) and tomorrow will see if I can't be brave and not burst into tears again. Don't know when you'll receive my letters but will write daily. I love you so and am sure it can't be long before we'll be together again. God bless you, dear, be good (no drinkin' or cussin') and I love you, don't ever forget, Hedy

P.S. Am a wee bit buzzy.

4 February 1945 Sunday

Dearest, 2 1/2 days you've been away from me, and I feel empty all the time. Am wondering now what you're doing and how you feel. Probably at this very moment, 8:45 pm, you're thinking of me. I'm sitting on the couch, the favorite one, with phonograph playing.

Last night spent a most domestic wifely evening hemming dish towels. Not for us but it made me feel very married! Came home early and read some stories from the Poe collection and scared myself to death. Kept hearing all sorts of weird noises.

Dear, am getting back into the old way of living with flannel pajamas, sweater, and bed socks, hair pinned up and oodles of cold cream. Al, I freeze to death without it all.

Today was a perfect day for skiing. Kurt, Casey, Greta and I all went out about 1:00 and came back at 4:30. You'll be pleased, Al. My climbing has improved, but I still can't plow or whatever it's called. We went all over Gärdet. Saw a lot of ski jumpers. There are three jumps, small, medium, and high. Whew! How can they do it?

Al, the news here is good, and I feel confident it won't be long. No Bill yet, and don't believe he's even near your parts. Am going to get busy now so darling, I close with all my love. Take good care, darling. I'll pray for you. I love you, Hedy XO

5 February 1945 Monday

Dearest Al, this makes three letters in three days. Try to beat that, hon.

Today the mail came in, and you received two from Grace, two from your sis, one from Mother Allen and one from Dad Allen. Will forward them on to you, dear. Al, are you sure you did right in having them give me your mail? No skeletons in your closet? Guess I know about them all, huh?

Darling, your Sis and Dad seem oh so pleased. And your Mom, too, except she asked about my accepting your faith. Al, dear, I can't help worrying there might be difficulties. We've discussed it so many times, but I still worry.

Grace asked for a picture of you which I will send. She also sent you a card. Quote, "When you come back again we'll paint the town red!" (That's what you think, thinks me!) I'll tag along, Herr Allen, if you don't mind, or even if you do!

Honey, these are short letters I write you, but they'll be almost daily to let you know I'm thinking of you always. Your loving wife, (hmmm— first time I've written those words. Sounds nice, eh?) Hedy

7 February 1945 Wednesday

Honey, I'm missing you so much. Last night, Al, I don't know what happened, but I got blue again. I wonder if I will ever feel happy here anymore. I just never feel that gay, silly way.

It seems too long since you were here with me. I wish time would fly, and I knew for sure you won't be leaving the States. I'm anxious to hear what will be decided.

The maid has been a darling. Fröken wants to stay every night, even if I don't get home until late. I'm really living the Life of Riley now, all meals made, all clothes taken care of. It's fun having everything done for me.

Honey, don't worry now because I'm not, but Al, no period yet. Today was the 31st day. Saw Doc Potter this morning. He laughed and told me not to worry and just wait patiently. He said his wife used to skip a whole month sometime. Well, that's what I'll do, wait patiently. But, ugh, Bill would crucify me if… I won't say it.

Good night now dear. God bless you and remember, I love you so very much, Hedy.

On February 10 and 11, there were blackouts in Stockholm. The legation sent everyone home at 3:45 in the afternoon. The first night, Hedy took a long hot bath. She was taking baths nightly, hoping to force her period to begin.

Am beginning to worry a bit. Not too much, though, because it would be so nice. I get all excited inside thinking it might be so, and then when I look at life in a practical way I know it would not be the best thing. Anyway, don't get too worried. I feel fine all the time, mornings too.

The next afternoon she and a friend went for a sandwich at Anglais, walked a bit, rode on the streetcar, and then had dinner at Berns. Next door at the *China Teatern* they saw Carmen Miranda in *Greenwich Village.*

When we came out of the movie it was pitch black, and neither of us had a flashlight. Cabs were unavailable, so street car it had to be. Certainly took me back to London days. I was scared walking home from the streetcar alone and feeling my way through those black streets. Got home safely though.

12 February 1945 Monday

> *Hon, I sent wedding pictures to the Count today, also three to Pastor Svantesson. The more I see of them, the more I resolve to stop eating, except for the fact I hate to hurt the maid's feelings.*
>
> *Bobby and Mab*[348] *have a baby girl, born yesterday morning. Bob was so excited when he told me about it. "The baby is almost six pounds, lovely complexion, most unusual in newborn babies." I must admit I egged him on a bit, but I got such a bang out of him. New fathers are so wonderful!*

Finally, Hedy began to receive news. Herman cabled as soon as he arrived in London, then his first letter arrived the following week. He had dined at one of her favorite restaurants, Claridge's in Mayfair, near Grosvenor Square. It was the swankiest hotel in London. Herman drank gin and lime and said it was a most expensive treat.

15 February 1945 Thursday

> *Dearest, your first letter came and was I excited! I've read it through 20 times already and will keep on until I get your next one.*
>
> *Al, still no curse after 39 days. Doc told me lots of people don't ever have morning sickness, so now I am worried. He said I couldn't find out anything until another month had gone by. So, am sweating it out. It would certainly complicate things no end.*
>
> *You have the cutest valentine from Gracie. A picture of a hula hula gal on top, and the words "gonna, gonna" open up and "Are you gonna or ain't you gonna be my Valentine."*
>
> *But you ain't gonna gonna.*

Hedy carefully wrapped all their wedding presents, including the many pieces of Orrefors glassware, in tissue paper and stored them in boxes. Herman had become good friends with Mr. Pråhl at the NK department store. NK didn't have anywhere to store the crates, but Pråhl agreed to make them ready for shipping. They would be insured and sent to the States when the time came for Hedy to be on her way home.

In an effort to save money, Hedy resolved to eliminate taxis as much as possible and take the street cars. She and Herman had 1700 kronor in the bank, and she was trying to save another 300 kronor each month from her salary. She went to look at a flat in Gärdet, an area a little farther north and less expensive than Herman's apartment on Garvargatan.

18 February 1945 Sunday

Darling, look at the date! Our one month anniversary. Al, it seems an age ago since that day in church. Never do I want to be as frightened as I was then. But the following two weeks, I live those over and over in memory. Darling, it's like a beautiful dream. To think that such a short while ago I was living up in the clouds somewhere. How silly we'd be and how we'd tease.

Honey, let's every year of our lives set aside two weeks and have a honeymoon. We'll divide the kids up and send half to one grandmother and half to the other. And we'll do something different every year—bathing in Miami, skiing in the Rockies, horseback riding, night clubbing. And then we'll come back feeling all wonderful, fetch the kids, and go back to our cute little house, and worry about David Richard's toothache, Pat's stubborn ways, etc. etc.

Last night Betty and I had dinner at KB's. Al, it brought back a flock of memories. Upstairs we were, with all the nasty pictures on the wall. Had an excellent meal, a nice long chat and got home early.

Well Hon, still no period. I'm being very casual about the whole thing now. Have to wait two more weeks though before Doc will be able to tell. I suppose if it's true, the gossip will fly!

Take good care, Al. Not much drinking, I hope. Write me everything you do. All your letters should be pages and pages long. Just look at how many I can fill writing about nothing. Yes, nothing except I miss you very much. Love you so darling, always remember that. God bless you, dear. Hedy.

20 February 1945 Tuesday

Darling, tomorrow, my dear, is the day we were to be married. It's still encircled on our calendar in the office. It didn't seem far off at the time we planned, but now it seems ages have passed. Bill wouldn't have been here to give me away anyway unless he comes back tonight.

Al, received your fourth cable. New York! Oh, how I wish I were with you. I have a hunch you sailed over. Tell me how the Statue and New York skyline looked. I bet you can't get many cigarettes now, at least from all the cartoons I see from the States about the shortage.

Good night, darling. Take care of yourself, Al. I love you so and I'm so lonely for you. Think I'll have a little cry now, and then I'll feel better. Write cheerful letters, dear. Your wife, Hedy.

23 February 1945 Friday

Dearest, Three weeks today, and it seems like three years! Bill came back this morning! It was wonderful seeing him again. He was sorry he missed you in London. He calls you "Blitz Allen." Ask him why. Said he had a feeling in Washington and consequently made arrangements for a new girl to come over (which we need badly anyway.)

No sooner had he come in the door and greeted us, "Are you pregnant?"

"NO!"

"Ohhh" (sigh of relief.)

"I don't think so."

"Uggh – !!$%&!!"

Edie and I knew we'd never have a chance to see him in the office, so we snatched him for lunch at Cecil's and had a two hour chat about the States, office, plus affairs, mistresses, etc. Know now what's been taking place in Washington and London, the gossip I mean.

You had five letters today, and I'll send them to you. Any explanations you may care to make or something you'd like to tell me, I'll be glad to hear. Am a bit puzzled. But I think you love me, and I know I love you so.

Had the nicest letter from Ace saying he wanted to be the first to welcome me into the family. I'm so anxious to meet him, Al, and everyone. Have to wait another week before I can have a consultation with Doc. Remember, dear, I love you, Hedy.

By this time, all three of the Allen boys were serving in the Army Air Force. Isadore, now known as Ace, was an aircraft engine mechanic at a base 70 miles north of Thurleigh.

28 February 1945 Wednesday

Dearest Al, just finished taking my last hot bath. Tomorrow all hot water is turned off. Gosh, I hate the thought of it. Heating water in kettles and then having half an inch in the tub! I've been in the tub for an hour now, reading and keeping the hot water running slowly the whole time.

Because of the continued fuel shortage, water could only be heated during authorized periods. This restriction didn't apply out in the countryside where homeowners had wood on their property. Suburbanites invited their Stockholm friends out for a "dinner and bath."[349]

> *Yesterday during lunch hour I went to Sturebadet. After a short conversation with Doc, decided no massage.*
>
> *Darling, got your 5th cable today. You'll be in Hibbing on the 5th! Am anxious to hear what you're going to think about the place.*
>
> *Last night saw* Conspirators *with Hedy Lamarr, written by Prokosch. Espionage! Was entertaining if a little fantastic. Then we all had dinner at Regnbågen. Brings back memories, huh?*
>
> *Al, I hope you don't leave the States. Let me know as soon as you know. Darling, I miss you more and more each day. Love you, God Bless you, Hedy.*

Hedy's biggest fear was that Herman would be sent to Japan.

1 March 1945 Thursday

> *Darling, 7:00 p.m. Am staying to write you. To think that one month ago, right now, you'd be popping in the door, "Operator 38 reporting." Wonder how long it will be before I get letters from the States. Am anxious to hear how it all seems to you. Bill was glad to get back. New York and Washington were too much for him. Jammed packed, no hotel rooms, no taxis, rude waiters and waitresses, etc. I guess Sweden is the most comfortable spot today. (Except for hot water!)*
>
> *Send me some pictures. Did you see Smithy? Good night, God bless you, and I love you, Hedy.*

4 March 1945 Sunday

Dearest, a Sunday in bed, reading and writing letters. Believe Betty and I will go to an early show tonight. She and Frances just came back from Persborg. The week we were in Rättvik, Al, was the best time. Don't forget, Hon, we'll take the children up there and show them where we spent our honeymoon. We'll take them skiing, sleigh riding, etc. and then put them to bed early!

Al, I hope it won't be long before we'll be back together. I feel so empty. Putting in time until we're with each other again. Bill says if what I suspect is true, I have to leave as soon as a replacement gets here. I love you, Al. Jag älskar dig, glöm det aldrig. Din hustru, Hedy

7 March 1945 Wednesday

Darling, we got a wedding present from Bill today. It's lovely! Pair of silver candlesticks! Plus a silver fruit bowl. Engraved on all three, "Hedy and Al—18 January 1945, Stockholm, Sweden, from Bill C." Bill made one of his touching speeches first, had me almost in tears. Kissed him at least five times.

Darling, sent you a cable this noon hour. What will people say? It just dawned on me this morning when I saw Cookie's doctor. Have thought it was true but didn't quite grasp it. When he examined me and said, "Yes, it's a baby all right," I beamed all over. Oh darling, if only we were together now. It's so wonderful.

The doctor filled out a form whereby I get extra egg, cheese, and butter coupons. Then vitamin pills, some other pills, and a few instructions. I'll take Doc Potter's advice on diet, as Swedish doctors don't pay any attention to it.

Don't worry about me, Al. I can't leave Sweden until July. Too dangerous to travel before then. Hope the new girl comes soon so she will be all broken in. Bill has been wonderful about it all.

Oh, received such a nice letter from Ace. The boys from the Propeller Shop chose me for their pin-up girl! Horrors! A married woman for a pin-up girl is bad, but a mother-to-be! Ace was so happy seeing you again.

Love, I'm going to bed now and sleep for two. Remember I love you, darling. Be good now and keep me posted. Good night, God bless you. Din hustru och lillan älskar dig, Hedy

P.S. Confession. Already have a couple of home-knit baby sweaters.

On March 7, Herman arrived in Hibbing to meet Hedy's family. They loved him immediately. He brought the wedding pictures and movies. Everyone laughed when they saw Hedy's beaming smile as she pointed to a large poster of a baby in the window display of a Stockholm shop.

Mama Johnson's neighbors, the Swedish ladies, came to meet Herman, and he charmed them all when he mumbled a few words of Swedish, probably all he knew.

Then, a Western Union telegram was delivered to their door. It read, "DARLING MISS YOU LOVE YOU DEARLY WRITING DAILY BELIEVE TWO OF US GOD BLESS YOU LOVE TO ALL. HEDVIG ALLEN." Herman couldn't have shared a more wonderful surprise with his new family.

18 March 1945 Sunday

Darling, it's a beautiful day, but I woke up with a horrible cold and decided I'd be wiser staying indoors. I don't think I'll read that approaching motherhood book anymore. It gives me the creeps, all the horrid things that can happen. When I read about the symptoms, I'm sure I feel this or that.

Now am doing what you and I planned to do so many times. Walking to work, back to the office from home after lunch. It's so lovely! Packs of people out walking or standing in the sun. And oodles of mothers pushing baby carriages. I turn to look at each one.

Thursday night a gang of legation girls went to see the basketball game. First Swedes played against Lithuanians, latter winning. Then U.S.A. versus Estonia, and the Estonians won but not without a fight. We girls yelled like mad, but there must have been half of the Baltics there because it seemed everyone in the bleachers rose when the Estonians scored.

Darling, bye for now, your wife who misses you so and who loves you dearly, Hedy.

Two days later, two cables arrived from the States, and Bill Carlson called Hedy into his office. He warned her to be calm, or she'd have a miscarriage. The first cable read, "DAD MET INSTANT DEATH IN MINE. FUNERAL TUESDAY 2 OCLOCK. MOTHER AND RUBY." The second was from Herman, "DEAREST WIFE DAD JOHNSON MET INSTANT DEATH MINE ACCIDENT DEPARTING FOR HIBBING IMMEDIATELY WISH POSSIBLE TO BE WITH YOU

THIS TIME SWEETHEART BE BRAVE LOVE YOU BOTH MISS YOU BOTH WRITING DAILY. HERMAN ALLEN."

Herman was in Washington State when he received the cable about Mr. Johnson's fatal accident. He immediately got on a bus and headed back to Minnesota.

Ruby wrote their brother Hedley that at 6:00 a.m. their father "*was walking from the coal dock back to the salt plant after putting in his report. It was foggy and raining, and he didn't have his flashlight on. The engineer couldn't stop in time. It means so much to us that he was killed instantly. Al is here and has been so much help to Mom. Easter may not seem what it should this year, but we all know what it stands for, and that's all that matters.*"

Alfred Johnson was 60 years old and had worked at the Oliver Mining Company for 30 years. Hedy was devastated to be a world away but grateful her father had learned three days earlier that he would be a grandfather.

28 March 1945 Wednesday

> *Darling, I've been so tired! We have so much packing to do. Fröken has been doing most of it. Saturday is moving day. I had your raincoat cleaned. I hope it was yours anyway.*
>
> *Our new apartment is tiny—two small bedrooms, living room and dining room combined, kitchen, and bath. Breakfast out on the balcony every morning. It's way out in Gärdet. Furusundsgatan, if you remember where that is. It will be so pleasant now that the weather is nice.*
>
> *Al, I hope time passes quickly and you won't leave the States. First part of July I'll be leaving here. Everything is going so nicely now, and the tacks on our map are really moving.*

Good night dear. I love and miss you. We both do. Doc laughs at me when I tell him I have a feeling it's going to be a boy. He's seen people have feelings before. But a girl will be wonderful too, won't it? God bless you, darling. Tell me everything about Hibbing when you write. I'm so worried about my mother. I love you so, Hedy.

3 April 1945 Tuesday

Darling, your letters came today, a slew of them! You have not an inkling of how happy they made me. I reread them all, and laugh sometimes, cry others. Also had a package from home. 15 bars of soap, make-up, nail polish, and a darling dress which is tight. I won't be able to wear it very long.

We moved, and what a job! I didn't carry anything heavy, but it still wore me out. Small but ample and 100 kr cheaper than Garvargatan (Doc Potter has taken it over, by the way.)

Al, the doctor said smoking would not hurt the baby in any way—just me! Liquor, I don't even feel like I want it, though Doc says it does no harm in moderation. I'm reading a book on prenatal care. One doesn't get enough advice from Swedish doctors. They merely say, "Carry on as usual."

I suggest you read a book or two on babies, dear, because it's your job too, don't forget. You must learn how to change diapers! We'll both have to get up a couple of times a night to feed the baby. I still can't believe it's true. Good night, darling, I love you dearly, don't forget. Din hustru, Hedy.

14 April 1945 Saturday

Dearest Al, I've had such a busy day. Roosevelt's death came as a shock. We had services at Storkyrkan in Gamla Staden at 2 o'clock, and then the legation was closed. Am enclosing the program. Everyone in uniform. The King and Crown Prince were there, and the rest of the royal family and all the diplomats from different legations.

I saw the doctor yesterday morning, and he's pleased with me. My blood pressure perfect, blood fine, fingernails and teeth good. He said I was unusually flat. You know, I'm pretty far along now, but no signs noticeable yet. I hope I'm out of here before it's obvious. Heavens! I can see myself gallivanting around the legation in a maternity dress. Horrors! For your information, I won't feel the baby move until about 4 1/2 or 5 months.

Take care and it won't be too long now. I love you, Al. Hedy

The death of President Roosevelt on April 12th should not have been much of a shock to the people around him. They knew he was ill and exhausted after his February return from Yalta, where he had met with Churchill and Stalin to discuss post-war Europe.

19 April 1945 Thursday

Dearest Al, I'm so lonesome. Seems time is dragging now. My heart starts pounding when I hear a cable is waiting for me, ever since that one. I'm so afraid I'm going to receive one saying you're leaving, even if you say you're certain you won't be.

Forgot to tell you I sold your bike. Believe I'll sell mine too. I don't think I will ride it this summer. The traffic is too thick now. Pleased dear?

I'm anxious to see what kind of Daddy you'll be. Men look so silly and act as though they're almost ashamed of being so thrilled over the baby. Darling, my letters to you now seem to only contain remarks about babies, babies, babies.

Good night, Love, take good care. We love you dearly. Have you read a baby book yet? All our love, Wife, Hedy.

21 April 1945 Saturday

Darling, I received the letters from your second stay in Hibbing. You are such a darling, and I love you so. My Sis wrote saying how much you helped my Mom and her through it all. That you could be there means everything to me. I feel so much better now.

Al, maybe it is best to have a slew of kids so someone will always be there. Well, I really don't mean it. Four at the most!

Santa Monica! Swimming, suntan, horseback riding, fishing! Oh, and here I sit! Pregnant in Stockholm and husbandless, working my fool head off! (I'm really not complaining, it says here in small print.)

Gas is rationed here too, so I'm not going to be able to toss any more boiling water down the drain. And Sturebadet is out for me.

The news, we don't miss a single broadcast now. And our tacks! Probably things will be cleared up by the time I leave, two months plus now. That seems too long, but perhaps it will go quickly.

> *If it weren't for Bill I'm afraid I'd be in awfully low spirits. We have such fun. He still refers to Jr. as "Little Blitz." Al, Bill says if you should ever wish to, when he goes back to his old work in London, you can work there.*
>
> *Darling, this is all for tonight! Won't be much longer. We love you so much, Hedy.*

Once he was back in the States, Herman's orders sent him first to Santa Monica, California, for a month of rest and relaxation. From there he went to Midland, Texas, to an advanced bombardier school with the intention of becoming an instructor. The dreaded prospect of going to Japan was always on his mind—and on Hedy's.

Work for Hedy and her colleagues did not slow down. By this time, Hedy was debriefing the Swedes who had been through Germany and then she typed up their reports.

26 April 1945 Thursday

> *Darling, received your package! All the things I needed! Lipsticks are nifty. I know you had the help of Mom Allen, else I would be shocked no end at your great ability to choose my colors.*
>
> *You'll be thrilled to know we're planning on one bridge evening a week here. Later on, you can teach me the finer points. It's not much fun playing blackjack with you anymore, seeing the money is all in one family.*
>
> *We're having difficulties with the gas rationing. Not enough to make two meals a day plus laundry and bathing. The maid is furious over it all, but the board or whatever it is will not*

call us three persons in spite of the fact that Fröken has all her meals here.

My dear, I am learning to knit! Half a year ago if someone had told me I'd be sitting with two knitting needles in my hand trying to make a pair of booties, I'd have said they were nuts. When I get back I'm going to take lessons from my Mom or your Mom. I'll have more time then, so perhaps will accomplish booties, sweater, and cap. I chose the color pink—girl's color, dear. I don't know why except if I struggled on for months in blue, feel sure it would be a girl. Awful I am.

To think—coming back after a year and a half, married and pregnant! Tut, tut. Laughed so hard at your story about meeting the boy who had been here. But then you let him sit there and discuss this "dish" (Dish!) before you explained you had married her. Men!

Bye for now, God bless you. I love you dearly, Al, your Hedy.

Chapter 15

Judgment After All

On the 28th of April, Robert Paulsson was sentenced to one year and ten months of hard labor and was to be removed from his position in the Aliens Commission. He was declared responsible for taking part in Lönnegren's unlawful intelligence activity and giving information about secret matters. His defense council protested, and subsequently Paulsson was released by the Appellate Court.

The sentence of John Lönnegren was two years of hard labor, and following a court-ordered mental examination, the verdict was upheld. John Lönnegren served his sentence. He died in 1949, a broken man.

Gray haired, portly, and always nattily dressed, during the war years John Lönnegren could talk for hours about a myriad of subjects. He had a sincere affection for a young American airman named Herman Allen. Perhaps in 1941, when Lönnegren was recruited by the German agents, he convinced himself that he was fighting on the right side and that Germany would prevail. When he realized it was impossible to disentangle himself, he got all caught up in the lure of the money, which brought him the gaiety and intrigue he coveted with the means to go out on the town and enjoy the company of his girls. When Lönnegren looked back on his actions, he knew he had done wrong.

The War in Europe is Over

After Hitler committed suicide on the 30th of April, his "Thousand Year Reich" soon collapsed.

The following week, Bill Carlson hosted a party for the legation crowd at his beautiful apartment on the upper floor of a grand house on Munkbron Square in Old Town. The translation for Munkbron is "Monk's Bridge" because of the bridge to the tiny islet Riddarholmen. On the islet sits Riddarholmskyrkan, a church originally built in the 13th century as a monastery that has served as the burial place of many Swedish monarchs.

Hedy, in her fifth month of pregnancy now, went home with Bill at 5:30 so she could sleep for a couple of hours until the rest of the guests arrived. The occasion was a farewell for several colleagues who were leaving Stockholm. The evening was wonderful, so wonderful that Hedy didn't get home until 3:00 the next morning.

Two days later, word came to Stockholm that Germany had signed military surrender documents. The war in Europe was over! The day was gloriously sunny. Church bells were ringing all over the city. Hedy and her friends joined the Norwegians in the throngs who paraded through Stockholm. "Ja, vi elsker dette landet," everyone sang in Norwegian. "Yes, we love this country."

From every office, workers were hanging out of their windows, throwing papers to the street below. They even emptied out their waste paper cans. Toilet paper streamers hung from the buildings. Confetti flew through the air and then fell like snow.

Open bed trucks and fancy convertibles overflowing with jubilant men and women drove slowly down the streets alongside the buses and trams. Everyone was in a frenzy, waving, singing, cheering, raising high their flags and bouquets of flowers.

The newspapers, even the Nazi-loving *Aftonbladet*, headlined "Extra Allmän TYSK capitulation," "General GERMAN Surrender." People stopped to buy the papers on the street and then paused to read. "Fred i Europa," they shouted. "Peace in Europe."

Hedy and her group made their way through the packed streets to the Hôtel Anglais at Stureplan. Along with the Americans, the Norwegians, Swedes and Danes jammed into the restaurant, dancing and singing. Champagne flowed like water. Hedy even danced the jitterbug.

She sat down to rest next to a Norwegian who, until three weeks earlier, had been in a German concentration camp for two years. He was so thin that it was hard for her to look at him, but they talked for a long time. "*I'll never forget his eyes; they were bulging*," she wrote Herman the next day. The legation crowd ended up at Hedy's apartment and stayed until 2:00 a.m. She slipped into her bed at midnight. She couldn't sleep but was able to rest her weary body. *"I listened to the broadcast from London. Would be wonderful to be there tonight. It certainly means everything to the people there. One doesn't get any such feeling here."*

The owner of her apartment building was furious about all the racket. The next day the owner told them that if any more noise came from their flat, they would be kicked out. Evidently some Swedes were not celebrating *Fredsdagen*, the Peace Day.

At the same time Hedy was partying on the streets of Stockholm, German Abwehr secretary Erika Wendt also went outside to celebrate. She marched down the main thoroughfare of Kungsgatan with a mob of cheering people. Everyone cried, "Fred!" Peace! A young man embraced her and said, "Now we have the German pigs, now they're dead!" Feeling she had no right to be there, she went home alone."[350]

Erika could hardly believe that she was free to go anywhere she wanted in the city. Börje, who worked with Ternberg, met her one sunny day soon afterward at Kungsträdgården, one of Erika's favorite spots. He said to her, "We're going to a cocktail party tomorrow at the home of William Carlson, the head of U.S. intelligence. He wants to meet you. He knows you are Uncle."

The next day Erika and Börje arrived at Carlson's elegant home on Munkbron and took the elevator to the top floor. Carlson was younger than Ternberg by nearly 15 years. He told Erika he was familiar with everything she had done for the Allies. The two were attracted to each other immediately. The cocktail party consisted of only one other person besides Börje, and the two of them discreetly left Erika and Carlson alone.

Before Erika left, Bill Carlson played the piano, first classical music, then folk songs that he sang in German. He took Erika's phone number and promised to invite her back for dinner. They did meet again soon afterward, several times in fact. One day, Bill's housekeeper packed a lunch, and they picnicked in a charming area south of Södermalm. Back at his home, he played for her again, jazz and American war tunes, and "Don't Fence Me In." She stayed all night. It was not for love, she thought, but for harmony and friendship, even if short-lived.[351]

Eric Siegfried Erickson

In May of 1945, Minister Herschel Johnson hosted a luncheon at Operakällaren, one of Stockholm's finest restaurants, located in the same building as the Royal Swedish Opera. Besides dignitaries from the American Legation, guests included representatives from the American

Chamber of Commerce in Stockholm, the press, many Swedish government officials, a member of the Swedish royal family, and representatives from OSS Stockholm.[352]

The guest of honor was an American oilman named Eric Siegfried "Red" Erickson. His presence was a shocking surprise to the audience, as Erickson was considered by most to be a traitor. As far as they knew, he had been working with Nazi Germany to provide them with oil, that most valuable commodity so necessary to fuel the Nazi's trucks, their Panzer tanks, and their planes.

In 1958, the book *The Counterfeit Traitor* by Alexander Klein was published. Two years later a movie of the same name starring William Holden was showing in theaters. Hedy shared with our family that it was about a spy named Red Erickson who had been in Stockholm while she was there.

Erickson was born to Swedish immigrants in Brooklyn, New York. Like Hedy, he spoke Swedish, and his language skill became a big factor in the path of his life. After serving in World War I, he received a degree in engineering from Cornell University. He worked for various oil companies all over the world and became an expert in the field. Erickson was also a flamboyant salesperson. After the Texas Oil Company sent him to Sweden, he started his own oil production company. Because of his close ties and dealings with Germany, as war spread over Europe he gained a reputation in both Swedish and Allied circles as a pro-Nazi traitor.

Around the end of 1942 or the beginning of 1943, Erickson contacted OSS Stockholm and set up a meeting with OSS Chief Tikander. He wanted to know what he needed to do to get off the pro-Nazi blacklist. When Tikander told him he would have to quit doing business with the Germans, Red insisted he wanted to do more than that. As a result of this meeting, Erickson's name remained on the blacklist, and he actively fraternized with the Germans and their Swedish friends.[353] He joined the German Chamber of Commerce in Sweden and socialized freely with the Nazis. He even blatantly insulted a Jewish friend in public.

Erickson's family was horrified. His new Swedish wife had a nervous breakdown. His brother Henry, who was working for the War Production Board in Washington, D.C., practically disowned him.

Few people knew that Red Erickson had become an Allied agent. His visit with Tikander was followed up by a series of trips to Germany, where he spied on almost every major Nazi oil refinery. He obtained detailed plans of their locations and operations, which he passed over to the OSS. In turn, this information went to the Allied Air Forces that later bombed the refineries.

In collaboration with Erickson was Prince Carl Bernadotte, nephew to the king of Sweden and cousin to Herman's friend Count Bernadotte. Erickson's royal connections helped give him access to the highest levels of the German business world. Because of Prince Carl's reputation as a wild playboy who had married a divorcee, Swedish associates believed that he too could be moving in Nazi social circles.

Germany was desperate for the oil supplies. In 1944, Erickson developed a lucrative proposition and laid it out for none other than Gestapo Chief Heinrich Himmler. Super salesman Erickson would build a synthetic oil refinery in Sweden. The fuel could be sold to the Germans with the profits shared with Himmler and his colleagues. This plan allowed Erickson access to refineries he had previously been restricted from seeing, as many of them had moved underground.

There is no doubt his efforts were an important factor in disrupting Germany's frantic quest for fuel. Their supplies were seriously dwindling. Their tanks couldn't move. Their airplanes couldn't fly. The war was soon over.

Erickson was honored by President Truman with the Medal of Freedom, the highest civilian award given to those who aided in the Allied war efforts. Truman recognized the valuable contributions Erickson had made with little regard for his own personal safety.[354]

William J. Casey, who served with the OSS and went on to be Director of Central Intelligence in 1981, described Erickson as Stockholm's most valuable asset.[355]

Years after the war, when Red Erickson talked with his family, he described how dangerous his involvement really was. As his nephew Joe explained, his uncle "was sure the Gestapo was on to him. Since he flew frequently between Germany and Sweden, he knew many of the pilots. He carried a gun when he boarded his last flight back to Sweden. After take-off, he was in the cockpit chatting with the pilot when orders came over the radio to return to the German airport. Eric took out his gun. The pilot said, 'No need for that, Eric. Germany is done, and I am done with Germany.' "[356]

Because of the publicity the book and the movie generated, Erickson's story is one of the better-known espionage cases to come out of OSS Stockholm. Erickson cooperated with both the book and the movie, and they represent with reasonable accuracy what really happened.

According to a 1959 report by Wilho Tikander, the people at OSS Stockholm most closely involved with the Erickson case were Dr. Robert Taylor Cole, Dr. Richard Huber, and Walter Surrey. However, a gentleman who worked there in 1944 told me that Bill Carlson also worked on the Red Erickson case. If this is true, Hedy typed the reports for her boss.

Tikander's report goes on to explain, "There were a few other high-ranking American officials involved in this project, but their identity cannot be disclosed even at this late date for reasons of security."[357] After the war, Carlson stayed to work in Stockholm for a while. When he moved to France to pursue business interests, he continued to work for intelligence organizations.

As for Red, he spent the last years of his life on the French Mediterranean coast and died in 1983 at the ripe old age of 92.

Chapter 16

Going Home

Repatriation

Sweden's official policy as a neutral nation was to intern both personnel and planes from belligerent countries until the end of the war. As time went on and the war situation changed, procedures became more and more flexible. Early on, the internees in Sweden were repatriated back to their home countries on a one-for-one basis. If one German airman was returned, so was one from the Allied forces. In many cases, the Germans went home immediately. However, as larger and larger numbers of Americans arrived in Sweden, piecemeal repatriation became impractical. There were so many more Americans than Germans to send home.

To help resolve the imbalance, the Swedes made deals with the Germans. For example, Allied airmen would be released in exchange for Sweden releasing interned *Luftwaffe* airplanes.

Later in 1944, when the outcome of the war was obviously in favor of the Allies, Sweden made another deal with Britain's RAF. Seventy-five of their crew members were sent back to England in exchange for 50 sets of radar equipment.

An American Legation message dated September 28, 1944, read that the Government of Sweden had decided to release 300 of the interned airmen "in anticipation of any Germans who might come into the country." The memo made clear that releasing the Americans was a gesture of friendship and goodwill to the United States. The message continued, "The Government regrets it is not feasible to release the entire number. From an internal political point of view, it would be embarrassing for the Government to empty all of the American camps at the same time."[358] Two days later, 270 internees were released.

Upon repatriation, the airmen were ordered to refrain from divulging to any unauthorized person the facts concerning their internment or their repatriation lest publicity hinder arrangements affecting the release of fellow airmen. They signed a document which read, "I also fully understand that I shall be bound by these orders and this certificate after the war, and I undertake to maintain complete secrecy and to refrain from publishing any article or book violating these orders, nor will I give to others any information which might be used by them for such purposes."

A few days after the September release, an account of an interview with two formerly interned officers appeared in the New York papers. As a London reporter recounted , they had been released from Sweden in exchange for two German airmen, and a number of other internees would be released in the near future on the same basis. The Air Force considered this information leak a breach of security and cabled the Military Attaché in Stockholm to request disciplinary action and to take steps to prevent a repetition.

To make the issue even more complicated, ambassador to Great Britain John Winant cabled the State Department that the British Foreign

Office was stressing the importance of keeping the Soviets fully informed on all negotiations involving the release of our airmen in exchange for Germans.[359] The Soviets were concerned that the released German soldiers would be used to fight against them.

Negotiations continued. The United States gave the Swedish government nine of the B-17s now in their country. Seven of these aircraft were converted into passenger planes for civilian use. Because one of the men who worked hard to put this deal together was Military Air Attaché Felix Hardison, the converted aircraft were known as "Airplanes Felix."[360]

The Americans also offered to bring over 50 P-51 Mustang fighters and leave the four already in Sweden.[361] An additional few hundred crew members were released. These men came out in October and November.

Working from the Office of the Military Air Attaché, Ted Borek and Herman Allen oversaw many of the logistical details of releasing the internees. When Herman had information that needed to be in the hands of Count Folke Bernadotte, he delivered the messages in person to Bernadotte's office.

The large groups of internees about to be released gathered in the suburbs of Stockholm, secure areas with facilities to house them all. Two of these areas, both south of the city, were Saltsjöbaden and Södertälje. From there, on an evening when the weather was bad enough for them to fly safely over German-occupied territories, the internees traveled to Bromma airport. Once cleared through customs, they boarded the dark green unmarked Liberators.

One airman wrote in his release form that, once on board, they were each handed an army blanket and a life preserver. He was shocked to see that there were no parachutes for the thirty men who squeezed together on benches in the bomb bay and waist area. It was a long cold six hours before the plane landed at Scotland's Leuchars airfield.

After the war with Germany was over, the American aircraft had to be repatriated. The Swedish Foreign Office released 32 B-17s and 44 B-24s from internment. Six ferry crews were sent to Stockholm, the departure point being the Västerås airdrome.[362]

As the planes left Sweden, they dipped their wings in salute as they soared over the American cemetery in Malmö where white crosses marked the graves of U.S. airmen.

Equipment was repatriated too. Roland A. "Ron" Lissner was pilot of a B-17 that force-landed in Sweden on February 3, 1945. In March, after Lissner mentioned to his commanding officer that he was bored, he was sent to work at Strandvägen 7B for General Alfred A. Kessler, Jr., who in December had replaced Felix Hardison as military air attaché.

From March until the end of August, Lissner was in charge of the interned salvaged aircraft equipment. This included engines, parachutes, guns, electric suits, and nearly one hundred leather jackets. Everything had to be packed up. The Swedish government asked that the equipment be sent to Oslo by train and then to England by ship.

When Lissner arrived in England, he remembers watching two or three B-17s being towed out into the Channel, their final resting place.[363]

One frequent question is whether released internees went back into combat. The answer is yes, for a while they did. Both the pilot and co-pilot of the *Liberty Lady* returned to Thurleigh in October of 1944 to finish up their missions. They were asked not to discuss their internment with the other airmen on base.

Soon after, the Air Force made a change. According to an official memo, "The large-scale evacuation of Army Air Force personnel from Sweden necessitates a change of policy relative to the final disposition of personnel. Effective Thursday, 12 October 1944, all personnel who are released from internment in Sweden and arrive in the United Kingdom will not be able to return to active combat status with their former units." Released internees were directed to proceed to the 70th Replacement Depot to pick up their new orders. For no more than ten days, they could visit their former units. Obviously, the *Liberty Lady* pilot and co-pilot returned to Thurleigh just in time.

Many former internees were sent to the States and, like Herman, anticipated they might next go to Japan.

Another question concerns how long the orders of secrecy lasted. The ink on surrender documents barely had time to dry when books and articles began to be published about every aspect of the war. The answer to the question depended on the importance and continued contemporary relevance of the information. When the war with Germany was over, most information the internees might have been privy to would not have been classified.[364]

On October 15, 1944, the internment camp at Rättvik officially closed. Leaving Rättvik was an emotional experience not only for the internees but also for their new Swedish friends. When it was time for the last men to say goodbye, nearly the entire town followed them to the train station. They all waved to each other as long as they could until the train disappeared.[365]

By 1945, the remaining internee camps were closing down one by one. The auxiliary camps at the airfields Såtenäs, Västerås, and Malmö were open as long as the American planes were there. Finally, Korsnäs at Falun, as well as an annex in Rättvik at the Turisthemmet, accommodated the late arriving airmen.

The last internee to be released and returned to the United Kingdom was James L. Howard. The date was August 12, 1945. His return completed the repatriation of interned American personnel.[366]

Herman and Hedy

9 May 1945 Wednesday

> *Dearest Al, A holiday tomorrow. Somehow these past few days have given all of us a permanent holiday feeling. It's safe for me to travel anytime now, but I suppose I'll be patient and work until the middle of June.*
>
> *My dear, I am getting a tummy. Monday I am taking off to shop. My skirts are getting tight. Can't get too many clothes here, too darn expensive. You know, I've been figuring my months wrong. Here's how. January 7 (last curse period), count back three months is October 7 plus ten days. October 17, approximate date of baby's birth. Do note that it is, tut, tut, one day minus nine months after January 18. I know, Hon, everyone is wondering. Really it doesn't bother me. In fact, it amuses me. Ty* (Tikander) *even asked Bill about it. People!*
>
> *Edie has hot water at her house today, so am going over pronto to sit in a deep tub. When I get back, I'm taking three tub baths a day, every day.*
>
> *So long dear, Hedy, who loves you very much.*

Hedy was finally able to leave Stockholm on June 1. She flew from Bromma to RAF Leuchars airfield in one of Bernt Balchen's Liberators. She was seated on a narrow bench and squeezed between two gentlemen who were as tired as she was, and there was little conversation. From Scotland, she took a train to London. Her transatlantic flight landed in New York, and from there she went to Washington, D.C. where, completely exhausted, she checked into the Carleton Hotel and the main OSS offices on Navy Hill.

Hedy's office took almost a week to secure for her a Pullman train reservation to Chicago from the busy capital city. Then Hedy rode another 600 miles by coach to Hibbing. She was finally home with her mother and Ruby on June 14.

Herman wrote from Texas that he was to be stationed at McDill Field in Tampa, training to be a radar commander. He and Hedy would look for an apartment there. A week later, Hedy traveled by train to Tampa and was finally reunited with her husband. The story of her arrival has been family folklore ever since.

Herman watched as a dark-haired young woman walked down the steps from the train. He wasn't sure if he was seeing the right person. Could she be his "dish" of a wife? She was pregnant and had swollen ankles. The permanent she had got in Hibbing had left her dark hair frizzier than he had ever seen it. He waved like crazy, though, and ran to meet her. Hedy was totally drained from two weeks of traveling and immediately began to sob in his arms. It had been a long five months.

Once they were together, Hedy didn't take long to recover. She was thrilled to see her husband, as was he to see her, and they were both looking forward to a glorious romantic reunion.

Since McDill didn't have accommodations for both of them, their first stop was to find temporary lodgings. Herman directed the taxi driver to stop at one of the nicer hotels not far from the airfield. They needed somewhere to stay while looking for a permanent place to live, and Herman wanted to give his bride a special treat.

When they walked up the steps to the lobby, neither of them could hold back a fleeting memory of the Grand in Stockholm or the Siljansborg in Rättvik. When they got to the large registration desk, Herman froze. Next to the registrar was a sign, GENTILES ONLY.

Herman was mortified. This was not a new experience for him, but it certainly was for his new bride. Hedy was mortified too. Her immediate reaction to the hotel desk clerk was, "Humph. We'll just go somewhere else."

Welcome home, Lieutenant.

Chapter 17

Thanksgiving 2007

And now it was Friday, the day after Thanksgiving, Hedy's fifth day in the hospital. The family was taking turns staying overnight. The doctors ordered the nurses to give her morphine whenever she needed it, and she was asking for it more and more often. We could talk with her for short periods between naps.

The family was gathering, the first time in many years that all five siblings had been together at Thanksgiving. Our tradition, for as long as I can remember, has been to celebrate on Friday. On Thursday, we cook and travel. Through the years, I've joked how convenient this schedule was. I could go to the grocery store on Thursday morning, and no one else was there.

We tried to keep visitors in Hedy's hospital room to a minimum, two at a time, if possible. The rest of the family gathered in a nearby waiting room with books and laptops open, soft music on. When my niece Emma opened her laptop and played an Andrews Sisters song, I burst into tears.

Mother hadn't eaten much of anything all week, just a bit of breakfast one morning. I asked her if she would like chicken soup, and she nodded, saying, "Yes, that sounds good."

Hedy had a special love for matzo ball soup, so my assignment was to make a pot for her Thanksgiving dinner. That morning, friend and Columbia real estate agent Jennifer Harding called Kathy to see how Hedy was doing. "She's resting comfortably this morning. Patti is looking for a recipe for matzo ball soup." Jennifer immediately said, "I'll have a pot of matzo ball soup ready this afternoon if Patti can meet me between appointments."

I did. It was delicious, and Hedy did have a few sips.

We didn't realize it at the time, but the soup would be her last meal.

Chapter 18

After the War

Before the month of May was over, OSS Director William Donovan received a memo from Wilho Tikander titled "OSS, Sweden, Winding up of operations." With the European hostilities over, most branches were closing out, and American subjects were either heading back to the States or awaiting other assignments with the OSS or with the State Department.

X-2 was the exception. Tikander wrote, "It appears this Branch will have to continue in operation indefinitely, and it is hereby recommended that it be made the successor to OSS Sweden. There is still a large amount of current work under process, and the prospects of increasing work are looming."

Tikander recommended William T. Carlson, presently Chief of X-2 Sweden, to succeed him as Chief, OSS Sweden. Edith Rising would remain as Carlson's secretary. Since Hedvig Johnson-Allen was returning to the United States in early June, Carlson would be given additional staff.[367]

In July of 1945, Donovan wrote a memorandum for President Truman outlining a summary of OSS activities in Sweden, the principal functions being to collect intelligence on Germany and to give support to active resistance in Norway and Denmark.

> OSS officers attached to the American Legation in Stockholm and to consular offices in other Swedish cities derived information both from clandestine intelligence chains and from sources available through Sweden's neutral position. Special agents, infiltrated by OSS as far as Berlin, Hamburg, and Leipzig, obtained more specific facts from these cities. OSS and British officers, cooperating with the Danish and Polish undergrounds, collated eyewitness accounts of conditions in German-occupied territory. Numerous refugees, Swedish businessmen, government officials and seamen arriving from Germany provided valuable general data on the changing economic and political situation inside the Reich.
>
> Intelligence gleaned from these sources was evaluated and processed for distribution to interested agencies. Reports on Germany, along with German documents and periodicals, were regularly dispatched to London and Washington. A blacklist of firms and individuals doing business with the enemy was kept current, and continuous investigations were made, tracing refugee German funds and investments seeking a safe haven in Sweden. Information on such enemy activity and on Nazis attempting to hide in Sweden was turned over to local authorities, who in several instances arrested the suspects. In addition, radio stations in Sweden provided a relay for messages between England and the resistance forces in Norway and Denmark.

> To aid resistance movements, OSS worked in close cooperation with the British Special Operations Executive. Supplies of arms, explosives, and equipment were clandestinely stored in Sweden and parachuted into Norway and Denmark or slipped over the Norway-Sweden border by sled. In this way, hundreds of tons of materials reached underground forces.
>
> These supplies were used in Norway in open guerrilla warfare against German columns in the north and in continuous sabotage attacks against railway lines connecting Oslo with ports along the southern coast and the Oslofjord. In Denmark, they were employed to blow up factories producing equipment for the German Army and to destroy enough track to bring railway traffic virtually to a standstill.
>
> The success of these activities was in large measure due to the attitude of the Swedish Government with whose knowledge and tacit consent they were undertaken.
>
> William J. Donovan, Director[368]

Operation Safehaven was the code name for efforts to track down Nazi-plundered valuables, for example, artworks, gold, and diamonds that might have been sent to neutral Sweden for safe keeping. Bill Carlson's X-2 was involved in the efforts to document such German transactions.

On September 28, 1945, Major General Donovan recommended that Capt. William T. Carlson be awarded the Legion of Merit. In his two-plus page endorsement, Donovan wrote about an accomplishment that had directly involved Lt. Herman F. Allen.

> ...During the course of the war, numerous American aviators were forced down within Swedish territory. Permitted a certain freedom of action by Swedish authorities, they became a natural target for enemy intelligence personnel who endeavored to learn from them vital information regarding American air strength and technical equipment. To Captain Carlson was entrusted the responsibility of ensuring their security; by constant vigilance and the utmost tact he was able to warn them of many undesirable contacts which they had been on the point of permitting to be established. Additional checks on the success of enemy efforts in this direction were maintained by sources available to Captain Carlson, and it can be said that no success was met with by the foe.[369]

Tikander reported that at one time or another there were 75 Americans attached to the OSS Mission in Sweden. In addition, a large number of foreigners worked for the various branches either directly or indirectly. Many of them had no idea they were working for the OSS. Their superiors asked them to do a job, and they did it.[370]

The End of the OSS

When he heard the news that President Roosevelt was dead, William Donovan was devastated. Roosevelt had been his friend and ally. Harry Truman was neither.

Donovan was finally allowed to speak to the new president about his ideas for a permanent post-war intelligence service. He sent memos and reports, trying to demonstrate the value of his organization. He embarked on a public relations campaign. The press was not on his side, however, and neither were most of Truman's advisers.[371]

Despite Donovan's efforts, on the 20th of September with Executive Order 9621 President Harry Truman disbanded the OSS effective October 1, 1945.

On September 28 Donovan bade farewell to more than 700 members of his staff at a converted skating rink just down from his Washington offices on E. Street. When the government could not find the money to pay for refreshments of Coca-Cola and hot dogs, Donovan personally covered the expense.[372]

"We have come to the end of an unusual experiment," Donovan said to the tearful group. "This experiment was to determine whether a group of Americans constituting a cross section of racial origins, of abilities, temperaments and talents could meet and risk an encounter with the long-established and well- trained enemy organizations … You can go with the assurance that you have made a beginning in showing the people of America that only by decisions of national policy based upon accurate information can we have the chance of a peace that will endure."[373]

It was a somber goodbye.

OSS Research and Development went to the State Department. The SI and X-2 branches were preserved in a new organization called the Strategic Services Unit (SSU). Within two years, personnel and assets went to an organization called the Central Intelligence Group (CIG) which in 1947 became the Central Intelligence Agency (CIA). In fact, the Washington, D.C. offices where Hedy worked in 1942 and 1943 were used for many years by the CIA.

No matter what their agency was called, many of those who transferred out of Donovan's group continued to call themselves "OSSers."

As Virginia Hahn, who served in X-2 Counterintelligence, wrote, "I was sitting at my desk in Germany doing the same sort of work, but then concerned with Soviet intelligence activity instead of the Gestapo."

The OSS trained many future leaders of the CIA, including four future directors of Central Intelligence—Allen Dulles, Richard Helms, William Colby, and William Casey.[374] Even though William Donovan had dreamed of heading up such an agency, it was not to be.

Earlier in the year, Donovan had joined the staff of the chief counsel for the prosecution of war criminals. Supreme Court Justice Robert H. Jackson discovered that the OSS, under Donovan's direction, had long been collecting evidence of wartime atrocities. Donovan was personally interested in seeing the criminals brought to justice, and he assigned other OSS staffers to join the team. When it was time to select a venue for the trials, Donovan pressed for Nuremberg, which is where the world's first international war crimes trial was held.

Unfortunately, many differences in strategy and personality developed between Donovan and Jackson. They couldn't work together. After an angry exchange of letters, Donovan left Nuremberg. The trials had just begun.[375] Still, the contributions of Donovan and the OSS to the Nuremberg trials were significant in securing a degree of justice.

With the OSS gone, Donovan returned to his law firm and civilian life. Always on the lookout for intelligence-related information, he passed along his ideas to the leaders of the newly formed CIA.

On February 8, 1959, William Joseph Donovan died at Walter Reed Army Medical Center in Washington. He is the only person to receive our nation's four highest decorations—the Medal of Honor, the Distinguished Service Cross, the Distinguished Service Medal, and the National Security Medal. When President Eisenhower heard the news of Donovan's death, he said, "What a man! We have lost the last hero."

The American Internees

In 1944, William W. Corcoran, U.S. Consul in Göteborg, Sweden, made charges that the neutral landings had increased to such an extent that they must be due to low morale. He wrote about speaking with airmen who had force-landed in Sweden and others who had escaped from enemy territory or enemy prison camps. They said, he reported, that they were done with flying. Even though he described their experiences as harrowing, he felt they now displayed a "complete lack of patriotism and continued sense of duty."

When Herman and his associates in the Office of the Military Air Attaché visited the site of a forced-landed aircraft, one of their jobs was to determine whether or not the crew had arrived under any but legitimate circumstances. Herman insisted that he always found their actions had been justified.

Military Air Attaché Felix Hardison strongly refuted Corcoran's charges. He noted that Corcoran had contacted only three airmen. On the other hand, Hardison was in daily contact with the men in the camps. Hardison noted, "On the whole morale was good, and the majority of our flyers express an earnest desire to get out of Sweden and return to active duty."[376]

Finally, Gen. Carl Spaatz, commander of the U.S. Strategic Air Forces in Europe, responded that in light of the large number of missions, casualties, and damaged aircraft, a very low percentage of crews were going to Sweden, less than one-half of one percent. He said, "We resent the implication by a non-military interrogator that any of these crews are cowards, are low in morale or lack the will to fight. Such is a base slander against the most courageous group of fighting men in this war."[377]

After the war, differing reactions to the experiences of the American internees continued. When tail gunner and internee William F. Powell was interviewed in 1992 by Dr. Gordon Pickler, he explained his thoughts on the situation: "Everybody wants to finish their missions. Nobody wants to go down. You want to finish, and you want to go home."

We have all read graphic accounts of air crews whose planes were badly damaged over enemy territory by fighters or by flak. Often the captain had no time to react except perhaps to give the immediate order to bail out.

Other options were not good. The crews could ditch in the water, land in hostile territory, or try to evade the enemy fighters waiting to finish them off. From their oft-burning bombers 30,000 feet high in the air, the pilots knew that the decisions they would make in the next few moments would decide the fate of ten men.

As the missions deep into German territory intensified, many crews were told that if they couldn't make it back to base, diverting to a neutral country might be their best option. In many cases, it was their only option.

The Liberty Lady

During March 1944, the partially destroyed B-17 *Liberty Lady* lay sprawled on the Mästermyr. The plane was fenced off and guarded day and night to make sure it was not plundered, for it seemed that everyone in town wanted a souvenir.

A group of Swedish Air Force technicians working under the command of legendary aviator Captain Albin Ahrenberg traveled to Gotland to investigate the plane. They removed valuable parts that could be used in Swedish aircraft. The airline ABA bought the engines to be rebuilt and used on freight and passenger planes. A carpenter was hired to build boxes to transport the weapons which were returned to the Americans.

The Liberty Lady on the Mästermyr.

The dismantling of the *Liberty Lady*. (from the collection of Stan Buck.)

Workshop owner Albin Larsson paid 250 kronor for the remains of the *Liberty Lady.* He guaranteed that no part of the plane would reach the hands of an enemy of the United States.

After key parts were removed, dismantling came next. The ground was too wet to transport the pieces of the plane. Some of the marshland was even under water. The work crew had to wait for the sun to dry the field.

Thick boards were placed on the ground so that the tractors hauling the parts could get over to the road. One day a photographer, Gustav Forsberg, came to the site to record their progress permanently. Albin Larsson proudly climbed atop the *Liberty Lady's* vertical fin and straddled it, his feet touching the triangle H that signified the 306th Bomb Group.

Albin Larsson atop the Liberty Lady.
(Svensk Flyghistorisk Förenings arkiv. Ola Forsberg Owner)

Young Lars Björkander had seen the *Liberty Lady* land in the farmer's field. One day Captain Ahrenberg drove Björkander, along with the son of Albin Larsson, to visit the crash site. As they passed the guard at the roped-off section gate, the two boys lay down on the truck floor so as not to be seen. They were laughing so hard that it was amazing the guard didn't hear them. Once inside the secure area, the boys were able to go right into the plane and see for themselves the work being done and what still remained. They were thrilled to be there.[378]

Nils Romin, a member of the Swedish Home Guard from nearby Havdhem, had arrived on the day of the landing, right after Albin Larsson. Nils guarded the plane at night so no one could steal any parts. Eventually, he was given the plane's shackle. Years later, his grandson Mattias Eneqvist noticed it hanging on a nail in his grandfather's workshop. The story of the B-17 inspired Mattias to begin researching the flight of the *Liberty Lady*.

Albin Larsson's shed was filled with miscellaneous plane parts. Rickard Melin, working for Albin at the time, asked for the landing lights. Albin agreed, and Rickard used the lights on his fishing boat. After Mattias Eneqvist placed an advertisement in the local paper to buy parts of the *Liberty Lady*, Rickard gave the lights to Mattias, who is sure they were the strongest lights ever to be used on a Gotland fishing boat.

Pieces of the *Liberty Lady* can be found all over Gotland. One of the local citizens even saved a pilot's leather helmet. For a while, scrap pieces of the plane were used to mark distances on a local shooting range. At a time when people were very frugal, nothing from the plane went to waste.

One of the wing struts is a roof truss in a Hemse store, the building that was originally Albin Larsson's workshop. As Björkander tells the story, Larsson, who always liked to tackle impossible projects, decided he wanted the beam to be put in place in one day. He bet it could be done, and there were plenty of bets that it couldn't. That evening, the men rigged the strut with ropes and braces to the spot where it hangs to this day. Albin Larsson won the bet.

The other wing strut is in a workshop in Havdhem, south of Hemse, also serving as a roof beam. Some of the aircraft's wiring was used in

Parts of the *Liberty Lady* still can be found all over the island of Gotland.

one of the houses. A museum in Visby displayed parts of the *Liberty Lady* for the curious to see.

Eventually, Albin Larsson had a scrap pile with a variety of metals he wanted to melt. He built a bonfire mixed with scrap lumber and ignited it with diesel fuel. Giant smoke rings rose up and blew in the evening breeze over to the village. To Lars Björkander, who related this story, this was the *Liberty Lady's* cremation. The smoke rings were her soul that soared up to the sky.[379]

Chapter 19

The Mediator

In April of 1945, delegates from 50 countries met in San Francisco to draw up a charter to create the United Nations, the commitment being to maintain international peace and security. The charter was ratified in October, and the first General Assembly met in January of 1946.

Challenges arose immediately. The Middle East was in turmoil. In November of 1947, the United Nations adopted a plan of partition to divide Palestine into two parts, one Arab and one Jewish with Jerusalem under international rule. David Ben-Gurion, head of the Jewish Agency, accepted the decision as a compromise, a beginning toward statehood.[380] Neither the Arabs nor the extremist Jews were happy with the partition.

Great Britain had been in charge of Palestine since a 1922 mandate by the League of Nations, but the British had failed to establish order. The mandate came to an end on May 14, 1948, and British troops departed Palestine, leaving responsibility for it to the United Nations.

At midnight that same day, David Ben-Gurion and his council declared Israel to be a Jewish state. The following day, Arab armies waged war. Extremists on each side were determined not to give an inch, no matter how long the battle took.

The United Nations' solution was to appoint a mediator to negotiate a peace between the Arabs and the Jews. Things moved quickly. One of the candidates considered was Folke Bernadotte of Sweden. After the White Buses rescue operation, he was known to be a humanitarian who could get things done.

When the position was officially offered to Bernadotte, he and his wife Estelle had just returned from a vacation on Stora Karlsö, a tiny island west of Gotland. Despite warnings from concerned Swedes that this would be a hopeless undertaking, Bernadotte accepted on May 20, 1948. He and Estelle thought that if he were to refuse, he might regret for the rest of his life that he had not tried to bring about a peaceful solution.

Bernadotte agreed to serve for six months but requested time off to be in Sweden for the August International Red Cross Conference in Stockholm. The United Nations made the announcement, and five days later Bernadotte was on his way.

Upon Bernadotte's appointment, he was informed that he would have an airplane at his disposal. He requested it be painted white and marked with the Red Cross and the flag of the United Nations. Similar measures had been successful in connection with the White Buses in 1945.[381]

The mediator made progress in his efforts, but neither side was satisfied with proposed compromises. The Arabs declared they were in Palestine first and would be giving up too much. Jewish leaders spoke of Bernadotte's former dealings with high-ranking Nazis.[382]

On the morning of the 17th of September, Bernadotte's plane landed on an airstrip north of Jerusalem. According to the United Press report,[383] the Swede's new cream-colored Chrysler was part of a three-car convoy going on an inspection tour of the front lines. During the morning travels, an Arab sniper shot at Bernadotte's car. No harm was done, and Bernadotte said he was not frightened.

In the same car with Bernadotte was French Air Force Colonel André Serot, a senior UN observer. In addition, there were other officials, including two UN truce observers and an American security officer. At Bernadotte's request, all were unarmed.

Serot had originally been sitting in the back. After their last stop, he asked if he could trade places with one of the men, an Israeli Army captain, so that he could sit directly next to Bernadotte. He wanted to thank him personally for rescuing his wife from the Dachau concentration camp in 1945.

As the convoy drove through the Israeli sector at about 5:00 p.m. Jerusalem time, the cars suddenly came upon a military jeep blocking the road. The driver thought he had reached another checkpoint. Three armed men dressed in Israeli Army uniforms jumped out of the jeep. One of them shot out the tires of Bernadotte's car. Then an assassin poked his submachine gun through the window of the third car and fired point blank at Bernadotte and the Frenchman sitting next to him. Hit 17 times, Serot died instantly. By the time he could be rushed to a hospital, Count Folke Bernadotte, nephew to the King of Sweden, was dead on arrival.[384] His family, at home in Stockholm, learned of his death when they heard the news on the radio.

Two years later, a news source from Stockholm headlined, "Israel Delivers Reply to Sweden on Bernadotte's Assassination; Admits Police Failure." A special Israeli committee established that Swedish criticism of the assassination was justified.[385] Yes, the Israelis did fail to take steps to apprehend the criminals. Yes, they did delay in thoroughly examining the crime scene. Yes, they were unable to apprehend the jeep used by the assailants. Yes, because of the war in Jerusalem, their government was in chaos.

The assassins were Jewish radicals who belonged to an underground group known as the Stern Gang. They would not accept the recommended peace terms and determined to prevent any concessions that would diminish Israel's prospects of becoming the nation they wanted her to be.

Israel's statement went on to say that the Jewish people have "every cause to be grateful to the people of Sweden especially to Count Bernadotte for their ceaseless activities during World War II on behalf of the victims of Nazi persecution. Israel, too, recalls with gratitude Bernadotte's sincere efforts for restoring peace to the Holy Land. …"

Count Bernadotte's role as the first United Nations mediator and his subsequent assassination are often ignored in the stories of those years of turmoil in the Holy Land, and the turmoil continues today.

On September 18, 1948, Herman walked out to his front yard in Bartow, Florida, to get the *Tampa Morning Tribune* for Hedy. The front page headlines blared, "Count Bernadotte, UN Peace Mediator, Slain in Jerusalem." The two were devastated. Hedy immediately wrote their condolences to the family. In October, an acknowledgement arrived from Stockholm with the return address Dragongården, Stockholm 5. It was signed simply "Estelle Bernadotte."

Today, if you explore the Stockholm island of Djurgården you may come across the Folke Bernadotte bust. Dedicated in 2011, it is near the water's edge, a short walk from Dragongården. There are other memorials, too, to this fine Swede who dedicated his life to service and died for it.

Chapter 20

Shoah

In 1907, Israel Nathan left his large family in Lithuania to settle in Canada. He never saw his parents again. I.N.'s father, Avraham Aharon (alternate spelling Aron) died in 1918. His mother Sara died in the 1930s. In the years that followed, many of his brothers and sisters left Rimshan[386] to live in North America, Mexico, Russia, New Zealand, and Israel.

Even though they were dealing with ever-increasing anti-Semitism in Lithuania, several families stayed behind. They hated to leave their homes, and they assumed they would be safe in the country where their people had thrived for generations. As time went on, however, and as the Jews were subjected to increasing repressions, it was harder and harder to emigrate. Where could they go? The United States would take in few Jews. The British enacted strict quotas for Jews who wanted to come into Palestine.

At the outset of World War II, Lithuania was brutally occupied for one year by the Soviet Union. The Germans invaded in June of 1941, and life got much worse for the Jewish people. Lithuania is where Hitler's Final Solution began, in one town after another. In the summer of 1941, the Nazis started going into the small shtetls and working with white

The Aharon family in Lithuania, around 1918. (from the family of Louis Allen)

armbanders, the local collaborators who could identify Jewish families. The Jews had to wear yellow stars on their clothing. Their money and valuables were confiscated. Yes, there were sympathetic Lithuanians, but the Nazis made it clear that anyone who helped the Jews would suffer their same fate.

Attacks on Jews were happening all over Lithuania. Jews were imprisoned in ghettoes. In Vilna, the cultural center of the country, of 80,000 Jewish residents in 1941, only two or three thousand survived the war. Many of the survivors had fled to the forests to join the resistance.[387]

On August 26, 1941, there was a roundup of the Jews living in Rimshan and several other small towns. Men, women and children, forced from their homes by armed Lithuanian volunteers, were told they were going to work on a farm. It is hard to imagine the confusion and the terror of packing small bags for the trip and trying to keep the little ones calm.

The Jews were to bring tools with them, along with food for the trip, but not too much food, because when they got to the farm, everything they needed would be given to them.

Among those driven from town were the aunts, uncles, and cousins of Herman, Lou, Dorothy and Ace. They were I.N.'s brother Nachman and his wife Shifra with their children Bila (five years old) and Yakov (seven); another brother Shmuel and his wife Berta with their children Tila (seven), Miryam (eight), Tuvya (11), Avaham (12); and I.N.'s sister Chaja and her husband Zarem.

The women, children and elderly rode on carts. The others walked alongside. After spending the night outside in the open, where likely few actually slept, they were herded to a cleared site off a dirt road in the forest northwest of Salok. It was by now evident that their destination was not a work farm. Long deep pits had been dug. Everyone was forced to undress down to their underwear. Many women, some carrying babies, balked at this order, but the Lithuanian thugs beat them and shoved them into the trenches. Anyone who protested or tried to run was immediately shot.

While German SS officers looked down from atop a hill, the Lithuanians fired their rifles and machine guns until all the Jews were dead, more than 2500.[388] The slaughter lasted until six in the evening. Jewish life in my grandfather's shtetl was gone.

After the mass killings, each of the white armbanders who fired the shots received a half liter of vodka. The homes and possessions of the murdered families were quickly confiscated for the use of either the Lithuanian collaborators or the Nazi invaders.

Others in I.N.'s family perished elsewhere during wartime. His sister Dvora and her husband Shalom were murdered in 1942 in Dolhinow, Poland. His brother Schneur and his family were killed near Braslaw, in what is today Belarus.

In 1949, I.N. returned to his hometown to search for his family. He could find no one. The Aharon homes were occupied by others. I.N. finally learned of their fate. Around 95 percent of the more than 200,000 Jews in Lithuania had perished.

Even then, no one wanted to talk about the Jews who had vanished. World War II was over, but Lithuania was occupied again by the Soviets, and people were afraid. Today, 70 years after the end of the war, Lithuanians are still grappling to come to terms with the legacy of the Holocaust.

Chapter 21

Ace Allen

Herman's baby brother, born in 1923, was named Isadore after a relative from his father's side. Everyone knew him as Izzy. The kids at school used to tease, "Isadore was a door, and now he is a screen door."

His uncle Walter was certain the name would be a burden to this top-notch young man and encouraged him to change it. When he got out of high school, Isadore went to court and legally became Ace Allen.

Ace was the baby, the Golden Boy, adored by his mother and watched over by his brothers and sister. He was gentle and studious, fun to be around in a quiet way.

At Thomas Jefferson High School in Tampa, Ace was a cadet in the Reserve Officers' Training Corps (ROTC) and, by his third year, was battalion commander and a skilled member of the rifle team.

To his mother Emma's dismay, in January of 1943 Ace became her third son to join the Army Air Force. After graduating from high school, he went straight into technical training to be an aircraft engine mechanic. Ace was a member of the 317th Service Group and saw service in England and France. While in England, he was stationed at Cottesmore, an RAF base turned over to the Americans. It was about 70 miles north of

Ace Allen

Herman's base at Thurleigh. Ace was an airplane propeller specialist doing repair work on C-47s, the huge transport planes that flew troops, cargo, and the wounded.

By July 1945, Ace was in France with orders to proceed to the Pacific. However, the surrender of Japan meant that Ace could go home, and he was officially discharged in November.

Wasting no time, by January of 1946, Ace had entered the State College of Washington in Pullman. Once again he was in the ROTC. He wanted to be an officer, like his brothers.

During Ace's senior year Emma received a letter that her son had been selected as a Distinguished Military Student, eligible to apply immediately for a direct commission in the Regular Army as a second lieutenant. On June 15, Ace reached his goal.

Because his college did not have an Air Force ROTC, this time around Ace was in the army. Years later, Herman made the comment that when Ace decided to join the army as a career officer, our country was not at war. If the Korean War had broken out first, he might never have joined.

The country of Korea is about the size of the state of Utah. For years, it was occupied, not so nicely, by Japan. As part of the Japanese surrender in 1945, Korea was divided into zones, one in the south controlled by the United States, the other in the north controlled by the Soviet Union. The people of Korea would not have long to celebrate a time of peace.

Over the next few years, relations between the north and the south deteriorated. The newly formed United Nations tried to orchestrate peace, but to no avail. The government of North Korea, sponsored by the Soviets, wanted to oust the UN Commission and take complete control of the country. The North Korean People's Army included in its ranks veteran Chinese Communist forces, and all were armed with Soviet Union military equipment. The South Koreans, though aided by the United States, didn't grasp at first the strength of their opposition.

The North Korean invasion of South Korea began on the 25th of June, 1950. South Korea was caught unawares, and the United States government was equally surprised. According to military historian Roy Appleman, "The surprise in Washington ... according to some observers, resembled that of another, earlier Sunday—Pearl Harbor, 7 December 1941."[389]

Five days later, President Truman announced in a press release that the United States was in the war. Ace and Hedy's sister Ruby had become good friends. They were together when they heard the news over the car radio.

Ace looked at Ruby and said, "That means me."

As June turned into July, the North Koreans successfully moved south and conquered city after city. The first American troops sent there had been stationed in Japan and were not sufficiently experienced in combat. The summer months in Korea meant temperatures reaching 110 degrees Fahrenheit. Men were literally dying of heat exhaustion. Rations were disappointing. Morale was low, losses were heavy, and their officers were crying out for replacements.

By the end of July and beginning of August, reinforcements were finally arriving. Ace was ordered to Fort Lewis on July 15 as part of the 9th Infantry Regiment of the 2nd Infantry Division. The regiment sailed from Tacoma, Washington, two days later, the first Army infantry troops to depart from the United States for Korea. On July 31, they landed in Pusan (today Busan), a southern port and the most important one in the country.

There had been no time for serious training. On the way to Pusan, the officers and soldiers were hurriedly taught, among other things, how to use the 3.5 inch rocket launcher, a newer and larger bazooka weapon.

The troops went first to a spot about ten miles southeast of the division headquarters at Taegu (today known as Daegu.) They had orders to be prepared to move out with an hour's notice.

The North Koreans were attempting, with some success, to cross the Naktong River in order to advance toward Pusan, the best port in the country as well as the origin of the vital railroad lines. A series of attacks back and forth from the hilly terrain and down to the valleys did not prevent the North Koreans from pressing forward.

At 4:00 p.m. on the 7th of August, Ace's regiment went into active combat. They were ordered to attack the North Koreans at a bulge in the river, the Naktong Bulge. There was fierce fighting in an atmosphere of chaos for several days, resulting in heavy casualties.[390]

In the early months of the Korean War, there wasn't enough time to keep detailed records of all that transpired.[391] Ace's family received a handwritten note that on the 9th day of August, "Lt. Allen was killed by enemy machine-gun fire as he led his platoon in combat. The incident occurred while his battalion was attacking near the Naktong River in the vicinity of Yongsan, Korea. Lt. Allen died instantly. This was verified by the medical aidman who was near him at the time. His remains are at the Military Cemetery in Miryang, Korea."

Second Lieutenant Allen was awarded the Purple Heart, the Combat Infantryman's Badge, the Korean Service Medal, the United Nations Service Medal, the National Defense Service Medal, the Korean Presidential Unit Citation and the Republic of Korea War Service Medal.

Emma never recovered from the loss of her son. She developed a tic in her eye that stayed with her for the rest of her life. As a dependent parent of a veteran who died in the active military, Emma received a monthly allowance from the U.S. Army of $36.02.

In the fall of 1950, new freshmen entering Washington State College (which became Washington State University in 1959) were told the story of Ace Allen. The editorial page of the September 7 issue of the *Spokane Daily Chronicle* read, "Hundreds who beheld the moving spectacle of the college stadium little more than three months ago must have been sobered by a sense of the transience of life when they read Wednesday of the death of Ace Allen. They could see him marching at the head of the crack drill squad of the ROTC, barking orders with precision learned in 30 months of service in the air force during the Second World War."

Chapter 22

Bartow

In my office sits a marble paperweight adorned with a photograph taken in Bartow, Florida. It reads "Bartow … The Place to Raise Your Family."

Herman's official date of discharge from active military service was September 18, 1945, just 16 days after the formal surrender ceremony which officially ended the war with Japan. As he explained, "They had a point system for when you could get out. If you were a Project X man, a POW or an internee or an escapee, then you didn't have to go by points. All you had to do was say you wanted out. I was the first in line. Hedy was pregnant, and it was time for me to settle down.

"So I got out, and we decided we would live in Florida. Maybe we should have gone back to Washington, my point of debarkation. They would have sent me there if I'd wanted to go, but the old man was in Florida. He painted a big picture for us. So we went into the department store business with him."

The newlyweds found a small place to rent in Haines City in the Skyline apartment complex. The day they moved in, Herman immediately traded the mattress for a better one he managed to find in an empty apartment. Their neighbors were all in the same situation, families with little money, trying to find their post-war place.

Hedy couldn't believe how hot Florida was. The temperatures were in the 80s and 90s, sweltering after the crisp cool days in Sweden. And she had never seen such bugs. In the Haines City apartment, she set the dining table legs into bowls of water so that at night the roaches wouldn't scurry up them. It was a whole new world, but Hedy accepted it as her new norm.

In September, her mother Helena traveled by train from Hibbing to help get ready for the baby's arrival. On the 16th of October, 1945, Hedy went into labor. Herman and his brother Ace rushed her to Winter Haven Hospital. Along with Helena, the three of them sweated it out in the waiting room.

Herman explained, "I was standing outside the delivery door in a state of nervous anticipation. All was quiet, and then suddenly came a husky cry. A tingling sensation hit my spine, and I sank into the nearest chair. There was commotion galore, with the nurses running in and out of the room. Then, all at once, a nurse came out with a bundle. She allowed me to peek, saying, 'It's a girl!'

"All along we thought the baby would be a boy, but now that was totally forgotten. A girl! Our first baby! I followed the nurse to the nursery and watched her give my daughter her first bath. Then she was asleep, just like that.

"In about half an hour, Hedy was wheeled back to her room. At first she couldn't understand the long months were over, her baby born, but when she did, she fell asleep too, content with the thought of a job well done."

The delivery was smooth and uneventful, but as was usual then, the new mother stayed in the hospital for ten days. The hospital charged $5 for the anesthesia, and $1.50 for each of nine days to take care of the baby named Patricia Dorothy. The total bill from the hospital was $102.

Since 1936, Herman's father had lived in the area and owned dress stores in several small towns in central Florida. In 1946, Herman and Hedy moved from Haines City to nearby Bartow. The official population of Bartow was less than 9000 people. Phosphate and citrus were the dominant industries.

In anticipation of working with Herman, I.N. had opened Allen & Sons, a store that sold clothing and fabrics, or what was then called dry goods. When Hedy gave directions, she always said, "On Main Street, between the two dime stores."

For the first couple of years, Herman and Hedy rented a small house on Hilmer Avenue. Around the corner lived Mr. Mathis and his yard full of chickens. Soon Herman brought live chicks to Hedy's back yard. After they grew into fryers, Herman slaughtered them and hung them on the clothesline, just as he had done during the Depression years. Hedy would take a deep breath and roll her eyes. She never cleaned one chicken.

Hedy and Herman on the porch of their home on Hilmer Avenue, Bartow. 1946.

In the beginning, there was no washing machine and there was no maid. Fröken was a Stockholm memory. Hedy soaked the soiled clothes in a tub, then used a wash board to scrub out the spots. She rinsed everything in the tub over and over and hung them out to dry on the same line that Herman used for the chickens. The organdy crisscross curtains were a joy to starch and iron, she insisted. The house smelled heavenly with the breeze coming through the screens, causing the curtains to flutter.

Barbara Ann arrived two years after I was born. Actually, our parents thought each of us would be "David" until finally David Fredrick was born in 1952, followed by William Paul in 1955. Hedy bounced each of her babies on her knee and sang to them in Swedish just as her mother had: *Rida rida Ranka, hästen heter Blanka.* Then whenever she and Herman wanted to have a private conversation that none of us could understand, they would break into Swedish.

These were the wonder years for us. We moved into a stucco house on Wilson Avenue, closer to town and the store. Our neighbors were our doctors, Herman's attorney, and Hedy's bridge club partners. The juvenile court judge lived right next door, so we were sure to behave. We could walk to every school we attended.

Hedy's sister Ruby met a young man named Vince at a party in Minneapolis. Like Ruby, Vince was of Swedish descent, and his last name was also Johnson. Their same last names were only part of the attraction, and Ruby and Vince married on May 24, 1952. Vince was a Catholic, and Ruby quickly became a Catholic too. Hedy always laughed that their poor mother had warned her children not to marry Catholics. Now Ruby had married a Catholic, and Hedy had married a Jew. Perhaps mother Helena was relieved when her son Hedley married Betty, a member of the Baptist Church.

Ruby and Vince went on to have ten children. Herman used to say that every time he picked up the telephone and heard Ruby's voice, he knew there was going to be another baby.

Herman with General Van Fleet in Bartow. March 17, 1953.

Like many of the returning veterans described so well by Tom Brokaw in his book, *The Greatest Generation*, Herman immediately threw himself into community affairs. Initially, the groups he joined were military-related. Bartow, like every town in the country, was filled with new veterans. During the war, Bartow Air Base had been used for pilot training. The war over, the base was returned to the City of Bartow to be used as a municipal airport. In 1950, the Air Force contracted to make that airport a flight training center for student pilots. When the first group of cadets arrived in the spring of the following year, the American Legion in Bartow sponsored a big welcome. Herman was post commander and drove all over town in a white Legion jeep.

One day Herman came home from the airbase with an old fuel tank. Next thing we knew, it was positioned upright against a tree in the side yard. It looked like a missile, similar to but smaller than those Hitler had sent to London. From that day forward, people in town knew the Allen house as the one with the rocket ship.

Bartow was the county seat of Polk County. Until 1963, Polk County was dry. The sale of alcohol was illegal, and no liquor could be served. Anyone who wanted to buy spirits had to go across the county line. On Saturday nights at the American Legion, the Cotillion Club held dances for the young couples. During musical breaks, everyone ran out to their cars, spiked their drinks and grabbed some snacks. Oh, how they loved to dance! The festivities went on until two or three in the morning.

A few hours later, at dawn, Herman woke up sons David and Bill to help him clean the Legion Hall. What the boys remembered were the millions of cigarettes. The building had to be spotless by nine in the morning because church services were held there.

Herman was paid to do this. He appreciated the work because money was so hard to come by in those days. David and Bill each got a few dollars too.

Every New Year's Eve, Herman and his friends went from party to party toasting in the New Year with shots of whiskey. Herman carried along a decanter music box that played, "How Dry I Am." Eventually, a Bartow policeman showed up to drive the partiers home.

Our grandfather I.N. lived in a little house about 15 miles away in Lake Wales. We visited him often, and I can still remember the smell of his home, that of an old man who had no one to look after him. Granddaddy would take us all to Morrison's Restaurant. We never went out to eat as a family without Granddaddy picking up the bill.

I.N. and our grandmother Emma, whom we called Granny Allen, had divorced in 1944. Emma lived on Guava Street in an apartment building owned by Mr. Woodard. Across the road from her front door there really was a guava tree. Barbara and I walked to her tiny home every Sunday after church, and she baked fresh apple dumplings for us.

Granny Allen, always looking like the perfect plump Grandma in a dark dress and with her hair pulled back in a bun, walked the two blocks to our house each night for dinner. If we heard that I.N. was on his way over, or if, heaven forbid, he arrived unannounced, Emma slipped out the back door and walked home. They never once spoke to each other after their divorce.

Each summer, Granny Allen took the airplane to Pittsburgh to spend a few months with Herman's sister Dorothy and her family. The year she was diagnosed with colon cancer, she stayed to be nursed by her daughter. I remember in 1960 when Aunt Dorothy telephoned to tell us that Granny Allen was gone. Daddy hung up the phone and went outside for a long time. He could never talk about his mother's death.

I.N. died nine years later. In his will, he left a college fund to be used by his grandchildren. As Herman explained, "My father graduated cum laude from the school of hard knocks, and he was always aware of the need and importance of a college degree."

The year I graduated from high school, Hedy was pregnant again. In September I was at college when Kathy was born, the fifth Allen child. Hedy would say, "Three is a little family; four is a large family. After you have that fourth one, people never know how many children you have."

Money was always tight. Hedy wrote to me one December, "Have done no Christmas shopping yet. Ordered a doll high chair for Kathy from Sears and a croquet set for the boys. Our financial shape, as per usual, doesn't warrant much shopping. The city and county taxes have to be paid. Everything is wonderful, and I have so much to be thankful for. If you have room, Patti, please bring home those shoes you said you never wore. My last pair of new shoes was five years ago."

After Herman's sister Dorothy and her husband Bernie visited one year, Bernie sent Hedy money to buy a clothes dryer. He couldn't believe she was still hanging clothes out on the clothesline. Hedy called Dorothy and explained that Herman would pick out an air conditioner for their bedroom instead. The cost was the same, and while a dryer would be great, she said, "You know how much an air conditioned room means when that dreadful heat comes."

Herman continued to immerse himself in extracurricular affairs, not limited to Bartow. He worked so hard on the 1956 campaign for Leroy Collins as governor that Collins paid the family a personal visit in Bartow.

In 1960 the *Polk County Democrat* ran a story titled "Polk Personality of the Week." The reporter wrote, "If there's ever a 'Mr. Bartow' contest, Herman F. Allen will probably be tagged It."

During the interview, the reporter asked Herman if he accepted his numerous obligations to establish some sort of record or to satisfy a personal ambition. Herman answered, "No, there's nothing like that. Honestly, I can't really explain how I get involved in these extracurricular activities. It's like a snowball. One thing just leads to another. It's been that way as long as I can remember." The list was long. According to the *Democrat*, it read like a census of Bartow organizations.

In 1961, when the world-renowned evangelist Billy Graham came to Bartow for the Easter sunrise service, Herman organized the event. Dr. Graham had been refused permission to preach the Easter service at nearby Bok Tower in Lake Wales "because of the flashlight bulbs, and those who use them, the apparatus of television, the police escorts to open lanes for the speaker to come and go … the necessary hubbub and confusion."[392]

When the day for the service came, the Florida Highway patrol officials counted 17,000 cars. The *Lakeland Ledger* wrote that the crowd was reported to be the largest ever assembled in Polk County.

A *Polk County Democrat* article described Herman's involvement: "Among the hardest workers of the many who were on duty all night long was Arrangements Chairman Herman F. Allen. The seemingly inexhaustible Allen was all over the place, seeing that everything ran smoothly. … Fatigue lines were dragging at his face and shoulders well before the 6 o'clock starting time, but he stuck to the job until the Graham Crusade team was ready to take over, then faded into the background."

As Hedy related years later, a reporter from one of the area newspapers mentioned in his story that the Billy Graham Easter Crusade was put on by a Jew. "It was a very nice article," Hedy said, "but Daddy did not know why they had to bring up the part about his being Jewish."

I assume most of my friends knew my daddy was Jewish, even though there were few outward clues. At home, we never learned about Jewish life or rituals. We celebrated Christmas and had Easter egg hunts.

Herman did not observe Jewish dietary laws. Only during the high holidays, he and his father would don yarmulkes and drive to the synagogue in Lakeland. More often, Herman showed up at the Episcopal Church, cooking pancakes or attending Christmas Eve services after a late night of partying. Hedy observed that Herman was still able to sleep standing up, just as he had done in Rättvik during their first Christmas together.

If we ever wondered, "Why doesn't Daddy run for elected office?" Mother answered, "Because he's Jewish, and he doesn't want that to be an issue."

Herman, Hedy, and I.N. at a Seder in 1946.

One day a lovely lady walked into the crowded store and asked Herman to kneel down and accept Jesus as his personal savior. Herman was polite and explained it would not be possible. He needed to wait on his customers.

Allen & Sons had not become the thriving business Hedy and Herman had dreamed about when they opened its doors after the war. There were plenty of Jewish merchants in the South who amassed great fortunes—the owners of Maas Brothers and Rich's Department Stores, even Phillip Berkovitz in Bartow—but Herman was not one of them.

In 1960, Herman was President of the chamber of commerce when Bartow's new Golden Gate Shopping Center had its grand opening. In addition to a brand new Publix grocery, the stores in the mall included a Grants and a Colony Shop.

At the ribbon cutting, Herman spoke to the crowd, "What helps Bartow helps us all," but what he told Hedy later was "When the ribbon was cut, I felt like it was my throat."

The mall opening was the beginning of the end for Allen & Sons. In the spring of 1962, Herman accepted a job as managing director of the Mid-State Tuberculosis and Respiratory Disease Association. Thus began his new career in the field of public health, one he entered into as eagerly as he had all his other ventures.

He began to come in direct contact with families who were suffering from various respiratory illnesses. My sister Barbara remembered a day when, "we went to a lady's home and picked up her child to take care of him for the day. We took him home and gave him a much-needed bath. Herman gave him a brand new outfit, head to toe, from Allen & Son's and threw in a couple of toys from the dime store next door."

This kindness was not an isolated incident. One of the reasons the store was failing was that Herman extended credit to anyone who asked for it, expecting they would pay him a few dollars each week. He and Hedy both remembered what it was like growing up when their families didn't have the money to buy what they needed.

At the end of 1962, Allen & Sons closed its doors. "It's no use." Herman explained. "The day of the little merchant has gone. It's impossible to compete. We're only sliding deeper and deeper into debt." It wasn't just the shopping center that was hurting Herman's business. Economically, times were tough in central Florida. The winter before, a big freeze had killed the budding orange trees. Many people were out of work.

At 9:00 p.m. on New Year's Eve day, Herman locked the doors of the store for the last time. The final sale had been a success, and most of the store's bills had been paid. He even managed to sell some of the showcases. What he kept for many years was the ledger of all the money owed to him. The book contained page after page of entries for a few dollars here, a few dollars there, never collected but never forgotten either. Nor did he forget his customers who came in to visit, to chat, to buy a pair of shoes or a yard of fabric.

The highlight of Herman's years as a community servant in Bartow came in April of 1969 when he was awarded the first Americanism Medal by the local Daughters of the American Revolution chapter. Bartow native Senator Spessard L. Holland presented the medal during a ceremony at the Civic Center. It was the first time the Bartow chapter had made the award. The *Polk County Democrat* reported, "The medal is presented by the National Society to a foreign-born citizen for outstanding community service and is considered one of the highest honors which can be conferred by the organization."

In August of that same year, Herman took a job as executive director of the South Carolina Tuberculosis and Respiratory Disease Association in Columbia, South Carolina, and the Herman Allen family left Bartow. Sentimentally, the move was heartbreaking. Financially, it had to be done.

The *Democrat* ran several articles at the time, naming Herman's contributions to the city. There was one anonymous letter in the *Democrat* that Hedy clipped and saved.

> PEOPLE ARE IMPORTANT TO HIM. Most citizens of Bartow know that the city is losing one of its most prominent citizens, together with his family. I refer to Herman Allen. Last night I had the privilege of attending and participating in one of the many farewell dinners given in his honor.

> Herman has received many deserved honors from various organizations here in Bartow, but I believe that one phase of his activities has been overlooked, and in my opinion it is a very important one.
>
> I wonder how many people know of the many so-called little things that he has done over the years. I know from personal association with him that on many occasions he has gone out of his way to do unasked favors for many people because he thought that he would be helping them when they needed help.
>
> The people involved did not have to be 'important.' All that was required was that there was the chance that they might need help and that he might help them. They were important to him because they were people.
>
> That side of Herman is just as important as the many things he did which people knew about and acclaimed at the time they occurred. If by calling attention to this, I have added anything to his stature, then I have accomplished one good deed.
>
> May God bless you and yours, Herman, now and at all times. I did not say goodbye to you last night. I said "Auf Wiedersehen," and that is what I meant. A FRIEND.

In her scrapbook, at the top of the article, Hedy wrote, "The only clipping that really matters."

Chapter 23

Columbia

Herman and Hedy settled in the Forest Acres neighborhood of Columbia, primarily because of its proximity to Fort Jackson, the large army base. Kathy entered first grade and the boys, David and Bill, enrolled at A.C. Flora High School.

The years flew by. I married an engineer whom I met at the University of Pittsburgh, and Barbara married a photographer from Winter Haven, Florida. David wed Karen, a nurse from Winter Haven. And Bill married another Barbara, also a nurse whom he met at the University of South Carolina Medical School in Charleston.

Before Herman's baby brother Ace went to Korea, he gave Hedy and Herman a bottle of Aquavit which they brought out on special occasions. They poured the liquor into shot glasses and toasted "skål" when each of us got married. Then Herman would secure the cork with candle wax. By the time Kathy got married, what little was left at the bottom of the bottle was nasty with bits of cork and wax. Nevertheless, we all enjoyed our final toast.

Hedy loved to share her memories of the war years. In her china cabinet she proudly arranged all the Orrefors glassware. The two most prominent items displayed were both wedding gifts from Count Folke Bernadotte—the etched decanter and an ornate Swedish Air Force officer's dagger.

Whenever Hedy met someone who was from Sweden, she would excitedly introduce herself with "Är du svensk?" Then she would beam and throw more Swedish words into the conversation.

Occasionally, Herman would join in on family conversations around the dining room table and reminisce about the crash of the *Liberty Lady*. Then he would close with the story of the arrest of John Lönnegren. He would shake his head, and sigh, "Oh Johnny. Oh Johnny."

Just as he had when they first moved to Bartow, Herman became involved with various military organizations. Hedy was the secretary for the American Legion, played bridge, and was active at the Episcopal church, St. Michael and All Angels.

And Herman continued the wild antics he had always been known for. In the winter of 1973, Columbia had a terrible snowstorm. There was no power for five days. The power company finally got to Forest Acres, but the crew reported to Herman that his house might burn down if they turned on the power. They wanted an electrician to certify that it was safe. Suddenly, Herman lay down on the driveway, right on the ice, blocking the power company truck. He refused to move unless they hooked up the power. He said he would take responsibility, and if the house burned down at least they would be warm. So the power company did, and all was fine, and the family took showers. Herman was everyone's hero, especially Hedy's.

During the 1980s, Herman was active in the South Carolina Public Health Association and even served as president one year. He was the first to suggest that SCPHA become a true example of good public health practice. Their education conferences must be smoke-free events. His suggestion was met with opposition, but Herman persisted. The group began by limiting smoking to social affairs. Then, in a few years, smoking was banned at all official events. Herman had become a pioneer in focusing on the adverse health consequences of smoking.[393]

Herman retired as executive director of the South Carolina Lung Association (formerly the South Carolina Tuberculosis and Respiratory Disease Association) in 1985. Retirement didn't last long. He took a job as coordinator of Aging Services at the University of South Carolina School of Public Health. On his first day, he asked his supervisor, "Where's my secretary?" They pointed to a computer and said, "Right there." With a little help, Herman taught himself how to use the software.

Herman and Hedy in the 1990s. (Photo by Bill Potthast, Potthast Studios, Winter Haven, Florida.)

For home use, he acquired a WordStar word processor and then an IBM computer. Suddenly he was creating columned newsletters for military organizations and sending out emails. First thing each morning, Herman printed the morning messages and brought them to Hedy, who would be sitting in her corner chaise, reading *The State* newspaper.

Then, out of the blue, Herman began to write poetry again. He arranged all his writings into notebooks, organized by the periods of his life. His poems were about family, aging, and his love for Hedy. She appreciated them all, saying "Herman has been writing poetry all his life. I always tell him the reason I married him was because he was so beautiful inside."

I asked a gift from God
I asked for the moon,
He gave me that
When I found you.

He gave me the comfort of knowing
That tomorrow would always be
As long as there was the moon
And you.

We all joked about Herman's part-time full-time jobs. He kept busy arranging university meetings at such resort areas as Kiawah and Ponte Vedra. Being the party planner was a project he did better than anyone.

Hedy and Herman enjoyed their cocktails every afternoon, always with the Swedish toast, "skål!" Herman continued to drink hard off and on through the years, a habit he picked up during the war and never let go.

The grandchildren came along, and the house at 4912 Westfield Road became the center of the extended family. David's and Kathy's children all grew up with Herman and Hedy around the corner. Herman regularly picked up the grandchildren after school. Long conversations followed. One day, Kathy's college-age daughter Meagen was introduced to a friend's mother who remembered her from the pickup line at school. She said, "I know you. You're the little girl who loves her grandfather."

In 1982, Bill Carlson, then living in Switzerland, came to Columbia for a visit. He had barely walked through the door when he sat down at the piano and began to play the old tunes. The family listened as Hedy, Herman, and Bill went from song to song. The first were in Swedish—"Albertina," "Där byggdes ett skepp uti Norden," and "När Jag Var En Ung Caballero." Next came the German songs, "Lili Marlene." and "Muss Ich Denn," years later made famous by Elvis Presley. Bill played American songs too, "You are my Sunshine" and "Don't Fence Me In." They were transported back to those glorious days in Stockholm, to the restaurants and the parties. The words had not been forgotten.

A favorite pastime of Hedy was to go to the movies with granddaughter Meagen. One afternoon, they visited the Nickelodeon, a little independent movie theater in downtown Columbia. Hedy had read that a Swedish film, *Kitchen Stories*, was playing there. The film is about a friendship that develops between two men in snowy, quiet, post-war Sweden. What made this movie special was not the endearing story or the confusing subtitles, but one particular tune.

A fun, quirky Swedish song started to play during the movie, and Hedy recognized it right away. Not only that, she remembered all the Swedish lyrics and started to sing along, out loud, right in the crowded little theater. On the way home, she told Meagen that the first time she heard this song, she was on a small pleasure boat with American journalist Nat Barrows along with half a dozen people from the Office of War Information. It was a wonderful afternoon with lots of frivolity, beer drinking and song, "Flickorna i Småland," "The Girls in Smaland." She hummed the tune all afternoon.

Forgetfulness began to affect Herman's daily routine. One day in 2001, he was driving in downtown Columbia and suddenly realized he was lost. Herman stopped a policeman and said, "I can't remember how to get home."

The policeman asked for his address, and Herman couldn't remember that either. He said, "I know I live near A.C. Flora High School so if you can get me that far, I'll be okay." This approach worked, but it scared Herman so much that he made an appointment with a well-known doctor he had met during his years in public health. The doctor's specialty was geriatrics.

After the appointment, the doctor spoke with Bill who sent out an email to the siblings. "Herman was tested and has been diagnosed with Alzheimer's. The doctor said it was slow progressing. Herman would probably die before it got bad."

In 2005, Herman suddenly began exhibiting some bizarre behaviors, more bizarre than usual. One night he opened up the refrigerator and said he was looking for his teeth. Hedy finally figured out that he meant his toothbrush and toothpaste. He still wasn't sure where to find them. The last straw was when he kissed her good night and asked, "Now where do I go?"

The next day he voluntarily checked into the Baptist Hospital and stayed on the psychiatric floor for a week. Hedy discovered that, even though she was managing his daily medications, he had doubled up on his sleeping pills. We thought this mistake was why he had gone off the edge. After Herman came home from the hospital, he gave up his car keys, and the question of driving was no longer an issue.

We bought the book, *The 36 Hour Day,* and read about caring for someone with Alzheimer's. We recognized our dad.

Herman spent most of his days in his office in front of the computer. He began to take paper off the printer and cut it up for scrap paper. Finally Kathy said, "I think you should cut it up and put a rubber band around every twenty or so and I will give them to everyone for souvenirs." Herman liked the idea.

Next he went to several stores to find how he could have the pieces of paper stick together like a pad. A lady at Walmart suggested he use a glue stick. So Herman spent hours putting together paper pads with a glue stick. Hedy smiled and rolled her eyes but said nothing. She loved that Herman was busy.

The 18th of January in 2007 was Herman and Hedy's 62nd wedding anniversary. Hedy was 85 years old, and Herman was 91. Kathy and her son Trevor planned a little party for the four of them. They walked into 4912[394] and announced, "We're here to celebrate your anniversary!"

Hedy announced back that they had already celebrated. She smiled at Kathy and said, "You know what I mean." Kathy and Trevor howled. Herman looked like the cat that ate the canary.

Chapter 24

Between Two Worlds

Years ago, my sister Barbara sent me the book *Between Two Worlds: Adult Children of Jewish-Gentile Intermarriage* by Leslie Goodman-Malamuth and Robin Margolis. She knew that my heart was torn between the faiths of our mother and our father.

When my parents moved to Bartow, Hedy attended the Presbyterian Church. In Hibbing, her parents had gone to a Presbyterian church because there was no Baptist church nearby. Herman always encouraged us to go to church and Sunday school.

There may have been three or four Jewish families living in Bartow. In the early years, Hedy cautioned us not to talk about our father being Jewish. "You never know when there's going to be another Holocaust," she would say. Even though it sounds irrational today, she had nightmares that someone would come and take away her children.

One Sunday morning, the Presbyterian Church honored the local American Legion chapter, and all were in attendance, including Herman. As usual, Mother was there that day with me and my sister Barbara. We were four and two years old.

During the sermon, the minister's message was that Jews would go to heaven only if they converted to Christianity. The minister knew that my father was in the congregation, and he knew Daddy was Jewish. His words changed our lives but not in the manner he intended.

The next Sunday morning, with her two little girls, all dressed up, in tow, Hedy drove to the Presbyterian Church. She could not walk through the front door. Around the corner was a little Episcopal church, and that is where we went to church from that day forward. Mother would tell us, "And that is why you are Episcopalian."

We, the children of Herman and Hedy, were tormented a little bit too. Friends might mention that Jews don't go to heaven. I guess they wanted to make sure we knew our father's fate.

When Herman was working for The Lung Association, a young man came to work as an intern. One night, after explaining that his father had been a preacher, he entertained our family on the piano, playing Christian hymns. With a little bourbon in him, Herman sang along with gusto.

Herman remembered these gospel songs. In later years, he taught Kathy all the words to his favorite: "He walks with me, and He talks with me, and He tells me I am his own." She didn't think twice about the fact that her Jewish father was singing about Jesus. We all tear up when we hear it.

Most of us, Herman and Hedy's children and grandchildren, have struggled with our faiths our entire lives. We have surfed through Episcopal, Quaker, Baptist, Unitarian, Methodist, Catholic, and others, including no religion.

In 1991, we began to have family Seders. A Jewish friend gave me a prayer book. I shortened the service slightly, typed it up, and made copies. We have had as many as 25 or 30 of us, Herman's children and grandchildren, gathered around a long table reading the story of the

Passover. *"We pray, as we sit here assembled in family friendship, that we shall become infused with renewed spirit and inspiration and understanding. May the problem of all who are downtrodden be our problem; may the struggle of all who strive for liberty and equality be our struggle."* In the early years, Herman began the service by reciting the Hebrew words. He wore his prayer shawl and took on the role of the Leader.

The Jewish Seder brought us together. In fact, after Hedy's heart procedure in January 2007, when she was being rolled from recovery to her room, and when she realized she was alive and awake, the first thing she said was, "We need to have a Seder this year."

Hedy was always quick to give us her opinion on heaven and hell. "My mother was a Baptist, but she snorted at Hell—no such thing. It was an attempt to frighten people into accepting Christianity. I just want to say how grateful Herman and I are for our wonderful family, for each other and all our children, their spouses, our grandchildren and great grandchildren. We have truly had our heaven here on earth."

I have been a reluctant Christian. Yes, I believe, but not *that* part. Not the part that says the only way a person can enter heaven is by accepting Jesus Christ as his personal savior. When I die, I want to be where Herman is. If I am a spiritual, God-loving person, it is largely because of my Jewish father.

In 2015, I joined an Inquirers' Class to learn more about the Catholic Church, the church of my husband John. The first evening, with no prompting from me, the leader suddenly announced that the next topic of discussion would be "Who is saved?" I could hardly breathe. Bottom line, she reassured, is that God saves and God wills the salvation of all. This, I learned, is the official teaching of the church, as represented by the Second Vatican Council. I have embraced the Catholic Church's emphasis on the Jewish roots of my Christian faith, and with that I am at peace.

Chapter 25

November 24, 2007

On Friday, it was my turn to spend the night at the hospital. I set up my laptop as before. This time there was a comfortable chair beside Mother's bed, but I was never able to sleep.

At 3:09 a.m., Bill emailed, "Hey are you awake?" I replied at 4:48, "She's been fine until about 4:30 when she had the worst pain ever in her back, chest, and head. The nurse just gave her morphine. Her blood pressure is up again, 150/90. Waiting for the doctor."

By the time Kathy arrived, about 5:30 a.m., she found me standing beside the bed, holding Mother's hands with tears running down my cheeks. Panicked, Kathy asked, "Is she okay?"

"We've had a long night, that's all."

After another full day at the hospital, going back and forth from the waiting room as often as I could, I drove back to the hotel to get some sleep. I had been awake for 48 hours. As my head hit the pillow, the phone rang. It was Barbara, who was spending the night at the hospital. "Patti, you need to come right away."

Ten minutes later, we were in the car. When I walked into the hospital room, it was nearly 9:00 p.m. There were a dozen people there. Mother was lying next to the safety rail on the right of her bed, hanging on, as she would have said, "for dear life." As I walked in, Barbara spoke to her, "Here's Patti, Mother." I'm not sure Mother heard anything. She looked like she was sleeping soundly, hanging on.

I remember thinking, "How beautiful you are, Mother."

Kathy walked into the room right after me. I looked up at the heart monitor, and I can't remember any of the readings, but they looked okay. The nurse stepped in, and Barbara said, "You can give her the morphine now."

Barbara explained that Mother had had an episode of severe pain, the worst ever. Her aorta had ruptured.

Soon the room was filled, and we were all standing around the bed, except for Herman. He was sitting in the chair next to Hedy, quietly holding her hand. Someone said, "We should sing. You know how much Hedy loves it when we sing." And so we did.

Someone's crying, my Lord, kum ba yah
Someone's crying, my Lord, kum ba yah
Someone's crying, my Lord, kum ba yah
Oh Lord, kum ba yah.

Verse after verse.

And slowly, slowly, slowly the line on the heart monitor weakened and straightened out and then it was flat. Shortly after 9 p.m. on Saturday, November 24, 2007, Hedvig Elizabeth Johnson Allen, our beautiful mother, was gone.

Chapter 26

Kum ba yah

On the day of the funeral, St. Michael's and All Angels Episcopal Church was filled with relatives and friends, nearly every child, grandchild, great-grandchild, nieces and nephews, friends, neighbors, and the wonderful church ladies.

The family sat in the front pews, but Herman did not leave Hedy's casket. During the entire service he stood by her at the altar, as he had done so many years before at their wedding in Stockholm.

Kathy, the youngest, gave the eulogy:

> "...My parents' marriage was amazing. Not only was it sixty-two years long, but it continued to grow stronger daily. My Dad is Jewish and my Mom a Christian. In the beginning, they decided to raise their family under one faith, and they picked Christianity. My Mom said they picked it because right after WWII, Christianity was an easier life.
>
> "What a day-by-day living example of being accepting of differences. My Dad would visit the synagogue. The rest of us attended a Christian church and both my parents

made sure we attended each Sunday. Our Mom stayed busy with altar guild, making cookies for church functions, and folding bulletins. In addition to my Mom's contribution to the collection each Sunday, my Dad handed her a five dollar bill to add to the plate from him.

"This Jewish/Christian bond has made me question religion perhaps more than someone who grew up with parents of the same faith. But I learned from my Mom that even though I may be sure in my belief system, I am not the judge of others. She loved everyone and found the best in them. And when she saw those accepting traits come out in her children and grandchildren, she teared up because she was so proud.

"My Mom's heart began to show signs of trouble ten years ago. It was a Monday, and we rushed her to the emergency room only to learn she had to immediately have emergency heart bypass surgery. When my Mom heard the news she said to the doctor, 'Whoa no, I have a hair appointment tomorrow morning at 9:30. We are going to have to schedule this surgery for some time later this week.'

"This past January, her heart gave her serious trouble again. We prayed for more time and we were given that gift. She played bridge and drove my Dad to Publix and Walmart regularly. But last week, her weak heart in her tiny 86-year-old body gave out.

"But you know you've done it right when you and your husband still adore each other after sixty-two years of marriage.

"You know you've done it right when each of your children and grandchildren are positive they were your favorite.

"You know you've done it right when your sweet and kind nature is engrained in the souls of your family and friends.

"You know you've done it right when as you are dying, twenty of your family members are surrounding your bed singing Kum ba yah.

Kum ba yah Mom. Kum ba yah"

We buried our mother that day at historic Elmwood Cemetery. After a short prayer service of both Christian and Hebrew scriptures, the family shoveled dirt onto her casket, a Jewish tradition. First Herman, then me, the eldest, then the rest of the family, one by one.

Chapter 27

The Atria

After the funeral, it became clear that Herman needed to have someone with him at all times. We made an appointment to speak to the staff at the Atria, an assisted living facility in the neighborhood, near the same Publix, the same bank.

David stayed in Columbia for the first two weeks after the funeral. He emailed, "Herman knows full well what is going on around him. This morning, I heard moaning in the living room at 4:15, and I found Herman sitting on his chair. He said he had a stomach ache, and I gave him two Tums. He is worried about leaving this house. I think this is the same feeling we used to have as kids when we had to go somewhere we didn't want to go. It gave us a stomach ache. He hates that we think he can't take care of himself. At the same time he knows the Atria is where he needs to be. He says, 'What choice do I have?' "

On the 5th of December, Herman, accompanied by Kathy and David, arrived at the Atria and selected his studio apartment. After lunch, he gave out Free Hug Cards. Before long, there was a big hug fest going on in the lobby. David said he watched one lady come back for five or six hugs, and then he felt a tug at his leg. He turned and a cute little lady in a wheel chair told him Herman was going to have to look out for the resident who was giving him all the hugs.

By this time, Herman's dementia was evident but under control. His days revolved around his calendar and his computer. As he had his entire adult life, he kept his schedule up to date in a business appointment book. Each activity, each visit, each trip to the doctor was carefully noted. It was important to him that his life run smoothly, by the clock, military style.

Herman had to stay busy and was always looking for projects. On one side of his room at the Atria was a card table with a paper cutter on top. This was his base of operations. He made hundreds of bookmarks, each with a saying glued to the top. We all sent orders with what we wanted ours to say: "Hubba Hubba." "It's important to have a twinkle in your wrinkle." I have a box of Herman's bookmarks. We all do.

Just as when he was living at 4912, Herman continued to make note pads. He went through the emails he printed and with the paper cutter, cut off any excess paper, not to waste an inch. Bill ordered special adhesive, perfect to bind the edges of the paper.

Herman saved his Kleenex boxes and labeled each with the varied sizes of the pads stacked inside each one. They were lined up on his window shelf, like a little store. When we came to visit, he became a salesman, "What size do you want? How many?" It was mandatory to place an order.

One day it hit me. When Israel Nathan left Eastern Europe to begin a new life in Canada, his first venture was to go door to door selling paper. Now, at the end of his life, like his father before him, Herman had become a paper peddler.

A doctor's appointment was always an experience for Herman. One day he began to complain about his throat. All of a sudden, out of nowhere, he would choke, gasping "Can't talk." His primary physician suggested a specialist to see if there was anything serious going on.

Kathy took the morning off. When she picked Herman up at the Atria, everything was fine. He was totally normal until they arrived at the doctor's office, and the nurse called his name. He took a few steps with his walker, and stopped. He looked up and starting crying out to the ceiling, "Father Abraham, Oh Father Abraham." Then he walked a little further and repeated, throwing in some extra moans. As he shuffled back to the examining room, every staff member turned to look.

When the doctor arrived, Daddy wanted to know what had taken so long. The doctor was kind and explained there were other patients he needed to see first.

Herman asked, "Did you not know I was here waiting?" The doctor smiled, "Believe me, Mr. Allen, we all knew you were here."

The doctor asked him to explain the reason for the visit, and Herman suddenly started talking in a high squeaky voice, "Can't you hear what is wrong?"

The doctor looked in Herman's ears and throat the best he could while Herman moaned, "Oh Doctor." Kathy got information on acid reflux and a prescription. They talked about coming back in a month, but all Kathy was thinking was, "Never coming back."

As soon as the doctor walked out, Herman was okay. He and Kathy walked back to the car in silence. He got in the car and said, "Well, I feel better."

In 2011, things began to change. Herman could no longer make pads and bookmarks. The paper store closed down. We worked hard to find games or easier projects. We telephoned more often.

One morning I arrived at his room and saw his computer equipment in the hallway, outside his door. He had cut the monitor cord with scissors. I knew it was because he couldn't figure out how to check his email. For so many years, reading emails had been his daily activity, first thing in the morning.

The staff took away his scissors. The head nurse recommended he move to their memory care unit as quickly as possible where he would have 24/7 attention.

The memory care unit was a much better place for Herman. Volunteers came in daily for activities. Herman got a wheelchair and enjoyed trips out to the garden. However, before long, he was eating very little and was losing weight fast.

There is so much that happened during those final months that cannot be written. They are the things you remember when you think, "The only thing worse than Daddy leaving us would be having to spend another day like this one." Herman knew it, too. One day, as Kathy was leaving his room, he asked her to please pray for a funeral. He asked, "You understand, don't you?" Kathy replied, "Yes, I do."

Herman had never joined a synagogue, but when Hospice learned he was Jewish, they asked a local rabbi to visit. On the day the rabbi came, Herman was on the toilet and wouldn't come out of the bathroom. Naturally, the rabbi was uncomfortable meeting someone for the first time in such private circumstances, but the two men talked. When I walked into the room, I heard Herman say, "Thy will be done on earth as it is in heaven." The very kind rabbi was nodding his head as Herman spoke this Christian prayer.

Over the course of a week or two, several grandchildren came to Columbia to visit and help. Herman had a second wind. On one of these better mornings, Meagan and Emma arrived and found Herman in the garden. He was sitting on the bench with his wheelchair by his side.

When he realized the two girls were there, Herman asked, "What are we going to do today? I need to buy some pants. Can we go to Walmart?" His attitude with the young entourage seemed to be that everything around him was new again.

Although Meagen and Emma nodded yes, they were thinking, "Kathy will kill us if we take Herman out."

Herman asked, "Do you have a vehicle? I need my gray tote bag and my list."

One of them answered, "Well, Keller will be here soon with his car, and on the way out the door, we can get the tote bag from your room."

The two girls pushed the wheelchair around and around the parking lot, hoping Herman might take a nap and forget about Walmart. Herman was amazingly calm, focused, and awake. He looked toward the sky and spoke quietly, "Thank you, thank you. I knew you would, I knew it." He seemed to have a personal conversation with God, as if He were there with him.

They were at the Atria's front door, chatting with other residents sitting in the row of rocking chairs, when Keller drove up. As soon as Herman recognized his grandson, he said, just as he would have done when it was he who was in charge, "Well, what are we waiting for? Let's go!"

The three grandchildren whispered back and forth about what they should do. Emma walked inside and asked a staff member if they could take Herman for a ride. Yes, she said. All they had to do was to sign him out.

Emma wrote his name in the little notebook. The three of them looked at each other and said in unison "Let's go, Grandpa."

As the car took off, Herman went right to sleep. He opened his eyes a few times, looked around and, reassured that the car was still in motion, dozed off again.

When they arrived at Walmart, Herman sat up straight, as if on cue. He looked in the direction of the front door and said, "Let's go!" Emma and Meagen wheeled him inside. As usual, Walmart was crowded with shoppers. No one seemed to notice the old man in the wheelchair. He would look up occasionally and exclaim, "Good, we're here!" and then nod off. When they were back in the car, Herman asked if they had bought everything they needed, and the grandchildren answered, yes they had.

Done with Walmart, Keller was driving around without much of a plan when suddenly, out of the blue, Herman sat up straight and looked over at Emma, who was in the back seat with him, "Is my bank still there? What is it called?"

"Wachovia?"

"That's right! Wachovia. Do they still know me there?"

"Of course they do, Herman. How could they ever forget you?"

Herman laughed, "We'll go there and reopen my account. Do I have any money?"

Emma wasn't sure how to answer this one, but not wanting to disappoint him, said, "Yes, certainly you have money, Grandad."

Herman clapped his hands, "Yes, I have plenty of money, I knew it! Emma, do you know where my new home is?"

Emma answered hesitatingly, "Yes, we know where it is."

"Can you take me there?"

"Yes, Granddad, we can take you there."

"What is it like? Is it nice?"

"Oh yes, it is beautiful."

"It is? Will I be able to approve everything before I move in?"

"Of course you will, Granddad. You can approve everything."

By this time they all felt like they were characters in Herman's dream.

Herman clapped his hands, "Yes, I knew it. We'll go by the dentist and we'll get my teeth fixed, and then we'll go to the eye doctor and get my eyes fixed. Yes, I'm back in town. We'll go to the bank. I have plenty of money. Do you need anything? You need a vehicle? Anything you need, I'll take care of it. You'll let me know, won't you?"

"Yes, we will, Granddad."

Herman called up to the front seat of the car, "Keller, do you know the way?"

"Yes, I know the way, Granddad."

Herman looked upward and thanked God, genuinely and with gusto.

Keller turned around in a driveway as they continued to drive around and around the streets of Forest Acres, the neighborhood where Herman and Hedy had lived for more than 40 years.

Herman looked over at Emma again, "Will I have a secretary? And I will need a driver! Keller, can you be my driver? How long will you be here?"

"A week "

"Well, that will work. You can be my driver, can't you?"

"Yes, Herman, I'll be your official chauffer."

"When we get there, I want you to call everyone. That's very import-ant. I need you to tell them where the house is. Tell them I'm back! Can you do that?"

"Yes, we'll make sure everyone knows."

"And invite them over tonight. We'll have a big supper, the whole family, all together."

"Okay, Herman. We'll tell them. We'll all be together."

"Now, I need to talk to Hedy. Can you call Hedy and tell her I'm here? Tonight I want to sleep in the bed with Hedy."

It was Herman's last road trip. When they returned to the Atria, he dozed for a while in his wheelchair. When he woke up and looked around, he realized where he was. He wasn't happy, and he told the three they could go home.[395]

Hospice began to visit every day. Herman wouldn't drink, and he wouldn't eat. His grandson Justin played CDs of World War II music, and while his children and grandchildren danced at the foot of his bed, Herman raised his arms in the air to conduct.

Col. Herman F. Allen died on May 26, 2011. On the day before Memorial Day, he was buried with military honors at the historic Elmwood cemetery in Columbia. He was finally next to Hedy again.

Come with me, my love, when it is time to go.
Come with me so we both will know
The whispering glimpses of the past
Which, somehow, do not last.

The memory of the years we were together
Through every conceivable format of weather,
We endured within the framework of our love,
Enhanced by prayers to God above.

So take my hand and I will travel at your side,
We will be together on this eventful ride.
We shall look around and watch the wave of friends
As they stand and cheer and know this is how it ends.

Herman Allen, May 3, 2000

Epilogue

William T. Carlson

By November of 1945 Bill Carlson was Chief of the OSS Mission in Stockholm. Erika did see him again. She had been living in an apartment on Brantingsgatan in Gärdet. When the landlady asked her to move out, Bill offered her the use of another apartment nearby that belonged to a girl at the embassy in Norway.[396] He knew the area well.

In February of 1946, Carlson moved to Paris to resume his activities as a businessman, but he continued to support the Strategic Services Unit (SSU) in their intelligence work.[397]

When he received the announcement that Hedy and Herman's daughter had been born he wrote a letter dated November 18, 1945, from Stockholm:

> *Dearest little Patricia,*
>
> *It was so nice to hear from you so soon after your arrival and to know that you have been such a very nice girl to your lovely mother, whom I hope you will take after. You know that if*

it hadn't been for you, we would still have your mother here! Everybody misses her, especially me.

To me, you look just like your mother, and consider yourself lucky. I hope you also inherited her disposition and charm. Then, if in addition to this, you get your father's stamina and brains, you sure will be some girl.

Tell your mama that I have not improved with age. In fact, I am slipping. I do not have the same interest in girls I used to and am a little tired of doing what I am doing and not doing. The *girls in the office give me a pain once in a while, and since your mummy isn't here, I don't get the real lowdown on the dirt, so I don't know what is going on behind my back.*

You might tell your mother the following news items:

Peggy has gone back to the U.S.A. broken hearted because her boyfriend George has jilted her and is planning to marry a Swedish girl.

Mr. and Mrs. Surrey are now in Washington, and C. Ravndal is also being transferred. The Minister is due to go to the States next week.

Edith Rising had a successful appendicitis operation yesterday after weeks of suffering.

Chuck is successfully playing one night stands.

Tell your pop that Johnny Lönnegren is still in jail but is trying to get out on the grounds of insanity.

Our office is now located in 7B, and I have the large office all to myself. I expect to be called to Washington any day for consultation.

Congratulations on having been born to such nice parents, and I hope you will grow up to be a lovely girl and that you have a most wonderful and happy life.

Love to you and mama and papa, Your Uncle Bill.

LIBERTY LADY CREW MEMBERS

Navigator Stan Buck fractured his right hand in October of 1944 and was sent to Santa Monica, California, to recover. When the war was over, Stan married Marcia and settled in California. He was an avid golfer and continued to ski for many years. Stan worked as a food broker until his death in 1981 of complications from a stroke.

Eighteen-year-old waist gunner Joe Paul, nicknamed "Virgin" by his crew, had the last laugh. He went back to the States, married, and fathered eight children.

Radio operator Victor Marcotte died in 1977 and is buried in Grand Rapids, Michigan.

Navigator Charles L. Stevenson was interred at what is now the Cambridge American Cemetery in England, then brought home after the war. On September 5, 1949, Charles' brother, Capt. Edwin R. Stevenson, was killed in the crash of a C-47 transport plane ten miles southeast of Anchorage, Alaska. Charles and Edwin's surviving brother, Howard, had been a fighter pilot and lived until 1999. Now, the three brothers are together, buried at the Beverly National Cemetery in Beverly, New Jersey.

As of this writing, waist gunner Don Courson is the last surviving member of the *Liberty Lady* crew. After the war, Don went back to Mississippi and retired from a career at the Agriculture Experiment Station.

Herman's pilot, Charles W. Smith and co-pilot Merle B. Brown both returned to Thurleigh in October of 1944 to finish up their missions. Merle became captain of his own B-17. He named it *Konditori Baby*, a fond memory the coffee shop in Rättvik.

By that time, Merle related, the P-51 fighter escorts were making it all the way to Berlin, so there were fewer close calls. On his last mission he was attacked by two of the first German jet fighters, the Me 262s. They were doing 500 miles per hour. He was flying 300.

When the war was over, Merle's Swedish girlfriend came to the United States so she and Merle could marry. As her ship pulled into New York harbor, a photographer happened to get a shot of a beautiful young woman perched on the ship's railing. His picture of Maj Britt was featured in the rotogravure section of the *Chicago Tribune* the next morning.

Merle's entire career was as a pilot of Lear Jets. Coming out of the war, he said, he was fortunate to be able to do what he loved the most. As he explained, "A lot of pilots came back and couldn't find a job. There were so many pilots."

At the age of 65, Merle retired but hardly slowed down. In 2005, he took his second parachute jump. The first had been in 1943 when both engines quit during a nighttime training flight in Oklahoma.

In 1991, Herman and Hedy flew to Minneapolis to see Hedy's sister Ruby and her family. Merle lived on the outskirts of the city so the two former crew members had a chance to spend a few hours together. Herman wrote, "The last time we saw each other was in Sweden in 1944. Nostalgia and memory go hand in hand!"

Merle Brown lived quietly in his home until he passed away on December 8, 2014.

After the war, Smithy went home and married Polly, the best friend of his younger sister. He had a series of jobs related to flying, taking him as far as Lima, Peru, while he and Polly had their three children. In 1977, Smithy retired and moved with Polly to their last home in Deer Isle, Maine.

Herman and Smithy never lost touch. In 1991, while visiting son David's family in Vermont, Herman and Hedy detoured to Maine to see Smithy and Polly. Herman wrote: "Prior to leaving our plane I donned my 1943/44 flight jacket, somewhat the squeeze for size, but all the jangled memories were there as we saw Smithy fronting the waiting crowd. He had not changed as I had not through these many years. I reached out and touched so many faces, heard many voices. My eyes misted as I shook his hand and hugged him close. I knew God was there as He was at our wingtips on each mission we flew.

"Smithy and I talked the night. A liter of bourbon was our constant companion—with branch water as the mix. Seize the day!"

Smithy died at the home of his son Geoff on November 24, 2008. He was three weeks short of his 92nd birthday.

Captain Robb

One of Assistant Military Attaché Robb's final projects with the internees was writing an official history, *Internees of the American Air Force in Sweden*. Professionally bound in an oversized hardback book, the history included an account of the activities of the internees in Sweden along with photographs and news clippings. The book was dedicated to "the boys who won't come back. They fought a good fight, died a brave death, and now lie in honored rest in the American Military Cemetery at Malmö Sweden. No more can be asked of a good soldier and no less can be expected of his friends than they carry on his fight to final victory."[398]

Captain Robb's wife Helene joined him in Sweden after VE Day. Robb continued to work in the same position at the legation, except now the focus was on the Soviet Union.

The following January the Robbs left Sweden. They sailed on the *S.S. Gripsholm* from Göteborg to New York, then returned to California. Robb worked in television and directed most of the car commercials for the Lawrence Welk musical variety show.

Sadly, Herman lost contact with his good friend and best man. He never knew that Robb was featured in a couple of "B" movies in the 60s and 70s. Captain Robb died in 1986. His Hollywood career never lived up to the excitement and intrigue he and Herman experienced in Stockholm when they were shadowed by the secret police and mingled with spies.

Others in Sweden

After his period in Sweden, fighter pilot Eldon E. Posey was seriously injured when his plane crashed during the Battle of the Bulge. After a long recovery, he went back to college and then established an academic career as distinguished as his military one. From 1965 until 1980, Professor Posey was head of the Mathematics Department at the University of North Carolina at Greensboro. He died on May 7, 2008.

Posey's son and I have hypothesized about the roaming raincoat. Perhaps in the pocket was hidden a map of Norway, an effort to keep the Germans guessing about the location of the coming invasion's landing sites. I will always wonder if Eldon Posey's trip to Sweden was really an accident.

Following the war, James Thomas Degnan was able to get his Swedish bride Ingegard to the States. He attended Rutgers University on the GI bill and graduated as a civil engineer, the first in his family to graduate from college. James and Ingegard settled in New Jersey with their two sons. He died in 1990 at the age of 68.

Erika Wendt remained in Sweden after the war. In 1993, she published her memoirs, *Kodnamn Onkel*, translated *Code Name Uncle*. Erika died in 2003.

Lt. Torkel Tistrand, the Swedish officer in charge of the internment camp at Rättvik, was unable to attend Herman and Hedy's wedding, but he sent a telegram from the Hotell Siljansborg: "You both got caught by the midnight sun, the very best and lots of fun." After the war Tistrand worked under Count Folke Bernadotte to manage Swedish Red Cross activities in Essen, Germany. Then he worked for the Swedish American Line shipping organization from their office in Göteborg. Tistrand passed away in 1999.[399]

By 1946, Wilho Tikander was back in Minnesota for an unsuccessful run for Congress. He then went to Chicago to practice law and became active in Finnish and Swedish organizations. Tikander died in 1965.

Prepared and circulated by Wilho Tikander in his own behalf. 16

Vote for

Wilho Tikander

DEMOCRATIC-FARMER LABOR CANDIDATE FOR

CONGRESS

EIGHTH DISTRICT MINNESOTA

He possesses the qualifications, background and record of experience necessary for YOUR Congressman

Primary Election July 8, 1946 - - - - General Election Nov. 5, 1946

(over)

OSS-SWEDEN

Herschel V. Johnson represented the United States as a deputy at the newly formed United Nations. One of the actions during his tenure focused on the topic of disarmament and atomic control. Johnson's family remembers he "had fits trying to deal with Gromyko."

Johnson and Gromyko were better able to work together on the Palestine question, both supporting partition, the division of Palestine into two parts, one Arab and one Jewish, with Jerusalem under international rule. In December of 1947, Johnson had a heart attack. He recuperated quickly but was no longer in the UN the following year when his friend, Count Bernadotte, was asked to become mediator to negotiate a peace between the Arabs and the Jews.

President Truman selected Johnson to be ambassador to Brazil, a position he held until 1953. Herschel Johnson retired in Charlotte, North Carolina, and lived there until his death in 1966.

The Chilean Nightingale, Rosita Serrano, entertained for a few years in Chile, the United States, North Africa and Switzerland. When she went back to Germany, the crowds enthusiastically received her, but the press called her the "Nazi Nightingale." Ms. Serrano finally returned to Chile where she died on April 6, 1997.

Kim Philby

In early 1944, even before D-Day, a new division known as Section IX was created by British Intelligence to combat Soviet espionage. It was clear to the Western Allies that the Soviet Union was to be the new threat. The greatest irony is that Kim Philby, the Soviet mole who worked in the same building as Hedy on London's Ryder Street, would become coordinator of this anti-Soviet intelligence operation.

Philby continued to cultivate his working relationship and friendship with James Angleton, a man totally dedicated to combating communism and soon to become head of X-2 in Italy.

In September of 1949, Philby was selected to go to Washington as MI6 Station Chief, and there he wined and dined with the "Who's Who" of the CIA and the FBI. Philby's old friend James Angleton was now in charge of the CIA's foreign intelligence operations and lunched with him at the famous restaurant, Harvey's, several times a week. These were lengthy affairs with much alcohol consumed, surely laced with precious details that Philby passed on to his Soviet handlers.[400]

It wasn't until 1963 that British agents had proof against Philby. He had been working in Beirut as a British news correspondent and was both a British agent and a Soviet mole. Late in the evening of January 23, 1964, Kim Philby fled Beirut by cargo ship to the Russian port of Odessa.

When the story of his defection hit the news, Hedy hung on every word. In our family, we all knew the name "Kim Philby," although we never appreciated the reason for our mother's strong interest in him.

James Angleton became the CIA's most paranoid mole hunter. The memory of his former friend, Kim Philby, tainted his life. In 1974, he was forced to retire to a life of fishing and raising orchids. After his death from lung cancer on May 11, 1987, he was noted by the *New York Times* to be one of the most fascinating figures in the history of the CIA.

Over the course of Kim Philby's 30-year career as a double agent, thousands of people died because of his traitorous betrayals. After his defection to Moscow, he was never given a meaningful job and continued to drink heavily until, one year to the day after Angleton's demise, he died from heart failure. The *New York Times* remembered Kim Philby as the double agent who betrayed his country.

Acknowledgements

There are so many people I need to thank. I never could have done this alone.

In 2008, I googled "Liberty Lady," and an Air Force group forum message popped up from two years earlier. Someone in Sweden was asking for information about the B-17 *Liberty Lady*. I immediately emailed him and asked, "Who are you? My father was the bombardier." Thus began my serious research. Mattias Eneqvist grew up on the island of Gotland, and his grandfather guarded the plane. With Mattias' assistance, I was able to pull together the details of the crash landing. He scoured the Swedish Archives for material. When my son and I visited Gotland in 2012 and when I returned with my sisters and brother in 2013, Mattias was there.

My son Johnny suggested in 2009 that I blog my research. At the time, I'm not sure I even understood what "blogging" meant. He designed my website, LibertyLadyBook.com, and I took off. Johnny was right. I have connected with people from all over the world, and they found me!

One of those people was Ulf Gahm from Gotland. In 2011, Ulf was an editor at *Gotlandsguiden*, the largest tourist magazine on the island. He was writing an article about the *Liberty Lady* because his father had been an early eyewitness to the landing. In 2012, my son Johnny and

I followed the footsteps of Hedy and Herman through England and Sweden. When we arrived at Gotland's tiny Visby airport, Ulf was there to pick us up. He and his family gave us a grand tour of the historical medieval city and drove us to the crash site. That day, Ulf confided that he was undergoing cancer treatment. My friend died in 2013. I did thank him but not nearly enough.

Another generous contributor is a gentleman I met through the OSS Society Discussion Group. Carl G. Finstrom was one of the leading authorities on OSS Stockholm and the American Legation. From 1986 until 1991, he served as army attaché in Stockholm. After that he studied, wrote, and lectured extensively on Scandinavian espionage, my area of interest. We shared our devotion to the memory of Bernt Balchen, the Norwegian-American aviator who knew Herman and Hedy. Carl patiently answered every question and sent email after email of information he thought might be important. Sadly, Carl died in October of 2015.

There are many others whose assistance I must acknowledge:

- Dr. Vivian Rogers-Price, director of the Research Center at the Mighty Eighth Air Force Museum, helped me in my initial search for Herman's mission reports.
- In addition to Carl Finstrom, the OSS Society Discussion Group members Jonathan Clemente, Matthew Aid, Thomas L. Ensminger, Virginia Cary Hahn, Roger Albrigtsen, John Richardson, and others have aided my research.
- The 306th Bomb Group Historical Association and its treasure trove of research material and fellow historians. The members of the Facebook group, "306th Bomb Group—First Over Germany" have kindly answered many questions.

- The Facebook group "American Internees in WWII Sweden," in particular Karen Cline and Dwight Mears. Both have written extensively on subjects important to my research. The members of this group, many in Sweden, have been an invaluable help.
- The regulars on the ArmyAirForces.com forum. How patient you were in the beginning when you had to know I knew nothing.
- Dr. Gordon Pickler shared his research and introduced me to the Air Force Historical Research Agency.
- Jim Root, who early on sent me a large package of material on OSS Stockholm.
- Lt. Col. J. W. Bradbury introduced me to Lars Gyllenhaal, noted historian of Scandinavian military history.
- From Sweden: Helena Engblom, Pär Henningsson, Tommy Jonason, Simon Olsson, Paul Wechselblatt, Raoul Granqvist, and Bo Widfeldt.
- Lasse Svensson, the photographer, and everyone on the island of Gotland who met us at the crash site. Several had been there in 1944 when the *Liberty Lady* came down.
- Jan-Olof Nilsson, Swedish author of books about the American internees.
- Hedy's roommates: Thelma Kane, Agness Gustafson Ricci, Katherine Hatter, and Ando MacDonell.
- Steven Koblik, author of *The Stones Cry Out: Sweden's Response to the Persecution of the Jews, 1933–1945*, took the time to speak with me about what Herman may have experienced in Sweden.
- Don Courson, Merle Brown, Charlie Huntoon, William Sapp Dixon, Thaddeus C. "Ted" Borek, Larry Jackson, Ron Lissner, all of whom were in Sweden.

- Families of the *Liberty Lady* crew and the other airmen in England and in Sweden.
- The Roswell Rotary Club and its Honor Air team.
- Monroe "Buddy" Stamps, navigator, who served in World War II and in Korea. A fellow Roswell Rotarian, Buddy went through Herman's mission diary with me, word by word.
- Jane Brown, copyeditor and excellent wordsmith.
- Elizabeth Evans, Smithy's daughter, for her keen proofreading eye.
- Suzanne Kingsbury, for your encouragement and advice.
- Johnny DiGeorge and Joshua Farr, my photo editors.
- Michael Potthast of Potthast Studios, Winter Haven, Florida.
- Jera Publishing, for guiding me through the process.
- My dear Aunt Dorothy, the historian of our family.
- And of course, my husband John, Johnny, Brian, Una, Felix, and the rest of my family who have been oh so patient.

This list doesn't begin to name everyone. Just know how grateful I am for your help. Writing this book has been the adventure of my life.

Pat DiGeorge
www.LibertyLadyBook.com

Bibliography

Agrell, Wilhelm. 2006. *Stockholm som spioncentral.* Lund: Historiska Media.

Aid, Matthew M. 2002. "'Stella Polaris' and the Secret Code Battle in Postwar Europe." *Intelligence and National Security* 17 (3): 17–86.

Air Force Historical Research Agency. n.d.

—. 2008. *The Birth of the United States Air Force.* January 9. Accessed June 12, 2012. http://www.afhra.af.mil/factsheets/factsheet.asp?id=10944.

Alexander, Jack. 1943. "The Clay-Pigeon Squadron." *Saturday Evening Post*, April 24: .

Allen, Louis, interview by Ace Allen. 1970s. *A Conversation with Louis Allen*

Allen, Yussel. 1966. "The Allens." Auckland, July.

Ambrose, Stephen E., and C.L. Sulzberger. 1997. *American Heritage New History of World War II.* New York: Viking.

Anderson, Matt. 2008. "Minnesota Historical Society." March 12. Accessed July 31, 2010. http://discussions.mnhs.org/collections/?s=Civilian+Conservation+Corps.

Appleman, Roy E. 1992. *South to the Naktong, North to the Yalu: United States Army in the Korean War.* Washington, D.C.: Center of Military History, United States Army. Accessed June 1, 2013. http://www.history.army.mil/books/korea/20-2-1/toc.htm.

Baedeker, K. 1895. *Baedecker's Norway and Sweden.* London: Leipsic: Karl Baedeker.

Bailey, Richard H. and the editors of Time-Life Books. 1978. *The Home Front: U.S.A.* Alexandria, VA: Time-Life Books.

Balchen, Bernt. 1958. *Come North With Me.* New York: E.P. Dutton & Co., Inc.

Bean, Maxine, interview by Pat DiGeorge. 2013. (June 20).

Berger, Susanne. 2005. "Stuck in Neutral: The Reasons behind Sweden's Passivity in the Raoul Wallenberg Case." http://www.raoul-wallenberg.eu/wp-content/uploads/2005/08/Stuck_25Oct05.pdf.

Bernadotte, Folke. 1951. *To Jerusalem.* London: Hodder and Stoughton.

Betts, Edward Ross. 1989. "Email sent to Karen Cline."

Bodson, Herman. 2005. "Downed Allied Airmen and Evasion of Capture: The Role of Local Resistance Networks in World War II." Jefferson, North Carolina: McFarland & Company, Inc.

Bove, Arthur P. 1946. *First Over Germany: A Story of the 306th Bombardment Group.* San Angelo, Texas: Newsfoto Publishing Co.

Breitman, Richard. 1993. "American Rescue Activities in Sweden." *Holocaust and Genocide Studies* 7 (2): 202-215.

Brinkley, David. 1988. *Washington Goes to War.* New York: Ballantine Books.

Casey, William. 1988. *The Secret War Against Hitler.* Washington, DC: Regnery Gateway.

Cassedy, Ellen. 2012. *We Are Here: Memories of the Lithuanian Holocaust.* Lincoln: University of Nebraska Press.

Center for Air Force History. 1991. *Combat Chronology 1941-1945.* U.S. Army Air Forces in World War II, Washington DC: Center for Air Force History.

Central Intelligence Agency. Dec 13, 2007. "A Look Back ... Julia Child: Life Before French Cuisine." *Central Intelligence Agency.* Accessed January 4, 2015. https://www.cia.gov/news-information/featured-story-archive/2007-featured-story-archive/julia-child.html.

—. 2008. *Central Intelligence Agency.* April 30. Accessed July 21, 2010. https://www.cia.gov/news-information/featured-story-archive/2008-featured-story-archive/office-of-strategic-services.html.

Chirnside, Mark. 2008. *RMS Aquitania: The Ship Beautiful.* Stroud, Gloucestershire: The History Press Ltd.

Christerson, Rolf. 1998. *Rättvik 100 år som turistort.* Rättvik : Rättviks kommun.

CIA History Staff. 2000. *The Office of Strategic Services: America's First Intelligence Agency.* Washington, DC: Central Intelligence Agency.

Claesson, Göran C-O. n.d. "From Prisoners of War to War Brides." http://salship.se/claesson/prisoners.php.

Cohen, Phil. n.d. *Charles L. Stevenson.* Accessed February 25, 2009. http://www.dvrbs.com/ccwd-ww2/WW2-CharlesStevenson.htm.

Cole, R. Taylor. 1983. *The Recollections of R. Taylor Cole.* Durham, North Carolina: Duke University Press.

Commemorative Air Force, Arizona Wing, Aviation Museum. n.d. *Crew Positions of the B-17G.* Accessed March 6, 2013. http://www.azcaf.org/pages/b17g_crew.html.

Conant, Jennet. 2011. *A Covert Affair.* New York: Simon & Schuster Paperbacks.

Crowdy, Terry. 2008. *Deceiving Hitler: Double Cross and Deception in World War II.* Oxford: Osprey.

Cunard. n.d. *Cunard Heritage.* Accessed June 11, 2012. www.cunard.com.

Cutler, Richard W. 2004. *Counterspy: Memoirs of a Counterintelligence Officer in World War II and the Cold War.* Washington, D.C.: Brassey's.

Degnan, James T. 1943–1944. "unpublished letters home."

Doerries, Reinhard R. 2009. *Hitler's Intelligence Chief: Walter Schellenberg.* New York: Enigma Books.

Dyreborg, Erik. 2002. *The Lucky Ones: airmen of the Mighty Eighth.* Lincoln, NE: Writers Club Press.

Elgueta, John Dzazópulos. 2010. *Rosita Serrano, el Ruiseñor chileno.* June. http://www.operasiempre.es/2010/06/rosita-serrano-el-ruisenor-chileno/.

Ell, May. n.d. *Biography for Rosita Serrano.* Accessed November 16, 2011. http://www.imdb.com/name/nm0785616/bio.

Eriksson, Herman. 1943. "Foreign Trade." In *Sweden: A Wartime Survey,* 83-94. New York: The American-Swedish News Exchange.

Faley, Luc Dewez and Michael P. 2009. *High Noon over Haseluenne: The 100th Bombardment Group over Berlin, March 6, 1944.* Atglen, PA: Schiffer Military History.

Fay, Elma Ernst U.S.R.C. (ret). 2000. "A Brief History of Red Cross Clubmobiles in W.W.II." Accessed March 19, 2013. www.clubmobile.org.

Finstrom, Carl Gustav. 23 February 2005. "The Secret War of the OSS in Scandinavia, 1942-1945."

Finstrom, Carl. n.d. "personal email."

Ford, Corey. 1970. *Donovan of OSS.* Boston: Little, Brown and Company.

Franklin, Ralph. 2011. "A Moonlight Serenade: Thanks for the Memories." *306th Echoes*, April.

Gardner, Pearl Greenberg. n.d. "Charles A. Greenberg."

Gay, Timothy M. 2012. *Assignment to Hell.* New York: New American Library.

Gilmour, John. 2010. *Sweden, the Swastika and Stalin: The Swedish Experience in the Second World War.* Edinburgh: Edinburgh University Press.

Goodall, Felicity. 2004. *Voices from the Home Front.* Newton Abbot, Devon: David & Charles.

Grand Hôtel Stockholm Sweden. n.d. "A glimpse into the long, colourful history of Grand Hotel Stockholm." Accessed June 9, 2011. www.grandhotel.se.

Gugeler, Russell A. n.d. "Combat Actions in Korea, Chapter Two, Attack Along a Ridgeline." *US Army Center of Military History.* Accessed June 5, 2013. http://www.history.army.mil/books/korea/30-2/30-2_2.HTM.

Hagglof, Gunnar. 1972. *Diplomat: Memoirs of a Swedish Envoy in London, Paris, Berlin, Moscow, Washington.* London: Bodley Head.

Hasselberg, Per-Erik. 2004. *Klippan 12 - en Strandvägsbyggnad.* Stockholm: Art & Auto Stockholm.

Helms, Richard. 2003. *A Look Over My Shoulder: A Life in the Central Intelligence Agency.* New York: Random House.

Hemingstam, Lars. n.d. *Captain Torkel Tistrand.* Accessed September 15, 2015. http://salship.se/tistrand.php.

Henningsson, Pär. 1999. "American Internees in Sweden 1943–1945." *Sweden After the Flak*, Winter: 5–6.

—. 1999. "The Story of Georgia Rebel." *Sweden After the Flak*, Summer/Fall.

Hewins, Ralph. 1950. *Count Folke Bernadotte: His Life and Work.* Minneapolis: T.S. Denison & Company.

Holmin, Georg. 1943. "The Defense of Neutrality." In *Sweden: A Wartime Survey*, 24–35. New York: The American-Swedish News Exchange.

Holzman, Michael Howard. 2008. *James Jesus Angleton, the CIA, and the Craft of Counterintelligence.* Amherst: University of Massachusetts Press.

Hoover, Calvin. 1965. *Memoirs of Capitalism, Communism, and Nazism.* Durham. NC: Duke University Press.

Hopper, Bruce C. 1944. *Logging the General to Neutrality and Back on Four Engines.* Air Force Historical Research Agency, U.S. Strategic Air Forces in Europe. Accessed October 20, 2010.

Hopper, Bruce. 1945. "Sweden: A Case Study in Neutrality." *Foreign Affairs*, April: 435–449.

Huntoon, Charles R. Jr., interview by Pat DiGeorge. 2010.

—. 1999. "Unpublished Memoir." *The Greatest Generation.*

n.d. *Ingmar Bergman Foundation.* Accessed July 6, 2013. http://ingmarbergman.se .

1950. "Israel Delivers Reply to Sweden on Bernadotte's Assassination; Admits Police Failure." *JTA, The Global Jewish News Source.* June 20. Accessed February 11, 2014. http://www.jta.org/1950/06/20/archive/israel-delivers-reply-to-sweden-on-bernadottes-assassination-admits-police-failure.

Iverson, Caroline. 1943. "Suzy-Q: The "Fightingest Flying Fortress" Comes Back From a Year of Action." *Life magazine*, January 18: 82-84, 86, 88, 90, 92.

Jablonski, Edward. 1965. *Flying Fortress: The Illustrated Biography of the B-17s and the Men Who Flew Them.* Garden City, New York: Doubleday & Company, Inc.

Jackson, Charles W. Johnson and Charles O. 1981. *City Behind a Fence: Oak Ridge, Tennessee, 1942-1946.* Knoxville: The University of Tennessee Press.

Jacobsson, Curt. 2003. "Historien om Liberty Lady." *Svensk Flyghistorisk Tidskrift*, May.

Joesten, Joachim. 1943. *Stalwart Sweden.* Garden City, N.Y.: Doubleday, Doran and Company, Inc.

Johnson, Albin E. 1944. "What I Saw in Sweden." *The Rotarian*, September: 8–11.

Jonason, Tommy and Simon Olsson. n.d. "The Enigmatic Josephine - the Spy Who Never existed. The Life of Karl Heinz Krämer." Accessed 2014.

Jonason, Tommy. 2014. "The German Legation in Stockholm." unpublished.

Kershaw, Alex. 2010. *To Save a People.* London: Hutchinson.

Klar, Lindsay. 2008. "Supporting the Air War on the Ground: The Ground Echelon Experience at Thurleigh, England 1942-1945." *306th Echoes*, October.

Koblik, Steven. 1988. *The Stones Cry Out: Sweden's Response to the Persecution of the Jews 1933-1945.* New York: Holocaust Library.

Krump, Jason. 2007. "Stories That Live Forever." *Washington State Cougars.* May 20. Accessed June 1, 2013.

Lan, Charles. 2013. "Berns salonger 150 år." *Populär Historia*, July 19. Accessed February 7, 2014. http://www.popularhistoria.se/artiklar/berns-salonger-150-ar/.

Landis, Carole. 1944. *Four Jills in a Jeep.* New York: Random House, Inc.

Larsson, Jan. 1995. *Raoul Wallenberg's biography.* Swedish Institute. http://www.raoulwallenberg.net/wallenberg/raoul-wallenberg-s-biography/.

Leyshon, John M. Redding and Harold I. 1943. *Skyways to Berlin With the American Flyers in England.* Indianapolis and New York: The Bobbs-Merrill Company.

Life. 1944. "War Prisoners: Allies and Germans are exchanged at the Swedish port of Göteborg." October 23. Accessed March 30, 2014. Google Books.

MacDonald, Elizabeth P. 1947. *Undercover Girl.* New York: The MacMillan Company.

Macintyre, Ben. 2014. *A Spy Among Friends: Kim Philby and the Great Betrayal.* New York: Crown Publishers.

Madison, James H. 2007. *Slinging Doughnuts for the Boys: An American Woman in World War II.* Bloomington: Indiana University Press.

Mangold, Tom. 1991. *Cold Warrior. James Jesus Angleton: The CIA's Master Spy Hunter.* New York: Simon & Schuster.

Martin, Joy. 2010. "Our parents before we were born is a mystery." unpublished document.

Marton, Kati. 1994. *A Death in Jerusalem.* New York: Pantheon Books.

McIntosh, Elizabeth P. 1998. *Women of the OSS: Sisterhood of Spies.* Annapolis, MD: Naval Institute Press.

McKay, C.G. January 2011. "Excerpts from McKay's Notes on The Case of Raoul Wallenberg." Accessed July 15, 2014. http://www.raoulwallenberg.org/mckay.pdf.

—. 1993. *From Information to Intrigue: Studies in Secret Service Based on the Swedish Experience 1939-1945.* London: Frakn Cass & Co. LTD.

McMath, Meredith Bean. n.d. "How to Grow a Mountain Man." *StoryRoot.* Accessed June 21, 2013. http://www.storyroot.com/MountainMan.html.

Mears, Dwight S. 2013. "The Catch-22 Effect: The Lasting Stigma of Wartime Cowardice in the U.S. Army Air Forces." *Journal of Military History*, July.

Melin, Ingemar. 1999. "Bulltofta: June 20–21, 1944." *Sweden: After the Flak*, Winter: 1–3.

Meyers, Jeffrey. 1998. *Gary Cooper: American Hero.* New York: William Morrow and Company, Inc.

Miller, Donald L. 2006. *Masters of the Air.* New York, NY: Simon & Schuster, Inc.

NARA. n.d. College Park, MD.

NARA. n.d. "William T. Carlson." OSS Personnel File.

Nilsson, Jan-Olof and Bengt-Arne Karlsson. 2002. *Anrop Red Dog.* Stockholm: Svenska Förlaget.

O'Donnell, Patrick K. 2004. *Operatives, Spies, and Saboteurs: The Unknown Story of the Men and Women of WWII's OSS.* New York, NY: FREE PRESS, a division of Simon & Schuster, Inc.

Office of the Military Attaché, Stockholm, Sweden. 1946. "Chronolocal History and pertinent facts pertaining to U.S. Military Internees in Sweden during World War II." Report to the Director of Military Intelligence, War Department General Staff, Washington, DC, Stockholm.

Official site of the City of Hibbing. n.d. *Hibbing>We're Ore and More.* Accessed June 30, 2010. www.hibbing.mn.us.

Olausson, Torbjörn. 1969. "They Came From The South." *Aerospace Historian*, AH/Autumn.

—. Special Issue November 1976. *Flyghistorisk Revy: Aviation Historical Review.* Stockholm: Swedish Aviation Historical Society.

—. 1999. "Loka Brunn." *Sweden After the Flak,* Winter.

Olson, Lynne. 2010. *Citizens of London: The Americans Who Stood with Britain in Its Darkest, Finest Hour.* New York: Random House.

Olsson, Kent. 2013. "Sagoslottsepok upp in rök ." *dt.* March 9. Accessed July 6, 2013. http://www.dt.se/nyheter/rattvik/1.5663346-sagoslottsepok-upp-i-rok.

Olsson, Simon. n.d. "email correspondence."

n.d. *Oscars Teatern Historia.* Accessed November 16, 2011. http://www.oscarsteatern.se.

Persson, Sune. 2009. *Escape from the Third Reich: The Harrowing True Story of the Largest Rescue Effort Inside Nazi Germany.* New York: Skyhorse Publishing.

—. 2000. "Folke Bernadotte and the White Buses." *Journal of Holocaust Education,* September 1.

Petri, Gustaf. 1943. "The Home Guard." In *Sweden: A Wartime Survey,* 36–42. New York: The American-Swedish News Exchange.

Pinck, Charles T. 2011. "Remembering The Last Hero." *The Harvard Crimson.* April 21. http://www.thecrimson.com/article/2011/4/21/war-oss-donovan-world/.

Posey, E.E. 2009. *World War II: Experiences and Memories.* Margaret Posey McQuain and Daniel M. Posey. Accessed February 3, 2011.

Price, Jeffrey Ethell and Dr. Alfred. 2002. *Target Berlin: Mission 250, 6 March 1944.* London: Greenhill Books.

Rooney, Andy. 1995. *My War.* New York: Random House.

—. 1982. "As reunions go, the 306th Bomb Group is special." *The Free Lance-Star,* October 12. http://news.google.com/.

Ryan, John L. 1984. "Recollections of Charles B. Overacker." *306th Echoes,* January. www.306bg.org.

Schwarze, Erika. 1993. *Kodnamn Onkel.* Stockholm: A. Bonnier.

Sirotnak, Joe. 1999. "This is Sweden?" *Sweden After the Flak,* December: 3–5.

Skoog, A. Ingemar. 2012. "Can a pile of scrap unmask a new high technology? The A4/V-2 No V89 Bäckebo+torpeden." *Acta Astronautica*, December 13.

Smith, Charles W. 2000. "306th Bomb Group: Weary Bones." unpublished.

Smith, Jean Edward. 2007. *FDR (Abridged, Audiobook).* Random House Audio.

Smith, John N. 2007. *Thurleigh and Twinwood Farm.* Peterborough, England: GMS Enterprises.

Smith, Richard Harris. 1972. *OSS: The Secret History of America's First Central Intelligence Agency.* Berkeley and Los Angeles, California: University of California Press.

Snyder, Steve. 2015. *Shot Down: The true story of pilot Howard Snyder and the crew of the B-17 Susan Ruth.* Seal Beach: Sea Breeze Publishing.

1942. *Winning Your Wings.* Directed by John Huston. Produced by Warner Brothers Studios. Performed by James Stewart. War Activities Committee of the Motion Picture Industry.

Strong, Russell. 1992. "Strong Speaks at Thurleigh." *396th Echoes*, October.

Strong, Russell A. 1982. "First Over Germany: A History of the 306th Bombardment Group." Winston-Salem, North Carolina: Hunter Publishing Company.

Sweden National Archives, Riksarkivet. n.d. "Lönnegren, John Alex:r, Född 12/12/-78, Yrke Fil.dr, Nationalitet Svensk." Stockholm. Accessed October 2011.

Talty, Stephan. 2013. *The Secret Agent: In Search of America's Greatest World War II Spy.* Amazon Digital Services, Inc.

Tavares, Ernest S. Jr. April 2001. "Operation Fortitude: The Closed Loop D-Day Deception Plan." Research Report, Air Command and Staff College, Air University, Maxwell Air Force Base. Accessed September 25, 2014. http://www2.warwick.ac.uk/fac/soc/pais/people/aldrich/vigilant/tavares_fortitude.pdf.

Taylor, Cal. 2011. "American Air Operations in Sweden, 1943–1945." *American Aviation Historical Society*, Spring.

Tennant, Peter. 1992. *Touchlines of War.* Hull: The University of Hull Press.

The Billboard. 1944. *Showbiz Carries on in Sweden.* August 12. Accessed August 19, 2011. www.billboard.com/archive.

2014. *The Disappearance of Glenn Miller.* Produced by History Detectives Special Investigations.

2011. *The Queen Mary: Royalty on the Seas.* Accessed August 13, 2011.

2005. *Thurleigh Memories: The 306th Bomb Group (II) in WWII.* Produced by Vernon Williams. www.oldsegundo.com.

Troy, Thomas F. 1981. *Donovan and the CIA.* Central Intelligence Agency.

U.S. Army Air Force. 1944. *Target: Germany, The U.S. Army Air Forces' Official Story of the VIII Bomber Command's First Year Over Europe.* British Edition. London: His Majesty's Stationery Office.

United Nations Department of Public Information. 1948. *General Lundstrom Gives Eyewitness Account of Bernadotte's Death.* September 18. http://unispal.un.org/ .

United Press. n.d. *French Officer Dies with Count, United Press, San Francisco Chronicle, Sep. 18, 1948.* http://cojs.org.

University of Virginia Alumni News. 2013. "The Hand That Held the Dagger." *UVA Magazine.* Summer. Accessed June 21, 2013. http://uvamagazine.org/.

Volkman, Ernest. 1994. *Spies: The Secret Agents Who Changed the Course of History.* New York: John Wiley & Sons, Inc.

Wallenberg, Olga. 1988. *Grand Hôtel Stockholm.* Stockholm, Sweden: Atlantis.

Waller, Douglas. 2011. *Wild Bill Donovan: The Spymaster Who Created the OSS and Modern American Espionage.* New York: Free Press.

War Department, Washington, DC. 1976. "The Overseas Targets: War Report of the OSS Volumel 1 and 2." New York: Walker Publishing Company, Inc.

n.d. "War Diary: X-2 Branch, OSS London, Vol. 2." Microfilm Roll 10, London Headquarters, National Archives Microfilm Publications.

Warg, Charlotte. 2013. *comment on the post "Hotell Lerdalshöjden".* March 2. http://libertyladybook.com/2012/08/19/hotell-lerdalshojden/.

Warner, Michael. 2000. "The Office of Strategic Services: America's First Intelligence Agency." Central Intelligence Agency, May.

Wegmann, Bo Widfeldt and Rolph. 1997. *Making for Sweden Part 1, The Royal Air Force.* Surrey, KT: Air Research Publications.

Weld, Alfred W., Sam S. McNeeley, Ralph W.F. Schreiter. August 1993. "368th Squadron Combat Diary 1942-45, 306th Bomb Group." 306bg.us.

Widfeldt, Bo and Rolph Wegmann. 1998. *Making for Sweden, Part 2.* Surrey, KT: Air Research Publications.

Widfeldt, Bo. 1983. *The Luftwaffe in Sweden 1939–1945.* Boylston, MA: Monogram Aviation Publications.

Williams, Vernon L. 2012. "Dr. Thurman Shuller's Leadership Changes the Course of History." *306th Echoes,* Fall, Fall 2012 ed.

Winks, Robin. 1987. *Cloak and Gown: Scholars in America's Secret War.* London: Collins Harvill.

n.d. *Yad Vashem Archives.* Accessed November 24, 2014. http://www.yadvashem.org/YV/en/about/archive/index.asp.

Unless otherwise noted, all photographs are from the personal files and scrapbooks of Herman and Hedvig Johnson Allen.

Endnotes

1. (Official site of the City of Hibbing n.d.)
2. (Anderson 2008)
3. (J. E. Smith 2007) chapter 79
4. The family was not related to the Freeport, Maine clothier.
5. (McMath n.d.)
6. (Bean 2013)
7. (McMath n.d.)
8. (University of Virginia Alumni News 2013)
9. (McMath n.d.)
10. (Bailey 1978) p. 21
11. (Brinkley 1988) p. 88
12. (O'Donnell 2004) pp. xii-xiii
13. (Central Intelligence Agency 2008)
14. (Waller 2011) p. 60
15. (McIntosh 1998) p. 5
16. (Troy 1981) p. 2
17. (Troy 1981) p. 81
18. (Pinck 2011)
19. (McIntosh 1998) p. 14
20. (Ford 1970) p. 121
21. (MacDonald 1947) p. 6
22. (O'Donnell 2004) p. xv
23. (MacDonald 1947) p. 19
24. (Conant 2011) p. 61
25. (Central Intelligence Agency Dec 13, 2007)
26. (Casey 1988) p. 3
27. (Meyers 1998) p. 205
28. (Cunard n.d.)

29. (Olson 2010)
30. (McIntosh 1998) p. 85
31. (Holzman 2008) p. 49
32. Today the address is 14 Ryder Street. This building was used in the filming of the movie *The Good Shepherd.*
33. (Crowdy 2008) p. 297
34. (McIntosh 1998) p. 94
35. (Cutler 2004) p. 13
36. (Olson 2010) p. 316
37. (Gay 2012) chapter 9
38. (Helms 2003) p. 153–160
39. (McIntosh 1998) p. 96
40. (Winks 1987) p. 341
41. (Goodall 2004) p. 266
42. (Crowdy 2008) p. 273
43. (Waller 2011) chapter 23
44. (NARA n.d.)
45. (NARA n.d.)
46. (Hoover 1965) pp. 199–201
47. (NARA n.d.)
48. (War Diary: X-2 Branch, OSS London, Vol. 2 n.d.) p. 38
49. (War Diary: X-2 Branch, OSS London, Vol. 2 n.d.) pp. 83–84
50. (War Diary: X-2 Branch, OSS London, Vol. 2 n.d.) pp. 127–128
51. (Y. Allen 1966)
52. (Gardner n.d.)
53. (L. Allen 1970s)
54. (L. Allen 1970s)
55. (L. Allen 1970s)
56. (Stewart 1942)
57. (Air Force Historical Research Agency 2008)
58. (Miller 2006) p. 39
59. (Miller 2006) p. 5
60. (Jablonski 1965) p. 5
61. (Jablonski 1965) pp. 6–11
62. (Cohen n.d.)
63. William Sapp Dixon, from comments on www.LibertyLadyBook.com on February 11, 2009.
64. (Miller 2006) p. 90
65. (Commemorative Air Force, Arizona Wing, Aviation Museum n.d.)
66. (R. A. Strong 1982) p. 54

67. (The Queen Mary: Royalty on the Seas 2011)
68. (Bove 1946)
69. (R. A. Strong 1982) p. 26
70. (Alexander 1943) p. 71
71. (Leyshon 1943) pp. 169, 182
72. (Leyshon 1943) p. 29
73. (Miller 2006) p. 74
74. (R. A. Strong 1982) p. 44
75. (Landis 1944) p. 66
76. (Miller 2006) p. 26
77. (R. A. Strong 1982) pp. 71, 80
78. (V. L. Williams 2012) p. 8
79. (R. A. Strong 1982) p. 117
80. (R. A. Strong 1982) p. 173
81. (Miller 2006) p. 246
82. (Thurleigh Memories: The 306th Bomb Group (II) in WWII 2005)
83. (R. Strong 1992) p. 18
84. (Fay 2000)
85. (Klar 2008)
86. (R. A. Strong 1982) p. 189
87. (Bove 1946)
88. (Franklin 2011) p. 8
89. (The Disappearance of Glenn Miller 2014) Dennis Spragg, senior consultant to the Glenn Miller Archive at the University of Colorado Boulder.
90. (Rooney, My War 1995) p. 105
91. (Rooney, As reunions go, the 306th Bomb Group is special 1982)
92. (Center for Air Force History 1991) p. 267
93. CQ= Charge of Quarters," also known as the "Walking Alarm Clock."
94. John M. Kelly
95. cloud cover
96. Ted Boswell, Jr.
97. Newspaper term for "That's the end."
98. Michael Kalish
99. (Miller 2006) p. 42
100. (Miller 2006) p. 253
101. (Center for Air Force History 1991) p. 260
102. (C. W. Smith 2000)
103. (R. A. Strong 1982) pp. 175–176
104. (Center for Air Force History 1991) p. 264
105. Gee fix, radio navigation system

106. (Center for Air Force History 1991) p. 275
107. (Center for Air Force History 1991) p. 276
108. (Bove 1946)
109. (J. N. Smith 2007) p. 35
110. (Center for Air Force History 1991) p. 282
111. (Miller 2006) p. 93
112. (R. A. Strong 1982) p. 187
113. (Center for Air Force History 1991) p. 284
114. (Miller 2006) pp. 249–251
115. (Bodson 2005) pp. 109–113
116. (Snyder 2015) for full details of *The Massacre at Saint Rémy*
117. (C. W. Smith 2000)
118. (Miller 2006) pp. 254–255
119. (Center for Air Force History 1991) p. 306
120. (R. A. Strong 1982) p. 158
121. Charles W. Smith unpublished account
122. (Center for Air Force History 1991) p. 313
123. (Weld August 1993) p. 53
124. (Faley 2009) pp. 8-9
125. (Miller 2006) p. 247
126. (Miller 2006) pp. 265-267
127. (C. W. Smith 2000)
128. (Price 2002) pp. 43–44
129. (Price 2002) p. 83
130. (Price 2002) pp. 86–89
131. (Jacobsson 2003)
132. (Jacobsson 2003)
133. (B. Widfeldt 1983) p. 44
134. (Petri 1943) p. 36
135. Lars Björkander letter to Ulf Gahm, March 2012
136. Letter from Gunnar Jonsson provided by the family of Charles W. Smith
137. (Cole 1983)
138. (McKay, From Information to Intrigue: Studies in Secret Service Based on the Swedish Experience 1939-1945 1993) p. 1
139. (Holmin 1943) p. 24
140. (B. Hopper 1945) pp. 437–439
141. (Hagglof 1972) p. 80
142. (Eriksson 1943) p. 84
143. (Joesten 1943) p. 59

144. (McKay, From Information to Intrigue: Studies in Secret Service Based on the Swedish Experience 1939-1945 1993) p. 4
145. The career of Torgny Segerstedt was the subject of the movie "The Last Sentence," released in 2012.
146. *Time* magazine, February 26, 1940
147. (Persson, Folke Bernadotte and the White Buses 2000)
148. *Time* magazine, October 5, 1942
149. (Baedeker 1895) p. 289
150. (NARA n.d.) 226-214-5, Accessed October 11, 2011. Memo August 8, 1944.
151. (Grand Hôtel Stockholm Sweden n.d.) p. 32
152. *The Rotarian* magazine, February 1946, A Visitor in Sweden
153. (The Billboard 1944)
154. (Johnson 1944)
155. (Cole 1983) p. 92
156. (B. Widfeldt 1983) p. 9
157. (Olausson, Flyghistorisk Revy: Aviation Historical Review Special Issue November 1976) pp. 3–5
158. (Olausson, Flyghistorisk Revy: Aviation Historical Review Special Issue November 1976) pp. 20, 66–67
159. (Wegmann 1997) pp. 10, 281
160. (Betts 1989)
161. (Wegmann 1997) p. 282–283
162. (Henningsson, The Story of Georgia Rebel 1999)
163. (Hewins 1950) pp. 80–81
164. (B. a. Widfeldt 1998) p. 239
165. (Office of the Military Attaché 1946)
166. (Iverson 1943)
167. (Hewins 1950) p. 81
168. (Hewins 1950) p. 11
169. (Marton 1994) p. 60
170. (Hewins 1950) p. 62
171. (Marton 1994) p. 65
172. (Hewins 1950) p. 72
173. (Hewins 1950) pp.79–80
174. (Office of the Military Attaché 1946)
175. (Melin 1999) pp. 1–3
176. Incoming Message 14 July 44: Sweden-Airfields for Forced Landings from Stockholm to USSTAF
177. (Melin 1999) pp. 2–3
178. (Office of the Military Attaché 1946)

179. (Balchen 1958) p. 19
180. (Balchen 1958) p. 195
181. (Balchen 1958) p. 214
182. (Balchen 1958) p. 265
183. *Time* magazine, December 13, 1943
184. *Time* magazine, May 22, 1944
185. Personal correspondence with Felicia Hardison Londre, daughter of Felix Hardison
186. (Skoog 2012)
187. (Ambrose and Sulzberger 1997) p. 292, 404, 484-484
188. (Office of the Military Attaché 1946)
189. (B. a. Widfeldt 1998) In their book *Making for Sweden Part 2*, authors Bo Widfeldt and Rolph Wegmann chronicled each and every United States Army Air Force aircraft and the fates of their crews.
190. (Air Force Historical Research Agency n.d.) Internees of the American Air Force in Sweden. Call 519.6143/1944.
191. (Olausson, They Came From The South 1969)
192. (Degnan 1943–1944)
193. (Martin 2010)
194. 2012 visit with Ebba Lindblad at her home in Falun
195. (Christerson 1998) pp. 186-187
196. (Warg 2013)
197. (S. Olsson n.d.) email correspondence
198. (Nilsson 2002) p. 104
199. For more such stories, see *Lucky Strike* by Jan-Olof Nilsson (2013)
200. (NARA n.d.) 226-125A-26. Espionage—Stockholm as Centre for Espionage Activities
201. (Gilmour 2010) p. 135
202. (Tennant 1992) p. 155
203. (McKay, From Information to Intrigue: Studies in Secret Service Based on the Swedish Experience 1939-1945 1993) p. 37
204. (NARA n.d.) 226-210-58, Accessed October 11, 2011
205. (Grand Hôtel Stockholm Sweden n.d.) p. 32
206. (Cole 1983) p. 76
207. *Time* magazine, February 28, 1944
208. (NARA n.d.) 226-210-327, Accessed October 11, 2011. History of the OSS Mission to Stockholm by Wilho Tikander
209. (Hasselberg 2004)
210. (NARA n.d.) 226-10-327, Accessed October 11, 2011. Wilho Tikander Questionnaire of May 16, 1960

211. (NARA n.d.) Legation Directory, obtained in the 1980s at the National Archives by Hedvig Allen
212. (McIntosh 1998) p. 38
213. (R. H. Smith 1972) p. 199
214. (C. G. Finstrom 23 February 2005) p. 3
215. (NARA n.d.) 226-210-327, Accessed October 11, 2011. Wilho Tikander Questionnaire of May 16, 1960
216. (Balchen 1958) p. 266
217. (NARA n.d.) 226-210-58, Accessed October 11, 2011
218. (NARA n.d.) 226-210-365, Accessed October 11, 2011. Communication Privileges for LIMIT
219. (C. Finstrom n.d.) November 30, 2009
220. (Gilmour 2010) p. 135
221. (NARA n.d.) 226-210-365, Accessed October 11, 2011. Censoring of Telephones in Göteborg
222. (NARA n.d.) 226-125A-7, Accessed October 9, 2009. Report on American Legation Security
223. (NARA n.d.) 226-210-365, Accessed October 11, 2011. Subject: Legation Security, dated 18 July, 1944
224. (Joesten 1943) pp. 31, 45
225. (Gilmour 2010) p. 17
226. (Joesten 1943) p. 36
227. (Waller 2011) p. 109
228. (Brinkley 1988) p. 92
229. (NARA n.d.) 226-210-245. Accessed October 11, 2011
230. (Schwarze 1993) Erika's story.
231. (McKay, From Information to Intrigue: Studies in Secret Service Based on the Swedish Experience 1939-1945 1993) p. 160
232. (T. Jonason 2014)
233. (Schwarze 1993) p. 68
234. (Schwarze 1993) I have chosen to use this spelling of Ternberg's name.
235. (T. Jonason 2014)
236. (Schwarze 1993) Erika's story pp. 15-110
237. Document from the Swedish Archives provided by Jan-Olof Nilsson
238. (NARA n.d.) 226-10-327, Accessed October 11, 2011. Wilho Tikander Questionnaire of May 16, 1960, pp. 12–13, 72
239. (Dyreborg 2002) p. 93
240. Escape and Evasion Reports, https://research.archives.gov/id/305270
241. (Air Force Historical Research Agency n.d.) Evasion and Escape, Europe. Call # 142.76213.

242. (NARA n.d.) 226-210-58, Accessed October 11, 2011
243. (NARA n.d.) 226-125A-27, Accessed October 13, 2011
244. (NARA n.d.) 226-A1-212-1, Accessed October 9, 2009.
245. (NARA n.d.) 226-125-26, October 13, 2011
246. (NARA n.d.) 226-125-26, October 13, 2011
247. (NARA u.d.) 226-125-26, October 13, 2011
248. From Personal interview with Charles Huntoon July 15, 2010
249. Interview with historian Steven Koblik, May 12, 2014.
250. (Koblik 1988) p. 47
251. (NARA n.d.) 226-210-327, October 11, 2011. Tikander Questionairre.
252. (NARA n.d.) This was retrieved from the National Archives in the 1980's by Hedvig Johnson Allen.
253. (NARA n.d.) 226-125-58. Preliminary report of R.V. Peel, accessed 10-22-2011
254. (NARA n.d.) 226-125A-3, 10-9-2009
255. (Ell n.d.)
256. (Oscars Teatern Historia n.d.)
257. (NARA n.d.) 226-210-365, October 11, 2011
258. (NARA n.d.)226-212-1, October 14, 2011, Swedish Spy on Refugees …
259. (McKay, From Information to Intrigue: Studies in Secret Service Based on the Swedish Experience 1939-1945 1993) p. 173
260. (NARA n.d.) 226-1125A-27, October 13, 2011
261. (NARA n.d.) 226-212-1, October 14, 2011
262. (NARA n.d.) 226-125–26
263. The name is found as Paulson or Paulsson. I am using Paulsson, as this is how the name is spelled most often by Swedish historians. In the OSS documents cited, I have left the name however it was spelled.
264. (McKay, From Information to Intrigue: Studies in Secret Service Based on the Swedish Experience 1939-1945 1993) pp. 26–27
265. (Schwarze 1993) pp. 156–157
266. (Schwarze 1993) pp. 156–158
267. (Gilmour 2010) p. 152
268. (Schwarze 1993) pp. 140, 153, 169-178
269. (Tavares April 2001)
270. (T. a. Jonason n.d.)
271. Harrington Aviation Museums The Dropzone, Volume 7, Issue 2. Summer 2009.
272. (NARA n.d.) 226-212-1, October 14, 2011
273. (Posey 2009)
274. (B. a. Widfeldt 1998) pp. 79-80.

275. (NARA n.d.) 290-55-582, December 17, 2012. MIS-X Section Case files of interned airmen.
276. (Posey 2009) pp. 155-156
277. Per Mrs. Eldon Posey
278. (NARA n.d.) Dwight Mears
279. (NARA n.d.) 290-55-582, December 17, 2012. MIS-X Section
280. All given names of John Lönnegren's female friends are fictitious.
281. Gävle is a city on the Baltic Sea about 98 miles north of Stockholm, and is an important iron ore exporting port.
282. (NARA n.d.) 226-212-1, Accessed October 14, 2011
283. (NARA n.d.) 226-212-1, Accessed October 14, 2011
284. (Sweden National Archives n.d.) Accessed October 2011
285. Fictitious name.
286. (NARA n.d.) 226-212-1, Accessed October 14, 2011
287. (NARA n.d.) 226-125-26, Accessed October 13, 2011, Sweden, C.E., German Air Intelligence
288. (NARA n.d.) 226-210-365, Accessed October 11, 2011. Memo from Saint Stockholm, USAAF Internees—Possible Penetration
289. Fictitious name.
290. Today the Strand is the Radisson Blu Strand Hotel
291. (NARA n.d.) 226-212-1, Accessed October 14, 2011
292. (Sweden National Archives n.d.) Accessed October 2011
293. (NARA n.d.) 226-212-1, Accessed October 14, 2011
294. Fictitious name.
295. (NARA n.d.) 226-212-2, Accessed October 14, 2011
296. (Hewins 1950) pp. 75-104
297. (Marton 1994) pp. 66-67
298. (Claesson n.d.)
299. (Schwarze 1993) pp. 184-190.
300. (Sweden National Archives n.d.)
301. Fictitious name
302. (NARA n.d.) 226-212-1, October 14, 2011
303. (Air Force Historical Research Agency n.d.) Medical Department History—Legation of the United States of America, Stockholm, Sweden
304. Trams pulled by small horse-drawn carriages began to service Stockholm in 1877. Then in the early 1900s, they were run by electric lines hung throughout the city. A model came out in 1943, nicknamed "jitterbug." A few years later, new trams called "mustangs" were introduced. These were named after the American fighter planes and were thought to be the world's most elegant

trams. (Thank you to the AB Stockholms Spårvägar Facebook group and to Patrik Blom)

305. (Aid 2002) My primary source for Stella Polaris
306. (Kershaw 2010) pp. 51-52
307. (NARA n.d.) 226-210-327. History of the OSS Mission to Sweden
308. (Breitman 1993)
309. (Koblik 1988) pp. 68–69
310. (Kershaw 2010) p. 55
311. (Kershaw 2010) p. 60
312. (Larsson 1995)
313. (Berger 2005) p. 26
314. (NARA n.d.) 226-212-2, Accessed October 14, 2011
315. (NARA n.d.) 226-212-1, Accessed October 14, 2011
316. (Balchen 1958) p. 278
317. (B. C. Hopper 1944) Dr. Bruce Hopper's history of this trip.
318. Letter dated June 8, 1978 from General Edward P. Curtis to Mr. Torbjorn Olausson
319. (B. C. Hopper 1944)
320. Personal correspondence with Felicia Hardison Londre, daughter of Felix Hardison
321. (B. C. Hopper 1944)
322. Both Herman's report and the Swedish police report note the date as 2 October. Carlson writes 3 October.
323. AB Aerotransport (ABA) Swedish airline, today part of the SAS Group.
324. (NARA n.d.) 226-212-1, Accessed October 14, 2011
325. (Lan 2013)
326. (NARA n.d.) 226-212-1, Accessed October 14, 2011
327. (NARA n.d.) 226-212-1, Accessed October 14, 2011
328. (K. Olsson 2013)
329. (Ingmar Bergman Foundation n.d.)
330. (Jackson 1981) p. xviii
331. (Wallenberg 1988) p. 63
332. (NARA n.d.) 226-212-1 Lönnegren-Paulson Case
333. (Schwarze 1993) p. 140
334. (Sweden National Archives n.d.) Född 12/12-78 Lönnegren, John Alex:r
335. The 500 kronor would have been the monthly income for, as an example, a customs officer and his family.
336. (NARA n.d.) 226-210-435. Swedish Request for the Recall of German Agents
337. (NARA n.d.) 226-210-435 Repercussions of the Lönnegren Case
338. (NARA n.d.) 226-210-435. Repercussions of the Wagner-Utermark Case

339. (Agrell 2006) p. 101
340. (McKay, From Information to Intrigue: Studies in Secret Service Based on the Swedish Experience 1939-1945 1993) p. 10–11
341. (NARA n.d.) 226-210-435, OSS report: Paulson Case.
342. (Persson, Escape from the Third Reich: The Harrowing True Story of the Largest Rescue Effort Inside Nazi Germany 2009) p. 10
343. (Doerries 2009) pp. 96–99
344. (Marton 1994) pp. 69, 76
345. (Persson, Folke Bernadotte and the White Buses 2000) pp. 90, 249
346. (Marton 1994)
347. (Doerries 2009) pp. 231–232
348. Count Carl "Bobby" Moltke and wife New York fashion editor Mab Wilson Moltke
349. *The Saturday Evening Post*, February 8, 1944.
350. (Schwarze 1993) p. 208. Erika's story of Peace Day.
351. (Schwarze 1993) pp. 210–214
352. (C. Finstrom n.d.) March 29, 2011
353. (NARA n.d.) 226-210-327, Wilho Tikander, about January 1959. Appraisal of book *The Counterfeit Traitor*.
354. (Talty 2013)
355. (Casey 1988) p. 40
356. Personal correspondence with Joe Erickson, nephew to Eric Siegfried "Red" Erickson
357. (NARA n.d.) 226-210-327, Wilho Tikander, about January 1959. Appraisal of book *The Counterfeit Traitor*.
358. (Air Force Historical Research Agency n.d.) 519.642 Memo to the State Department signed by Johnson.
359. Memo for Chief of Air Staff: American Airmen Interned in Sweden. 13 October 1944
360. (Henningsson, American Internees in Sweden 1943–1945 1999)
361. (B. a. Widfeldt 1998) p. 243
362. (Air Force Historical Research Agency 2008) Report titled "Repatriation of force-landed aircraft from Sweden to the United Kingdom." Call #519.8021-6.
363. Personal interview with Ron Lissner, October 2013.
364. Correspondence with Dwight Mears, military historian.
365. (Nilsson 2002) p. 124
366. (Office of the Military Attaché 1946)
367. (NARA n.d.) 226-110-327 Memo to Major General William J. Donovan
368. (NARA n.d.) 226-210-68, Accessed October 10, 2011. Memo For the President
369. (NARA n.d.) 226-E224-0107, Accessed October 13, 2011

370. (NARA n.d.) 226-10-327, Accessed October 11, 2011. Wilho Tikander Questionnaire of May 16, 1960
371. (Waller 2011) pp. 317–338
372. (Winks 1987) p. 306
373. (CIA History Staff 2000) p. 43
374. (Warner 2000)
375. (Waller 2011) Chapters 31 and 32
376. (Mears 2013)
377. (Mears 2013)
378. Lars Björkander letter to Ulf Gahm, March 2012
379. Lars Björkander letter to Ulf Gahm, March 2012
380. (Marton 1994) p. 25
381. (Bernadotte 1951) pp. 1-6
382. (Marton 1994) pp. 158-159
383. (United Press n.d.)
384. (United Nations Department of Public Information 1948)
385. (Israel Delivers Reply to Sweden on Bernadotte's Assassination; Admits Police Failure 1950)
386. Between the wars Rimshan was known as Rymszany, Poland.
387. (Cassedy 2012) p. 68
388. (Yad Vashem Archives n.d.)
389. (Appleman 1992) p. 37
390. (Gugeler n.d.)
391. (Appleman 1992) p. x
392. As quoted in the Spartanbug Herald, January 18, 1961, referencing a letter to the Lake Wales Ministerial Association from the son of the building of the Bok Tower.
393. Told by Linda Jacobs from Lugoff, South Carolina, a former co-worker and president of the SCPHA
394. Our family shorthand for the home at 4912 Westfield Road.
395. From the account of Herman's last road trip by Emma Allen, his granddaughter.
396. (Schwarze 1993)
397. (C. Finstrom n.d.)
398. (Air Force Historical Research Agency 2008)
399. (Hemingstam n.d.)
400. (Macintyre 2014) chapters 8 and 9

Index of Names

S

T

U

W

CPSIA information can be obtained
at www.ICGtesting.com
Printed in the USA
LVOW01s2007231016
509637LV00003B/4/P

9 780998 257006